Oneida Community

An Autobiography, 1851–1876

A YORK STATE BOOK

Oneida Community

An Autobiography, 1851-1876

EDITED, WITH AN INTRODUCTION
AND PREFACES, BY

Constance Noyes Robertson

ONEIDA COMMUNITY MANSION HOUSE/
SYRACUSE UNIVERSITY PRESS

First paperback edition 1981
92 93 94 95 96 97 98 99   6 5 4 3 2

Library of Congress Catalog Card Number: 75-115417

ISBN 0-8156-0166-2

This edition was published with the assistance of a grant from Oneida Ltd.

The paper used in this publication meets the minimum requirements of American National Standard for Information Sciences—Permanence of Paper for Printed Library Materials, ANSI Z39.48-1984. ♾™

Manufactured in the United States of America

To my brother
PIERREPONT TROWBRIDGE NOYES

with my deepest admiration and love

Author of nine published novels including a book club selection, *Fire Bell in the Night,* CONSTANCE NOYES ROBERTSON has unusual qualifications for preparing this book. John Humphrey Noyes was her paternal grandfather, and both her parents belonged to the Oneida Community generation called Stirpicults resulting from the experiment in eugenic breeding. Her father, Pierrepont B. Noyes, played an important part in rescuing and reanimating the fortunes of the joint stock company that succeeded the old Community, now the modern silverware plant, Oneida, Ltd. Mrs. Robertson has lived most of her life in the Oneida area and has known personally many of the members of the old group. Having absorbed the traditions and word-of-mouth history of the old Community since childhood, she observes, "Happiness is the real theme of this book."

Contents

Illustrations

Preface

This book is a labor of love. I am a third-generation product of the Oneida Community. Both my parents were born in the class of children that the Oneida Community called Stirpicults, in their experiment in eugenic breeding. My grandparents and great-grandparents on both sides were among the founding members of the Community. My paternal grandfather was John Humphrey Noyes. I have heard the history of the old Community ever since I can remember. I love its spirit, its past, its present, its future.

To make this book I have chosen out of the prolific writings of the Oneida Community those excerpts, mainly from the *Circular,* the *Daily Journal,* and the *American Socialist*—their own periodicals—that seem to me the most characteristic, the most revealing, the most evocative of the truth of their lives and of their experiment. This, by their own testimony, is what these people were like; this is what the Community was like for the first twenty-five years of its history. I have called this book an autobiography because it is an account of their own lives, written by themselves in their own publications; not a single autobiography by one man telling about himself but a multiple autobiography by two- or three-hundred men and women telling about themselves and each other.

The period here dealt with covers the years from 1851 through 1876, the period of the publication of the *Circular*; from the days of their first, near-starvation struggles to keep alive to what must have seemed to them, indeed, a kind of High Tide of both the Flesh and Spirit, when they were prospering so astonishingly that they felt obliged to remind themselves that money and worldly success were not their aim; that they were, after all, "doing business as unto the Lord." As their leader admonished them, they must hope never to see the day when they would not have to depend on the Lord for money.

Because, during my own childhood, my grandmother used to tell me stories of her childhood in the old Community, the scene comes to me, I suppose, as more romantic, more glamorous than it may have been. I used to listen fascinated to the story of "Good Dinner Days," when the frugal menu was made glorious by the addition of a pat of butter apiece. I loved to hear about the bees when the children braided straw hats or picked strawberries. An only child myself in those days, the idea of a flock of children living together, playing together in the Children's House, seemed wonderful to me.

That I am a biased witness cannot be denied. I do not apologize for this. I can honestly say that although the Oneida Community was certainly radical and may have been wrong-headed in some of its theories, I know it to have been deeply sincere, courageous, and, in a curious sense, innocent. The members of the Community were willing to risk everything they had, willing to face the world's disapproval, willing to make great sacrifices, spiritual as well as practical, for what they believed. I have known some of these people in their later days and could recognize their peculiar quality; a quality which I used to think was like the rounded pebbles in a brook, all harsh edges and sharp corners smoothed away so that their relations with others were sweet, gentle, loving, tolerant. My maternal grandmother, who had been one of the dissidents at the break-up, told me in her old age that there had never been such happiness as they knew in the old Community. I believe that this was honest testimony.

One last word I should like to add on my own account—perhaps a naive one. Most of the principal facts of this history I have known, some of them from early childhood; they could not surprise me. But the new and over-mastering impression I gathered from reading the story of those early years, as the Oneida Communists told it, is of all-pervading happiness.

In the beginning they were desperately poor, they had little enough to eat, they worked—men, women, and also children—

like galley slaves. They were threatened and even attacked by out-side groups who disapproved of them. But they had an unshakeable faith in their creed and their leader so that they did not fear the future. They worked together, they lived together, they loved one another and above all—or because of this—they were simply happy. They were gay; they played as well as prayed. They saw all of life as good and their own lives as especially fortunate. So—until the last days—they were happy.

And in this age when we have a thousand physical advantages which they lacked, when we have a government which insures us against want, when we have innumerable mechanical devices to substitute for hard physical labor, we are not content. We fear the future, with good reason. Many of us have no abiding faith to cling to. We are alienated, apprehensive, unhappy. Happiness, I believe, is the real theme of this book; the autobiography of a happy people.

CONSTANCE NOYES ROBERTSON

Kenwood, 1969

Acknowledgments

Mere thanks, written or uttered, are not sufficient to discharge my debt of gratitude to the several persons who have, during the three years of my labor, helped and heartened me. My first thanks must go to my husband, Miles E. Robertson, who, though not a birthright communist, has championed this book from its inception, has read and criticized and approved and been its staunch advocate. The grant from the Robertson Foundation, so to speak, has financed hours of dictation, miles of copying, reams of Xeroxing. In this case thanks are not required or expected, but it gives me great pleasure to render them.

To my cousins Charlotte Noyes Sewall and Imogen Noyes Stone I am indebted for hours of reading and for many valuable suggestions. Both have great stores of knowledge of the old Community, derived partly from early association with their father, George W. Noyes, who made the subject a life study. This they have shared with me most generously. Two other cousins, Stephen R. Leonard, Jr., and Mary Leonard Beagle, have most kindly lent me material collected by their father, Stephen R. Leonard, whose collection of material and knowledge of the Community was encyclopedic. I wish I might still thank my mother, Corinna A. Noyes, and my father, Pierrepont B. Noyes, both for what they told me long ago and what they have written as their memories of life in the old Community and, especially useful in the preparation of this book, for their legacy to me of complete files of Community publications.

Several other persons have given me help far beyond the call of duty. I wish to thank my friend Winifred Halsted who has read at least three versions of this book—a monumental job which I had no right to extort from a working writer but which I am more grateful for than I can say. My sister, Barbara Noyes Smith, has shuttled the manuscript three thousand miles back and forth to California, time after time, to give me advice I could not have done without. Helen Dick Davis, herself a writer, has not only read and advised from a distance, but came from Mississippi and spent two months working with me over the final revision. I have no words to thank her.

Others who have helped like heroes are my nephew, John F. Robertson, who supplied me with his invaluable dictaphone which simply saved my life, and his wife, Margaret Robertson, who read and copied and cheered the work. I must thank Rupert Smith for spending so much valuable time in making the many excellent reproductions of aged photographs used in this book. Marie Magliocca not only copied at length but did a thousand helpful things for me during the course of the work. Nora Anthony not only did several most complicated jobs of Xeroxing for me but shrugged them off as though they were nothing. Helen deFrees, at the very beginning, copied from some very amateur dictating which I know was a trial to her but which she did for old friendship's sake. Virginia Rann—this is truly prodigious—copied the whole manuscript through twice. I look upon her not only with gratitude but awe. I hope that all these kind people, not adequately rewarded by my thanks, will finally receive the golden crowns which are their due from John Humphrey Noyes in his particular heaven.

Oneida Community

An Autobiography, 1851–1876

Community Song

(Sung to the tune of The Braes o' Balquither)

Let us go, brothers, go
To the Eden of heart-love,
Where the fruits of life grow,
And no death e'er can part love;
Where the pure currents flow
From all gushing hearts together,
And the wedding of the Lamb
Is the feast of joy forever.
     Let us go, brothers, go!

We will build us a dome
On our beautiful plantation,
And we'll all have one home,
And one family relation;
We'll battle with the wiles
Of the dark world of Mammon,
And return with it's spoils
To the home of our dear ones.
     Let us go, brothers, go!

When the rude winds of wrath
Idly rave round our dwelling,
And the slanderer's breath
Like a simoon is swelling,
Then so merrily we'll sing
As the storm blusters o'er us,
Til the very heavens ring
With our hearts joyful chorus.
     Let us go, brothers, go!

Now love's sunshine's begun,
And the spirit-flowers are blooming;
And the feeling that we're one
All our hearts is perfuming;
Towards *one home* let us all
Set our faces together
Where true love shall dwell
In peace and joy forever.
     Let us go, brothers, go!

Introduction

How does one describe an experiment like the Oneida Community? What can it be compared to? Where is there an analogue or even a partially similar model? Among the sixty or seventy contemporary social experiments of the nineteenth century, where is one which compared in any important particular with Oneida? To what leader, from Fourier and Robert Owen to Brigham Young, can Oneida's Noyes be likened? The biographer's task is not an easy one. His subject has been called everything from "crazy" to "the most impressive genius of the period." In order to understand Noyes and the community which he led for more than thirty years, it is necessary to know something of his history and the religious theory which he devised and believed in.

John Humphrey Noyes was the son of the Honorable John Noyes and his wife, Polly Hayes Noyes. Their forbears on both sides had come to America, the Noyeses from England, the Hayeses from Scotland, in the early seventeenth century and settled in the several New England states. The elder John Noyes, of the fifth generation from Nicholas, the original immigrant, was born in Atkinson, Massachusetts, in 1764, where he taught school and prepared himself for college, graduating with honors from Dartmouth in the class of 1795. For the next two years he acted as tutor at Dartmouth where Daniel Webster was one of his pupils. After a brief period as a minister, he went into business in Brattleboro, Vermont, and it was there, in 1804, that he married Polly Hayes, the daughter of Rutherford Hayes, keeper of a popular tavern and grandfather of Rutherford Birchard Hayes, the nineteenth president of the United States.

1

The first son of this marriage, John Humphrey, was born on September 3, 1811, at Brattleboro, Vermont. Of his father, John Humphrey Noyes wrote many years later, "In the family circle and in the highways and byways of business, he was a born Solomon, with a college education added. I have never seen his equal in conversational teaching. He charmed everyone with his political wisdom and did more to make me a thinker than all the disciplines of the schools and colleges." His mother, educated only as a young woman of that period would be, was, even so, perhaps the most important influence in her son's early life. "Vital, inquisitive, imaginative, she no sooner saw a principle than she must attempt to realize it in practice." This description, written a generation after she died, by her grandson, George W. Noyes, in *The Religious Experience of John Humphrey Noyes,* identifies a characteristic which Polly Hayes Noyes passed on to her eldest son and to his son after him. Not all of her descendants inherited this unimpeded transmission of ideas to action, but it was the fortunate legacy of her eldest, John Humphrey; a scholarly mind—this, perhaps from his father—and, once convinced, an uninhibited translation from conception to performance.

Unfortunately the original records in the form of letters, diaries, journals, and even a later memoir dealing with the boyhood and youth of the young John Humphrey, have been destroyed. We do know that he was a precocious learner and thoughtful. As a child he used to say that he wanted to go to bed early because he wanted to think. His mother noted that he had a quick temper and was a natural leader among the children. His early education was obtained in the schools of Brattleboro, Dummerston, and Putney, Vermont, plus a term at a school in Amherst, Massachusetts, and another at the Brattleboro Academy to complete his preparation for college which entered at the age of fifteen. Excerpts from a diary he kept during his years at Dartmouth (cited by George W. Noyes in *Religious Experience of John Humphrey Noyes)* show him to have been a good student, a normally lively youth, pleasure-loving but ambitious and sufficiently competitive.

After John's graduation from Dartmouth in 1830, he spent the next year studying law in the office of his brother-in-law, Larkin G. Meade, in Chesterfield, New Hampshire. Until this time his most notable characteristics would seem to have been a turn for self-examination and a painful bashfulness in the presence of young ladies. This last was apparently hereditary since there is a family legend which claims that the Noyeses who lived in the village of Atkinson, Massachusetts, where John Humphrey's father was born, were so bashful that they were unable to propose to any girls but their own cousins, and this "Atkinson Difficulty," so-called, was one of the crosses which the young John Noyes had to bear.

Time, however, must have disposed of this difficulty, if such it was, for the next year, in 1831, a new and powerful force entered his life. This was the year of the second Great Awakening, the most potent revival to shake America since the days of Jonathan Edwards. Coming on the heels of Lyman Beecher and Dr. Asahel Nettleton, Charles G. Finney was the most powerful revivalist of the period. Central and western New York State were tinder to his flame, and in that region known as the "Burnt-over District," it was estimated that in the year 1830 alone, one hundred thousand converts joined the church. Inspired by Finney's example, a host of minor revivalists entered the field and it was one of these who held a "protracted meeting" in Putney, Vermont, the home of the Noyeses in 1831.

At this time, John Noyes, as he wrote in his diary, "looked on religion as a sort of phrenzy to which all were liable," and he feared lest he should be caught in its snare. He attended the meeting reluctantly, only because his mother was, as he wrote, "extremely anxious that he should receive the word, although he told her plainly that she would be disappointed." The result was electrifying. After four days of wrestling with Satan and the spirit of unbelief, "light gleamed upon his soul," and by nightfall he had decided to devote himself to the service and ministry of God. Like his mother, George W. Noyes writes, John could do nothing by halves. Having arrived at his decision, he assumed as a matter of course that he must abandon the law and become a minister, and he began at once to study Hebrew preparatory to entrance to the Andover Theological Seminary. As he wrote in his diary, "Hitherto, the world, henceforth, God!" He vowed with all his inward strength that he would live in the "revival spirit and be a young convert forever."

Thus, the young John Humphrey Noyes in 1831, at the age of twenty, in a statement to his mother and later to "his friends in private and to all who would hear him in public meetings," declared his new-found faith. Son of a well-born, well-educated, well-off, and somewhat unreligious member of Congress, John Humphrey must have astonished his parents. This declaration was the first of many such statements by him, shading from the so-called eccentric to the openly heretical, during the years that followed.

Andover was a disappointment to the passionate young idealist. Instead of a group of equally passionate young believers, he found there what he called "a professional spirit" among the students. The actual courses of study for the first year, as he wrote later in his *Confessions of Religious Experience* (1849), were excellent, and one lesson he learned and carried away with him to his great profit. A "select society" called the Brethren performed a weekly exercise which consisted in a frank criticism of each other's characters. The member whose turn it was to submit to the criticism held his peace while the other members, one by one, told him his faults in the plainest possible way. "This exercise," Noyes wrote, "sometimes cruelly crucified self-complacency, but it was contrary to the regulations of the society for anyone to be provoked or to complain."

The Andover Seminary was not enough to satisfy John Noyes, however, and the next year he transferred to the Yale Theological School in New Haven. Here he studied under Professor Nathaniel W. Taylor, a popular teacher thought to be somewhat heretical since, as Noyes wrote, he "affirmed man's entire ability to meet the demands of the divine law" which, he added, "gave an excellent opening to my theory."

In August, 1833, Noyes, together with the rest of his class, received his license to preach, and during the six-week vacation which followed he labored as pastor of a little church in North Salem, New York, preaching his first sermon and thereafter preaching six times a week. For this labor he received twenty-five dollars which, with seven dollars he earned by preaching in another small church, was, he records, all the pay he ever received for ministerial labor.

What with Taylorism and Abolitionism, the Free Church, in

which he was very active, and an assortment of revivalists of every shade and color, young John Noyes lived in an exciting ferment of new ideas. A revival which, he wrote, "promised to shake the whole city," was under way in New Haven, and John Noyes with several of his confreres was in the thick of the battle. The effect upon him, as he wrote in his *Confession,* "was the immediate cause of his conviction and conversion to Perfectionism."

Perfectionism, which began as an offshoot of Wesleyan Methodism, had for a number of years been preached by revivalists, especially in western New York, New England and New Jersey, and through the Burnt-over District. Although its exponents advocated the way of perfect holiness, that church which called itself perfectionist did not expect or require sinlessness of its members. To the inflexible logic of John Noyes this made no sense. After months of intense study and strenuous debate not only with his fellow students but with his pastors and masters in the college, he reached his decision and made his statement: "He that committeth sin is of the devil." The next morning a fellow student came to labor with him. "Don't you commit sin?" Knowing that his answer would plunge him into the depth of obloquy, John Noyes replied firmly, "No." Within a few hours the word passed through the college and the city. "Noyes says he is perfect," and on the heels of this went the report, "Noyes is crazy."

After a stormy hearing before the faculty association, the young heretic was allowed to resign his license and shortly was asked to withdraw altogether from the college premises. As he wrote, "I had now lost my standing in the Free Church, in the ministry and in the college. My good name in the great world was gone. My friends were fast falling away. I was beginning to be indeed an outcast. Yet I rejoiced and leaped for joy. Sincerely I declared that 'I was glad when I got rid of my reputation.' Some person asked me whether I should continue to preach now that the clergy had taken away my license. I replied—'I have taken away their license to sin and they keep on sinning. So, though they have taken away my license to preach, I shall keep on preaching.' "

Noyes's confession of sinlessness was made on February 20, 1834, a date always celebrated in the Oneida Community as the High Tide of the Spirit. From this time onward the next several years were a period of trial and tribulation for the young convert. Cut off from his college, his church, and his family, his license to preach rescinded, dropped by many of his seeming friends and adherents, he wandered, often on foot and without money, the length and breadth of New England and New York, preaching, exhorting, spreading his new faith.

From 1834, Noyes and James Boyle published a paper in New Haven which they called, daringly, *The Perfectionist.* "Let us," said Noyes, "rescue the name from the disrepute into which it has been thrown." The first number was issued on August 20, and thereafter a number was published on the twentieth of each month until the spring of 1836, but after six months Noyes and his partner, Boyle, disagreed and Noyes quit the paper, leaving Boyle in control. Three years later, in 1837, in Ithaca, New York, he undertook an independent venture in publishing and called his paper *The Witness;* "to such as choose to buy it, for one dollar for twenty-six numbers; to such as prefer to receive it as a gift, gratis." Three numbers were published in Ithaca; after that there was an interruption of more than a year.

This interruption, itself caused by a kind of misunderstanding, was one of the most important episodes in Noyes's life. In that year, 1837, John Noyes wrote a letter to David Harrison, a trusted young friend and disciple, "in the nakedness of privacy." Private it did not remain. Harrison read it to a few friends including Simon Lovett, an erstwhile confrere of Noyes's, who "borrowed the letter to peruse at leisure," promising to return it without delay. Instead, Lovett showed it to a fanatical young female named Elizabeth Hawley who insisted upon sending the letter to Theophilus Gates, no friend to Noyes and the publisher of a new paper to be called *The Battle-Axe and Weapons of War,* aimed at attacking the institution of marriage. Noyes's letter to Harrison was grist to Gates's mill and he published it—without permission—in his second issue. Since the letter had been published anonymously, rumor attributed it to Boyle, but Noyes had the courage to acknowledge its authorship in the next number of *The Witness.*

The gist of the letter was this statement: Noyes advocated neither a plurality of wives nor a community of wives, but a *nullity* of wives. "When the will of God is done on earth as it is in Heaven, there will be no marriage. Exclusiveness, jealousy, quarrelling have no place in the marriage supper of the Lamb. God has placed a partition between man and woman during the apostasy for good reason: this partition will be broken down in the resurrection for equally good reasons. But woe to him who abolishes the law of the apostasy before he stands in the holiness of the resurrection! I call a certain woman my wife. She is yours, she is Christ's, and in Him she is the bride of all saints. She is now in the hands of a stranger, and according to my promise to her, I rejoice. My claim upon her cuts directly across the marriage covenant of this world and God knows the end." This was written a year before Noyes, himself, was married.

The furore created by this statement can only be imagined. Converts fell away. The subscribers to his little paper, *The Witness,* disappeared; indigence stared Noyes in the face. At this point he was rescued by Miss Harriet Holton of nearby Westminster, Vermont—financially because she was well-off and emotionally because she was a true and faithful believer in his inspiration and his cause. At the lowest possible moment, when the printers were clamoring for payment and he could not even pay his board bill, John Noyes opened a letter from Harriet containing eighty dollars—the exact amount of his debts. Later there were other donations and in his letter of thanks he begged her to "stop running me in debt or make sure that you look at my heart . . . for evidence that your generosity is not misplaced."

This was in March, 1838. In June he sent her what must be one of the strangest proposals ever received; as heterodox, as frank as the *Battle-Axe* letter, and as specific. "We can enter into no engagement with each other which shall limit the range of our affections as they are limited in matrimonial engagements by the fashions of this world." The letter was sent on June 11, 1838, and the next day she accepted. It was recalled that several years before someone had suggested that she might marry John Noyes. Harriet had retorted, "I should as soon think of marrying the morning star!" To John's proposal she replied, "I only expect to be placed in a situation where I can enjoy . . . your society and instruction as long as the Lord pleases and when He pleases."

The young couple were married in Chesterfield, New Hampshire, on June 28, 1838, and after a brief honeymoon spent in Albany buying a printing press, they returned to the Noyes home in Putney where they, with the help of John's two adoring sisters, Charlotte and Harriet, taught themselves to set type and print the first issues of the new volume of *The Witness*.

As one biographer, Robert Allerton Parker, has written in *A Yankee Saint*, "To intertwine into a single pattern strands fundamentally alien and conflicting, to create a tough, enduring yet pliant fabric—here is the problem of every creator, whether in art or in life. Between 1838 and 1848 John Noyes toiled to create his own pattern in human lives, content to begin with the humblest elements and those closest at hand." His aim, which sometimes seemed impossible to achieve, was the creation of a commune of true believers. His own family was the original nucleus; his wife, his sisters, Charlotte and Harriet, his brother George. They met at John's house and called their group the Society of Inquiry, designed, as Noyes wrote in *The Witness*, February 22, 1841, "for discussion and exhortation."

John Skinner joined the group in 1839, George and Mary Cragin in 1840, and gradually a number of other local persons, some of whom dropped out after a short time. There were no set rules for this combination until January 31, 1841, when a constitution of the Society of Inquiry of Putney, Vermont, was drawn up, and the six formal Articles were signed by the members. (This Society was an outgrowth of what had earlier been called the Putney Bible School.) During the next month, February, 1841, the available capital, which included John Noyes's inheritance from his father, Harriet Holton Noyes's patrimony, the inheritances of Charlotte, Harriet, and George Noyes, plus smaller amounts from John R. Miller, John L. Skinner, and the Cragins, totaled $38,000 and was called the Putney Corporation. Later, a number of other persons who could make no contribution in property were admitted to the society. At the end of March 1843, there were thirty-five persons being supported by the common purse.

In 1845 a contract of partnership was followed by a detailed constitution with officers elected and a board of directors. By 1846 the little group of Putney Perfectionists had been associated in religious faith for seven years and had advanced toward external union as far as communism of property. But until this time there had existed two obstacles in the way of implementing Noyes's theory of Complex Marriage, as set forth originally in the *Battle-Axe* letter of 1837. The first stumbling-block was theological. He had always insisted that the resurrection of the body must precede Complex Marriage. Now, after nearly ten years, he arrived at a new conception: increased life tended to improve environment and improved environment tended to increase life. Ergo, Complex Marriage, which would accomplish these ends, was a means by which the resurrection power would be let out into the world.

The second difficulty was physiological. Noyes agreed with Malthus on the absolute necessity for control over propagation. The solution to this problem, which he had arrived at by his own personal experience, he called Male Continence. He described this experience in a pamphlet published first in 1848 and again in 1873.

During the first six years of the marriage of John Noyes and Harriet Holton, out of five births, four were stillborn. Their only living child was Theodore, born in 1841. This, perhaps, was not an extraordinary statistic for that time; men must work and women must weep, and suffering was the natural lot of women. This John Noyes could not accept. Should women be forever the victims of brute nature? It was a challenge which he accepted. The Shaker answer was absolute celibacy. This Noyes rejected. In his careful analysis of the whole sexual arrangement, he recognized two separate functions, the social and the propagative. To separate the two and to provide a safeguard for the woman, he found that self-control, *coitus reservatus* or, as he called it, "Male Continence," was the solution. As he wrote (*Male Continence,* 1848), "It is the glory of man to control himself and the Kingdom of God summons him to control all things."

Here was a great victory over the tyranny of nature. Nearly a hundred years before birth control was practically accepted socially or religiously in the world, Male Continence was one of the major tenets of the Oneida Community, without which neither their social theory nor their experiment in Stirpiculture—a eugenics program—would have been possible.

In the spring of 1846 Noyes "saw many reasons for thinking that the time has come to take the final step out of marriage." In March of that year his sister Harriet wrote in the *Spiritual Magazine*: "Although far from sanguine in my disposition, the improvement that has been made among us the past winter is so palpable and universal that I cannot forbear acknowledging it. There has been among us a marked increase of union. We know in our souls that it is not transient in its nature and that time will but confirm and extend the brotherly love that exists."

On or about November 1, 1846, they signed a Statement of Principles.

We, the undersigned, hold the following principles as the basis of our social union:

1. All individual proprietorship of either persons or things is surrendered and absolute community of interests takes the place of the laws and fashions which preside over property and family relations in the world.

2. God as the ultimate and absolute owner of our persons and possessions is installed as the director of our combinations and the distributor of property. His spirit is our supreme regulator.

3. John H. Noyes is the father and overseer whom the Holy Ghost has set over the family thus constituted. To John H. Noyes as such we submit ourselves in all things spiritual and temporal, appealing from his decisions only to the spirit of God, and that without disputing.

4. We pledge ourselves to these principles without reserve; and if we fall away from them, let God and our signatures be witness against us.

> Geo. Cragin
> Harriet A. Noyes
> Charlotte A. Miller
> Harriet H. Skinner
> Mary E. Cragin
> John L. Skinner
> John R. Miller

George W. Noyes notes, in *The Putney Community*, that "On November 4, 1846, the Putney Perfectionists carried through a consolidation of Households. There was much glorious testimony of the love and union that exists among us."

Half a year later, not only those original signers but the whole enlarged Putney Commune agreed that "the increasing intimacy of communion with God's invisible kingdom" which had been conferred upon them was proof of God's pleasure and purpose concerning them. At a meeting of believers in Putney, on June 1, 1847, John Humphrey Noyes made a "new and further confession of truth," published in the *Spiritual Magazine,* July 15, 1847:

> With a mighty hand and marvellous wisdom God has gathered us together here. We have been able to cut our way through isolation and selfishness in which the mass of men exist and have attained a position in which before heaven and earth we trample under foot the domestic and pecuniary fashions of the world. Separate households, property exclusiveness have come to an end with us. Our Association is established on principles opposed at every point to the institutions of the world. . . . Therefore it is unanimously adopted as the declaration of the believers assembled that the *Kingdom of God Has Come!*

In the Baptist Meeting House in Lairdsville, Oneida County, New York, a Perfectionist convention opened on September 3, 1847, and continued for three days. Present were delegations from various Perfectionist colonies in New York State, from Newark, New Jersey, and from Putney, Vermont, this last represented by John H. Noyes and Harriet A. Noyes. Jonathan Burt, of whom more later, was moderator. After a stormy session during which Noyes's theory and the conduct of the Putney Community were the centers of attention, so great was the enthusiasm of a certain group of members that plans were discussed for the formation of an association of the Putney type in central New York, one site especially considered being Jonathan Burt's sawmill property at Oneida Reserve. At that time there was no thought of abandoning the establishment at Putney, and a group of three families from Beaver Meadow, New York—the Ackleys, the Nashes, and the Hatches—began a semi-communistic settlement which two weeks later moved to the Burt farm near Oneida.

It was at this point, October 26, 1847, that certain pious citizens of Putney, having heard rumors of the scandalous goings-on in the Perfectionist association in their town, arose in wrath and charged John Humphrey Noyes with adultery. Bail was given and Noyes was released until his trial which was set for the following April. His response to this charge was that "it was a controversy of principles and would have to be settled at last by priests and philosophers" (from a letter from Harriet H. Skinner to her mother,

October 29, 1847, cited in George W. Noyes, *Putney Community,* p. 283).

How this controversy would have been settled by such worthies cannot be known since the occasion did not arise. On November 26, John Noyes and his brother-in-law, John Miller, were summoned by another brother-in-law, Larkin G. Mead, to come at once to Brattleboro where they learned that warrants for the arrest of two of the members, Mr. and Mrs. Cragin, had been issued. There was also a rumor that the incensed citizens of Putney were on the point of a mob attack on the little commune. Mr. Mead advised that Noyes and all members who were not residents of the place should leave at once. This plan was followed, Noyes and the Cragins going to New York City and the other members dispersing to their places of residence.

Although it was some years before the various Vermont properties belonging to the association were finally sold, and during this period members of the Oneida family actually returned to Putney as a branch commune, carried on business at their store and mill, and reported that most of those who had been most hostile to them in 1847 were now very friendly, this dispersal was the real end of the Putney commune. Good fortune, or what John Humphrey Noyes liked to call "special Providence," led, during the next three months, to the various steps in the group's transfer to a new setting. At the invitation of Jonathan Burt, Noyes visited the tiny settlement at Oneida Creek, found the pioneer communists living in crowded and primitive conditions but happy and strong in faith, and it was then he decided to bring his Putney family and any other converts to join the Oneida group.

As he wrote to Mr. Cragin, February 4, 1848 (George W. Noyes, *Putney Community,* pp. 387–88):

Everything conspires to bring about concentration here. I have the enthusiastic confidence of all now on the ground. . . . Now for the temporalities. Do you recollect a small timber house across the road from Brother Burt's? There is one comfortable room with a buttery, a back kitchen for summer, a bedroom upstairs, a good barn, a small shoemaker's shop and twenty-three acres of land. . . . I think you can live at least as comfortably there with your children as the Beaver Meadow folks in their shanty (and I assure you they are happy) until we can build a Chateau. There is some romance in beginning our Community in the log huts of the Indians.

George W. Noyes continues (p. 392):

Abandonment of Putney was finally resolved upon. Purchase of land and buildings adjoining Burt's were immediately begun and soon a domain of one hundred and sixty acres with two houses and two log cabins were secured. . . . A rough board shanty was quickly built for a young men's dormitory. During the summer and fall the Mansion House, a wooden structure sixty by thirty-five feet with three storeys and garret was erected. (A member) Erastus Hamilton from Syracuse, who had studied architecture made the plans and superintended the work. The saw mill and timber on the domain provided the materials. All the work except the plastering was done by the Community. Most of the lathing was done by the women. When free from other duties all worked merrily on the house and many valuable lessons in making industry attractive were learned. The building was ready for use before winter.

Why or how this building, completed in 1849, came to be called the Mansion House is nowhere stated in their publications. Later, when the first section of the brick building which succeeded it was built, other names were discussed. The *Circular* for October 3, 1861, says, "If we were Fourierists we should call it the Phalanstery. We are not a Phalanx, but a Community. How would Communistery do? Or koinistery, from the Greek *Koinonia*—fellowship, communism? Or Koinonia Hall? What shall it be? Perhaps some of our readers can suggest a name. Communism certainly needs a distinctive name for its dwelling."

Apparently none of these suggestions suited the family, and the new house and its successors, built respectively in 1861, 1863, 1871, and 1878, were known then and forever after as the Mansion House.

With their occupation of the new Mansion House, the first communal organization of the children began. The larger of the two houses originally on the place was converted into a nursery for the children between two and twelve years of age, of which there were seventeen, and with them, of course, the necessary nurses, housekeepers, and teachers. The other small dwelling was also converted into a nursery for the six babies, also with their nurses and housekeepers.

As Harriet Worden, one of these children, wrote some twenty years later in "Old Mansion House Memories" (*Circular*, January 30, 1871), "The separation from the main household proved very favorable to the comfort and good-breeding of the children, at the same time saving the older people from much noise and confusion. The women who served as 'mothers' and attendants of the children found the business not a burden but a pleasure. At first the real mothers experienced considerable distress in giving up their little ones to the care of others, but a new sphere of existence opened to them and they now found time for educational pursuits. Besides, the improvement in the behavior and general condition of their children was of greater value than the luxury of a sickly maternal tenderness.'

As *The First Annual Report of the Oneida Association* states, "The Oneida Association regards itself as a branch of the kingdom of Heaven, the exponent of the Principles, and servant of the spiritual will, of that kingdom. It has no written constitution or by-laws— no formal mode of electing officers. In the place of all formulas, it relies on inspiration, working *through* those who approve themselves as agents of God, and *by* such apparatus of instruction and criticism as has been described."

Except for the Contract of Partnership of 1846 when John R. Miller was elected president, John L. Skinner secretary, and John Humphrey Noyes, George W. Cragin, and George W. Noyes directors, it was not until 1876, when Noyes announced his "resignation as president of the Oneida Community," that any member, including himself, was ever referred to by the title of president, secretary, treasurer, or whatever.

A group of persons—men and women who, generally speaking, were among the older members and often those who had been among the original founders—were called the Central Members. John Humphrey Noyes was, from the beginning, spoken of as the leader. When he was absent from Oneida and residing either at Wallingford or Brooklyn, one of these central members was appointed by him as father of the family, and a leading woman was the mother of the family. Committees were appointed either by him or these surrogates to manage and serve in the various departments. The only discipline was what they called Mutual Criticism which was conducted by committees, either in public meeting or privately.

The statement entitled "The Oneida Association" appeared in the first volume of their new publication, the *Circular*, for January 30, 1851, and gives a complete resumé of the aims and situation of the Oneida Association, as it was then called, as of that date. It does not go into any particulars about either their religion or their social theory, but both are stated by inference, i.e., "The Bible is our only written constitution," and, farther on, "We teach [husbands and wives] the law of love" and "are not troubled with involuntary propagation." It answered one question which was asked of them with stupefying regularity for the next twenty years: "What do you do with the lazy ones?" The answer was that the "lazy ones" rarely lasted long enough to give trouble in the Community.

A word should perhaps be said here about the nomenclature of the Community. In the beginning they called themselves the Oneida Association but later changed their title to the Oneida Community and called themselves communists. In recent times when that word has come to have for many a pejorative connotation, it should be remembered that the Oneida members were, as they constantly told the world, *Bible Communists* and that it was *Bible Communism* which they practiced and preached.

On September 21, 1853, the *Circular* printed on its first page a description of the Community at Oneida and of each of the other branch communes then extant. Briefly, they cited *"Oneida,* 250 acres; 130 persons in residence, including 40 children. Horticulture and various manufacturing and mechanical pursuits. *Brooklyn Commune*: 25 members, including children. Occupation, mainly preparing, printing and free distribution of the semi-weekly *Circular*. Has been occupied for about five years. *Newark Community*: 15 members. Established over a year in connection with a machine shop. *Wallingford*: a gardening and agricultural Community. 18 members, established 2 years. *Putney* and *Cambridge, Vermont*: small associations, the 1st suitable for gardening, the 2nd for dairy purposes."

On February 3, 1859, the *Circular* began to carry on its front page a longer and more detailed description of the Community as it was then.

THE ONEIDA COMMUNITY, WHERE AND WHAT IT IS

The Community consists of about 200 members, comprising men, women, youth and children, nearly in equal proportions. They cultivate 386 acres of their own land in the Town of Lenox and Vernon, in the State of New York. The Community has been established here eleven years and is self-supporting. There are two branch communities, one located at Wallingford, Conn., and the other at Putney, Vermont, which are also self-supporting.

The Community takes its origin from religious faith and thorough devotion to the teachings of the Bible. . . . The social organization is that of entire Communism like that of the day of Pentecost, when "no man said that aught of the things he possessed was his own, but they held all things in common." The relation of the sexes is placed, not like that of common society, on the basis of law and constraint, neither on the opposite one of mere freedom; but on that of *inspiration, truly derived by communication with the spirit of God.* . . . The object of the Community is to lead a true life.

The true life, unfortunately, was not to be won without a struggle. At the end of their first year at Oneida, John Humphrey Noyes, as Parker says, "the inveterate and indefatigable propagandist," printed and circulated his *First Annual Report of the Oneida Association* in which he recounted frankly and freely their history, their financial situation, their aims and intentions, their religious credo, and—here came trouble—their Theory of the Sexual Relation. The next year, 1850, complaints were made to the magistrates of both Oneida and Madison Counties, claiming that "immoralities" were practiced in the Community. The Grand Jury of Madison County, having been advised also that the communists were industrious and law-abiding, refused to notice the complaint.

However, hostilities were not at an end. The authorities of Oneida County—which actually had no jurisdiction since the Community dwelling was in Madison County—summoned Community members to Utica and put them through a grueling examination. For sensitive and well-bred women, especially, it was a horrible experience, but their courage, their dignity, and their gentle manners carried them through. It was demanded that they break up the Community and go away, to which they agreed if it was the will of their new neighbors that they should do so.

But to test fairly the question whether neighbors really wished them to "clear out," the Community circulated the following document (from *A Yankee Saint,* by Robert Allerton Parker):

TO THE DISTRICT ATTORNEY OF THE COUNTY
OF ONEIDA AND ALL WHOM IT MAY CONCERN:

This is to certify that we, the undersigned, citizens of the towns of Vernon and Lenox, are well acquainted with the general character of the Oneida Community, and are willing to testify, that we regard them as honorable business men, as good neighbors, and quiet, peaceable citizens. We believe them to be lovers of justice and good order—that they are men who mind their own business, and in no way interfere with the rights of their neighbors. We regard them, so far as we know, as persons of good moral character; and we have no sympathy with the recent attempts to disturb their peace.

Nearly every one to whom they appealed willingly signed this document, and one influential landowner declared that he considered the Community members the best class of citizens in the region and that he regarded it as a blessing to have them in their midst.

Another tribulation befell them when, in 1851, a religious paper in New York, *The Observer,* launched a virulent attack against them as a moral eyesore. Various other New York and local newspapers took up the battle which grew so hot and attracted so much unfavorable notice that in March, 1852, the Community issued a manifesto agreeing to abandon their practice of Complex Marriage. Exactly how long this voluntary embargo held is not stated, but by August of that year they published what they called a Theocratic Platform among whose planks were "Abandonment of the entire fashion of the world, especially marriage. . . . Dwelling together in Association of Complex Families, and Cultivation of Free Love."

Whether this was intended as the formal notification to the world that the embargo had been lifted is a matter for conjecture, but it is certain that the Community practiced its peculiar social theory almost to the end of its existence. The only printed argument for this stand followed St. Paul and the Primitive Church in holding that since believers in holiness died in Christ and were resurrected in Christ, they were past death, absolved from divorce, and were in a posthumous state. Monogamy was a part of the grand Apostasy of Christendom. In the resurrection state, Pantogamy or Complex Marriage recognized the continued existence of the sexual relation but excluded ownership.

The most significant fruit of *The Observer*'s crusade of pompous verbiage is a letter it drew from the elder Henry James. James made it clear to the editor of *The Observer* that he was no champion of the doctrines and practices of Noyes. "I told them candidly that any man of common sense must be given short shrift in his regard to a deity who elected men to the privilege of leading disorderly lives; but at the same time I saw they were in no way amenable to the tribunal of common sense" (from *A Yankee Saint,* pp. 192–93). James came to the defense of the Community, actually called at the Brooklyn commune, which had been the particular target of *The Observer*'s fire, and rebuked the attacker, calling it "an unmanly sight to see a great prosperous newspaper . . . gather together the two wings of its hebdomadal flatulence . . . for a doughty descent upon this starveling and harmless fieldmouse!" The *Circular* for March 7, 1852, remarked that it was "a pretty serious thing to lie under the general and outspoken censure of mankind."

With the continuing increase in the number of members, more room was required, and beginning in 1849 additions to Oneida's first wooden Mansion House were made as needed. A new two-story wing was erected in that year, and later other additions for sleeping accommodations, kitchen space, and laundry rooms; and a new building called the Children's House was built just north of the Mansion House and connected with it by an underground passage.

Such patches and additions were no more than temporary expedients, but it was another ten years before the Community was prosperous enough, in 1861, to risk investing in a really adequate permanent dwelling. In 1862 they moved into what would eventually become the north wing of the large brick Mansion House which they ultimately constructed. More room was needed also for the burgeoning young industries which the Community was carrying on, as well as conveniences for the household, and for this a sort of all-purpose building which they called the Tontine, meaning "a building designed for miscellaneous occupations," was erected just west of the new main building in 1863. It was primarily intended to accommodate the washing department, the bag business and the printing office, although it later passed through a number of other phases of usefulness.

In 1864 the trap business, having overflowed its quarters in the old mill, required the building of a new brick factory on a farm property the Community had bought a mile from the Mansion House in the region then called Turkey Street, which the Community renamed Willow Place in memory of their original Brooklyn branch. It was, they wrote in the *Circular* for October 17, 1864, "of brick, the main part 124 feet by 26 feet, two storeys high, with wings, one of two storeys and the other of one storey. It makes a large and showy building and is to be fitted up in all its parts in the most perfect manner. When all is completed and the building in running order, it will be one of the most interesting factories in the country."

The new south wing of the brick Mansion House was begun in 1869, and the family moved into it the next year. Since it was no longer needed and its nearness to the new house was considered a fire hazard, the old wooden Mansion House was demolished in 1870. The third and final addition to the new brick house was a wing running west from the north wing and built in 1878.

It is possible that the communists resented being called a "starveling fieldmouse" even by a kindly critic, but it must be admitted that during those early years they were hard put to keep afloat. It is not altogether to be wondered at. On the same page of the *Circular* of February 3, 1859, which carried their proud report of growth, they also published their Business Platform which consisted in the quotation, in full, of the sixth chapter of St. Matthew, "Consider the lilies of the field," which would seem almost too hopeful, even for a group of true believers.

Although the first Annual Inventory, taken in 1857, showed that during those first nine years, from 1848, they had invaded their capital to the extent of $40,000, they were not dismayed. As they wrote (*Circular,* January 6, 1865), this sum was an investment in their own education which would be lucrative afterwards, "if they struck oil." "Communism," they announced, was "an institution of the Holy Spirit; the social order of Heaven. Its Foundation: God owns all things. Its mode of distribution: by Inspiration. Its Government: Free Criticism. Its result: Unity and Immortality."

In the beginning the intention of the communists was to support themselves by horticulture, as did many of the other communistic experiments of that period. Neither they nor their contemporaries were able to succeed in this endeavor, but in their case, fortunately, Yankee instinct pointed the way before it was too late. The Oneida Community prepared to enter "business as unto the Lord."

There were other ways of making a living, and at one time or another they tried a curious assortment of them. In their earliest days they raised broom corn and made it into brooms which they sold. In the Brooklyn branch they made gold chain. They made and sold rustic seats, wagon-wheel spokes, hoes, mop handles, palm-leaf hats, and "satin sprung cravats," whatever they may have been. They early began to send out what they called peddlers, some on foot, some in wagons, to sell vegetables and fruit from their gardens and, more importantly, to sell silk thread which they bought from a manufacturer in New York until they began to manufacture it themselves in 1866. The bag business—both carpet traveling bags and lunch bags from a patent invented by Mr. Noyes—was begun at Wallingford and later taken over by the Oneida group where it developed into a fairly lucrative affair for a number of years. Fruit and vegetable preserving, which was a natural extension of their farming industry, was begun early and continued, with one break in 1868, to the end of the Community and beyond.

The foundry, besides providing castings for the trap business, also made and sold sleigh shoes, wagon fixtures, architectural columns, window caps, agricultural castings, and sash weights. Workers in the machine shop not only invented and constructed necessary machinery for the trap and silk works, but sold such machines to other manufacturers.

Although horticulture could not support them, it continued for many years not only to supply the family table and as far as possible the fruit-canning business, but also to bring in a modest income from the sale of fruit trees, grape, and raspberry vines from the nursery garden, plums, peaches, and apples from the orchards, and, for a number of years, a handsome return from the sale of straw-berries, both to the city markets and as the Community's famous strawberry shortcakes which they served to visitors.

The four major industries which gradually made obsolete those early efforts were the trap, silk, fruit-preserving, and later the sil-verware businesses. From a precarious, hand-to-mouth affair—when, as they said, an order for five dozen traps was an occasion for rejoicing—the trap business grew in the course of these first twenty-five years into a highly profitable industry and made the Oneida Community a prosperous institution. The silk thread busi-ness, from its start in 1866, prospered, and although it never really competed in profits with the trap business, it did very well. The fruit-preserving business contributed a steady if small income. The silverware business, which was a late-comer, began at Wallingford in 1877 and continued there until, after the break-up of the Com-munity, it was moved to Niagara Falls, New York. More than thirty years later, in 1912, it was finally moved to Sherrill and Oneida, New York, where, unrecognizably enlarged, it still remains. The Community throve and grew in size; new buildings took the place of their primitive beginnings; new members joined. The Oneida Community was widely known.

It was also, in some quarters, widely disapproved. Its social theory, which maintained that no property should be held in selfish-ness by one individual, also set aside what they considered the selfish monogamy of the world, and members substituted for it their own system which they called Complex Marriage. This system they distinguished sharply from the much-vilified and frequently disastrous cults of Free Love, so called, which were prevalent in many contemporary communities. In Complex Marriage, each was married to all. At the same time they declared that "exclusive idola-trous bonds between two members were pernicious to the whole system of Complex Marriage."

Partly to prevent these exclusive attachments which they called Special Love, and, more importantly, to protect the members from social approaches which might be unattractive, a third party, gen-erally an older person, acted as intermediary between the two members who wished for a closer relationship. The women were at all times free to decline without embarrassment. Certain members remained celibate all their lives. As John Humphrey Noyes stated many times, Complex Marriage was as binding a relationship as conventional marriage, and the whole group held themselves responsible for every child born to the group.

When later the Oneida Communists entered upon the eugenic experiment which has interested so many students of modern sociology, the children thus produced were brought up according to the most careful theory, for theorizing, on almost every subject, was one of their predelictions.

From the beginning Community children, either Community-born or those brought in by parents who joined from outside, were cared for all together in a children's department under the supervision of selected nurses and teachers. Their own parents were freely allowed to see them but the responsibility for their care was taken by the appointed guardians, and their mothers were able to continue whatever work they had previously undertaken. The so-called Stirpicults took their father's name as long as the Oneida Community lasted. Later, in some cases, they took their mother's name or that of their step-fathers. On the evidence of some of those children, until recently still living, they had a happy, healthy, and untroubled childhood.

The labor of the Community was all done at first by the members themselves. Committees were appointed to manage the kitchen and dining room, the laundry, the Children's House, the farm, and the heavy work. And all this labor was a free-will offering; there was no pressure exerted to demand it of the members. Actually, the Community disapproved of such pressure or a sense of what they called "legality" in the workers, with the result that these people worked willingly and with enthusiasm.

Later, as the various business projects expanded and required more workers, the Community began to hire outside labor, although their own people continued not only to manage and direct the growing enterprises but actually do a considerable portion of the work. In the offices and in some of the lighter duties of the manufactory as well as in the management and care of the communal home, women shared the labor and, in fact, the Oneida

Community was one of the first groups to grant full equality of position to women.

Education of their children was a subject of the greatest importance to the communists. Various systems of schooling were tried; teachers, curriculum, age-group, and hours of study were the subject of experiment from year to year, but the steady level of instruction was certainly higher than the average in the outside world at that time.

This in itself was admirable, but more remarkable for that period was the emphasis on adult education. With *improvement* the Community watchword, it was not enough that the children should be well educated. Every member, young and old, not only was encouraged to learn, but, as classes in a dozen subjects were formed, a real passion for learning swept the Community. As early as 1853 middle-aged women were studying English grammar, German, and French. Two years later, "Greek and French languages, mathematics, grammar etc." were "in vogue after supper, varied occasionally by a writing bee."

This was only the beginning. Ten years later there was talk of a Community University in which girls should have all the advantages of boys. For a start, they were being taught to swim and, on the intellectual side, they were urged to cultivate "a taste for solid reading." The university, unfortunately, never materialized, but to the very end, next only to spiritual improvement, education was the grand ambition of the Community.

This, then, was the birth, growth, and development of the Oneida Community. In 1849 its membership was 87; in 1851 it was 205; in 1875 it was 298, and in 1878 it was 306. At various times branch communes were essayed; only the one at Wallingford, Connecticut, was maintained to the end of the Oneida experiment. In the beginning, the majority of the members were New Englanders; later, members from the local area and other sections of the country joined. To a nucleus of teachers, preachers, lawyers, and doctors was added a sturdy complement of farmers and artisans, engineers and merchants, practical men and women to leaven the lump of what might have been unrealistic fanatics to produce the wholesome bread of communism.

The relation of the Community to the outside world, both its immediate neighbors and the great world beyond, was surprisingly amicable. Locally most of the farmers and the citizens of the small towns and villages nearby, if not wholly approving, were for the most part friendly. When the Community was under attack by the clergy in 1873, a half-dozen of the local newspapers defended them handsomely. There was criticism of their social theory but none of their honesty, industry, or decorous public behavior. During the summer, crowds of men, women, and children, not only local but from a distance, thronged the Community's lawns and buildings, ate their strawberries, listened to their music. When the growing Community industries obliged them to hire outside help, there is no record of any but friendly relations between the workers and the communists who paid better than ordinary wages, supplied night schools for any employees who wished them, and introduced piece work and the eight-hour day.

The *Circular* of March 9, 1876, contained an announcement which astonished the religious and journalistic world. The Oneida Community *Circular,* it said, would no longer be published, and in large black type, a Prospectus announced the forthcoming publication of a new paper entitled *The American Socialist,* devoted to "the progress of socialism everywhere," to be edited by John Humphrey Noyes. This in itself was not too surprising since Noyes had been the *deus ex machina* of all the Community publications, but the real bombshell was the added announcement of the resignation of the editor-in-chief of the new weekly from the presidency of the Oneida Community, in order, it said, "to be free henceforth to devote himself wholly to editorial labor." It also announced that he was to be succeeded by his son, Theodore Richards Noyes, as new president of the Oneida Community.

To what would seem an extraordinary degree, considering the size and remoteness of the Community, the press, not only locally but in New York and other large cities, reported and speculated at length upon the cause and possible results of this change. Had there been dissension in the apparently prosperous and serene Oneida Community? And, they asked even more frequently, could the Community hope to live and prosper without its original genius and prophet?

These questions the new publication did not answer. It did, as promised, devote most of its space to socialistic matters, with only an occasional article dealing with the Oneida group, making no mention of its internal politics. For nearly four years longer, from March 9, 1876, to December 25, 1879, the new periodical continued to be published and the Oneida Community continued to exist in more or less its old form. Then, with the issue of December 25, the *American Socialist* bid farewell to its subscribers:

> Respecting the future of the cause to which the *Socialist* has been devoted, we may say for ourselves that we still believe in the continued progress and ultimate triumph of Socialistic principles. We still believe that Christianity requires that "the strong should bear the burdens of the weak" and that just in proportion as this is done will genuine Communism prevail. We still believe that the principles of Cooperation, Mutual Insurance and Christian Brotherhood are more and more modifying all the relations of mankind, and winning new and glorious victories in every field of endeavor and will yet make "divinely real" our highest ideal.
>
> And now, with malice toward none and good-will toward all, we bid our readers adieu.

On August 28, 1879, the Oneida Community had announced a change of social platform: that is, the end of the practice of Complex Marriage and the return to the marriage customs of the world. It was their intention at that time to continue the other forms of communal life: the common ownership of their businesses and other properties, the continuation of their common homes at Oneida and Wallingford, the communal care of the children. They would now look, they wrote (*American Socialist,* August 28, 1879), "for the sympathy and encouragement which have been so liberally promised in case this change should ever be made."

To what extent they received this sympathy—how much praise from their previous critics, how much lamentation from their outside partisans—is not documented. The Community continued to operate on this new basis until January 1, 1881, when they made the radical change from communism to joint stock and incorporated a company which they called Oneida Community, Limited. The assets of the old Community were divided in the form of stock in the new company on the basis of a mutually agreed-on combination of the amount of money contributed by each adult member upon joining, plus a percentage of the capital according to the number of years of membership per individual. All children under sixteen years of age were given a yearly income and a guarantee of support and education until that age was reached. At sixteen, they were given a lump sum to assist in further education or the learning of a trade.

At this time some members left Oneida, temporarily or permanently. The majority remaining continued to dwell in or near the old Mansion House and to work for, or to be supported by, the new company. John Humphrey Noyes, who had left the Community in 1879, removed to Niagara Falls, Canada, where he spent the remainder of his life. A pleasant house was bought for him and a number of his closest friends and relatives joined him there for longer or shorter periods. He died there in 1886, at the age of seventy-five.

His son Pierrepont Noyes wrote of him (*My Father's House*):

While the Community was writing "finis" my father gave an impressive demonstration of that genius for interpreting misfortune or disaster as victory, which heartened his followers through all the trials of their great experiment and which preserved their belief that such were merely incidents in God's inscrutable plan for educating his chosen people—preparing them for their eternal birthright. He wrote:

"We made a raid into an unknown country, charted it and returned without the loss of a man, woman or child."

Could anything be more dramatic—a man now in his seventieth year, standing amid the ruins of his lifework, shouting "Victory!"

I

Where They Lived

After the Community's first rude accommodations at what was then called Oneida Reserve—two small farm houses, two log cabins left by the Indians, and a shed—the first wooden Mansion House which they built with their own strenuous labor during 1848 must have seemed the height of luxury. One of the members, Mr. Erastus Hamilton, had been trained as an architect, and, as Harriet Worden wrote (*Circular,* January 16, 1871), "One beautiful moonlight night, he and Mr. Noyes, with the aid of the North Star, staked out the ground for the foundation walls of their new abode." Their own sawmill and wood lots provided the lumber, their own carpenters and joiners did the work. Even the women worked, completing most of the lathing of the interior. The building, though not wholly finished, was ready for occupancy before cold weather. It would be worth, they wrote proudly, the sum of $3,000.00. Beyond this they owned property—farmland, the mill, and others—amounting to $9,400, but they were nearly out of ready cash, with a house to finish, a printing office to support, and a hundred persons to feed and clothe (*Circular,* January 16, 1871).

In their partly finished Mansion, the problem of dormitory space for the members was partially solved by the invention which they called the Tent Room. This room, of which they were understandably proud, gave rise to scandalous stories, but the Oneida Community stood firm. The Tent Room was "private enough for persons of sound morality." Later, when their finances were less straitened, the Tent Room was succeeded by separate bedrooms. In 1849, also, a separate building for the whole family of children was constructed just north of the Mansion House.

27

There remained various problems of inconvenience, among them bathing and the family laundry. In 1857 a bath house was proposed but not carried out. The men bathed in the flume of the mill or in the creek, but this was available only in summer—and not to the women. One member—probably a woman—said wistfully (*Circular,* June 4, 1857) that if the men did not have access to the creek they would soon have a new bath house, but nothing was done about it. The family laundry, in the beginning, was done in the most primitive way, often out of doors. Later, as more room was provided in the various wings, a cistern was built and the washing was done indoors by a company of men and women whose names were drawn by lot each week. Various improvements were introduced from time to time, culminating in the Universal Clothes Wringer, until, in 1863, a new brick building was built somewhat west of the new Mansion House to accommodate the laundry.

The need for this addition had been discussed for some years, since, with the growing family, the laundry had entirely outgrown the old conveniences. There were other reasons for investing in a new building; the bag business also had outgrown its present accommodations, a new printing office was desired, and ultimately a new dining room and kitchen would be required. It was decided that a building large enough for the washing, the bag business, and the printing, plus cellar space for the fruit department, would be more economical than a smaller building. This building was named the Tontine, and the ground between it and the New House was graded, grassed, and landscaped (*Circular,* May 9, 1864) to "make a nice little place to step into on hot sunny days." Half of the Tontine was devoted to the washing department and provided a steam engine, a boiler, two washing machines, an ironing room, and mangle. Still later, the requirements of the silk department made it necessary to move the laundry to the old mill where a brick wing was built to accommodate it (*Circular,* April 10, 1871).

By 1860–61 the Community was prosperous enough to build the north wing of the new brick house—the "Chateau" Mr. Noyes had written about in 1848—into which they moved, with great rejoicing, in the summer of 1862. In 1864 the new trap factory was built in Turkey Street and named Willow Place, after the old Brooklyn home. This property, a mile and a half north of the Mansion House, had been bought the year before from a Mr. Wager and included a water power on Sconondoa Creek, a sawmill, a stone quarry, an iron foundry, and a good farm house which they moved farther east and transformed into a small branch commune for those of their members who worked in the trap shop.

Work was begun on the south wing of the brick Mansion House in 1869, and the next year the family completed its move from the old wooden Mansion House into the new, thankful especially for the spacious and convenient Children's House, so-called, which occupied a large part of the lower floor of this new wing. The old Mansion was demolished in 1870. In this same year an addition was made to the Willow Place factory to accommodate the ever-growing businesses, especially the new silk thread business which had been begun in 1866 (*Circular,* August 6, 1866).

Construction of the Midland Railroad, which was first projected in 1868, was a matter of some concern to the Community since the survey proposed to run more than a mile through the center of their home domain. With some reluctance they finally agreed to exchange the right of way for a depot for their own use. The railroad was opened from Oswego to Norwich, a distance of about one hundred miles, in late November of 1869 and promised two passenger trains and a freight train each way, daily. Later, by an arrangement with the Central Road, the Community people were able to reach New York City in twelve hours and, by a connection with the Albany and Susquehanna, to get their coal by rail from the Pennsylvania mines. With these conveniences, plus a telegraphic communication from the depot, they were obliged to admit that the Midland was an invaluable addition to their lives. Even aside from travel to distant points like New York and Wallingford, their business at Oneida Village which had required two or three daily trips by the Oneida Community Express—horse-drawn—could now be done by a five-minute train ride instead of a four-mile circuit by road. They did not then anticipate the hordes of visitors the railroad would bring them and perhaps some other drawbacks. It was reported that as a train stopped at the new depot someone, possibly not the conductor, called out, "Cars stop for fifteen minutes for stealing fruit." This announcement, the *Circular* (October 11, 1869) said indulgently, was "probably made for the fun of it." The influx of visitors and "excursions" overflowed the Community's domain from spring to fall. The "Strangers' Guide," reprinted below, was for the direction of these visitors and a somewhat more severe "Notice to Visitors," given in another section, suggests that their guests were not always considerate.

The entry in the *Circular,* July 19, 1875, describing the telegraph line just introduced between the Mansion House and the factory at Willow Place, seems an astonishingly modern note, and one can imagine half the members, with their invariable enthusiasm, finding practical telegraphy an interesting study for all classes. This little line, they confidently expected, would ultimately be connected with other lines so that they could confer with people the world over. The Oneidans might live a life withdrawn from the World but there was nothing parochial about their thinking.

First Annual Report of the Oneida Association, January 1, 1849

The Oneida Association is located in a secluded valley on the Oneida Creek, in the towns of Lenox and Vernon, and counties of Madison and Oneida, in the state of New York, three miles south of the Oneida Depot, which is the half-way railroad station between Utica and Syracuse. The post office address of the Association is Oneida Castle, in the county of Oneida. The lands of the Association are part of the territory reserved till recently, to the Oneida Indians. The State purchased the territory in 1840 and '42, and disposed of it to white settlers, receiving part payment and giving articles securing deeds to the purchasers in full payment. The Association holds most of its lands under these articles. The domain, consisting of 160 acres, lying on both sides of the Creek, is mostly alluvial soil of good quality. It includes an excellent water privilege, which is now occupied by a saw-mill and other lumber machinery, and affords abundance of power for a grist-mill, machine-shop, and other works, already projected by the Association. This water privilege and the land immediately adjoining, has been paid for in full, and is held by deed from the State.

ERECTION OF THE MANSION HOUSE

It stands on an elevated part of the domain, commanding a very extensive view of the surrounding country. It is sixty feet long, thirty-five feet wide, three stories high and is surmounted by a cupola. The lower story, or basement, is divided by partitions across the whole width, into three apartments of equal size, viz., 35 feet by 20. The first of these apartments runs back into a rise of ground on which the house abuts, and is a cellar. The second or middle apartment is the kitchen. The third, or front apartment, is the dining room. The second story comprises a parlor over the dining room and the same size (i.e. 35 by 20), a reception-room, a school-room and a printing office. The third story is devoted to sleeping apartments for married pairs and for females. The garret, extending over the whole house and without partitions, is the dormitory of the unmarried men and boys. The edifice now gives comfortable quarters to about sixty persons and might easily accommodate one hundred.

When the Mansion House came to be occupied . . . the best of the ordinary houses, that nearest the Mansion House, was converted into a nursery, and all the children between the ages of two and twelve (seventeen in number), with the necessary house-keepers and teachers, were established there, by themselves. The other principal dwelling house, previously occupied by Mr. Burt, was also converted into a nursery, and given up to the infants (six in number) with their nurses and house-keepers. This arrangement proved to be very favorable to the comfort and good-breeding of the children and at the same time, saved the main household of the Association from much noise and confusion. The women serving as attendants of the children for short periods only, and in rotation (except in cases of special taste and qualification), found the business not a burden but a pleasure.

COMMON TABLE

The meals of the Association, at the Mansion House, were served at one table, extending through the dining-room, and were alike for all, not differing materially in quality from the meals of respectable households in ordinary life. The business of waiting on the table was left open to volunteers, and became a very attractive service, making occasion for lively competition.

THE TENT ROOM

It was the wish and intention of the Association, from the beginning, to make the Mansion House its winter quarters . . . but as winter drew near and the finishing of the house lingered, it became evident that this intention must be abandoned unless some new method of constructing dormitories, more expeditious than the usual one, could be devised.

One half of the third story, i.e. a space of 35 feet by 30, was finished as a single apartment. Within this apartment, twelve tents (each about 7 feet by 8, large enough for a bed and all other apparatus necessary for a dormitory) were erected against the walls of the room to form a hollow square. The tents were made of cotton cloth, supported on upright wooden frames about seven feet high, and open at the top. The space between the tops of the tents and the ceiling of the room (about 2 feet) gave free circulation to air and light. The interior of the hollow square, a space about 18 feet by 14, became a comfortable sitting-room for the occupants of the tents. One large stove in the center of this sitting-room was found sufficient to warm the twelve rooms around it and two reflectors suspended in the same apartment gave light enough for all ordinary purposes to the whole.

On trial all parties were delighted with the arrangement. "Christmas Eve" was the first evening of the occupation of the tents; and the Association celebrated the occasion in the sitting-room of the encampment, with music and sentiment, in the midst of green festoons and with mirth like that of the "feast of tabernacles."

Second Annual Report of the Oneida Association, February 20, 1850

NEW BUILDINGS

The Association has erected during the last year a house for children, 24 feet by 43, and two stories high. Cost $800.

A building for a store, printing office, etc., 34 feet by 44, two stories high, with a cellar under the whole and cost $1,200.

Also a wing to the Mansion House, 16 feet by 45; and another 16 by 25 feet—both two stories high, and cost $1,000.

Total cost of the Mansion House, $3,000.

The children take their meals in the large dining-room and Mansion House, so that no part of the Children's House is used for kitchen or dining purposes. It is devoted exclusively to sitting and sleeping-rooms.

These two buildings, with an ordinary farm-house one story and a half high, valued at $600, are all the buildings used as *dwellings*, and are found sufficient to accommodate the present number of forty families.

The total cost of these three houses is $4,400. Adding $600 for wells, fences, etc., the gross amount is $5,000. The total cost of the houses which would be necessary for these forty families in the ordinary state of isolation, at the low estimate of $500 each, would be $20,000.

In this one item, then, of dwelling-houses, there is a saving made by this Community of $15,000, or three-fourths of the ordinary expense. The amount thus released from useless investment can be profitably employed in various branches of business and production.

Circular, April 25, 1852

Much might be said of the increased sociality of the Tent Room, as compared to the cold isolation of ordinary apartments. The curtained sleeping rooms are left plain, simply furnished for the retirement of rest; and the common room into which they open is intended to be the social resort of the inmates. It is furnished with books, center table, etc., and the reunions here, for study, conversation, and music, form a constant social element, both improving and delightful.

Circular, October 25, 1855

We do need more room. Never were 170 persons found before living in one family under so small an amount of roof as ours. It is a grand part of our discipline, however, that we have been called, and in a sense compelled, for several years to aggregate so closely. Smallness of space has served as a compress on excessive individuality, and brought out only the more divinely the qualities of that charity that is the social element of Communism. But a larger school room for the children, says one, would be so convenient; and what shall we do, says another, for some who want rooms with a fire in them during the winter months? We must apparently give up the sewing room for this purpose, and then where will the bag manufacture betake itself? Our parlor is full in the evening, so that it is difficult to secure ventilation without exposing some persons to cold current while others are plied with too much heat. Our dining tables at their utmost capacity will not seat one-half of the Community, the other half being necessarily put off till the second table, etc., etc. But what then? We shall go along first grade, as we have done, with our present accommodations, until we can make them better. We want money for executing the various improvements and embellishments that suggest themselves in our surroundings, and we take this as hint from the Lord to go to work vigorously and make money, which we shall endeavor to do. In due time we are confident that the interior life that is given to us will also have the means of clothing itself in fitting forms of external excellence and beauty.

Circular, September 24, 1853

A few rods from the north front of the Commune is a tasteful, convenient building, of smaller dimensions which they call the Children's House. There suitable persons are employed in taking charge of the children, for whom daily a real parental care is exercised.

Circular, April 9, 1857

We are contemplating an extension of our accommodations to the amount of about 24 beds, to make room for the expected addition to the family from Putney. The space allotted for the purpose, having been cleared of its heterogeneous accumulations, the family indulged in a general dance, previous to partitioning off the area, which, being very spacious, admitted of nearly the whole dancing together.

Circular, March 28, 1861

The ground for the New House, cellar and foundation has been broken, the stones are nearly all on the ground, and perhaps half of the brick. The joiners are busy making window frames and doors; and in two or three weeks we may expect to see the first stones of the walls laid in their long resting places.

To give our readers an idea of the building we propose to erect, it may be mentioned that it will consist of a main part 45 by 60 feet, three stories high, the longest line being east and west. On the north side of this main part will be a wing 41 by 57, also three stories high. On the northeast corner of the wing will be a tower four stories in height, 18 feet square. The whole building fronts east. In the first story of the main part there will be a large Reception Room with a number of bedrooms adjacent, for the accommodation of visitors. There will also be two other large rooms in the rear part of the same story which may be used as schoolrooms, or for other purposes. In the second story there will be a large hall or assembly room in size about 42 by 52, 22 feet high, with gallery and stage. The remainder of the building will be mainly occupied with sitting-rooms and dormitories.

Circular, June 19, 1862

The Hall is nearly finished, though the room presents a somewhat chaotic appearance yet. The band has already tried the effect of the music there, and has now suspended playing until it is quite completed. We are much pleased with the taste and nicety with which the German artists executed the work of frescoing the room, which, being quite high, enhances the effect of the painting overhead. There are paintings in oil of symbolic figures representing Justice, Music, Astronomy and History only without the wings usually attached to such illustrations. There is a large stage at the east end of the apartment, with a proscenium arch of wood, delicately frescoed; and on the other three sides there is a gallery which will amply accommodate all our own people with seats.

Circular, June 26, 1862
OPENING OF COMMUNITY HALL

Our new Hall being finished, with the exception of a few minor items, last week, it was thought best to begin its occupation as a Community Assembly Room with a few appropriate exercises. Accordingly, on Sunday, the Hall was set in order. At 6:45 o'clock p.m. the family assembled in our Old Parlor, to bid adieu to the place which for so many years has been the home-center of the Community. Mr. Inslee read the 33rd Psalm. Mr. Burt then made a few valedictory remarks, giving some reminiscences of the past in relation to our accommodations for Community assemblage. He mentioned the fact that during the first summer after the Community started, the meetings were held in a barn. Afterwards a large board shanty was built, and a portion of that was thus occupied. After this the Mansion was built, and in that, with the enlargement three years ago, we have been accommodated until the present time.

The Community hymn was then sung: "Let Us Go, Brothers, Go."

Circular, May 28, 1863

Ground has been broken for the cellar of our new building which is to accommodate the Washing Department, the Bag Business, and perhaps the Printing Business. The teams are carrying sand; much of the requisite lumber is on the ground, and the work will now go steadily forward. The building is to be seventy-two feet long by thirty-six feet wide, and two stories high besides the basement. One half the building will be devoted to the Washing Department, furnishing rooms for washing, drying and ironing the clothes. The other half of it is proposed to occupy as follows: Basement for a fruit room: First story above the basement, Bag Shop: Third story or second above the basement, Printing Office. The building will be situated on the slope west of the New House, and the basement opens on the west side on the level with the road through that part of the grounds.

Since the new library room has been fitted up with alcoves and shelves, the librarian has thoroughly reorganized our library. All the books in the Community have been catalogued and numbered, and nearly all have been definitely arranged in their places on the library shelves. A Library Register is kept in which persons record the books which they take out, so that all books are accounted for, and may easily be found, either in the library or in the possession of the persons who are reading them. A committee has been appointed which has the superintendence of the buying of books and pictures.

Circular, October 17, 1864

Of the doings of the Community, perhaps the most interesting part is that of the Trap factory inaugurated and perfected by Mr. Newhouse. The building is situated on Oneida Creek, is three stories high and provided with various kinds of machinery ingeniously contrived for the purpose of manufacturing traps. So large is the demand for these goods, that another factory is being erected by the Community on Sconondoa Creek at a cost of over twenty thousand dollars. This building is being rapidly enclosed. It is of brick, the main part 124 feet by 26 feet, two stories high, with wings one of two stories and the other of one story. It makes a large and showy building and is to be fitted up in all its parts in the most perfect manner. The vast deal of labor was here being laid out in construction of the dam and in leading the water down to the factory. When all is completed and the building is in running order it will be one of the most interesting factories in the country, since fine mechanical skill and inventive genius are here developed in curious and wonderful machines which do their work rapidly and in the most perfect manner.

Circular, August 19, 1867
WILLOW PLACE

These works are a mile and a third north-easterly from the Oneida Community, and on the old turnpike leading from Syracuse to Utica. Should the traveling public ever enforce its demand for a more direct railway communication between these two cities, then Willow Place will be almost exactly on the line of the new road. The material used in the construction of this factory is mainly brick. The shop consists of two ells, attached to a transverse building 124 feet long, 26 feet wide and four stories high, including a stone basement which contains the wheel-pit. The two-story ell on the right is 105 feet long and 50 feet wide. The lower part is used as a Machine Shop and Office. The upper is filled with silk machinery in full operation, and now produces about seventy pounds of machine twist per week. The rest of the building is devoted to the trap business, which at present employs about 70 hands. The power is supplied by water taken from the Sconondoa Creek, and held in a large reservoir from whence it is carried underground to a breast-wheel 20 feet and 6 inches in diameter and 10 feet face. These works, and the necessary bands and aqueduct were built in 1864, at a cost of $32,000, not including any machinery except the water-wheel.

A little to the right, is a large, beautiful farmhouse surrounded by fruit and shade trees. This is the home of the Willow Place family who moved in there last spring. They now number about thirty, and are chiefly employed in the shops. A quarter of a mile east is another water power belonging to the Community. Here is a foundry consisting of two stone buildings, two excellent store-houses, and a vigorous little sawmill. Between these two water privileges is a bit of water, rock and umbrageous scenery not surpassed by anything in the neighborhood. Combined with all is a farm of one hundred acres, on which are two good stone quarries, and the necessary farm buildings. Besides these there are a half dozen or more small tenant houses which are rented to our workmen.

Circular, May 4, 1868

Opposite to the main Community dwelling, 20 rods distant, is the O. C. Store, with its two wings, one occupied by the business office and the other by the shoe shop and tailor shop. The office is the place for the receipt and dispatch of mails, and the headquarters of book-keeping and finance. Its affairs with the varied business correspondence of the Community are mainly executed by three young women.

Sixty rods down the road by the flower garden and the avenue of elms you come to another bridge over the creek with the two or three cottages and the mill. First the mill was occupied as a saw and grist mill with a printing office and carpenter shop in the upper stories. Singular has been the transformations of the old mill. After the removal of the trap and silk works to the new factory at Willow Place, nearly the whole of the mill was transformed into a bag and satchel factory. Six months ago the building was a hive of industry in this department. Today we are invited to go down and attend the *last "Bag Bee."* The business is closed up, the hired hands are discharged, the stock is to be sold, and the building forthwith given up to the horticulturists for a fruit-preserving factory. Let us look in upon the Bee. Here are a score or two of persons and a half-dozen sewing machines, putting the finishing strokes to the tasteful bags and satchels with which travellers arm themselves for distant journeys. The upper parts of the building display large pyramids of fruit cans which are made in the attic, two men deftly soldering, at little bench-furnaces, five or six hundred a day.

Circular, July 26, 1869

It is with peculiar interest that we watch the growth of the new wing to our main building. Day by day one can see its numerous walls grow— except on Sunday, when all is as silent as a church on week days. Never did we witness the erection of so large an edifice where the work was accomplished with so little noise and confusion.

Circular, October 25, 1869

This day is made memorable in the annals of the O. C., by the introduction of steam into the Mansion for heating purposes. There have been weeks of preparation; thousands of feet of conducting pipe have been fitted, and placed in position ramifying through the building from cellar to attic, and making as complex a system as the arteries and veins of the human body. A score of "radiators" and "coils" flank the walls of halls, sitting-rooms and sleeping rooms.

At six-thirty o'clock all was in readiness and the signal given to "let on steam."

Circular, January 17, 1870

Several divisions of the new-wing cellar (it has a labyrinth of compartments) have lately had cement floors laid down. This cellar, light and airy, connects, by a short arched passage, directly with the kitchen and dining-room in the basement of the Old Mansion. This passage is much used especially in stormy weather. It might puzzle a stranger who had no knowledge of the ebb and flow of this underground current, which at mealtimes is at flood tide, to divine how communication is kept up between the two houses; but this will explain. With another longer, arched passage, we have access to the Tontine, and in this way can visit our three principle buildings without exposure to the elements, or wetting the soles of our feet.

Circular, March 21, 1870

STRANGER'S GUIDE TO O.C.

Visitors on arriving at Oneida by New York Central Railroad, may proceed to the Community (distant about four miles) either on foot, or by carriage hired at the livery, or by the cars of the Midland Railroad. The pedestrian follows the most of the distance the straight path of the railway track. The carriage route is through the main street of Oneida, to Oneida Castle, a village of many Indian reminiscences, and thence up the valley of Oneida Creek a mile and a half through a well cultivated district to the Community domain. Time, three-quarters of an hour. By the Midland cars, which make two trips a day, the traveller is set down in about seven minutes at the O. C. Station, within a stone's throw of the Community dwellings. Fare, fifteen cents. Visitors from the north or south have no change to make, as the Community Station is on the new route from Oswego to New York (nearly completed) and is a stopping place of all the trains.

Reception-Room

A walk of three minutes from the station brings the visitor to a rear entrance of the Mansion, opening into a small summer court. Passing through it he enters a hall on the right which conducts to a reception-room, where he will usually find a gentleman or lady attendant who will answer his inquiries and give him directions for making a tour of the place. If they are absent a word addressed to any person on the premises will bring the required attention. No pay is taken from those who merely wish to see the institution, but every facility is freely accorded to them.

Directly opposite this reception-room is the visitor's dining room, where refreshments are served. Persons wishing for dinner should procure their ticket as soon after arrival as convenient, to give the Kitchen Department suitable time for preparation.

Those who desire to see the public rooms will now be furnished with a guide, or with directions by which they may go alone.

The Main Pile

Returning to the vestibule on the ground floor by which we entered, we may now pass out through an eastern door to the lawn in front of the main building. The latter is seen to be of brick, with stone trimmings, and to consist of a center and two wings with a tower at either end. The southern wing has been recently built, and with its mansard roof gives three habitable stories. The towers are four stories in height.

Parlor and Library

The principle entrance, through the portico of the central building, leads to various public rooms. On the right as we enter is a parlor; on the left a cloak room and office with toilet conveniences for gentlemen. The parlor contains a stereoscope with views, a few engravings and a register wherein visitors commonly write their names. Further on, the entrance hall is crossed by another, leading to the wings on either hand. Next we come to the library on the left of the main staircase. This is a cozy room for the student, containing a collection of 3,300 volumes. It is always open for the use of the Community and its guests. The reading tables are supplied with files of many of the leading newspapers and periodicals of the day.

Museum

Ascending the staircase we enter a vestibule which contains a dozen interesting pictures, and the nucleus of a museum. Among the curiosities are a few animal remains, including the well-preserved tooth of a mastodon, some stalactites, old books, relics from Pompeii and Egypt, medals, Indian weapons, etc. A case of birds prepared by a member of the Community may be examined by persons interested in taxidermy.

The Meeting Hall

From the vestibule, doors open into the Hall or Chapel, a large room 21 feet high and frescoed. A stage and curtains on the front give conveniences for concerts, lectures and dramatic entertainment. A piano and harmonium, always present, invite to musical practice by the Community members or by visitors. During the summer, music will generally be given here at a certain hour each afternoon, at which visitors may be present. The main use of the Hall is for the social meetings of the Community, which are held in it for an hour every evening. Here by converse on all topics of interest, the members cultivate the spirit of brotherhood which binds them together.

The Wings

The part of the building we have now seen comprise all the public rooms which are ordinarily open to visitors. The north wing of the building contains the living apartments of the family, and the south wing is occupied by the children, their attendants and others. The quiet of the occupants requires of course that these portions should be closed from intrusion. To visit them, persons should first obtain permission from an attendant.

Circular, April 11, 1870

The "Old Mansion House" has been under sentence of demolition for some weeks, and the execution has only been delayed until the new wing should be completed.

Circular, June 13, 1870

The Community leaves today the Dining-Room and Kitchen in the old Mansion House, where for more than twenty years its members have gathered daily to partake of the frugal meal, or surround the festive board, and takes possession of the rooms that have been newly fitted up in the Tontine. The new Kitchen is provided with a "dumb waiter," speaking-tube, improved fixtures for cooking by steam, and, in short, with most, if not all, the modern improvements in this department. It is anticipated that the labor of preparing meals for two hundred folk will be materially reduced by means of these improved conditions, and a change is made with gladness, notwithstanding the many old and pleasant associations which we leave. The Dining-Room is too small to accommodate all at "first table"; but there is an adjoining room that will duplicate it when we are ready to move the silk-spooling which now occupies it, and then we shall have ample room.

Circular, October 10, 1870

A GLANCE AT THE NEW CHILDREN'S HOUSE

Would you like to walk through our new Children's House; it is really a portion of the new wing at the Mansion House that has just been completed. We will enter the Tower door on the south side.

The veranda is 35 feet long and 9 feet broad. It affords the children a convenient place for amusement when it rains, or when the ground is wet and muddy.

This is the main southern entrance, leading into the Ground Corridor, as we have called this lower passage-way or hall, extending north and south through the entire building, with doors on the right and left, opening into these several rooms. The stairway near the south end of the Ground Corridor leads to the main corridor and the next floor above. Observe that the walls of the passage-way are "hard finished," and that the wainscoting, as well as the stairway, is made of black walnut, oak, ash and cherry.

Opening the first door on the right hand, we enter a spacious room called the Children's Parlor. Its walls also are "hard finished," and its woodwork is similar to that of the corridor. It has a pleasant bay window on the south side. It contains no stove, but in yonder wall is a neatly finished hot-air register, which affords all necessary heat. The two doors on the north side of the room open into two large bedrooms.

Returning to the Corridor, and crossing it, we enter the Home Parlor, in size and appearance like the room just described, with the exception that it has no bay window. The three windows look out on the veranda already mentioned. This is a play-room, and the place where the children gather before going to their meals. Here, too, children's meetings are held.

From the Home Parlor we pass into the West Avenue. Here are large and pleasant bedrooms; but the first door on the right opens into a room having a zinc-lined bathing tub and an iron sink, both having hot and cold water faucets.

The next room on the same side of the Avenue is a convenient room for washing the little hands and faces, for which purpose polished marble basins are set in a marble slab. Here, too, are hot and cold water faucets.

Returning again to the Ground Corridor, let us pass on northward, and open the door of the nursery, where are, of course, the youngest members of the Children's Department with their mothers and attendants. Nearby are a pantry, a small kitchen, and convenient bedrooms.

If you would like to look still further, walk into the main corridor on the second floor. We call this the Main Corridor because it leads directly into the large Assembly Hall of the main building. In style and finish it resembles that below. Doors on either side open into bedrooms, of suitable dimensions. The interior of these rooms contain a bed, a bureau, a table, three common chairs, one rocker, and a looking-glass, while the walls are ornamented with a few pictures, and a number of books are on the table or book shelves. Most of the bedrooms are like this, furnished with a small closet for clothes.

One room on this floor is called the Children's Clothes-room. A door on the opposite side of this room opens into a bathroom, furnished with many conveniences. Our children have a bath every day. There is still another corridor above this one; the rooms in the upper story are all dormitories for the use of children and adults. From the three principal corridors, running north and south, branch off several avenues, running east and west and leading to distant parts of the building.

The walls have generally a surface of "hard finish"; a few have been painted; considerable of the woodwork has been grained in imitation of black walnut, oak, cherry, etc. There is but a single stove (that in the Nursery Kitchen) in the entire building—all being heated by the aid of steam pipes and registers. Here, too, winter will have few terrors for the little ones, for any desired temperature may be kept in all the rooms during the coldest weather.

We have a large and conveniently arranged house for our children; it is really one of the best things Communism has given us.

The space bounded by the Mansion House on the east, by the new Children's House on the south, by the Tontine on the west, by the reservoir and flower garden on the north, has been designated "The Quadrangle." It is kept smoothly shaven by the lawn-mower and here the children can be seen, during many hours of the day, running, leaping, jumping the rope and so on.

Circular, February 27, 1871

One may wander through our huge brick dwelling house from cellar to attic, and except in one room will find nothing to remind him of the days of stoves and housekeeping. There are, however, so many occasions in the daily life of a large family demanding the use of a stove, that, when our house came to be heated by steam, a room was appropriated in which it was arranged that all the little wants requiring a stove should be gratified. The room is on the first story of the new wing, and is called the *Nursery Kitchen.* There is a medium-size cooking stove in it with a tea-kettle and a variety of iron-ware; a sink, with faucets for hot and cold water, rack for washing dishes, etc.

The room contains two tables, the smaller one being fitted up as an ironing-table; three or four plain wooden chairs, a large cushioned armchair, and a comfortable lounge; a little what-not is in one corner, containing bluing, starch, soap, etc. On the east side of the room is a door opening into a buttery furnished with a small assortment of crockery; cans containing dried herbs, glass jars of molasses, arrow-root, ground flax-seed, vinegar, and various other articles; neat wooden pails with covers, in which there are wheat flour, coarse and fine, Indian and oat meal, crackers, sugar, etc.; little boxes filled with ginger, cayenne pepper, "composition," and the like. In short, the shelves of this buttery are filled with nearly everything that is needed in the care of an infant or an invalid. Hither, also, come all who have a bit of washing, starching, ironing, or pressing to do, and, in a family of 200, including 70 women, there are countless such little jobs. One can readily imagine that this room is almost constantly used. "What should we do without it," is the frequent exclamation, "with the wash room a quarter of a mile off, and the public kitchen and dining-room a good two minutes walk from some parts of the house!"

If you were to know the multifarious uses to which our "pocket-kitchen" is put in the course of a day, I think you would at least smile. In the first place, it is generally understood that this is where the "mothers," and those who care for the children, have the first prerogative.

And now it is found to be a great convenience for all of us—for notwithstanding the luxury of steam, who does not like the warmth of a good stove now and then? This little kitchen, therefore, is generally patronized, and we must acknowledge it to be one of the snuggest, coziest, handiest places within our ken. Here a weary one finds a handy place to "rest for a little while" on the comfortable sofa; and here in fact, is where one flees in moments of distress, whether afflicted with toothache, earache, or some other ache—he is sure to find something adapted to his ills.

Besides all the conveniences we have enumerated of our "pocket-kitchen," we think it might very appropriately be called "hub"; for if we have a general rendezvous, here it is. Here the women and girls are wont to collect in little groups to talk over topics of latest interest, and to rehearse the news, if any there be. Indeed, if you wish to see the greatest number of persons in the shortest space of time, just take a seat in our "pocket-kitchen" for a little while.

Circular, May 18, 1874

The South Sitting-Room is the coziest place in all the house—a room in which you may take "solid comfort." It is not a very large room; K. says a large room can never be made cozy and "homey"; however, some of us hope that the arts of Communism will be able to bring those two elements into the great room in the great assembly. But this room is small, and feminine taste and tact preside over it and render it attractive. If anyone has a choice flower, a picture, or anything new and curious to exhibit, this is the very place to bring them, for half the family, at least, will see them before the day is over. The windows are filled with heliotropes and geraniums; pictures and maps adorn the walls, and the center table is well supplied with choice reading matter. You may spend a pleasant half hour here anytime with your favorite author. Of late a new attraction has been added to the room in the shape of a music-box, which when wound up will play eight tunes without stopping. The airs are sweet and the music is enticing. Young and old come in groups to listen and do not seem to tire of hearing the melodies for the hundredth time. There are other attractions in the South Sitting-Room. In the evening the lamps are lighted and people drop in by twos and threes for social chit-chat, or gather about the tables for games of dominoes, squails, or whatever game happens to be in fashion. For an hour after meeting there is generally a constantly-changing throng in this room, making, through friendly contact and interchange, a pleasant ending to the day.

Circular, December 14, 1874

The new addition to the Dining-Room is almost ready for use. The carpenters are building the dumb-waiters and putting on other finishing touches. So that we now have a large and commodious Dining-Room where the whole family—table-waiters alone excepted—can sit at a time. No more "second table," or "second table-waiters"; unless it be those who wait on the waiters—no more re-setting of tables—but ample accommodations for men, women and children. After twenty-five years we have for the first time hit on a plan which makes practical the long cherished idea of a "Family Dining-Room."

II

How They Lived and Worked

The Evening Meetings, from the reports of which many of these excerpts are taken and which are often referred to and described, were, as they said (*Circular*, July 17, 1863), "the most cherished part of our daily lives." In the early days, when the bell rang at half-past seven in the evening, the members gathered in the parlor of the old Mansion—later, at eight o'clock in the Hall of the new Mansion House—and then ensued the reading of correspondence, articles from the *Circular* or other publications, and "much edifying conversation and discussion" (*Circular*, February 23, 1854). Criticism also occupied a prominent part of the meetings, and business was freely discussed by the whole family.

"Partly social, partly intellectual, partly industrial and partly religious in character" was how they described these meetings (*Circular*, February 10, 1859). They were entirely informal; the women brought their knitting, braiding, or sewing, and small tables with lamps on them dotted the Hall. There was no regular preaching but often one of John Humphrey Noyes's *Home Talks* was read aloud or, if he was there in person, he spoke to them. If no one was inspired to speak, a hymn was called for and everyone sang. As the various industries grew more absorbing, orders were reported or a change of method in the shops was discussed.

What they described as "A Raid at Legality" (*Circular*, April 25, 1864) was an occasional sudden change in the meetings. This was one of the most refreshing attitudes of the Oneida Communists; their inveterate opposition to what they called legality, by which they meant routine, the pressure of sameness, of convention, of oppressive order, of being conscience-driven. It was a point of belief with them that when one kept in the same track or rut he was especially exposed to attacks of evil—the Devil knew just where to find him.

The daily schedule was fairly spartan; breakfast at six o'clock, Bible reading at quarter to seven, after which persons went to their different places of business—the trap shop, the machine shop, the mill and so on. There was music by the band every other day from twelve to one, supper at half-past five, then classes in French, algebra, arithmetic, etc. between suppertime and a general reading at seven, varied by an occasional lecture until the evening meeting at eight which closed at nine o'clock. The hour after supper had been devoted to classes and business meetings but it was remarked that there was a tendency to allow business discussions to "spin out and encroach on time which might be more profitably spent" (*Circular,* May 3, 1855). While working for money was necessary, it must not be allowed to take the place of more improving occupations.

From the beginning the Community believed in work; not legally—that is, work forced upon the worker as a duty—but work freely chosen, as they said, "under Inspiration." It is probable that their system of mingling the sexes in labor had something to do with making the work of every kind, from the household laundry to picking up stones in their fields, agreeable occupations. It was not the *kind* of work that dignified a man but that a good spirit and good manners dignified every kind of work.

Anyone with a special aptitude or experience in any sort of manufacture was immediately put to work at his specialty. In the 1850's one member, a mechanic, had a hobby of making rustic furniture out of cedar sticks (*Circular,* September 19, 1852). No sooner said than done. Immediately the art of making "rustic seats, tables, chairs, etc. for garden use and ornament" was made a Community project and the product sold so readily that a two-carload lot was sent to Syracuse and sold, and another lot was sent to the State Fair in Utica where it won a silver medal, which was gratifying, especially since that city had been the scene of the recent abuse of the Community by the District Attorney of Oneida County.

In 1853 the horticulturists were still hopeful. Six men were regularly engaged in the garden and each gardener had a boy under his charge; in addition, some of the other men worked with them a portion of the time and occasionally the women made a bee when there was work for them to do. Everybody worked hard and they sold what they raised, but it was not enough to support the Community family.

By 1855 other industries, though in their infancy, began to occupy an increasingly large proportion of the Community personnel, both men and women. They were making and selling animal traps, traveling bags, and preserved fruit, and it became apparent that these businesses represented time more profitably spent than even the most romantic, Garden-of-Eden kind of digging and delving. The important thing was to make a living, any kind of honest work that would keep the Community afloat.

In 1858, a year of financial depression in the country, although they admitted that the prospect was not promising, the Community had faith that they would soon be able to realize their hearts' desires. They were never dismayed. Hard times just now should be looked upon as a Special Providence, since the lull in the trap business freed many of the men to engage in preparation for the New House they were all looking forward to (*Circular,* August 26, 1858). Brick was the favored material and there was no reason why the force which had been employed in the trap shop could not make brick instead. Before fall they had set to work on this new project, although the actual construction of the New House did not begin for another two years.

Working together by the ordinance of bees was another reason why the communists enjoyed work. Often the bell rang before five o'clock in the morning to summon all hands to any of a variety of bees, for gathering broom corn, for apple paring, for making bags, or, most charming of all, to gather cowslips for dinner. This system, when applied to those monotonous kinds of work which, done alone, would tire out one or two workers and take a great deal of time; if "done by storm," that is, by a large company, such chores were completed, it seemed, in no time at all and were nothing but fun.

One of the advantages of communism to which they often alluded was frequent change of employment which gave freshness in every department and opened the way to inspiration. Another advantage was in the matter of the difficult question of precedence. Since all were equally rich, wealth could not cause envy or jealousy. There remained a human desire to hold positions of influence, which was only objectionable when prompted by pride and *personal* ambition. In their case, Providence had solved the problem by smothering them with offices. Their only difficulty was in pushing the young people forward to accept the responsibility (*Circular*, July 19, 1869).

In 1864 the printing of the *Circular* was moved from Oneida to Wallingford. Prior to this time the branch Community had been engaged in making chains for the steel traps manufactured at Oneida, but it was found more convenient for the chain-making to be carried on in direct connection with the trap-making. Also, as the trap business increased and required more space, the printing office had been crowded, so that the move was expedient for both groups. This arrangement was continued until 1868 when a new wave of economizing counseled concentration, and the printing department and some of the members were moved back to Oneida. However, it was remarked that the two Communities were so entirely one in character and interests that they kept no accounts with each other except as a prudent man kept account with himself (*Circular*, March 12, 1864).

The Community did not regard Sunday as more sacred nor did they observe it more religiously than any other day (*Circular*, April 4, 1864). In their first years they tried the experiment of holding Sunday meetings for the benefit of outsiders, but decided that it did not amount to much and abandoned the idea. For themselves, they distributed their religious services equally through the week instead of laying in enough religion on Sunday to last for seven days. They preferred to receive a fresh portion every day. After they employed outside help, in deference to their feelings, the Community shops were closed on Sunday and the communists occupied themselves at home with business meetings and study.

The quantity and quality of the fare provided at the Community table would seem a clue to its scale of living. Possibly because during the early years they were of necessity on light rations, the whole subject came in for a good deal of attention. As early as

1855 it was suggested that they needed "a gastronomical chemistry full as much as an agricultural one" (*Circular*, April 5, 1855). After "some dullness in the evening meeting, owing to the over-tempting cookery of a good supper," the bill of fare was probably modified, although at that period it was certainly not lavish (*Circular*, February 22, 1855). Dullness, especially what they called the "Sunday Stupor," was sharply criticized, and steps were taken to provide the day with light meals and commendable activities (*Circular*, September 21, 1856).

Alimentiveness, a favorite word, was often criticized as a besetting sin of certain members, just as gluttony was a cardinal sin in medieval times, and at various periods a day of fasting was appointed for all. "The Devil," they wrote (*Circular*, September 10, 1851) "has managed to make the table to a great extent a snare, when it should be the scene of a sacred ordinance." It is difficult to see how, for instance, "Supper: a truly sumptuous blackberry shortcake; enough of it; nothing else on the table but water" (*Circular*, August 30, 1855) could have been an enticement of the Devil, but the communists took no chances.

The subject of visitors at Oneida recurs so frequently in the Oneida *Journal* that it deserves special comment. As early as 1853 (*Circular*, January 26, 1853) they speak of Oneida's habitual hospitality and say that it is very rare that the family is without visitors. In 1859 (*Circular*, June 23, 1859) they first mention the fact that the visitors came to eat strawberries and cream or strawberry shortcake. This institution, which grew to be enormously popular, began by accident for the benefit of certain visitors who asked for it and went on until it was understood by the public that this delicacy could always be had there in season. Presently, to serve the large number of excursionists brought in by the new Midland Railroad, they began to serve vegetable or fruit dinners and to provide a concert by the band to amuse their guests.

The Fourth of July was a time of the greatest influx which, as it grew in numbers, was an increasingly difficult problem. Generally speaking, visitors were courteous and asked only questions which the communists were glad to answer. It was only occasionally that they were obliged to rebuke their guests or to remind them that the Mansion House was, after all, a private home. The story is told that when one of these over-inquisitive guests asked what was the faint perfume he detected in the Mansion House, the Community woman who was acting as a guide answered quietly, "The odor of crushed selfishness."

One of the extraordinary features of Community life which comes through unmistakably in their own unstudied accounts of their daily doings is the universal interest in what they called "Improvement," not only spiritual, which might have been expected in a religious organization, but intellectual. Only a modest proportion of the communists had had a higher education; many of them had been farmers or artisans of only a minimal education. But in the Community there was a rage for Improvement; they read and read well, they spent their meagre funds, even at first, not only for the publication of their own paper but for books and newspapers and magazines. In their meetings they discussed topics of the day and books of the hour. They were interested in ideas; they corrected their own grammar, and at one time started a big push to make everyone a good speller. They were interested in words. When they noted that stewed pumpkin for pies was among the products of the fruit department, they added the amusing note that they were "always distressed as to the proper name of that great, homely, honest old yellow fruit of the *Cucurbita Pepo* which we have always called punkin, reckless alike of orthography and good taste." The dictionary said *pompion* was correct but what did it rhyme with? Pumpkin rhymed with bumpkin and they preferred it.

After closing the several small branch communes in Vermont and New Jersey, the Wallingford Commune was the only branch for some time. It was never large—forty or fifty members the extent of it—but even aside from their useful production of chain, bags, printing, and so on, it was always useful to the Oneida group as a variation, a place to which the Oneida members could go for rest and recreation. Therefore the Wallingford family was continually changing, and its spirit remained lively and cheerful. During a time in the mid-sixties (*Circular,* June 4, 1866) the Community maintained an agency in New York which the young men who ran it called "Moffat Abbey," themselves being the "Monks." They worked hard and successfully during the day and studied together in the evenings, with "a spice of jollity" often increased by the addition of two Community boys who were studying medicine and law at Columbia and Yale. A house in New Haven was later purchased for these students.

The last Community branch was instituted in what had been the Wager farm house in Turkey Street in Oneida County, one mile north of the Community Mansion House and immediately adjacent to the new Willow Place factory built in 1864. It, too, was called the Willow Place Commune and was a lively and practical addition as a residence for those members who worked in the trap, silk, and machine shops in the new factory.

In 1868 there were at Oneida, including Willow Place, 210 members; at Wallingford, 52, including the students at New Haven, and 16 in the New York Agency, making a total of 278 members. Before the end of that year, in the interest of economy, a part of the Wallingford group was moved to Oneida, together with the New York Agency, and the house in New Haven was sold.

A word should be said here about what they called "seceders," a term obviously lifted from wartime speech. What was meant, of course, was the men and women who joined and later decided to leave the Community. As of 1867, the number having seceded was 115 in the past eighteen years. Generally speaking, these partings were accomplished with little ill-feeling and no litigation. In a few cases the seceders claimed not only whatever money they had brought into the Community upon joining but also claimed remuneration for their time and labor during their stay there. This evidently, was inequitable since, during their residence at Oneida, their living expenses had been paid, and, if they had children with them, the children's education had also been provided. After a few such experiences the Central Committee drew up a contract for all entering members which stated the terms under which they might, if they later desired, leave, and what the financial arrangement was to be.

The Community's finances during the first few years when they were building their communal home and trying to support themselves by horticulture had been all outgo and very little income. Religious fanatics though they might be, they were still hard-headed Yankee stock and they made a change. They experimented with making one product after another until they found those able to support them, on a slender income at first, but as time went on the Community began to grow and prosper. There were ups and downs even then, bad years when it was necessary to economize and good years when they adjured themselves to remember that they must learn, as St. Paul wrote, "how to abound as well as to suffer need." Their numbers grew, their houses grew to accommodate them. They became well-known and, with some exceptions, respected.

Circular, Brooklyn, N.Y., November 30, 1851

The Oneida Association

The business men at Oneida who sometimes travel about the country had frequently expressed a wish that we would furnish them with a pamphlet or print of some kind, containing, in the shortest possible compass, all necessary information about the history, principles, and condition of the Oneida Association, which they might present to inquirers, and so save a world of talk.

QUESTION 1—Where is the Association located?

ANSWER—On the Oneida Creek, in the town of Lenox, Madison County, N.Y., three miles south of Oneida Depot. The post office address is Oneida Castle, Oneida County, New York.

Q 2—What is the number of members?

A—About 150; of whom ⅓ are men, ⅓ women, and ⅓ children.

Q 3—Do all these live in one house and eat at one table?

A—You see in the picture on this page all the buildings occupied as dwellings by the Association. The main building is 60 feet long, 35 feet wide, three stories high, with a habitable garrett. The basement is divided into three equal rooms, the first is the dining room, where we all eat together. The second is the kitchen. The third is the cellar. Over the dining room is a parlor of the same size for general gatherings. The rest of the house is divided into sleeping rooms; which, with those in the children's house and out-buildings, accommodate the whole family.

Q 4—How long has the Association been organized?

A—Nearly four years. Many of the first members, however, were immigrants from Putney, Vermont, where they had been organized as an Association 9 years previously.

Q 5—What are your principles?

A—Our fundamental principle is religion.

Q 6—What denomination do you belong to?

A—To none of the popular denominations. We are generally called Perfectionists.

Q 7—Who is the founder of your system?

A—John H. Noyes, a graduate of Dartmouth College who studied theology under Professor Stuart of Andover and Doctor Taylor of New Haven, and in 1834, while a student and licentiate of the Yale Theological Seminary, became a Perfectionist.

Q 8—Do you believe in the Bible?

A—Most heartily, and study it more than all other books. It is, in fact, our only written creed and constitution.

Q 13—What are your rules and regulations?

A—The Bible, as I said before, is our only written constitution. We have no systematic code of by-laws. Or rather, we have no statute book. Unwritten by-laws are constantly growing in us and among us by the suggestion of experience. Wisdom, evolved by trials and established by precedence, is the common law of all countries; and this is our code.

Q 14—You must have officers. How do you elect them?

A—We do not elect them—we find them out. God and education make officers; in an adjusted society, they are sure to reach their places by a natural process.

Q 15—What do you rely upon for the regulation and discipline of members?

A—On religious influence, free criticism, and education.

Q 16—What are your means of religious influence?

A—We have meetings every evening, and they are generally devoted to religious conversation and reading though business and other topics are not excluded. Then we have a religious meeting on Sunday open to the public. The Bible is the daily study of men, women, and children.

Q 17—What is your system of criticism?

A—We tell each other plainly and kindly our thoughts about each other in various ways. Sometimes the whole Association criticizes a member in meeting. Sometimes it is done more privately, by committees, and sometimes by individuals. In some cases, criticism is directed to general character, and in others to special faults and offences. Generally, criticism is invited by the subject of it and is regarded as a privilege. It is well understood that the moral health of the Association depends on the freest circulation of this plainness of speech; and all are ambitious to balance the accounts in this way as often as possible.

Q 18—What are your provisions for education?

A—We have a daily school for children in which common learning is taught in connection with the fear of God and the law of love. But it is understood among us that the whole Association is a school; and all members, old and young, are supplied with books and addict themselves to various branches of learning as they have opportunity.

Q 19—Do you hold to Community of property?

A—We believe that all of the systems of property-getting in this world are vulgarly called the "grab game," i.e., the game in which the prizes are not distributed by any rules of wisdom and justice, but are seized by the strongest and craftiest; and the laws of the world simply give rules, more or less civilized, for the conduct of this game.

Q 21—Do you separate husbands and wives?

A—No, but we teach them the law of love. Thou shalt love thy neighbor as thyself; as the results of our social system, we live in peace, have good health, and are not troubled with involuntary propagation.

Q 22—Do parents take care of their own children?

A—Yes, if they please. But members as fast as they become intelligent come to regard the whole Association as one family and all children as children of the family. The care of the children, after the period of nursing, is committed to those who have the best talent and the most taste for the business, so the parents are made free for other avocations.

Q 23—What are your regulations about labor?

A—Labor in the Association is free; and we find that free labor is more profitable than slave labor. Our men and women organize themselves or are organized by the General Managers, into groups under Chiefs for the various departments of work. These groups are frequently changed and constant rotation goes on so that all have variety of occupation, and opportunity to find out what each one is best adapted to.

Q 24—What do you do with the lazy ones?

A—This sort of person cannot live under our system of religious influence, criticism and education. We have to criticize members for working too much, oftener than for being lazy.

Q 25—What amount of capital has the Association?

A—We have not the means of an exact estimate but it is safe to say $50,000., including all the outside property such as lands, notes, etc., belonging to the members. About half this sum is invested in permanent, available property at Oneida.

Q 26—Are you involved in debt?

A—We owe the State for lands, about $800. Otherwise we are clear; and we make it a general rule to pay as we go.

Q 27—How much land have you?

A—About 275 acres, mostly very good meadowland.

Q 28—What do you raise?

A—Most of the articles commonly raised by farmers. We have this year a considerable stock of broom-corn which we shall manufacture for market. We have large orchards of various and choice fruit trees growing, and our vegetable garden has been very productive and profitable.

Q 29—Are you engaged in any manufactures?

A—We have a mill, three stories high, on good water power. In this building there is a sawmill, a gristmill and a machine shop. The gristmill makes the best of flour and is obtaining a large run of custom. The machine shop is doing some business and getting ready for more. Then we have a shoe shop and a blacksmith shop in active operation and are preparing for wagon-making.

Q 30—What are your expenses?

A—The only estimate we have made is recorded in our Second Annual Report, according to which the expense for board is 45¢ per week for each individual; or about $24.00 per year, and for clothing $10.50 per year.

Q 31—Does the Association support itself?

A—During the first three years, we were engaged in preparatory labors, building mills, etc., and could not be said to have supported ourselves, except that we increased the value of the homestead. This year we have begun to use our preparations, and expect to be able to show in our Annual Report in February, that the Oneida Association is a self-supporting institution.

Circular, November 30, 1851

TOLERATION

The following is an extract from our Second Annual Report, written nearly two years ago. The correctness of the views presented in it, and the justice of this compliment to the legal profession, are verified by our recent experience:

What have been the results of our experience on the point of toleration? Is the world prepared to allow our experiment, and give us fair play? Our experience at Oneida has established one fact, viz., *that Putney does not present an average specimen of the civilization of this country.* We are willing to look upon the foolish and mean transactions of 1847 with charity for the mass of the people there, and to attribute their proceedings to the imposition of a dark malignant influence, which they were then unable to resist. But, whether their misfortune or voluntary crime, the *character* of the facts stand unchanged; the disgraceful index remains, and there is one receding point in the midst of an advancing world. Their brutal strokes at our press, at our private Association for Reform, at free opinion and free discussion, all belonged to the past age; for which, if they can forgive *themselves*, and regain the self-respect and moral security which should attend a right course, we certainly can freely forgive them.

Circular, January 4, 1852

A FAMILY PRESS

We have been interested in the fact that while the *Circular* is offered freely to the public, so there is no paid labor in its production; from the Editor without a salary, to the little hands that claim a share in the last manipulations of folding it for the mail. It goes forth from the bosom of a family, who find their happiness and reward in the service. The Editor's sanctum is in the most sociable corner of the sitting room; a pencil and bookcover serve for his *escritoir*. The compositor's work is "upstairs," and is reckoned in the program of family arrangements as much as the cooking. Two or three have regular work there, but all are women, and the children not too young are learning; and alternate between the different departments of domestic care and setting type. And they count the last as the cream of their work. In this way more than twenty have a share in getting out the paper. The press-room is in the back-yard, but a step from the hall door—a building erected on purpose. Convenient to this is the door of our dining room, where there is a long stationary table: and here it is we fold the *Circular* of a Saturday afternoon for the mail. So we serve our reader from the dinner board which God spreads for us day by day. Much pains have been taken to make this room a place of worship and elevated associations, and we consider this among others a consecrating ordinance.

Circular, October 10, 1852

We begin to think that Community planting, and cultivation in the right spirit, has a positive influence on the growth of crops. Besides the more faithful attention which they receive in Community, they are surrounded by a genial magnetism, which we suspect is quite important to the highest development of plants. Love is a better element for anything to grow in than selfishness; and this, together with the electrical touch of free labor, may produce results in vegetation which will astonish all previous science. Let us watch the experiment.

Circular, February 16, 1853

THE PLODDING SPIRIT

The *plodding spirit* is much honored in our Associations, as the first requisite to all improvement. If I were asked to define it, I should say it is the spirit that is willing to learn little by little; it does not wish to jump at once into the attainment of the good we desire, but is willing to dig as for hidden treasures; it has everlasting perseverence in it, and does not despise the day of small things. It seeks improvement for its own sake, and has fellowship with God in so doing. It enjoys the details of the process as well as the result. We have found that there are wonderful force and execution in this spirit. Persons who have felt that their natural talents and capabilities were small have surprised themselves and others with their improvement under its influence.

Circular, May 18, 1853

Henry James, when he used to call on us from time to time, a few years ago, never lectured us on our "disorderly lives," as he said he did, in his controversy with the *Observer*; but he did lecture us on our narrow-minded views of the value of the Bible; and also on the foolishness of our slow way of propagating our sentiments, advising us to operate in the public mind through such established journals as the *Tribune.*

Circular, October 8, 1853

We find inspiration working particularly nowadays, in reference to business. At the same time, we feel roused to new earnestness to favor the *mingling of the sexes* in labor. We find that the spirit of the world is deadly opposed to this innovation, and would make it very easy to slip back into the old routine of separate employments for men and women. But the leaven of heavenly principles about labor, resists, from time to time, this backward tendency, and brings forth a new endorsement of the truths contained in the Bible argument on this subject. We believe that the great secret of securing enthusiasm in labor and producing a free, healthy, social equilibrium, is contained in the proposition, "loving companionship and labor, and especially the mingling of the sexes, makes labor attractive."

Circular, February 23, 1854

EVENING MEETING

At about one-half past seven o'clock when the family are all in, the first thing which usually calls the attention is the reading of correspondence which has been received by that day's mail from the other Communes, from outside friends and inquirers. These frequently draw out much pleasant and edifying conversation. Three evenings in a week we receive the *Circular* from which articles are read aloud and discussed. We also have the semi-weekly *Tribune,* the *Home Journal,* and several local papers from which the most interesting articles are read. Criticisms of character and spiritual edification occupy a prominent place in the evening meetings; also all business and other matters of interest to the family are here discussed and all are free to express their opinions.

Formerly we rang a bell at half past seven to call the family together and held our meetings usually 'til about 9 o'clock, but now it is left free for all to follow their own attractions about coming in and going out. After public exercises are over, each one spends time as he chooses, and the evening usually ends as it commences; in reading and writing and private conversation. One after another retires until about 11 o'clock when the room is usually empty. The "watch" whose duty it is, then extinguishes the light, sees that everything about the house is safe and in order and then retires himself.

Circular, August 29, 1854

I have been here a few days at work in the machine shop. I find when I get nervous or worn out by literary confinement, that to come over here and go to chiseling and filing black dirty iron, in the midst of the rattle of machinery, is better than going to the Springs. I have more good and refreshing thoughts while working at the vise in one day, than I should have in a week if I had nothing else to do but think. It helps me to have good sleep, a good appetite, and a thankful heart. Indeed I am abundantly proving the truth of the axiom that if we trust in God he will certainly take care and provide for us whatever is necessary in the way of *criticism, praise,* and *change.* I have adopted that as an everlasting platform of contentment, that my condition be such as it may.

Certainly we could not wish for better surroundings for a child, to make him—not indeed a distorted professional, or a hard-faced speculator—but to make him a gentle, thoughtful man of use and improvement. I hope he will be ever kept from the mercenary idea of doing things for pay, or making riches for himself. I am not afraid of its leading him to poverty. On the other hand, let him remain free from the absurd notion that one kind of employment is more honorable than another, which causes so much mischief in the world. He will be taught in the Community that it is not the kind of work that dignifies a man, but that by good spirit and good manners the man dignifies *every kind* of work; and that he is the truest gentleman who is capable of doing the most useful things.

Circular, November 16, 1854

When we learned nearly a week ago that the Brooklyn family had abandoned the use of tea and coffee, I made up my mind at once to do the same, but I confess it was something of a trial and seemed anything but attractive. The next morning I awoke early and was up some time before the bell rang, with an unusual appetite for some coffee and my breakfast. I knew I could go down to the table and willfully refuse to drink it, and put myself under law, but this I could not bear to do. I went to God in earnest prayer for deliverance, with the determination not to go to breakfast till I could go a free man—till all that hankering was removed and I could thankfully and with a good appetite take cold water. It was nearly eight o'clock when I went down to the breakfast table but my appetite for coffee was entirely removed, and I have not enjoyed my breakfast so well for a month as I did that morning. I have enjoyed my meals better ever since, and have not had the least appetite for tea or coffee.

In my meditations that morning I felt clearly that there was no need of suffering in my body by the change as I did before, and I felt like asking God for such a victory over habit that I could make any change that was called for and not suffer by it. I have been conscious that my prayer was answered, for I am not aware of the least inconvenience in consequence of the change.

Circular, February 22, 1855

A MEMBER'S LOG

Arose when the bell rang. Dressed and put my bed to air—took breakfast, then studied Bible lessons; knitted while the Bible exercises were attended to. Went to my chamber and assisted to put the room in order, then attended to ironing until about 11 o'clock. Wrote about half an hour, then studied next Bible lesson until dinner. Gave a lesson on the piano from 1 o'clock until 2, another from 2 o'clock until 3; then practiced, myself, from 3 o'clock until 4. Then read in "Plurality of Worlds," took the evening repast, worked a short time; read a Home Talk on keeping accounts. Listened to a lecture on grammar, in which an independent spirit of inquiry was recommended, and the simple doctrines of common sense were held up in preference to the mere words used in the science. Attended evening meeting; worked a little at knitting, then retired, grateful for being permitted to enjoy the benefits of this school. Awoke early on Thursday, exclaiming with joyful spirit, "Blessed art thou among women!" This made so vivid an impression on my mind that I believed it was the spirit of truth that brought it.

Circular, February 22, 1855

Winding up of our carpet-bag work for the present, having exhausted material on hand. The Bees after dinner have been very popular. Elbow has touched elbow all over the parlor sometimes when one hundred needles were flying, and a bee-hive would best describe the hum and liveliness of the scene. Seasons of industrial communion they may be called, and we have found them as truly edifying and as attractive to the influx of Christ's spirit as meetings for religious communion ever were. To continue the Bees we shall take up braiding palm-leaf hats, at which our children have worked two hours a day through the winter. We have enough experienced braiders to commence the hats, and to initiate the raw ones. It would be too much like losing a "sanctuary privilege" to suspend the Bees. There is more or less tendency in Community to make a hotel life of it—the hotel feeling would take the place of the family, home feeling, if it was not resisted. We find that unitary industry is a good promoter of the family spirit. There is more of the freedom of home in our Bees than in our evening meetings. We continue to experiment in the way of finding out the two parts of industry, and harmonizing them so as to make good music in all our work.

Circular, March 15, 1855

By the way, our water-power building, containing besides the grist-mill, a printing-office, a room for rustic seat manufacture, a trap-saloon, a wagon and general wood shop, together with the rudimentary elements of a broom factory and a machine-shop, deserves some better designation than "mill"; suppose we name it comprehensibly the Circularium?

Circular, May 17, 1855

It is customary during this season to appoint Bees for specific jobs of work nearly every morning at 5 o'clock, which call together a large party of men and women volunteers, and no part of the day is more pleasantly spent than this gregarious hour before breakfast. Anyone who has the responsibility of a job or has a special interest in having it done, mentions it the evening before with an invitation to a general Bee, and the red rising sun of the next morning greets us in the field. One morning it is the kitchen group which invites to a Bee in the meadows for gathering cowslips for dinner. The system is particularly useful applied to those monotonous kinds of work which in detail would tire out one or two workers; done by storm by a large company, they are, as the phrase is, "nothing but fun."

Circular, July 12, 1855

The Community has recently started a peddler's wagon stocked with our various manufactures. The short trips which it has made in the neighboring villages have been successful and the enterprise promises to be a growing one. The vegetable wagons have begun their daily trip.

Circular, December 20, 1855

December, with its changeable weather, furnishes but limited opportunity for outdoor labor, and the great majority of the Community have to content themselves in this respect with an occasional bee. But what is lost in one direction is gained in another—labor in the different workshops goes off all the merrier. The *Circularium* (as this building has been termed) presents in its different rooms just now a picture of lively and attractive industry. Over 30 persons are here employed in the trap shop, machine shop, wood shop, grist mill, and printing office. As we write, our ears are seranaded by a curious medley of sounds, made by revolving wheels, whirling saws, clinking hammers, etc. which is by no means unpleasant. The printing office hands, as a healthy variation of a somewhat monotonous exercise of type-setting, usually have a short recess (in which, for a few days past the other departments of the *Circularium* have fraternized with us) spent in such lively entertainment as may be suggested for the occasion. One day a circle is formed, and each one opens the Bible and reads the first verse that attracts his attention. The next day perhaps a run over to the shoe shop is suggested. Again, the time is spent in discussing the nice lunch which our sisters have so generously furnished (many thanks to them!). And again a dance in the unoccupied garret is tripped off—all with their inky, sooty hands—then all return immediately to their different employments, and again the music of labor is heard throughout the building.

Circular, February 14, 1856

Arose at the ringing of the first bell—a quarter to six. In addition to other motives which would induce me to be prompt, I wait on the children's table which makes it necessary. This service after my own breakfast commonly occupies me till time for bible-game. After bible-game, I go immediately to milking. Have enjoyed this chore very much this winter. Mr. L. appears to be disposed to carry out the bible principle of rewards, and because I have been faithful over one cow to give me more. He has sent me over two already, and talks of giving me three or four next summer.

After milking, sung half an hour with E. and S. Then we three women went to the trap-shop where I heated irons for G. to weld. His dexterity required me to mind my business well. S. reported to me some conversation she had with Mr. J. at the forge. He expressed himself pleased with the spirit growing amongst the women to earn something, and thought they rendered substantial aid in the trap-shop, contributing considerably to the increase of the weekly profits.

At noon waited on the first table; listened to the music; sewed from one till two. At two joined the bee for braiding palm-leaf hats. I usually spend from three to four o'clock in a kind of school with the girls; but to-day, as they had a lesson to study, I braided till half past three. At half past four went to milking again. After milking sewed till supper time, then helped serve the supper in the parlor, eating my own with the other waiters in the cellar, and enjoying the pleasant conversation with which it was enlivened. After supper helped J. study his Greek; attended class and the evening gathering in the parlor. I have lately desired the elevation of my attractions, and feel a confidence in the confession of Christ that it will effect in me what I desire.

Circular, September 11, 1856

It has been warm, some of the time raining, and with all a very *busy* day, with little chance for us to be annoyed by the Sunday spirit. By this we mean a feeling that prevails in common society on this day. That is, sleepy and listless and averse to serious thought and reflection or action of any kind. We commence the day with washing as usual, which was finished before noon. In the meantime, a card was placed upon the bulletin board giving notice of a meeting for reading at 2 o'clock, a bag bee at half past three, and singing school at a quarter of seven. Our Sunday occupations do not vary very materially from other days of the week.

Circular, March 12, 1857

It is now about 2 years since the Community resolved by unanimous vote to restrict the use of butter and cheese in our family to the production of our own dairy. This resolution has obliged us to have many meals without either. Our weekly consumption for the past year has been not more that 90 pounds of butter and about 50 pounds of cheese, but we have been far from shortened in respect to milk and cream. We have been pleased with this experience; it has had a wholesome effect in refining our alimentiveness, and it has developed considerable culinary skill, leading to the invention of new dishes, and increasing our taste for fruit. Some, indeed, have been disposed to think it would be retrograding in return to the common use of butter and cheese, but after considerable discussion of the subject of diet this spring, the legitimacy of their use for the present, during the transition at least from no meat to the maximum of fruit, has been settled and this evening something like the following proposition was received with popular applause. That is, that we consider milk, butter, cheese and eggs as good and proper food for the Community, at least until we get tired of them in the natural way, and we now propose to ourselves to supply our table, as soon as we can do so by our own production, with these articles in *unlimited abundance*.

Circular, June 25, 1857

Commenced the strawberry harvest, which is always a kind of garden jubilee. Picked 88 quarts in a short hour after supper. In addition to the usual financial report, we had a report from the kitchen department this evening, showing the cost of our Community board for a week. A strict account was kept of all the articles consumed, estimating them at the full market price; to this was added the value of the labor expended in the kitchen and dining room, also the cost of the fuel used, and the rent of house and fixtures. The whole amounted to $165.13, which divided by 197, the number of our family, allows 83¢ and a fraction to each member as the price of board and lodging for a week. The cost of the table fare amounted to $130.09, of which $51. worth was supplied from the Community dairy, and about $25. worth from the garden and farm, which left $55. for foreign productions, flour, sugar, etc. Garden supplies are at their minimum now, and we use probably more sugar and flour than at any other season.

Circular, July 16, 1857

A large company of the folks have gone out to pick peas. Last night it was mentioned by the head gardener that the season for this market article had barely commenced and the question with him was how to get the 10 or 12 bushels which the vines would yield every day *attractively* picked. The job would be tedious and dragging undertaken by a few, but a storming company, such as we can easily raise when anything calls out our enthusiasm, would do it with ease and make a pasttime of it.

Circular, October 29, 1857

Volunteers for milking called for; that is, a few extra hands to allow the present number these dark mornings to get through for Bible reading. Our milking is done altogether on the volunteer system. One man has the general care, and he keeps his corps good by calling for new recruits as old ones wish to quit. Volunteers are never wanting. This evening, probably on account of winter's surly front, there was some hesitation, but the number was presently complete. It was observed, if we propose to enlarge our dairy as we must extensively to have all the milk we want to use (for butter is quite a rarity on our table nowadays) there should be more alacrity in answering the call for milkers. Mrs. N. who is a constant milker, said that she enjoyed milking in the winter. Instead of curling up over the register, she liked to straighten herself up in the frosty morning air—it put courage into her for all day. If a woman wants to slip out of her effeminacy, she cannot take a more effectual way than to milk in the winter.

Circular, April 15, 1858

Conversation about receiving members. It was generally thought that some rule should be adopted which will relieve the Community from the embarrassments which are occasioned from time to time by members becoming dissatisfied and demanding at once the refunding of all of the property they brought into the Community. We do not object to returning to persons who leave us their property: indeed, when it becomes apparent that a person is not prepared for Community life and wishes to withdraw, we always cheerfully help him carry out his wishes, desiring to have among us only the whole-hearted; but it does appear to us unreasonable that persons in withdrawing should crowd us up to immediate payment. It was thought a rule should be adopted in regard to receiving future accessions, which will enable the Community and not the seceder, to say *when* his property shall be refunded.

Circular, February 10, 1859

The bell for the evening meeting always makes a pleasant break in the more or less sameness of one's individual experiences, and to a certain degree calls him to assume his public or organic character. A growth in the Community spirit in the young, newcomers, and in fact, in all, is indicated by an interest for and liberty in our public evening gatherings. Partly social, partly intellectual, partly industrial, and partly religious in character, their touching points of interest are not a few. Some of us, not strongly religious naturally, have felt that we were much indebted to the inspiration of the Community in our striving to realize a better experience. The evening meetings have been a powerful means by which this help has been given. Freedom and a sort of at-homeativeness have had to be achieved by most of us. We notice that the women are the last to acquire and the slowest to use their liberty in our meetings. They are exhorted to speech rather than to silence. Most of them bring their sewing, knitting, braiding, and other womanly industries, some of the boys and men assisting them in braiding. Tonight no one being inspired to introduce any topic, someone calls for a hymn and the Community hymn is sung in this way, sure to strike every cord of loyalty. It was written years ago by JHN, and sung to the air, *"The Braes o' Balquither."*

Circular, June 23, 1859

Today we have had a great many visitors, who come for strawberries—most of them eat strawberries and cream here. This institution of strawberries and cream is the growth of accident, beginning without any design. Indeed, all this visiting, which comes now with summer as sure as the flowers, is accidental so far as we are concerned. In gathering here and trying to live a true life, we did not intend to set ourselves up for a curiosity or show of any kind. We were doing as we should, had there been none to see but ourselves. This serving of strawberries and cream commenced with complaisance to occasional visitors who asked if we would favor them, which went on, till it grew to be understood that they could be had here, and now we expect from twenty to thirty calls a day. We are sometimes an object of amusement no doubt to our visitors, and, on the other hand, we are amused with them sometimes.

Circular, July 7, 1859

Strangers were coming in and going out all the afternoon, perhaps to the number of two hundred, all of them pleasant, civil people, not one that gave us any offense. We are lionized, without setting ourselves up to be anything but a very common sort of people, living in a homely way, so far as any attempt at show or style is concerned. But we are likely to be known for what we are, at the rate things are going. And to be sure there is plenty of misunderstanding to be corrected. The atmospheric opinion of us, as it may be called, that which is in the common mind by impression and vague report, is bad. We are thought to be a set of Mormons, or worse than Mormons—to be guilty of Convent cruelties, immuring hapless victims, and secreting persons from their friends. One of us was asked the other day if the little children knew their own parents? We are asked if we are obliged to cut off our hair—and a lady inquired lately if the women were obliged to wear calico? By many little expressions of surprise and disappointment, we understand what odd notions the people have about us. We are willing therefore for the sake of the truth which we wish to see prevail, to let the people correct their impressions by observation; and though it is said a lie will get halfway around the globe while truth is putting on its boots, we are very well contented with the prospects of the chase at present.

Circular, August 18, 1859

We are sometimes asked how we make our fruit trees bear so luxuriantly. We sometimes say in answer to these questions, "Our soil is probably good and there is skill and attention used in its cultivation"; but I think that our trees and plants grow well because they are *noticed* and *praised* and *nurtured with human society and magnetism.* They love it and thrive by it. That little pear tree that you see nearly covered with pears is an argument for my theory. We have plently of others equally good or better but none of them bear like that. The reason is that the tree stands by the entrance to the garden where it is brushed and petted by all passersby. Instead of purring like a cat, which it probably would do if it could, it sends up its fruit as a return.

Circular, July 11, 1861

We looked to the Fourth with some trepidation not knowing what amount of company we should have on that day, or how we should be able to entertain them. Some preparation had been made in the culinary department, and in the organization of persons for the different departments of waiting, and nearly the whole Community held themselves in readiness for the demands of the occasion. The family dinner was taken informally in the laundry, as persons could find opportunity, while the Dining-Room was given up to guests through the middle of the day. The schoolroom was trimmed with evergreen and extemporized into a saloon, where strawberries and cream were distributed while Miss B. furnished lemonade, beer and mead for the thirsty, from a window in the basement. It was supposed that nearly a thousand persons were present in the afternoon, while others were coming and going through the day. On the whole the day passed off as smoothly as could be desired. The crowd was an eminently quiet and decorous one, the people amusing themselves with strolling through the grounds or attending the musical performances with which the day was interspersed. In the afternoon, after the performance of the regular program, the room was vacated by the audience and filled again by a second audience of those who could not gain admission before. The evening comes at last, and our visitors leave, and then the gardens are filled with our own folks, who come out to enjoy the coolness and freedom of the open air. The President's message was read in the evening and was received with applause—and it was thought Lincoln continued to deserve his title of "Honest Old Abe."

Circular, September 11, 1862

To give an idea of the various operations of the Community would be somewhat like describing the industry of a village. The farmers and dairymen are occupied with their crops and herds. The fruitmen have one group cultivating strawberry plants, another gathering fruit, and a third in the preserving house. The teamsters are drawing coal. The carpenters have had a month's job of repairs at the mill. Rooms are being partitioned off in the large apartments of the old house, for increased accommodation. The library of the New House has been fitted up, and with its well-lighted reading table forms an attractive gathering place at all leisure times. The silk men are on the wing for the far west. The manufacturing departments are usually active, particularly the bag-making (which by the way has its principal work room directly across the main entrance hall from the library). Trap-making only has been suspended during the summer, but in the place of it a beginning has been made in the manufacture of mops and fruit boxes. Printing, bookkeeping, teaching, the culinary and household arts, etc., etc., are all represented in our system of industry. A strong group has been required most of the summer to dispense hospitality to visitors, whose increasing numbers require somewhat the system of a hotel. This synopsis of the Community industry gives the summer picture, and brings us to the change which generally comes in the fall, when pleasure travel drops off, farm labor closes, and external activity calms down to more interior pursuits.

Circular, March 11, 1863

In the evening Mr. Hamilton gave a report of his visit among the Shakers. There was a great deal of interest and curiosity manifested by both men and women with whom he came in contact to find out about our Community, its principles, measures, etc. Some of them seemed to have quite an idea of our doctrines. One of them admitted that they would either have to come over to us or we to them. He was treated with uniform courtesy and friendliness and great attention, except in one case, that of their Minister, who seemed a little crusty and disputative. No charges were made for his entertainment.

Circular, July 2, 1863

NOTICE TO VISITORS

It is for the interest of those who make this a place of summer resort, as well as for the interest of the Community, that such regulations are necessary to the quiet and comfort of well-bred people and to the preservation of the houses, gardens, and grounds from injury and pillage, should be faithfully and cheerfully observed. A disorderly place cannot long be attractive to respectable visitors; and the Community, rather than allow their home to become a scene of dissipation and confusion, would by all means prefer to withdraw from the business of entertaining visitors. They hold themselves bound by their allegiance to Providence, to make and keep it a wholesome, well-ordered business, or abandon it altogether. They believe it can be made permanently pleasant and profitable to all parties; and to this end they respectfully ask the co-operation of their visitors, and invite their special attention to the following suggestions:

1. *The Community do not furnish spirituous liquors or tobacco in any form*; and would prefer that they should not be used on the premises. *Smoking in the Mansion House* is especially offensive, and ought to be wholly avoided.

2. *Card-playing* in the house or on the grounds, is offensive to the Community and to many visitors.

3. *Purloining of fruit and flowers* in the gardens, is contrary to good morals, and if generally practiced would soon strip the place of its attractions.

4. *Careless driving* of carriages on the borders of the lawn, and *swift driving* in the midst of crowds, are serious annoyances.

5. *Boisterous talking,* and *heavy tramping* in the house, and especially in going up and down the tower stairs, are needless disturbances of both inmates and visitors.

6. *Scribbling* on window casements or the walls of rooms, is not in accordance with the tastes of the Community.

7. If visitors, in walking about the premises, leave the paths, and *trample cultivated grounds* among vines and fruit bushes, they make bad work for the gardeners.

8. In rambling about the house, visitors should remember that all of the small rooms are occupied by the family as *private apartments.*

9. The *trap works* in the factory south of the house, are not open to the public; and visits to them are regarded as intrusions, because they interfere with business.

10. The Community in order to preserve its own habits of diet, has found it necessary to decline furnishing *tea, coffee, or meat* to visitors, and respectfully asks to be allowed to keep its rule in this respect without being solicited to the contrary. If warm drinks are wanted, malt coffee and cocoa will always be ready on call, and eggs can be furnished to those who require animal food.

11. The Community closes the labors of the day with a family *meeting* at eight p.m., and asks to be excused from waiting on visitors after that hour.

12. The Community does not refuse to entertain visitors on *Sunday* because many find it difficult to come on any other day; but its education and habits dispose it to prefer giving up that day to rest; and its respect for public opinion leads it to desire that as few as possible may come on that day, and that they who come may be as quiet as possible.

A religious meeting of the family is held on Sunday at two p.m., to which visitors are made free.

While an experience of several seasons has shown the necessity in particular cases of calling attention to such suggestions as are given above, it has also shown that the great mass of those who come here are spontaneously polite and considerate; needing no law to put them upon good behavior. The Community cheerfully and thankfully bears testimony to the general respect and kindness with which it has been treated by its visitors, and hopes to be more and more able to make them a good return.

Circular, July 9, 1863

On the Fourth of July, the number of visitors was supposed to be 1500 to 2000. The Community as a body were organized to receive and entertain company on that occasion, and stood the onset of friends throughout the day with soldierly steadiness and discipline, broken only by a momentary panic among the stabling corps, from a failure of ammunition in the line of checks (which was soon checked however); but there is a limit to the power of the best constituted armies, and it is judged that nothing but a lucky shower in the middle of the day saved us from being routed by stress of numbers. When it is considered that we have no servants in the household affairs of the Community, but that all work is done by our own sisters and their assistants, and that the propensity of the public to make our place a summer resort increased, it will be seen that a new problem is presented for our study. We must not over-work ourselves, we must not refuse the hospitality to which Providence seems to call us. The solution of this matter begins to engage the attention of our thinkers.

Circular, August 16, 1863

By what some call luck, which we cannot but recognize as a Providential direction, the Military Draft which took place in this district the present week, passed the Community by without calling for a man. We had expected to be hit, and held our business arrangements in suspense for a considerable time to provide for the expected contingency of a call for several of our members; and when at the close of our meeting last evening, a messenger arrived with a list of the drafted names (amounting to 212 in this town) it was at first difficult to believe that no Community man was included among them.

Such, however, was the fact; and it is explained by the circumstance that through a mistake of the enrolling officer concerning our residence, the names of the Community men were not taken in the spring enroll-ment. This mistake again is due to a singular circumstance, that is that our residence is so situated on the border of two Counties and two Con-gressional districts, that it is easy for persons not familiar with the locality to place us in the wrong county and district. The topography of the place is as follows: Oneida Creek, which forms the boundary between Oneida and Madison Counties, makes a sharp curve in front of the Com-munity, and is crossed by bridges in the road at a short distance on either side of us. The consequence is, that while we are left in Madison County, our neighbors on a straight road both sides of us are in Oneida County, and hence the ambiguity by which the enrolling officer was led to suppose that we belong to another district. The discovery of the facts in relation to this affair at first caused some natural effervescense in the town, but we believe all are disposed to look upon our exemption good-naturedly, as one of those turns of fortune, which like the draft itself, causes "one to be taken and another left."

This view is the more judicious, if it be true, as we suppose, as a mistake which leaves us out of the draft, increases no other man's risk of being drawn, except in an infinitesimal degree. Assuming that the proportion of the town's quota if founded on the number of its enrolled men, the addition of the eighteen names, more or less, of our members who are liable to the town enrollment, would neither diminish the num-ber of conscripts, nor change the risk of others in any way, but would only add three or four more soldiers to the number called for. A circum-stance which gives a certain propriety to the accident (if accident it must be called) which makes the Community free from the operation of the draft is that we do not vote or hold office under the government. We stand somewhat in the relation of peaceable foreigners, without paupers, paying our taxes and supporting our own schools, thus seeking none of the rewards of political citizenship. That we should acquiesce in the fair-ness of an arrangement which leaves the fighting of the government to those who enjoy its honors is not strange. Still this unsought exemption we regard as no particular indulgence. Mankind is so much a unit that the griefs and burdens of one's neighbors must be in part his own, and no formal discharge can release true-hearted men from the wish to bear their share of a common responsibility. We consider ourselves fellow-conscripts with the new-made soldiers, but drawn to serve in a different field. Indeed, while most of them have been enjoying life in the usual way, we have been encamped for the last sixteen years, pioneering in a grand struggle against worse foes to the common welfare than the southern secesh. And while they go to war, we will still continue to work in the not less noble task of making human society a better place for them when they return.

Circular, October 1, 1863

It is but a short time since the Community performed the labor of farm, household, and work-shop, almost wholly within its own ranks and without hiring. Two years ago we commenced another system by hiring two Englishmen to do ditching on the farm. Now the Community employs in the different departments of work a force of twenty-seven hired hands, that including the masons and carpenters that work on new buildings. Arrangements have been made this week with a neighbor for the boarding of most of this company. Two weeks ago we could have said that the new system had not even then invaded our household. But *mores mutantur*; there are now assisting in the laundry for two or three days in the week a couple of young colored women from the vicinity. Whether this will prove to be an entering wedge for the extended hiring of domestic service as the two Englishmen did on the farm remains to be seen.

Circular, January 12, 1864

In the Evening Meeting Mr. Noyes took occasion to define the object of the proposed transfer of the *Circular* to Wallingford and the establishment there of a University, etc.; and also his own relation to the movement and the relative *status* of the two communities. He should regard Oneida as the dynamic member of the duality, and Wallingford might be the conspicuous member, *if she could be*! To establish a school successfully it is necessary that there should be a quiet place to study, and this cannot be so well secured here at Oneida as at Wallingford owing to our increasing business operations. Said he found himself called upon to break up the tendency in himself to settle down in one spot and become a fixture, and thought that in this respect we ought all of us to become soldiers, ready to go at all times anywhere that the public service required. He further proposed, if the financial men would consent, to spend one month at Wallingford and the next at Oneida, and so on through the next year, alternating between the two communes every other month. Thought this would be economy in the end, as it would conduce very much to the unity of the two communes. To this proposal there was a very general expression of approval.

Circular, April 4, 1864

SUNDAY AT ONEIDA

Sunday is a characteristic day in the Community, marking our time into weeks, but we do not regard it as more sacred or observe it more *religiously* than other days. Work in the shop and out of doors is suspended, and the men are at the house. It is a day of books and pens, of music and meetings, and sometimes of industrious committees. At nine o'clock, if you think to find a seat by the register in the Hall, you will fall upon the Rhetorical Club. They are reading a passage in Shakespeare perhaps, or one of their number is making a speech, or reciting a piece of poetry. They are mostly young men. Whether our ambitious young women think utterances native-born with them, or that speech-making is out of their sphere, we will not say, but we have not observed any of them in this class. Women in Community gradually overcome the awe of numbers, and are free to speak conversationally in the hearing of two or three hundred.

If at eleven you make a call in the "lower sitting-room," you will find yourself in the Business meeting—the financial board, the foremen of the departments, and others presenting and hearing proposals in the fashion of a city council. The doings are noted and reported in the evening meeting.

At three o'clock you may chance to stumble on a women's business meeting. This is called irregularly as occasion demands, once a month or so. They talk about the dish towels and spoons, and general order about the house. Criticism is free; each one speaks by turn—a conservative regulation not so necessary in meetings of the more taciturn sex. The Community women comprise all kinds of housekeepers, educated under different conditions, but the tendency in living together is to level up to the highest standard. The grand arrangements for the distribution of work and family responsibilities are not made in this meeting, but are made by a board. This meeting is chiefly for fault-finding, and for questions of order, economy, and convenience. It has one or two offices in gift, that of waiting upon beggars for instance. Mrs. B. at the last meeting, wished someone would take her place in the discharge of this duty, as she has served a long time and they called for frequent attentions. It included waiting on the Indian women who come almost daily. They have conceived a great liking for the wheat bread of our oven, and bring their baskets in exchange, which have been taken until we are stocked and overstocked.

Circular, April 25, 1864

A RAID AT LEGALITY

It is a point of belief with us that when one keeps constantly in the same track or rut, he is specially exposed to attacks of evil—the devil knows just where to find him; but that inspiration will continually lead us into new channels by which we shall dodge the adversary. Our evening meeting last Wednesday, instead of beginning with the usual singing, was introduced by a few remarks from Mr. B., in which he deprecated routine as stagnation and death. Immediately upon Mr. B.'s sitting down, there entered upon the stage a trio with *fife and drums,* which filled the room with the rhythmical vibrations of martial music. The next evening at the same time, C. gave us on the tenor drum a representation of a battle, with its confused noises of musketry, roar of cannon, and battery broadsides. Friday evening Mr. A. opened with a declamation, and Saturday evening Mr. C. gave us an oratorical impromptu. Sunday afternoon, in the place of the usual exercises, we had an impromptu concert, music by the orchestra, songs, etc. We are out upon routine and bores, and are set upon learning to shift our sails for the breeze of inspiration.

Circular, May 2, 1864

Another idea which the Community broach and maintain is that grandparents should wisely abstain, unless in circumstances of necessity, from taking charge of their own grandchildren, and indeed from having much to do with them. Philoprogenitiveness is so strong a passion, particularly in women, that one who has had a family of her own needs rather to devote her after life to recovering herself from the disorders which it has brought upon her, than to continue the cultivation of it by taking possession of the second generation. The second growth of this passion must be in some respects much more perverting than the first. The position most becoming to aged parents is that which Paul assigns to widows, when he says: "She that is a widow indeed and desolate, trusteth in God and continueth in supplications and prayers night and day." In this position a woman who has fulfilled the place of a mother and blessed her children with her own care may bless her grandchildren and the whole church by bringing upon them the care of God. In saving her own soul from the disorders of philoprogenitiveness, she becomes a medium of heavenly spirits to her descendents and to all around her. Such at least is the teaching of experience in Communism.

Circular, August 1, 1864

Among the many classes of visitors that are entertained at the Community, there is one class who come with *malice prepense*, to *pump* us and spy out whatever they can. They seem to imagine that we are a secret society, and their curiosity is piqued. Under the mystery which they throw over us they conjure up evil, such as is imputed to the Spanish Inquisition, to Nunneries and Free-Masonry. We have published frankly our social principles, and our paper is a constant exposé of our life; besides we are never without, as one may say, a "visiting committee" inspecting our family order. If all the fruits that are manifest are wholesome and good, why should persons take the trouble to imagine that there is some secret root of mischief?

Inquisitors of the class mentioned will ask, "Are you perfectly contented here?" Well, we say "we are," without asking them if they are perfectly contented at home, which would be the natural retort. They imply by their questions sometimes, that we are staying here upon compulsion, and that we are little better than galley slaves. "Do you have to work here, whether or no?" "Well, did not your father and mother work when they were beginning life, before they had a competence?" The Community was not born to a fortune, and we have worked heartily through our narrow circumstances; but are fast growing into circumstances of ease and leisure. If we do work, we are comparatively without care, in consequence of the division of responsibility which our system affords; and we average less hours than the industrious classes in the world. We don't *have* to work; that is, one has the same chance to be lazy as members of any common family have.

To show what simple things can be made a mystery of, the strangest suspicions have been overheard as to the object of our *doors being numbered!* As though it were possible to misconstrue so manifest a convenience! In a house of 60 rooms, subject to occasional change of occupants, the obvious method of distinguishing them is by numbers, and if persons see any more occult meaning in the figures over our doors than that, they are deeper than we are.

Not far from the library window is the reservoir, from which water is distributed to our dwellings. The walls are of stonework and rise above the ground about eight feet. It is octagonal in form, and perhaps 30 feet in circumference; the top is overgrown with grass, and a beautiful tracery of ivy is fast obliterating the masonry on the sides. The observations of the curious upon this structure are various and amusing. It is a "monument," an "altar," a "dungeon." The other day a group stood speculating upon it, and as one of the family passed, inquired what it was. The person answered, "a reservoir," and walked on. Presently another of our folks coming along, they made the same inquiry of him: "a reservoir," was the reply. A third comer was plied with the same question, and when he answered, "a reservoir," they were heard to say, "They all tell the same story." They had heard perhaps, that we have a dungeon in which we incarcerate refractory members (as that is a current story, we believe, on some of the outskirts of credulity), and one company supposed they had discovered it in an underground archway which serves to connect the cellars of two of our buildings.

Our Children's Department is a great bugbear to the ignorant. "Oh, it is awful! The poor little darlings are taken as soon as they are weaned, and put into a separate house and never know their own mothers after that." *We* should not think it was *very* awful, if it were true that our little children did not know their own mothers from others that are just as good; but there is not a shadow of truth in the story. Is it a possible thing, when mothers visit the Children's House and take their children to their own rooms when they please, and are themselves detailed as matrons and attendants at the Children's House from time to time? The mothers say they enjoy their little ones vastly better than if they were with them continually. A party of frolicksome girls was passing under the windows of the Children's House the other night about sunset, when one was heard to say, "The children are all gone to bed, I suppose." "Oh yes," said another "of course—they choke them every night to make them go to sleep." This was sheer fun, but it was as near the truth as many of the ideas abroad, about our domestic customs.

A new puzzle for the inquisitive is a cottage built this summer at the northern limits of the lawn for the relief of an invalid who is unpleasantly affected by the noise incident to the visiting season here. Mr. D. was a machinist, to whom we owe much of our improvements in the trap manufacture; but he has been confined now two years with a nervous difficulty which makes him very sensitive to noise, and his comfort has been studied in building him a sort of hermitage for the summer months. We understand the curious are uncertain whether it is a pesthouse for cases of smallpox, or a cell for lunatics.

Well, we expect to be questioned and cross questioned as anyone should expect who professes to have made a valuable discovery. We expect to make it a part of our business to explain our science of life for the good of mankind; but we prefer inquirers of a less *imaginative* kind.

Circular, August 8, 1864

INQUIRERS—CLASS SECOND

We have mentioned the class of visitors of the Community who come with excited imaginations and calculate to make some shocking discovery, to search out some trap-door or blue-chamber or other. There is another class we will now introduce, who are not less inquisitive and determined, but whose range of investigation is somewhat more elevated. They do not quiz us as though we were imposters and knaves, but they are exceedingly mystified as to how we *manage our affairs*, financial, industrial, and domestic. Their questions do not imply that we are wicked, but that we are *awfully legal.* They assume that we have a code of the most minute and stringent regulations, as the only conceivable way to make our machinery work.

"You all have to get up exactly at the same time, don't you? Your breakfast bell rings at six, and nobody is at liberty to oversleep, I suppose?"

Our breakfast is ready at six, to be sure, and those whose business makes it more convenient or whose taste inclines them to be up with the sun can sit down at that time; but the breakfast lasts till half past seven. The waiters are assiduous till then, and the loiterers after that, though they may have to wait on themselves, find breakfast without much trouble. There are five tables—we take our seats in order, and fill one table after another, so that I can tell about what time it is when I come down, by the seat that I find waiting for me. I am down generally about seven, and find the fourth table nearly filled.

"Well, you all have to eat the same thing?"

Very much as members of one family do elsewhere. Do you and your wife have different dishes? We have the ordinary variety of food (minus meat, but plus fruit) and we have a rotation of cooks in the kitchen, which gives us an admirable chance to find out the best ways of preparing food. Besides, there is all the latitude desired for individuals to cook for themselves. Most of us enjoy our meals best at the general table. We believe in living well, and mean to exalt cooking into a rank among the fine arts. The table is a subject for criticism in the family meeting from time to time, when everyone has a chance to find fault and suggest improvements.

"Well, how is it about dress? Some persons want to dress a great deal more than others. Do you have a certain sum appropriated to each one, or how do you insure equality?"

We are not careful about equality in this thing. There is a clothing committee which has power to veto any great extravagance, but generally persons have what dress they wish for, and some more than others. There is no sum appropriated, and no rule of equal distribution—and no prescribed uniform.

Circular, August 7, 1865

We had a christening at the meeting last night. A baby was named— that is, the name selected by the parents was submitted to the approbation of the Community. When a new baby comes, we have this little form of acknowledgment of Community ownership—the name is offered for general acceptance; or for objection, if such there should be. Any ceremony of baptism or dedication would be supererogatory. Our children are dedicated from the first, by our referring the question of parties becoming parents, to the sanction and sympathy of the church. In ordinary society, the family is one thing, and the church is another, so that when a child is born into a family, it is proper to go through some ceremony to transfer to the church, which is the meaning of baptism. By this ordinance, a child is supposed to be transferred from the family to the church, and the church becomes professedly responsible for it. But here the church is the family, and the family is the church, and the child that is born into the family is born into the church, and there is no occasion for formal transfer. Still, it is comely that parents of a new-born babe should make some recognition of the Community sponsorship, and this is done as far as we have any form, by making the name a matter of general choice.

Circular, February 19, 1866

It should be understood that the Community, while favoring simplicity in all things, is also in favor of having its members well fed and well clothed. The tendency of the Community has been, in respect to all such matters, to rise above the common standard. Those who fared best before coming hither in the above particulars have now no cause of complaint, while those who are less fortunate have certainly occasion for contentment, as there is no partiality exercised in the distribution of the comforts and luxuries of life.

The average cost of food per week for each individual in the Community, during the past year of high prices (estimating the productions raised by the Community for their own use at the market value, but not including the labor of persons in cooking and preparing them), was $1.42 per week. In 1857 it was only $.63 per week.

The average cost of clothing in 1865 (including wages paid to hired laborers, but not including labor performed in this department by the Community) was $38.62, or a trifle over $.74 per week. In 1858, the cost of clothing material for each individual was $16.98 for the whole year.

In order, however, to obtain a correct estimate of the whole cost of living in the Community, there must also be considered the expense of keeping the buildings in repair, the cost of keeping the furniture good, expenses of the library, music, dentistry, lights, fuel, laundry department, stationery, postage, etc., etc. Taking all these things into account, the actual cost of living during the past year (not including household labor performed by the Community members), was $2.62 per week. Eight years ago it was estimated at $1.33 per week. The difference in these rates is accounted for fully by the improvement in fare, which has come with increased means, and partly by the enhanced value of all articles of food, clothing, etc.

Daily Journal, June 29, 1866

Fifty-nine dinners were furnished to visitors yesterday. It has been decided to charge from 75¢ to $1.00 for meals according to quality. A good dinner will be furnished for 75¢, while for a first-rate meal $1.00 will be charged.

Daily Journal, July 7, 1866

The sky is clear but not cloudless. The temperature is on its way up towards the nineties. The hills look beautiful in the the hot clear atmosphere. The woods seem to invite one to their shadows and cool retreats. We hear the music of the mowing machines in the Elm meadow and know that the farmers are haying. We see lines of carriages on the road and know that visitors are numerous. Below our window the steam engine keeps up steady motion and works tirelessly for the cooks, the bathers, and the fruit-preservers. The Depot team comes a little after ten o'clock with the mail, and the semi-diurnal load of cherries. The fruit men tell us they have put up more than their quota of cherries and the season will soon close. The quality of the cherries received this year is the best of any we have ever had, and they have arrived here in the best condition. So, with cherries in our mouth we bid you goodbye until next week.

Circular, July 16, 1866

FOURTH OF JULY—COMMUNIZED LABOR

Many well-disposed persons have been inclined to think that our principles did not afford sufficient stimulus to productive industry and enterprise; that where people worked from attraction, and not to get a living or make money, they would be likely to become lazy and inefficient. The simple view of the amount of labor performed here on the Fourth of July would certainly dispel any such illusion.

In the first place the strawberries picked the previous day on our own fields and upon several of our neighbors (which the Community have undertaken to market), amounted to about four thousand quarts, or about one hundred and twenty-five bushels. All of this food had to be disposed of either by table use, canning, selling here, or shipping abroad. Two double teams carried to the one o'clock A.M. train about two thousand quarts, thus taking the day by the very forelock. Another load of some eight hundred quarts went down to the half-past eight train. Four hundred and fifty-two quarts were picked over, hulled, put in cans and sealed; the balance were sold at retail here or used for strawberry short-cake, or served with cream for visitors. Seventy-five bushels of cherries had been received from the western portion of the State by the day previous; a portion of these had to be picked over and canned on this day. A Bee was called for this purpose at half past four o'clock in the morning. And many bushels were sold by the single quart to the crowd of visitors. Beside the home housework, some three hundred extra dinners had to be furnished; nearly a hundred visitors were supplied with strawberries and cream, to say nothing of the ice cream furnished, the lemonade drank, etc. Several men were busily engaged all day in looking after visitors' teams—putting them into the barn, feeding, etc. Early in the morning of the same day, the goods of our little stores were moved into the large building just completed for a store and other purposes; the shelves were partly filled with samples of our own manufacture, including bags, traps, fruit, etc. In addition to this labor several men and women were engaged in selling goods all day. Of course, a certain number had to be detailed for police service, to see that there was no disorderly behavior; still another group were employed in showing the curious over the buildings and around the grounds. Then a large number were engaged no small portion of the time in furnishing our friends with such music as they could in the Hall, and on the lawn. We had little hired help on that day, excepting a group of strawberry pickers, who of course required more or less superintendence.

Yet all this was done cheerfully, voluntarily. I do not think a man, woman, or child had to be urged to do anything. Everything "went off like clock work," as the saying is; and yet no one had to be "wound up" with any promise of extra wages or by any coercive measures. We had no drill exercises as in an army, and yet on such occasions as the one in question, our *esprit de corps* seems to pervade all ranks, and each is only anxious to do the best thing and please the Lord. It is edifying to us to notice that it is becoming more and more easy to *mobilize* the forces of the Community for such an occasion as the one under consideration. Men and women are more and more free to leave any post and take hold in the helping spirit wherever most needed. It is grand to see two hundred thus engaged, working cheerfully, joyously, animated by the same purpose and seeking the same objects.

Circular, October 7, 1867

Nothing of the kind could be more delightfully informal than are our new meetings. The practice of convening at midday for religious exercises was at first so novel a proceeding that our meetings were characterized by considerable stiffness. The "Go-to-meeting spirit" put an extra whale-bone into our backs and made our faces slightly solemn. Some of us were even harassed with drowsiness, and occasionally one would yield the palm of victory to Morpheus, while with drooping head he napped the meeting through. For one day Mr. Noyes said this was a "free country" and if we could not feel at liberty to go to sleep, to talk or to keep silent on these occasions, our meeting had not reached the true standard. "Let's all take a nap together," he said; "that will be something new." So we all commenced nodding like so many poppies in a shower; but as each kept an eye open to see the maneuvers of the rest, a hearty laugh soon ended the fun. Since then we have relished our meeting as much as our dinner. The mail which comes most propitiously between these two ordinances furnishes many a topic of interest. Letters are read, and comments are made upon intelligence received in the newspapers, or upon notices they contain of the O.C.; frequently Mr. Noyes delivers a pithy home-talk; sometimes we converse upon matters of business, and occasionally we adopt the style of the Quakers, sitting in silence, each one busy with his own thoughts. We think these gatherings have attained a state of simplicity as nearly approximating the artlessness of private family circles as is possible in so large a society; and when we start for the Hall at the ringing of the bell, we look more like a flock of children let out of school at recess, than we do like starched-up religionists, going to church.

Circular, January 2, 1868

After working in the shop about one month I was assigned to a combination of light duties at the O.C.; the principal one being that of nurse to a man who had had a paralytic stroke. Here I will dwell for a moment upon another advantage of Communism. If by any means one of the family is injured in body so as to become unfitted for active service, he does not need to worry, and think that his work is suffering for attention, and his family becoming destitute. But he feels that his affliction is a call to him from God to turn inward and seek humility and patience. Every facility is offered him for doing this work of heart-searching. His business and family interest being one with those of God and His church, he rests assured that all will go just as well as though he were well and strong. Sufficient help is also appointed to attend to his every necessary want and comfort. In many cases the patient is urged to cease all thought and anxiety about becoming able to assist in the visible labor, and devote his whole time to heart culture.

Circular, January 6, 1868

COMMUNITY HOUSEWORK
By a new member

On arriving at O.C. I had some curiosity to know what were the manners and customs of the family in regard to the affairs of everyday life.

The kitchen is divided into two rooms. In the main one is a large coal stove, on which bread can be toasted, griddle-cakes baked, potatoes re-warmed, etc. Joining this main kitchen is a smaller one, on one side of which is a large zinc oven capable of baking two bushels of potatoes at once. Near this is a wood stove used for various purposes. At the end of the room and on part of one side are cupboards.

A door leads from the kitchen to the bakery, which is an institution by itself. It is supplied with large mixing-boxes, seasoning-cupboards, flour-sifters, and a zinc oven of the largest pattern, which is capable of baking sixty five-pound loaves of bread at a time, or in all three hundred pounds. Operating this bakery is the exclusive business of one man; and when necessary, he is aided by a company of young women.

At the head of the kitchen department is a man whose business it is to see that all necessary articles in the shape of provisions and table furniture, dishes, etc. are provided.

Next in order come the kitchen men. These men alternate in rising at half-past four A.M. for the purpose of building the kitchen fire and making the preparations for breakfast. They aid during the day in all the various labors of the kitchen.

The cooking department is headed by two women, one of whom is chief counsellor and manager, while the other is her assistant. These women occupy their position usually for four weeks at a time; so that it does not become an irksome task, and gives all an opportunity to try their skill at a variety of dishes. These women make out the bill of fare, which is always ample, and in my estimation equal to any first-class hotel. They superintend all the cooking and have charge of the kitchen generally.

Next come the table waiters. These consist of young women, in age ranging from twelve to thirty. They are appointed to their position and alternated at stated periods by a committee selected by the family to attend to such matters. Waiters are in attendance at the main tables of the dining room until eight o'clock. And should you be an hour later you could still find plenty to eat on a side table.

At twelve noon the bell again rings the signal for dinner, which lasts until one o'clock in the dining room after which time you will find a table set in the back kitchen for an hour longer. At half-past five a large hand-bell is rung telling you that supper is ready; but you will be well served if you do not go until seven. Thus liberal time is given to suit all taste and business.

The dining room is capable of conveniently seating one hundred and ten persons at once. On opposite sides of the room are four oval tables, each seating eight persons. The middle of the room is occupied by two long tables; one seating twenty-six, and the other twenty persons. The rule is to fill up the farthest table on the west side of the room first, then the next, and so on, in regular order. This associates old and young, male and female, in a good and wholesome manner, and tends to diffuse a spirit of politeness and sociability not otherwise attainable.

The next thing in order is to clear the tables and wash the dishes, an operation which is provided for by itself, and is not under the supervision of the kitchen corps. Half an hour after the bell rings for any meal, part of the tables are ready to be cleared. This is performed by four women aided by one man. The women brush the refuse of the table in the pans and place dishes in piles. The man carries them to the washing-room either in his hands or in a small three-wheeled cart made for the purpose.

Circular, March 21, 1868

Mr. Woolworth remarked that they had a pleasant time burying Florilla this morning. Everyone appeared cheerful and light-hearted; and the whole thing seemed to him more like a picnic than a burial. He believed it was more pleasing to God than long, doleful faces, and the shedding of a good many tears; and also more in keeping with real faith and the spirit of resurrection.

Circular, December 28, 1868

We have one room which most embodies our idea of *home.* It is the Upper Sitting-Room in the brick house. High, airy, embracing two stories with three large windows touching the floor, soaring thirteen feet, and catching the rising sun; surrounded on the north, west, and south by a double tier of bedrooms, one above the other, with a white overlooking corridor between, in the panels of which hang the framed heads of Greek poets and philosophers; warm, with a mammoth sheet-iron stove on one side and a hot-air register on the other; convenient, with its book-strewn center table, its sofa, chairs, and bureaus; it is the room of all others in which the true home feeling finds the freest play. The Hall is grand for concerts, lectures, meetings, and all occasions when the whole family assemble together; but it is too cold and stately for constant, familiar resort. It is to the Upper Sitting-Room that one runs to find a missing friend; it is here that the Willow Place folks gather after meeting to pass a pleasant word and say good-night. But, above all, here, if in any place, is the source of the ever-flowing fountain of Community life, for here Mr. Noyes spends the greater part of his time. It is this circumstance which has made the room the delightful place it is this winter. Here he writes, now and then spending a half hour in conversation with a group around the stove.

Circular, February 22, 1869

There is scarcely anything left to remind the O.C. of its early privations in regard to diet; yet there are some droll reminiscences among the present generation of a period when brown bread and applesauce, beans and milk-gravy were the staple, if not the only articles of diet. The class who were boys then seem to retain the most vivid recollections of that regimen—probably because it bore upon them at the stage in which persons are the most omnivorous. One of this class relates with great gusto how a new boy, having become an inmate of the Children's House by his father's joining the Community at this time of low diet, declined the lunch of crackers which was given to the children, remarking naively that "he did not like crackers, they were too dry; he preferred something moist, *like pie*." Pie was an unheard-of-luxury at this time, and his remarks seemed so astoundingly presumptuous to the children that it has been a standing joke to this day. A long dispensation of beans and milk-gravy (a substitute for butter) gave to the former the name (among the boys) of the "staff," and to the latter the "consolation."

Circular, August 2, 1869

Among the many advantages arising from Communism is the opportunity we find of frequently changing employments. Such an advantage not only relieves the hardship of following an occupation after the taste for it has ceased, but it gives a freshness to every department, that facilitates progress and opens the way for inspiration. To many it may seem a waste of talent for a machinist to be looking after milk, a carpenter to work in a kitchen, or a mechanic to pare potatoes, but experience proves that such talent carries improvement where they would scarcely reach if those departments were regarded as exclusively the province of women. A first-class joiner who worked in our kitchen invented a mop-wringer which saves a world of work, and our women now think that they could not do without it. He also introduced a system of washing potatoes by means of a circular cage revolving in water; and now a young mechanic from the trap-shop, conceiving that potatoes may be rid of their jackets on the same principle by which we "tom" the rust, etc., from the iron, has introduced pieces of brick into the circular cage. In revolving, the bricks rub the potatoes, until their skins are taken off more completely than by paring, and considerably less labor and much saving of the nutritious parts of the potato.

Circular, February 28, 1870

Some of our ingenious mechanics have made us two new tables for the Dining-Room, which are constructed very differently from those commonly used. The tables are circular, with revolving centers, and therefore are in two parts, though resting on one framework. The outside part of each of these tables is about a foot wide, and made like a ring. On this ring is placed the plates, knives, and forks. The revolving centers are about an inch higher than the surrounding outside tables and fill up the space left by the latter, only allowing room for the former to revolve and the tablecloths of each to fall between. These revolving centers are for food, drink, extra dishes, etc., etc. When you go to your meal you sit down at the stationary table, turn over your plate, and arm yourself with your knife and fork, and then, if you observe anything on the revolving table that you want, you can turn it as you with wish, with the slightest touch, and lo! the desired dish is before you, and all you have to do is to help yourself.

But every invention has its drawbacks, they say, and this is no exception. If you don't look out, or rather, if others don't look out, as you are conveying a spoonful of gravy for instance from some dish on the center table to your plate, someone opposite to you may give the table a whirl, and before you are aware the dish from which you are dipping is two or three feet away, and you are lucky if you get a chance to put the spoon back. Still, as these revolving tables are set with duplicate dishes, one does not have to turn far to get a dish, so there is not so very much danger of such accidents occurring. After using them two or three weeks we pronounce these tables very convenient and attractive, and far preferable to the ordinary stationary table.

Circular, April 18, 1870

Among our various experiments is one relating to dining arrangements. Two of our meals, that is dinner and supper, are taken picnic fashion. That is to say, instead of a formal setting of the tables, with waiters and numerous duplicate dishes of food scattered here and there, we have the food massed in an attractive way in the center of one table, and the plates, knives, forks, tumblers, and so forth massed on another table, and the manner of dining is for each one to help themselves to just what he wants and sit where he pleases. During the warm months it may be fashionable to take one's supper out on the lawn, or make a convivial party under the cherry trees. Another part of this plan is to cultivate less dependence on hot food. The question whether dinner shall be hot or cold is left to the convenience of the cooks, and one form is received with as much favor as the other. The advantage, which we think is gained by this arrangement, is that it saves labor, allows the cooks to take time for preparing food, when it can be done in the most favorable manner, and provides us with more variety and better meals than ever before.

Circular, June 6, 1870

Superstitions have the life of a polyp—cut them in two and they will not die. So with the stories among the vulgar about the O.C. There are certain stories about our customs and domestic arrangements, not half so probable as that the moon is made of green cheese, which are always in circulation and come round to us fresh as new laid eggs every visiting season, having done so for twenty years at least. One of these stories is that we distribute ourselves at bedtime by lot. Another is that our children do not know their parents. Another, that we bury our dead secretly. Another, that we all sleep in one bed; one great *circular* bed, is a particular version of this story. A gentleman from a neighboring village, and not a stranger to our place, called yesterday with a lady who had never been here before, a clergyman's wife we understood. After going the usual round the gentleman asked the guide if it would be proper to take them where they could see some of our bedrooms, "for," said he aside, "the lady with me has the most damnable ideas about your arrangements for the night—she believes you all sleep in one bed"; then in an apologetic tone, "she was once an old maid." Are all old maids demented? Nobody of any sense could believe such a thing. Imagine it, anybody who can! In order to be comfortable at all, the beds should be fifty feet square, and, to have decent ventilation, there ought to be a dome over it a hundred feet high!

Well, how do we sleep? We inquire of our attendant for this department, how many beds we make up every morning? She says 189 here and at Willow Place. Substracting from this fifteen beds for the children who sleep two together, or one with an adult, and five for spare beds, we have 169 beds for our adult population which numbers about 200. This is almost a bed apiece. Where two sleep together they are of the same sex. The beds are mostly one in a room. There are ten or a dozen rooms perhaps in which there are two. We believe in the right of retirement as one of the most sacred rights of existence. We have respect to the command, "when thou prayest enter into thy closet," and mean to provide for easy obedience in our home arrangements, by giving all rooms by themselves. So instead of all huddling into one bed, as the story goes, we rather carry our refinement to the standard of royalty. The king has his own apartment, and the queen has hers. In the etiquette of high rank, it would be a vulgarity for husbands and wives to occupy the same bedchamber.

Circular, November 14, 1870

Many who visit us seem to studiously misrepresent us, as, for insance, a certain New York writer who lately said, in speaking of our Library, that it contained no light reading, we deeming novels pernicious. However true the latter statement may be, the facts are that thirteen shelves in our Library are devoted to novels, and among them may be found the writings of most of the standard novelists—Scott, Dickens, Thackeray, Cooper, Bronte, Bulwer, Reade, etc., etc. Besides this, three of the largest shelves in the Library are devoted to poetry; and the observer sees such names as Keats, Cowper, Burns, Milton, Pope, Young, Longfellow, Bryant, Whittier, Tennyson, etc., as well as translations of Homer, Virgil, Goethe, etc.

Circular, November 21, 1870

The proportion of males and females in our Communities is as follows:

Age	Male	Female
Under 1	5	2
From 1 to 10	14	7
From 10 to 20	7	15
From 20 to 30	21	35
From 30 to 40	28	20
From 40 to 50	16	22
From 50 to 60	15	20
From 60 to 70	16	13
From 70 to 80	6	6
From 80 to 90	0	2
Total	128	142

Circular, February 20, 1871

A great deal of our outdoor and indoor labor has, during a course of years, gradually devolved upon hired help, while our own people have in several departments served only as superintendents. This has been brought about not because we have felt above manual labor, but because all our own help has been absorbed in more renumerative employments pertaining to manufacturing. We have not allowed ourselves to get lily-fingered, and have always stood ready, and always intend to stand ready, to do with cheerful zeal anything that our circumstances seem to call for. As an illustration of this, our family have found themselves so much at leisure this winter, owing to the change of the spooling-room from O.C. to Willow Place, and for other reasons, that we have recently undertaken to do our own laundry work, a task that for several years has devolved upon hired help with only two or three Communists for superintendents. The change has proved to be a most satisfactory one. Though only the same number of our women have been put into the department to make good the help dismissed (and be it remembered that our women do not work so many hours a day as hired help), the week's work has been shortened two days. This is partly owing to a charming feature of the new arrangement that ought not to pass unnoticed. Two or three times a week a "grand Bee" consisting of both sexes of all ages, assist an hour in the afternoon at the ironing-room. The men and boys fold sheets and tablecloths, or mangle towels and pillow cases, while the women and girls sprinkle and fold, or starch and iron: all are in unitary fever of cheerful industry; and the work accomplished at Bee is surprising.

Circular, July 10, 1871

ADMISSIONS

These communities are constantly receiving applications for admission which they have to reject. It is difficult to state in any brief way all their reasons for thus limiting their numbers; but some of them are these:

1. The parent Community at Oneida is full. Its buildings are adapted to a certain number, and it wants no more.

2. The Branch-Communities, though they have not attained the normal size, have as many members as they can well accommodate and must grow in numbers only as they grow in capital and buildings.

3. The kind of men and women who are likely to make the Communities grow, spiritually and financially, are scarce, and have to be sifted out slowly and cautiously. It should be distinctly understood that these Communities are not asylums for pleasure seekers or persons who merely want a home and a living. They will receive only those who are very much in earnest in religion. They have already done their full share

of labor in criticizing and working over raw recruits, and intend hereafter to devote themselves to other jobs (plenty of which they have on
hand), receiving only such members as seem likely to help and not
hinder their work. As candidates for Communism multiply, it is obvious
that they cannot all settle at Oneida and Wallingford. Other communities
must be formed; and the best way for earnest disciples generally is to
work and wait till the Spirit of Pentecost shall come on their neighbors
and give them communities right where they are.

Circular, December 11, 1871

"How do we get our clothes?" is the question often asked. This is
the way we get them now. The clothing committee (which by the way,
is large enough to understand the wants of the family) has prepared two
printed lists of clothing—one for the men and one for the women. You
take one of these blanks, fill it out according to your wants for the coming year, sign it, and return it to the committee. This enables them to get
at our wants and purchase accordingly.

Circular, May 27, 1872

There never was a time when all departments of business in the
O.C. were carried on so harmoniously and with so little worry as now;
and still we have more to do then ever before. There is an increasing
trap trade, urgent demands for silk, extensive plans for building, farm
and garden work, besides the numerous cares incident to a great household; and yet no one is anxious or worn out. After supper most of our
folks are at home. The orchestra meets for private practice, a quartet
meets to sing, a lively company have a Bee to improve the grounds, the
children romp on the lawn; and so the time is filled up until meeting at
eight o'clock.

Circular, October 14, 1872

The Visitor's Register shows by names recorded that 3,699
strangers have visited the O.C. since the beginning of the year. This is
really a small minority, probably not more than one-third of the transient
callers that we have had, as many visitors neglect to record their names.
There were on one occasion as many as seven hundred visitors on the
O.C. grounds at one time during the past summer.

Circular, October 28, 1872

One of the signs of the unity and flexibility of the Community, of which we have lately spoken, is seen in the hearty readiness with which new and revolutionary manners are adopted at the suggestion of the scientific and spiritual. Up to the twentieth day of October, 1872, the Community, like most families, has taken three meals per day; and the routine of breakfast, dinner, and supper has been as practically invariable as the rising and going down of the sun. Today, after the presentation of scientific physiological reasons by Doctors Noyes and Cragin, and the more cogent spiritual reasons suggested by Mr. Noyes, behold a new regimen begun without opposition, almost without discussion. The family breakfast hours are now from eight to ten instead of from six to eight as heretofore, and the dinner and final meal for the day is served at three P.M. The medical men say that eating of three meals per day is a habit and not a natural instinct, and that it has been conclusively proved that better digestion, better assimilation, better sleep, and brighter faculties are the rewards of those who limit themselves to two meals. The physiological view of the change commends itself to us, but we are happily reminded by one whose eye is always on spiritual things that the great boon of correct dietetic habits is not primarily good digestion but a clearer spiritual life.

Nor is this change of mealtimes the end of the turn-about. The evening meeting, the choicest hour of the day, has been put forward an hour, and is now held from seven o'clock till eight instead of from eight till nine as heretofore. The result of these changes thus far has been to promote sociability and break up habit in a manner that is eminently pleasing to the spirit of Communism. Habit is a tyrant, and it is good to rebel against it from time to time. Furthermore, we have a notion that it is possible to really hoodwink the devil when he thinks he has got you started on some track, where he will be sure to find you for all time, by suddenly switching off and making him lose the scent.

Circular, November 4, 1872

How does the O.C. like the new regimen? After a ten days trial of the system of two meals per day, Mr. Woolworth in the evening meeting invited the family to say what they thought about it. The expression in favor of the new manner of life was at once hearty and unanimous. Some spoke of aches and pains that had disappeared since discarding the third meal, and other testified to a more equable spiritual life. Clearer heads, lighter spirits, and a new delight in food make all rejoice in the era just begun; and we seem to be nearer to eating our meat with gladness and singleness of heart than ever before.

Circular, July 28, 1873

SOUNDS ON THE LAWN AFTER SUPPER

The click of mallets and balls on the croquet ground; the rolling of carts and wagons in the distance; the music of piano, clarinet and cello playing in the Hall; a quartet singing in the cottage at the foot of the hill; children's voices laughing; boys playing horse; cows lowing at the barn; sheep bells tinkling; lambs bleating; frogs peeping in the pond below the garden; birds singing; wind whistling through the trees; the roar and rumble of the cars on the Midland; the ringing of the car bell which announces the arrival of our friends from Joppa; a merry meeting of the newly arrived; the high note of the whistle which calls us together for an hour in the Hall.

Circular, August 18, 1873

A PANORAMIC VIEW

Five o'clock! Stillness reigns from attic to cellar. Six o'clock! The whistle sounds. Little bare feet pattering along the main hall on the way to the Children's Room to be dressed—the first glad sound of the morning. Laughing voices ringing through the empty halls and corridors arouse the sleepers from their dreams. Half an hour and there is the noise of footsteps, some light some heavy, constantly hurrying up and down the long stairway from the Mansard; the noise of chairs and tables hastily shoved about, and the rumble of bedsteads in the many chambers around the house. Another half hour and the women are at their several callings—bed-making, sweeping halls, tidying up the parlors, mopping and dusting the library, and putting things to rights generally. Meanwhile a trio of active cooks are getting breakfast for the fifteen "titmen" of the family, who file out to the Dining-Room at seven o'clock. Some of the men go to the shop, some are packing silk, some are out on the farm, some are at the barn, one or two are in the printing-office, a few may be seen on the croquet ground, a few sitting on the portico, a few are reading in the library, and the rest are in their rooms until eight o'clock when the whistle calls one and all to breakfast. By the hour of nine the people are scattered to their various assignments—trap-shop, machine-shop, silk-room, business office, printing-office, kitchen, dining-room, laundry, company room, etc. The children with their guardians start off for the lot east of the road, and the people who remain are tending our youngest, or making their clothes, or taking care of the various concerns of the household. Company comes in on the train at ten—a slight bustle ensues. Just at noon a few more are added, and consequently more bustle. Cooks and waiters stepping lively to get dinner in readiness at one o'clock. At twelve the bell rings, and the older children go to school, and the younger ones to bed. Stillness reigns for the next two hours. At three the whistle calls to dinner; there is a thronging towards the Dining-Room and the two hundred discuss the viands temptingly laid out. Dinner over, and many resume their labors until six o'clock, when the family are all again at home. People are meeting in the court, vestibule, or in the sitting rooms to tell the latest news; young and old mingle in croquet on the lawn, or at dominoes in the house, as the case may be. Many are reading or studying or writing; the children are frolicking below stairs; it is a time of rest and relaxation and the home feeling predominates. All concentrate in the Hall at eight for a family meeting; some interesting topic draws out the enthusiasm of all who are present. Meeting closes at nine, and people disperse, some to the library, some to the Sitting-Room upstairs, some to the Sitting-Room downstairs, some to the South Sitting-Room; some to the nursery kitchen, and some to their own bedrooms. At ten o'clock the house is still. The watchman goes quietly round on his mission; he locks the doors—puts out the lights—darkness and tranquility till morning.

Circular, March 2, 1874

Our readers often get glimpses from the nursery and the Children's Room, showing the effects of Community education on those fresh young lives. Perhaps someone would like a glimpse of the opposite extreme, showing what Communism has done for the old—that part of human life commonly unlovely, because enveloped in the spirit of old age and disease. Lady C., nearly ninety, is confined to her room and bent under the accumulations of her long journey. We passed her room this morning. She was alone. Singing greeted our ears and we stopped to listen. It was not like the voice of the swan singing its death-song; nor the carol of the lark, nor the song of the caged bird even; but the voice of one who had found God and whose faith and truth were anchored on the eternal rock, victorious in Christ. There was something electrical in the whole scene, and I was thankful that there is a life beyond the power of disease and old age.

Circular, May 18, 1874

One pleasant morning last week we strolled over to the "Villa" for a short visit. Arrived there, we rang the doorbell and were shown into a neat and cozy parlor by Miss Ida who then ran to summon Mrs. W. the "mother" of the family from whom we gathered the following information: There are at present but sixteen persons in the family, which consists regularly of nineteen. The men and women are about equal in number. Mrs. W.'s ideal of a small family is to have all ages represented, children, youth, the middle-aged, and the elderly. The main object of the family is to make a pleasant home for the foremen and others who manage our businesses at the Willow Place factory. They don't keep chickens. A row-boat on the pond furnishes an opportunity for simple aquatic exercises. Their evenings are described as seasons of pleasant social enjoyment. After the usual evening meeting they frequently amuse themselves with such light games as dominoes and squails; sometimes, for variety, cake and wine are passed around, and often songs go to heighten the cheer. Twice a week at least they all attend the evening meeting at O.C.; this is a time-honored custom.

Circular, July 13, 1874

In an ordinary family the mother usually has the care and superintendence of the whole household; the furniture, bedding, washing, baking, sewing, etc., etc. A Community family, though in many respects like a common one, is so large as to make it necessary to divide the care; and so arise various departments, clothing, washing, furniture, bedding, and so on, each having a competent head appointed to the office. If you need a new window curtain, stand-spread, an easy chair, a foot-stool, a different bedstead, a looking-glass, or a larger bureau, just apply to Mrs. S., who has charge of the furniture, and she will be sure to do her best to accommodate you. When the carpet in your room grows threadbare and shabby, let Miss K. know of it and she will provide you with a better one. If anyone of the 200 beds needs a tick mended, more husks supplied, a new mattress, a wider counterpaine, larger or smaller pillows, in short if in any way it needs changing or repairing, she who needs it has only to speak to Mrs. N. and as if by magic the work is done. If one of your dresses is new and you would like to have it carefully washed, or you need a piece of cloth bleached, mention it to Mrs. K., and you will find yourself as well served as though you had not left it to others. Mrs. C. will furnish goods for your own clothing, and Mrs. V. will provide for your children. But of all the offices thus filled that relieve us of burden, that of superintending the kitchen is the one most appreciated. This post is filled by two of our women (changing quite often), while all the others go to the table entirely free from the loss of appetite occasioned by the responsibility of planning, and the anxiety of preparing the food. No wonder we women of 30 are mistaken for Misses when we are saved from so much care and vexation.

Oneida Circular, August 31, 1874

The Oneida Community is unique and stands on a basis of its own. The failure of a thousand Fourierist or Owenite Communities in the past or the future does not affect this chance of success an iota. It is founded on a religious basis and we who have labored in it our whole lives must be admitted to know how necessary its religion is to its existence. We have often said that without its religion it would fail, established and prosperous though it be. We acknowledge that selfishness must be rooted out before men and women will be fit to enjoy our style of Communism, and it may take a long time to do it. We mean to help all we can by showing the way.

Circular, March 8, 1875

Twenty years ago when all the traps we made were forged out in a little old blacksmith's shop, and finished off with a footpress and file, when silk-manufacturing was undreamed of and fruit-preserving hardly known anywhere in the world; when the O.C. was indulging in the pastoral fancy of making our living by raising fruit and vegetables to sell—in those good old times, we were never troubled for plenty of good, hard work outdoors, for great and small. Plenty of digging and hoeing and weeding all summer long, for the girls as well as the boys. Plenty of work in the barns and at the wood-pile for men and boys all winter. Then, the main problem was how to get a living. We had no need to worry ourselves about proper physical development. As we have gradually enlarged our resources, our occupations have changed. Superintending the trap, silk, and fruit-preserving businesses, the farm, carpenter's shop, etc., work in the counting-room, in the printing-office and other sedentary employments now engage many of our men. The importance of a first-rate physical basis is becoming apparent, and we occasionally sigh for the good old times when we hoed corn and dug ditches. But the most interesting question before us is about our children. Will they learn to work, and so get the vigorous, hardy constitution of the farmer boy, when there is no spur of necessity goading them on? This problem we have taken upon ourselves to solve.

Oneida Circular, April 12, 1875

O.C. HISTORY

As a community we are constantly growing. Our family slowly increasing in number; our old business enterprises expand year by year, and new projects are undertaken almost constantly. Things are never at a standstill with us, but, on the contrary, the events of each week or month will form important chapters in our history. Although the O.C. has been in existence well nigh thirty years, there are still many problems in this scheme which we cannot claim to have fully worked out. For one thing, all the world is predicting and expecting that if we ever undertake to change leaders by appointing some other person to succeed Mr. Noyes our organization will soon go to pieces. We have no present intention of changing leaders, but if it ever becomes necessary, we predict and expect that our affairs will go smoothly forward, without any dangerous disturbances. Other similar points might be mentioned. It remains to be shown that the young folks who grow up in the Community will uphold the faith of their fathers in its integrity and maintain the principles on which our institution is founded, thus making it a permanent home. For these reasons it may be desirable to wait many years yet before attempting to write and publish a full history of the Oneida Community.

Circulator, May 17, 1875

Instead of arising the moment our evening meeting hour is closed, and scattering to their rooms in the different parts of the house, the majority of the family remain in their seats, and the transition from meeting to after meeting is mainly marked by a buzz of cheerful conversation. The stage is always well lighted by two blazing chandeliers. On it, after an interim, perhaps, appear some of the musicians, and favor us with vocal or instrumental solos, duets, quartets, and quintets. Mayhap someone repeats a poem. The other evening by special request Mr. Warne had a few of his scholars recite pieces. Their recitations were received with applause, and we were delighted by a promise of more from the children another time. This custom helps to keep warm and bright the family feeling in our big household, and prevents our meetings from becoming, or seeming, stiff and formal.

Circular, September 6, 1875

We are reading at our evening gathering the "First Annual Report of the Oneida Association," published in 1849. At the time the report was written, our present remunerative businesses were unborn, and we only carried on in a small way a grist-mill, a machine-shop, and a saw-mill. There were but 87 members of the Community on the First of January, 1849. The professions of the men are given as follows: "four are farmers; two are carpenters and machinists; two are cabinet-makers; two are shoe-makers; two are blacksmiths; two millers; two have been school-teachers; two were bred to the ministry; one is a painter; one is a wagon-maker; one is a gun-smith; one a lead-pipe-maker; one has been a merchant and publishing agent. Some of the members are conversant with several other professions, such as those of editors, architects, harness-makers, etc."

How oddly this all sounds now that we have double and treble the number of members in the family that we had then, and of course many more who have or did have professions.

At that period the Community was made up entirely of young people and persons in the prime of life. The oldest member of the family then was but fifty, and the majority of persons were under forty. All were in the vigor of youth. Over a quarter of a century has intervened and marked the change! Those who were in the prime of life then are well advanced in life now; and though most of them are well and able to serve efficiently in some way, there is still quite a number who are not able to take the responsibility of our heavy businesses, or to assist at manual labor as they did 25 or even ten years ago. The "young people"—those between the ages of 16 and 25—and those who were "the children" at the beginning of our effort, are now the workers and managers of various departments of business in the Community; and not only so, but they are the fathers and mothers of the large household of children which have been born in the Community within the last fifteen years. And so it is plain that the Community has not retrograded but gone forward; its members have not lost their interest in "bees" or any other needful business, but rather their interests and responsibilities have increased. In those early days we had few children, and no aged persons. It is simply a work of time and progress—years have been added to the people, and our offspring have multiplied. We have a large proportion of young and able-bodied persons in middle life now, who have added cares of not only looking out for the wants of those who have grown old in the service, but the still greater responsibility of nursing and rearing and educating the fast-increasing company of little ones who are born in the Community. This we consider the most important work before us, and one which occupies the attention of "every adult member" at the present time more than any other, as will be seen from the conversation on this subject.

III

What They Thought

What they thought seems to me almost more important than what they did or how they lived or any other category in the lives of the Oneida Communists. They had come together and pledged their lives, their fortunes, and their sacred honors, much as did the Founding Fathers in framing the Declaration of Independence, on the basis of what they thought and what they believed. The announcement which appeared in the *Circular* for January 17, 1854, states their credo concisely. After that, the items here cited are less basic but are still, however applied, the crux of what they believed, what they thought. Their ideas were many and varied but alike in the quality of originality which appears in all of them.

Fifty years before modern psychiatry had conceived of the subjective and objective states of introverts and extroverts, the Community, in a criticism of the state of matters in the trap shop where they thought "some dissipating influences have been at work," remarked (*Circular,* July 23, 1857) that "two spheres of activity are open to man; one is outward and from himself upon the material world, and the other is more or less inward and towards himself . . . every man is naturally more biased towards one of these spheres than to the other. . . . Both these men are one-sided—distorted. Accordingly, any undue preponderance of one bias over the other is felt by the body and promptly regulated by our system of criticism."

When John Humphrey Noyes wrote or spoke, the Community read and listened. On the subject of old age he was particularly interesting. In 1858 (*Circular,* April 29, 1858) he wrote: "The thought occurred to me whether we could not create an opposite atmosphere—one which would repel and resist the advances of old age and make it more easy and natural to grow youthful than to grow old and infirm." Seven years later (*Circular,* August 14, 1865) he spoke on the same subject. "Say to yourself (whatever your age) 'I am 22 years old and shall never be any older.' " This attitude, or something like it, must have inspired not only Noyes but many of his adherents, those hopeful spirits who began to study algebra and Greek at eighty years of age and who sought improvement until the day they died.

Not all the subjects discussed by the members were weighty in tone. The discussion of what they called the Meat Question occupied a good many of their evening meetings for several years. One view is really delightful. The question was raised (*Circular,* February 25, 1858) whether there was any truth in the idea that "we partake of the nature of animals by eating their flesh." The opponents of this theory thought it would be as reasonable "to suppose that we should become like cows by feeding on beef."

Once again the question of legal, systematic efficiency came under discussion, and they decided that it was better to be partially disorganized than to come into a legal, cramped Shakerish kind of order. Pliancy or a flexible will in small matters gave the social atmosphere "a more than downy softness" (*Circular,* January 20, 1859). A person obstinate in small things is to be marked as a man "who takes a pin-hole view of the universe."

At a time, 1862, in the very heart of Victorian repressiveness of most amusements, from the theater to card playing, the Community remarked that they had already learned that true sport and pleasure did not belong to the superficial and irreligious. In the future, amusements, recreations, diversions, whatever you pleased to call them—"the playful action of life as distinguished from its more weighty pursuits"—would sustain a more prominent position. This was not to be mistaken for mere frivolity. It was evidently a law of the universe that there could be no unalloyed happiness that had not in it the element of worship.

In the statement of General Principles to govern the care and treatment of infants and young children (*Circular,* January 29, 1863), one of the most original and characteristic principles asserted that "Amativeness takes precedence of Philoprogenitiveness, and parental feeling becomes a usurpation when it crowds out a passion which is relatively its superior."

They state further that the rearing of children should be carried out in connection with self-culture, and "The appetite for universal improvement must not be allowed to seriously encroach upon them." This dictum chimes perfectly with their chief theme of improvement in every department of character, but still comes oddly from a group then and always so deeply devoted to the breeding and rearing of their children.

The episode of the visit of William Hepworth Dixon (*Daily Journal,* August 16, 1866) is an example of the guilelessness, as well as the openness of the Oneida Communists. Dixon, an Englishman and an editor of the London *Athenaeum,* arrived at the Community with a letter of introduction from Horace Greeley. It was explained that Mr. Dixon had some knowledge of the Community gathered from fragmentary issues of its publications in the British Museum and was "considerably interested in socialistic questions." He apparently entertained the communists with his conversation and gave them a lecture on the Holy Land. They accepted him as a friend of the socialistic movement and made themselves pleasant to him. It was, as they wrote some months later (*Daily Journal,* March 21, 1867), when Dixon published a scurrilous account of his visit, "difficult to restrain our wrath on reading . . . what Dixon said about Mr. Noyes; everything about it was so untruthful." The book which Dixon later wrote, *"Spiritual Wives,"* is certainly not a favorable or accurate view of either the Community or his hosts.

The article on *Diotrephiasis (Circular,* February 25, 1867) explains itself and is included particularly because it is an example, too, of the lightness and humor which was a part of their lives. Another naming which was especially delightful was the title of the annual celebration of the great day on which John Humphrey Noyes had declared himself sinless—as they used to say, "The Twentieth of February, the Day We Celebrate," or, as they named it, the "High Tide of the Spirit." This, the perihelion of the year, was opposed by the aphelion, or the Twentieth of August, which they named the "High Tide of the Flesh" and on occasion they took steps to quell the Carnal Man at this season (*Circular,* August 28, 1871).

Just as small families often have occasional words of what might be called a private language, so the large family of the Oneida Community had a number of special usages which occur frequently in these excerpts. One which appears many times in many connections is the good old New England word *bee.* It was an ordinance exactly suited to Community life; a bee would be announced at dinner or perhaps on the bulletin board; "A bee in the kitchen to pare apples"; or "A bee to pick strawberries at five o'clock tomorrow morning"; or "A bee in the Upper Sitting Room to sew bags." Often, to make the occasion more interesting, a reader would be appointed and they got through a great number of books, much to their pleasure and edification.

Other words either peculiar to the Oneida Community or used by them in a special way are *legal* and *legality,* which they used to indicate acting under the pressure of duty instead of freely, from Inspiration; *principality,* which could mean a state of mind, an influence, or even a habit—all usually to be criticized, as "a coughing principality" which they advised its victim to avoid; *amativeness* and *alimentiveness* which explain themselves, i.e., excessive amorousness and excessive interest in or desire for food; *philoprogenitiveness,* the love of children, only criticized when carried to excess; *at-home-a-tiveness,* certainly a homemade word of obvious meaning and *Diotrephiasis* which was coined by Noyes to mean the love of preeminence, or, as he said, the "who-shall-be-greatest mania." All of these words have the special flavor of Community speech and writing.

From a letter from Noyes to an inquirer, in 1860, there is the first discussion of "the conjunction of *faith and science*" as noted in the *Circular* (April 4, 1870). He advised that "the spiritually minded look favorably towards science, and the scientifics look favorably towards faith." They would then, he said hopefully, "be the beginning of a new class of scientists" who would "cast their crowns at the feet of faith and turn their whole strength into our religious meetings."

Certainly, while John Humphrey Noyes was at the helm of Community living or thinking, no part of it was allowed to become stale or humdrum. The law of fellowship, ascending or descending, was one of his most original concepts (*Circular,* August 16, 1875). Ascending fellowship: companionship so that the drawing of the fellowship is upward; descending, the drawing of the fellowship downward. The balance would seem to be a delicate matter, but, as they said, any one could tell whether he had reached a spot where the inspiration of a superior being worked through him in a way to make descending fellowship safe for him. Even the children were instructed in this science and were frequently criticized for "horizontal fellowship," too much of which, they found, could lead to trouble.

In the 1870's there were plenty of disturbances in the outside world both at home and abroad, but the Community gave to political matters only enough attention to keep themselves reasonably well informed on the progress of events. Their minds were in pursuit of more important matters. They admired and approved of those who labored at the great issues of the world but found it took more heroism to turn resolutely away from outside turmoil than to become absorbed in it, taking part, heart in hand. It was their business, they said (*Circular,* April 17, 1871), to seek the peace of God and blow it upon the world.

The Community was sometimes twitted upon its unanimity, as when one of the newspapers remarked that if Mr. Noyes took a pinch of snuff, all the Community sneezed. There were many other advantages. Every particle of knowledge which any member had was at the service of all; if one could sketch or paint or play an instrument or sing or do a dozen other things well he was ready to teach others who wanted to learn. If art was but a reflection of life, they might reasonably look for some new art development as a result of communism.

Good times and sudden prosperity, the Community reminded its members, offered as many snares as hard times and discontent, made it too easy to sail off on the wings of imagination into a thousand new ventures. They must remember, Mr. Noyes said (*Circular,* October 5, 1868), that if they were ever to learn to walk wisely without being compelled to it by suffering, they must begin by keeping sober and chaste and continent in enticing circumstances; to be prompt yet modest, bold yet cautious, victorious yet humble. They were able to do more work without being tired because, since they trusted in Providence, they worked without worry. In the Community they relied on one another and trusted in Providence. Thus faithfulness took the place of care and made labor light.

Circular, January 17, 1854
[Announcement on the first page]

The *Circular* is published on Tuesdays, Thursdays, and Saturdays at 43 Willow Place, near the South Ferry, Brooklyn, N. Y. The topics which have heretofore chiefly occupied its columns and which will still be the main element of its most serious discussions are comprised in the following schedule of doctrines and measures: *Salvation from Sin, The Gift of the Gospel.* "Thou shalt call his name Jesus: for He shall save his people from their sins." *The Second Coming of Christ.* A.D. 70 or "immediately after" the Destruction of Jerusalem at the close of the Bible record and the Apostolic Age. "Verily I say unto you, there be some standing here which shall not taste of death till they see the Son of Man coming in his Kingdom." *The Kingdom of God,* founded in the invisible "mansions" of Christ and his followers 1800 years ago, and now being extended to this world and Hades, uniting three worlds on the plan of the Second Resurrection. "Thy Kingdom come, Thy will be done on earth *as it is in Heaven. Communism, an Institution* of the Holy Spirit— the social order of Heaven. "All mine are thine, and thine mine." "*Deliverance from Disease and Death,* foretold by Prophets and fulfilled by Christ." "He will swallow up Death in Victory."

SUMMARY THEOCRATIC PLATFORM

Sovereignty of Jesus Christ, dating from His Second Coming, A.D. 70. Co-sovereignty of the Primitive Church, raised from the dead at the Second Coming.

Unity of all Believers, in this world and in Hades, with the one Kingdom in the Heavens.

Resurrection of the spirit, overcoming Disease, renewing Youth and Abolishing Death.

Community of property of all kinds, with inspiration for distribution.

Dwelling together in Association or Complex Families.
Home Churches and Home Schools.
Meetings every evening.
Lord's Supper at every meal.
Free Criticism the Regulator of Society.
Horticulture the leading business for subsistence.
A daily press divorced from Mammon and devoted to God.

Circular, August 12, 1854

PRACTICAL COMMUNISM—A PLAN FOR EMPLOYERS. NATURAL AND PRACTICAL IMMEDIATELY, FOR ALL SORTS OF BUSINESS AND IN THE BUSINESS SOCIETY AS IT IS.

This plan is founded on the simple proposition to substitute the family relation for the system of hiring. As the opposers of slavery say to the slave master, "Emancipate your negroes, and carry on your business by paying them wages," so it is now said to the hireling master, "Stop hiring, and carry on your business by taking your workmen into your family." In other words, let every distinct form of business which employs and supports a number of workmen be the gathering point of a *family* sufficient to man the business, and carry on all the domestic affairs without hiring. Let the employer, whatever his line of business, *live* with his men, and make them interested *partners* instead of holding them by the mere bond of wages, in supporting families scattered abroad.

The material advantages of this business condensation would be in part as follows: 1. Opportunity of acquaintance and constant consultation between the workmen. 2. Enthusiasm, induced by aggregation and entire community of interest. 3. Saving of time and labor in traveling to and fro, in the care of domestic affairs. 4. Relief from complicated accounts and arbitrary money payments.

The educational and religious advantages of this plan would be manifold and complete. 1. Every important business would be the gathering point of an extensive *family*. 2. That family, embracing of course persons qualified to instruct, in having constant opportunity for meeting in mutual help, would become a *school*. 3. That school, rising into the knowledge of God and having the best possible facilities for mutual criticism and religious culture, would become a *church*. Thus business would become a truly sacred institution—the very platform of the worship of God. The four great interests of mankind—business, family affection, education, and religion—would join hands and dwell together wherever human beings have a home.

Circular, July 9, 1857

Some criticism of disorder and slackness which had manifested itself in certain quarters. The Community, while it affords an admirable field for the utmost perfection of order and neatness, at the same time offers more or less opportunity for individual negligence to those who are thus predisposed. In a family of 200, a person may say to himself: if I neglect this thing it will never be felt among so many; if it is not done by me, some other one will do it equally well. But this evil is progressively disappearing, not so much by the exercise of any outward regulation or constraint, as by the growth among us of a *conscientious will*—a purpose in every heart to do all things as under the Lord, and to discharge every duty with reference to his pleasure.

Circular, July 23, 1857

Some criticism of the state of things in the trap shop. Some dissipating influences have been at work there, the most noticeable of which was the passion for music. Then followed a general criticism of the musical appetite. It was thought that music had in some cases become insubordinate to the true Community interest, and had, therefore, become more or less distasteful. Communism continually shows itself to be a harmonizer—a regulator of the opposite, and perhaps somewhat antagonistic influences in attractions of human nature. Two spheres of activity are open to man: one is outward, and from himself upon the material world, the other is more or less inward and towards himself. Both are followed by corresponding outward or inward results. Every man is naturally more biased towards one of these spheres than to the other. If he follows the first bias, he becomes the simple worker and man of enterprise; if he follows the second one, he becomes the man of culture—poet, musician, and lover of general literature, etc. The former becomes rich in all material and outward results, but poor in himself. The latter becomes rich in himself but deficient in all the acquirements of the former. Both of these men are one-sided—distorted, even positively weak and doubtless liable to spiritual maladies and unhappiness. Brought together by the love of truth and our relation to God and the infinities, yet possessing our particular biases we find ourselves subject to a harmonizing power, and conscious of a more natural poise of spirit. Accordingly, any undue preponderance of one bias over the other is soon felt by the body, and promptly regulated by our system of criticism.

Circular, February 25, 1858

The meat question has occupied several evenings this week. Freedom of discussion has been the motto, and all opinions have been heard. The query whether there is any truth in the idea held by some that we partake of the nature of animals by eating their flesh was discussed. On one side it was thought it would be as reasonable to suppose that we should be turned into squashes and cabbages by feeding on these vegetables, as that we should become like cows by feeding on beef; and if we must choose between them one would rather be a cow than a squash.

We may feel free, so far as our consciences are concerned, to eat *anything,* and yet it is right we should inquire what is really the best kind of food. What is most congenial to our nature? Our favorite object is unity, and we must expect to be persuaded alike on all questions. The subject is still open and the discussion will probably be continued to the point of unanimity, at which we are very apt to arrive in all our debates.

Circular, April 29, 1858

I have had many thoughts during the past year and some rather anxious ones upon the subject of *old age* in connection with our hope of victory over death. The subject has forced itself upon my attention almost in spite of myself, and has given rise to some suggestions of this kind: We may fairly consider that we are in a great measure superior to the principality of disease. Experience tells us that if the person afflicted be a man of determined faith, the atmosphere of health which surrounds him, acting in conjunction with his own belief, will, in a large majority of cases, defeat the enemy and set the sufferer free. A disease is a positive, overt agent, we know exactly where to direct our resistance; and the concentrated power which is thus brought to bear is almost irresistible. Not so with old age. It is insidious—underhanded—steals upon all alike, constantly, and by imperceptible degrees—when we are asleep and defenseless—when we are at work and elsewhere. It is like the atmosphere surrounding us on every hand, and pressing in upon us incessantly, with never-ceasing vigilance. The thought occurred to me whether we could not create an opposite atmosphere—one which would resist and repel the advances of old age, and make it more easy and natural to grow youthful than to grow old and infirm. Can we not by our combined faith generate an element which will reverse the process and make it difficult to lose our youth and become withered and decrepit. Our feelings and imaginations on the subject of disease and old age have a great tendency to realize themselves. The whole subject is thickly covered with imaginations that bind us with chains to the old-fashioned testimony. I have sometimes thought the younger class among us are more subject to worldly imagination in this respect than the older class. It is quite a favorite doctrine with the young that it is a privilege to be young. When I feel truthful and honest as a believer in Christ, instead of wishing myself only sixteen years old, if I wish at all, I wish I was a thousand years old. Good is before me—not behind me. Not the younger but the older I am, the better I am. I have no sorrow on account of my age. I think that forty-six years is considerably sweeter than "sweet sixteen."

The subject has presented itself to me in this shape: There is a strong feeling (and it is a worldly imagination) that youth is the bright time of enjoyment; and persons expect after they arrive at a certain age that their enjoyment will decrease—that they will lose their susceptibilities to pleasure. I think this is a false view, and feel like resisting it in my heart and cultivating the feeling that as believers in Christ we are entitled to growth and increasing enjoyment.   J.H.N.

Circular, June 10, 1858

The financial committee met this forenoon and took into consideration our wants. It led to considerable feeling and desire to have everyone take a right attitude in regard to our finances, recognizing the fact that God has the control of them. We need to become sympathetic with one another; we must feel alike, and act alike on this question. The truth is that our means are rather limited at the present time, and we cannot spend much without running in debt. That is the fact and I take it to be God's word to us. Now shall we accept it as such and accommodate ourselves in a good spirit to the circumstances he provides, or shall we ignore them?

There needs to be more sympathy on the part of everyone—more cooperation. Each one should see, not only what he wants, but should take an equal responsibility in measuring our means for getting it. It should be a religious thing with us.

Circular, July 15, 1858

It is better that things remain as they are, partially disorganized, than that we should come into a legal, cramped, Shakerish kind of order. The *law of love* among us is to take the place of legality and forced restraint. It will doubtless take longer to get it in successful operation; but it will be worth a great deal more in the end. We have reason to be satisfied with the result thus far. There is much more good order among us now, than there was two or three years ago. The Association is only ten years old, and a boy of that age is not expected to be very systematic.

Circular, December 16, 1858

I do not suppose the art of politeness will grow up among us on the ordinary basis. Our society is different and our motives are somewhat different from those which men and women are generally under. There is not the same influence with us to polish the outside that they have; yet there is ground enough in our society for great improvement. We should expect to attain, finally, to the highest standard of politeness—that which will make us at home in the society of Heaven.

Circular, January 20, 1859

Talk in the evening meeting upon the cultivation of a flexible will in small matters. Pliancy of will seems to be especially pleasing to Christ; it gives the social atmosphere a more than downy softness. It is one of the peculiar blessings of Community life, that it tends to make us pliant in will. To many people this suppleness of the will in small matters looks like a loss of individuality—a sort of death: in reality it is found to be no such thing. What better index to the inborn nobleness of a person's character, or the reverse, than to know in what sphere he uses his will. If he is obstinate about small things you are tempted to mark him as a man who takes a pin-hole view of the universe.

Circular, October 10, 1861

While building the New House, it is well to have before us this practical question: Is the Community spiritually strong enough to convert its own children and bring them up in the nurture and admonition of the Lord? If it is, we are building the house for a good purpose, and the Community will be a perpetual, an everlasting, and a renewing institution; if it is not strong enough to do that, it will perish in the second generation, and our house will go to strangers.

Circular, June 26, 1862

Our society is evidently destined to contrast widely with that of ordinary society, in many respects, but perhaps in few more strikingly than in its relation to amusements. We have already learned that true sport and pleasure do not belong to the superficial and irreligious, but rather to those who can make the best use of them; that as Christ-seekers we may hope to enjoy all the good things of this world; that it is proper and expedient for the old as well as the young to mingle in sports; and that it is altogether proper for the fair sex as well as the homely sex to engage in most outdoor and indoor amusements. This is a great advance; and we have followed up our theory with corresponding practice, to some extent; but if I conceive correctly, we are yet far short of the true standard in this respect. I think that in the future, amusements, recreations, diversions, whatever you please to call them—the playful action of life, as distinguished from its more weighty pursuits, will sustain a more prominent position. Our theory indicates this result; our circumstances invite it. We are daily throwing aside the influences which in ordinary society keep under restraint the sportive, spontaneous action of life. But let us keep in mind, that we are invited by Providence to enter this fair field of promise, not that we may merely obtain our own pleasure, but that we may more acceptably serve and please God. It is evidently a law of his universe, that there can be no unalloyed happiness that has not in it the element of worship. All things are ours, *if* we are Christ's. All things are good, if they are received with thanksgiving.

Circular, May 29, 1865

THE COMMUNITY AND THE WAR

It would be difficult to explain how far we have sympathized with the war without reverting to the previous attitude of the Community towards the government of the United States. So long as our government stood with one foot upon the neck of the slave, and with the other trampled upon the rights of the red man, we had no sympathy with it. Such practically was its position while under the control of the Slave Power. In consequence of this, the Community had for many years previous to the breaking out of the Rebellion asserted their independence of the government and in heart and spirit disclaimed allegiance to it.

Our interest in the events of the war was very deep; and as it progressed our sympathies were drawn out towards it just in proportion as we saw it tending to develop in the people and the government a recognition of the rights of man, and providence of God in the affairs of the nation. Of late this recognition has appeared to us very genuine and hearty, on the part of both government and people. So far as the war has been the means of producing this state of things, so far have we sympathized with it.

Nor has the sympathy of the Community been altogether of an unsubstantial character; for it has borne its full share, we think, of the burdens and losses incident to the war. We have responded to repeated calls for aid to the poor soldier, have loaned our town money to aid in raising volunteers, and our direct United States war taxes have amounted to more than $10,000.00. Besides this, our state and county taxes have more than quadrupled, in consequence of heavy bounties paid by the state and counties for volunteers.

It may appear somewhat singular to some that we should so far sympathize with the war, and so readily help sustain it, and still none of us personally engage in it. This apparent inconsistency will disappear, we think, when it is understood that we considered ourselves already enlisted in another army, which, under the command of Jesus Christ, was engaged in the general battle with the hosts of evil. Under such circumstances, it would have been entirely out of character for us to leave our place in the line, and go off independently to assist in taking one of the outposts of evil, slavery, unless we had distinct orders from our commander to do so. Such orders we did not receive, and accordingly remained at our post. Our objection to personal service in the war was consequently not on the ground of disbelief in the rightfulness of war, in itself considered, nor in the use of carnal weapons, though we think war is a very poor way generally to overcome evil or settle difficulties; but mainly on the ground of want of orders from the supreme Government of God.

Without stopping to discuss the question whether God instituted the present war, or whether the same results which it has accomplished might not have been secured in a peaceful way (which we fully believe), we would say that we regard the war as a great fact, allowed of God, and consider that under his good providence, it has been the means of elevating the nation to a much higher plane, morally and spiritually, than that on which it previously stood, which augurs well for the future.

Circular, August 14, 1865

Mr. Noyes said: "In order to keep your spirits bright, in order to maintain a state of ripe vivacity, you must be just as busy with the great purposes of heroic accomplishment as you were at 22, or as true, heroic youthfulness always is. You may measure and judge your spirit by this test: If you are saying to yourself, 'Well, I cannot accomplish anything, for I shall not live but a little while; I am getting to be old; my best days are gone; great purposes are for the young, and I have got by them'—

if that is the way you are talking, you are surrendering to old age and the devil. The way you should talk is, 'I am 22 years old now and never shall be any older; as great a field of hopefulness and improvement opens to me now as there did at 22, and my heart is as open to great plans now as ever it was. The idea that I have seen my best days come to their end is all humbug. The heart that is open to God's plans and inspiration will have immortality, and its purposes will have no end."

Circular, August 16, 1866

Mr. William Hepworth Dixon, Editor of the London *Athenaeum,* arrived here yesterday, bringing a letter of introduction to Mr. Noyes from Horace Greeley. He is accompanied by two friends, Mr. and Mrs. Haywood, of London. Mr. Greeley's letter was as follows:

New York, August 10, 1866

Dear Sir:—The bearer, Mr. Hepworth Dixon, Editor of *The Athenaeum,* has come from London expressly to study our people. He wishes especially to know *your* people, having long been familiar with your writings. I commend him to your confidence and hospitality.

Yours,

[Signed]

Horace Greeley

To Mr. Noyes, or his successor, Oneida Community. Mr. Dixon has gained some knowledge of the Community from fragments of our publications in the British Museum. He appears to be considerably interested in socialistic questions. He is on a tour of observation, and intends to visit Brigham Young's dominions before returning to Europe.

Circular, December 8, 1866

In catering for this column, we of course choose the agreeable and often superficial incidents which are characteristic of Community life. But it must not be thought because we put these pleasant things foremost that everything goes perfectly smooth like a pleasure-boat on an unrippled sea in our societies. On the contrary we have this fall had a great deal of spiritual strain and struggle, some tempestuous passages and thundering criticisms, which to outsiders would have seemed sufficient to rock any weak foundation to its base. But as old seamen preferred gale to a calm, so we count our criticisms and heart searchings among the best part of our experiences. They only settle us the firmer in our faith, and prove as the poet says, that "where the share is deepest driven, there the best fruits grow."

Circular, December 13, 1866

We were very much interested in Mr. Noyes's talk last evening on the "inspired use of natural means" as agents sufficient to overcome all difficulties, old age included. This view of the "situation" takes from us all excuse for imbecility of mind or body, and should nerve us to greater activity of heart and faith, to avail ourselves of the resources that lie within the reach of all.

Daily Journal, January 3, 1867

The Inventory being read, Mr. Hinds observed: "I think we have reason to be thankful for this showing. Perhaps it is not all some might wish, but taking everything into account, our expenses here, with those at Wallingford and New Haven, of the educational and publishing departments, the Communities it appears to me, have much occasion for gratitude."

Mr. Hamilton joined in this and then said: "In reflecting on this subject of our business, I compare it to the human body. Money, in one sense, is like the blood in the body, and I am not very much of a physiologist; but I believe the blood is mainly manufactured by the stomach. I don't think it is God's purpose to make us immensely rich, in the sense that many men and companies are in the world. It seems to me that individuals and corporations, when they begin to amass property that does not play an important part in their business, and in a moral influence in society, are like persons who are getting a big, overgrown belly. Now a man does not want to carry around a larger belly than is necessary to help furnish all the blood he wants. I should think from all I hear that the Shakers are pot-bellied. They are immensely rich, but this wealth does but little good in society. I like to be in good condition and see others so and I am ambitious to see the Community grow strong and acquire a great deal of power, but I don't believe God purposes to have us become pot-bellied."

Circular, February 25, 1867

DIOTREPHIASIS

St. John in his last Epistle complains of a man in the church called Diotrephes. This man's disease was *love of preeminence,* or, in the Greek, *Philoproteia—love of primacy.* This is a disease that deserves a special name; and we have been searching the Greek lexicon for the proper compound. It might be called *Proteiasis,* or *Philoproteiasis,* or the *Diotrephian Philoproteiasis*; but on the whole we prefer to designate it simply by the name of the man who was the most notable victim of it. We call it *Diotrephiasis.* In English it might be called the *preeminence mania,* or the *"Who-shall-be-greatest" mania.* It is kindred to, if not identical with, *lust of office,* in its more virulent forms. The *Presidential mania,* for instance, which prevails among high politicians in this country, probably sometimes passes into true *Diotrephiasis.* But it is to be regarded as primarily a *spiritual* and *ecclesiastical* disease rather than political. As such it has assumed in this country a very interesting type within the last thirty-five years. Like modern *bronchitis* and *laryngitis*—the "Minister's sore throat"—it has become so distinct and virulent as to require a special name and special treatment. It seems to be even contagious and epidemic. We were told years ago that there were not less than three hundred persons among the Spiritualists, each of whom believed himself to be "The Coming Man," that is, the central medium of modern inspiration, and the predestined inaugurator of the "good time coming" period. The number must be much greater now. We ourselves saw among Perfectionists, before Spiritualism was born, probably not less than a hundred victims of this disease—persons who suddenly became inflated with the insane notion that they were Christs, and had the destiny of the world on their shoulders. The stages by which the disease progressed were sometimes curious. In a little clique of illuminati there would arise a strife to outstrip each other in startling testimony. One would claim to be *a* son of God; another, going a little beyond the first, would testify that he was *the* son of God; the third, pressing on for the primacy, would affirm that he was the *only begotten*; and a fourth would cap the climax by announcing that he was God himself, Very Father in person! We use the masculine pronouns in the above descriptions, but the persons engaged in these races were as often females as males.

We may laugh at these phenomena as eccentricities, or scold at them as blasphemies; but the truer and better way is to study them as diseases. These monstrous swellings of egotism have causes as subtle and as real as the causes of *goitre*, and are almost as involuntary. They are states of the brain and solar plexus, affected by evil spirits, and though generally harmless enough to keep out of the Lunatic Hospitals, are actually forms of incipient mania, and often pass into real insanity. All Lunatic Asylums are full of patients who believe themselves to be soul potentates. In fact this enlargement of the *ego* is the most constant symptom of virulent mania.

Signed, J.H.N.

Circular, March 18, 1867

DIXON ON THE ONEIDA COMMUNITY

"Many of the Saints having been at Putney, they had some experience in the ways of grace; and Noyes laid down for them a rule in their new home, which a Gentile would have thought superfluous at Oneida Creek—the duty of enjoying life. At Putney, said he, they had been too strict; studying overmuch; dealing too harshly with each other's faults. In their new home, heaven would not ask from them such rigours. If God, he asked them, had meant Adam to fast and pray, would he have placed him in a garden tempted on every side by delicious fruit? Man's Maker blessed him with appetites, and turned him into a clover field! And what were these Saints at Oneida Creek? Men in the position of Adam before the fall; men without sin; men to whom everything was lawful because everything was pure. Why, then, should they not eat, drink, and love, to their heart's content, under daily guidance of the Holy Spirit?"

Footnote by the editor of the *Circular:* This is fine writing, but almost wholly imaginative. Nobody in the Community remembers any such change of rules.

Daily Journal, March 21, 1867

It was with difficulty that we could restrain our wrath, in reading in last week's *Circular,* what Dixon said about Mr. Noyes, everything about it was so untruthful.

Circular, June 17, 1867

FROM A NEW MEMBER

During a few meetings I have attended here, I have noticed a very significant testimony which I never heard elsewhere—the confessions of *a soft heart.* I have attended many meetings where persons came together for the express purpose of relating their experience, but don't recollect the confession of a soft heart. I think it was given nearly a dozen times last night, and hardly a meeting passes but I hear it. I think this soft heart is closely allied to what Paul designates as the fruits of the Spirit, gentleness, meekness, etc. At any rate, there is an influence here which tends to soften the heart, which I never realized elsewhere—an influence which causes an involuntary welling-up of tears, not of sorrow, tears of joy, joy that is unspeakable. I confess a soft heart.

J.H.N.—I don't know but we may think of Christ's saying "Except ye be converted and become as little children, ye can not enter the Kingdom of Heaven," as meaning that we must have soft hearts. I want a heart that is quick to receive impressions, quick to take fire, to be effective, to manifest emotions, quick to laugh when there is occasion for it, and quick to weep when there is occasion for it. That is the soft heart. And people have lost it by losing their childhood. I don't know as anybody but God can restore it to them. God can restore the soft heart.

Circular, July 28, 1867

Theodore remarked that his father said a short time ago that the true kind of improvement is to be doing something all the time that requires courage. There has been a great victory gained by the young women in getting freedom to speak, but that should not be the stopping place. They must look around for something to be done that requires the same courage. Let those who have only made confessions try to bring out some new idea every time they speak.

Circular, December 2, 1867

There is a constant movement toward the advancement of the second generation—the children of the sturdy pioneers in Communism who have so long borne the brunt of the battle. The prospect is that a young man not more that twenty-seven years old will be placed in the position of father of this great O.C. family. We believe that every such office carries with it the inspiration necessary to an acceptable fulfillment, so we have no fears of his doing otherwise than well.

Circular, March 23, 1868

FROM THE EVENING MEETING

After the Talks from Wallingford had been read, Mr. Woolworth said he hoped we should fulfill Mr. Noyes's expectations, and learn to be watchful, sober, and chaste in the use of our tongues. He thought the

Community still suffered more or less from the gossiping spirit. Barrenness is the state of reaction from gossip. When people come to meeting with nothing edifying to say it is probable they have squandered their best thoughts in idle talk.

Circular, July 19, 1869

Happiness is usually associated in men's minds with positions wherein individuals can control persons and things around them. It is therefore generally expected that such positions will excite more or less of envy, jealousy, and strife. It might be interesting to some of our readers to know how the O.C. manages to settle this difficult question of precedence. One of the points in which we differ from the world, touching this matter, is the fact that wealth has no connection with office.

We are all equally rich in that kind of goods that is measured by money, therefore wealth cannot act as a stimulus to envy or jealousy. It may however be truly said that there is in human nature an innate desire to hold a position of influence. This propensity certainly cannot be complained of, if it proceeds from an unselfish desire to serve, and can be made an incentive to improvement. It is only when prompted by pride and personal ambition that it can be found fault with. It appears that Providence in dealing with this passion among us has adopted the plan of smothering it with offices. Instead of having but one or two great officers and an anxious collection of rank and file hungry for their positions, we are all the time pushing people forward and urging our young men and women to accept the responsibilities of office.

Probably the most difficult business position in the Community is that of the committee whose duty it is to distribute offices; and their difficulty consists in finding the persons to fill them; so that though we may not be born great, we are pretty sure to have greatness thrust upon us.

Circular, February 22, 1869

The facts stated in the last *Circular*, which by the way was fairly drawn out, that never a couple has eloped from the O.C., is very remarkable; if not to persons outside, it is to one inside, who never happened to think of it before. Knowing, as we do, the great proportion of young folks we have always numbered, and knowing that the discipline of the passions is more radical here than even with the Shakers, inasmuch as total abstinence is often more practicable than moderation, we wonder at the fact; and still it is true. A hundred young folks have passed the age of temptation at the O.C., and yet there has never been an elopement.

Circular, April 4, 1870

FROM A LETTER FROM J.H.N. TO AN INQUIRER

My impression, from all our experience, is that the day of *meetings,* in the old simplistic, religious sense, is over and gone; and that what is coming is a conjunction of *faith and science,* which will make our meetings very different things from those of the churches generally, or even of the Primitive Church. You speak of the scientific training that is going on among our young people, as distinct from that which we need in our meetings. Probably it is so at present; but many things indicate to me that we are the body in which God designs to bring science and religion together and solder them into one. It is only in this way that our religious meetings can become the arena and home of our educated classes, and without this they are likely to be dull.

I should advise, therefore, that the spiritually minded look favorably towards science, and that the scientifics look favorably towards faith, and see if God will not bring the hearts of these long-separated classes together. Then I think we shall have lively meetings. I am not sure but there is more real divine inspiration going in the scientific world than in the religious world. Cant and legality and timidity are death to inspiration. If we want lively meetings, we want inspiration; and if we want inspiration, let us follow it where we find it. If it is among the scientifics, let us honor it there, even if the scientifics themselves think it is only their own zeal and sagacity. For my part, I consider the success of our young men in science as the effect of inspiration, and I claim their victories as the victories of faith. And we must train these young men to see and acknowledge that it is so. Then they will be the beginning of a new class of scientists, more humble and more successful than the world has ever seen; and then they will cast their crowns at the feet of faith, and turn their whole strength into our religious meetings. J.H.N.

Circular, April 17, 1871

In a recent evening meeting the conversation turned upon our attitude towards the present disturbances in the outside world. There are conflicts in the field, disruptions in the Cabinet, quarrels in commercial affairs, and so on, which excites somewhat our interest; but we believe that our true course is to give to political matters only that amount of attention which will keep us reasonably well posted in the progress of events, and anchor our minds in the pursuit of more important truth. In taking such an attitude we are not cowardly or inclined to shirk our share of responsibility in the great issues going, for all that is good and of service to the world in these issues has for a foundation single-eyed digging for the truth on the part of somebody. We find that it requires much more heroism to persevere in turning resolutely away from outside turmoil than to allow ourselves to be entirely absorbed by it, taking part, heart in hand. It is our business to see the peace of God in our hearts and blow peace upon the world.

Circular, August 28, 1871

THE 20TH OF AUGUST

Bible Communists have long been accustomed to regard this day as a turning-point of the year—the aphelion of man's orbit around the great spiritual center. External allurements are now the strongest. Pleasure-seeking and self-indulgence demand a loose rein. Saratoga, Newport, Long Branch, and other summer resorts are thronged with pleasure-hunters. Horse-racing, boat-racing, and "champion" contests culminate in interest. Earth tempts the appetite with new and beautiful fruits. Now of all the year the inducements are strongest to let the outward prevail over the inward—the carnal over the spiritual—love of sensual pleasure over the love of righteousness.

Two advantages at least result from a knowledge of the fact in spiritual astronomy that we have mentioned. First it enables persons to more easily and effectually guard against the temptations that thicken as they approach the aphelion of their yearly course. Dangers that are foreseen lose a portion of their terrors. Secondly, it enables them to take the utmost advantage of the better influences that prevail as they approach the perihelion or opposite point in their yearly orbit: they are like a ship's crew that is prepared to avail itself to the utmost of wind and tide in its course towards a desired haven.

Circular, September 4, 1871

When the Community started it relied on the spirit of improvement for its animating principle, on the Bible for its textbook, on education and criticism for its government. For the securing of its properties against the claims of seceders it had this simple rule:

On the admission of any member, all property belonging to him or her becomes the property of the Community. A record of the estimated amount will be kept, and in case of the subsequent withdrawal of the member, the Community, according to its practice heretofore, will refund the property or an equivalent. This practice, however, stands on the ground, not of obligation, but of expediency and liberality; and the time and manner of refunding must be trusted to the discretion of the Community. While a person remains a member, his subsistence and education in the Community are held to be just equivalents for his labor; and no accounts are kept between him and the Community, and no claims of wages accrues to him in case of subsequent withdrawal.

As might be expected some of the superficial and selfish have been attracted to our movement. They came, stayed a while, and went again. Sometimes their claims on leaving have been reasonable and sometimes vexatious. They have always been settled with, according to this agreement. This rule was a new thing to the world at large, and we ourselves hardly knew whether it would stand the ordeal of a court-room. We have been threatened with law-suits, but Providence has always kept us from getting into the meshes of the law. It now appears that the Community has "builded better than it knew." Some years ago Judge Towner of Cleveland called our attention to the decisions made in the United States courts in favor of the communities at Economy, Pennsylvania, and Zoar, Ohio, and against seceders from those societies who had demanded a division of property and wages. Since then we have felt that God has put a rock beneath our feet. We cannot be unmindful of the inspiration that led us to adopt a rule that had, unbeknown to us, stood the test of law.

Circular, September 11, 1871

The evening meeting was taken up with expressions of thankfulness. In our view thankfulness is not a lazy, good feeling that comes into us of its own accord in consequence of some pleasant arrangement of circumstances. It is a thing to be sought for in a voluntary, resolute way, and not put off till greater blessings and greater mercies compel us to be grateful.

Circular, November 20, 1871

Those who take it upon themselves to carp at Communism, however varied the style and matter of strictures, always seem to agree upon one point, that is that Communism is the grave of individuality, the sepulcher of originality; that "the member is very apt to get the better of the man"; that it tends, in short, to make people all alike, and, from the very necessity of its organization, is in a state of society in which a few ruling minds

> Sit on their thrones
> in a purple sublimity,
> and grind down men's bones
> to a pale unanimity.

This special fling at Communism is heard so frequently, both from the wise and unwise, that it has really come to sound trite and not a little monotonous.

It is our candid conviction that individuality (and by this we mean the mannerisms, the originalities, the inventive powers, the thousand and one little peculiarities which, combined, make everyone a genius by himself) is increased by Communism, and that materially. Why not? The unity which cements us together and which we confess we esteem above everything, makes gentlemen and ladies of us—makes us love harmony rather than discord—makes us rather provoke others to love than seek our own pleasure. That is all. It does not make us all alike. Because we have "one Lord, one faith, one baptism, one God and Father of all, who is above all, and through all, and in us all," we do not think that the next step in the syllogism is that our minds should all run in the same groove or our souls be all cut after the same pattern, any more than that we should dress in uniform or have the same colored eyes and hair. No, indeed! The more complex you get your unit, the more varied its component parts will be; and then, besides all the divers natural peculiarities of taste and disposition among us, do we not, spiritually speaking, have "gifts differing according to the grace that is given us?" Certainly, we find it so.

Circular, December 25, 1871

TESTIMONY OF MR. W.

I have had a new sense lately of the happiness that is accessible to us. There is a world of happiness that we can enter into if we can learn the art of doing so—happiness that doesn't depend on anything of an external nature. In my experience I have touched it from time to time. I can hardly explain it. It is not produced by anything external; but I seem to have access to a spirit that is happy and victorious. It is a real art to be happy, and one that will bear study. "The fruit of the Spirit is love, joy, peace," and happiness is the "fruit of the Spirit."

Circular, June 2, 1873

Mr. Noyes said in meeting, "We ought not to make prayer a solemn thing, but go to work in a fox-hunter's spirit. Start a fox—get something to pray for—and then make it a lively struggle in the real spirit of sport. Get your health and education by it, and learn to know God by it. No matter what you pray for, if it is something God is interested in. God himself will start a fox for you if you really want to be a hunter: He will start a fox that will really draw out your heart and you can learn to make a splendid game of it."

Circular, June 30, 1873

I tell you I don't believe that this universe is an old dog-eared arithmetic full of "hard sums" that I must "do," or else die. I used to think it was. I believe it is God's home, and my heart is saying "God, God, God," all the times I go around this part of it. If I can find him often enough I shall be strong and satisfied and there won't be any problems left worth speaking of.

Circular, September 22, 1873

One of the many things for which we are thankful is that we have pleasant neighbors. Those around us years ago were not always disposed to treat us with friendliness or even tolerance. But time has wrought a change; some, who were formerly bitter, have moved away, and circumstances seem to have affected the feelings of others who remain, till now, we often gratefully acknowledge favors shown us by them. The present mutual good feeling is pleasing, and we trust it will never be less.

Circular, November 3, 1873

FROM MR. NOYES AT THE RECENT EVENING MEETING

I do not look upon the Community as separate from the world; nor is it possible for it to be separated from the world. I never have had any idea of saving myself or the Community by keeping ourselves in a monkish kind of segregation. We are not a sect; we are nothing but a large family. There is no sect in which the parents allow their children the freedom of reading books written in the spirit and interest of other sects that we do; nor do they encourage them in freedom of thought as we do. We keep ourselves saturated all the time with worldly influences through our library. It is true that our people are comparatively free from personal communication with the world, but we keep our library crammed with the ideas of the world. We feel about as much sympathy with one sect as with another. We feel about as liberal towards Positivists as towards church members. We meet the world with freedom in music and in literature, and keep ourselves separate only as far as is necessary to retain our organization.

Circular, March 23, 1874

Mr. Noyes said in the evening meeting, "It seems to me that the great value of wealth is not that it gives us the privilege of living without work, but that it enables us to find work that is good and attractive and healthy. That is the use we are going to make of riches. They give us liberty and power to find good healthy work. Working ten or twelve hours a day under compulsion in the work-or-starve system I do not think is good or healthy. But for people who have abundance of means and could live without work, to turn to manual labor for profit of the soul as well as the body and work so much as will prove best for their bodies and souls—that is something the Lord is pleased with, and something that we are going to do. I judge that about six hours labor is as much as anybody ought to do on hygienic principles. My impression is that six hours continuous labor is enough for anybody. Labor reformers talk about eight hours, but I would reduce the working hours to six, and have them come between eight o'clock and three, or between breakfast and dinner, and give the rest of the time to study and recreation. I believe a large association working in that way would accomplish more than under the eight or even ten hour system. This gives you six hours for study and plenty of time for eating and drinking and amusement and sleep. I think with this arrangement we can support ourselves well, do all the business that is necessary and at the same time carry on home education. Everyone can get a liberal education and pay as he goes."

Circular, May 18, 1874

Out of mere curiosity someone began a year or more ago to look into the the antecedents of the Community members. The result of the investigation was a long and formidable document which was read at our meeting not long ago, causing the greatest amusement. "Well," said one, "we are some pumpkins after all!" Really, though, we don't feel any bigger than we did before, but perhaps those good people who have been disposed to regard us as a pack of social and religious fanatics—the scum and offscouring of the earth—will feel better towards us to know that members of the O.C. are connected by birth or marriage with: 1 Sculptor; 1 Consul; 1 President of the United States; 4 Missionaries; 6 Scientific Professors; 6 State Officers; 7 Poets; 6 Members of Congress; 7 Descendants of European Aristocracy; 8 Editors; 21 Members of State Legislatures; 22 Authors; 23 Justices of the Peace; 26 Judges; 48 Army Officers; 58 Lawyers; 67 Physicians; 115 Ministers (of all denominations but Roman Catholic). One lady however has an aunt who is Lady Superior of a convent at Gibraltar. [Under that is a list of many O.C. members whose ancestors had been officers in the Revolutionary War or the War of 1812.]

Circular, December 13, 1875

NOTE FROM WALLINGFORD—HOME TALK BY J.H.N.

If we have primarily in view to make money, we shall get no enthusiasm from heaven. That is the snare that besets the Community at Oneida. They are great business men there, and are engaged in big enterprises; but there is a great danger of their losing sight of the idea that the object of business is *education*, and of taking up the idea of the world, which is that the object of business is money. Here and there and always, the temptation is to shift from our true purpose and take up the great object which the world has in business. We start in business under inspiration and with objects that are pure and true, perhaps, but the spirit of the world broods over us and about us, and works among us continually, turning our attention to the object of making money; to the external, objective result instead of the subjective, which is education and development.

The truth is that all whose object in business is to make money are hirelings. I don't care whether they are working for somebody else, or are doing business for themselves; if their object is to make money I say they are hirelings and are working in the hireling spirit. It is only as we turn to the other object, the education of ourselves and our children, the development of ourselves as mediums of inspiration in business, that we cease to be hirelings. It is only when we take up that object that we rise into freedom—into the noble spirit of sons of God.

Circular, August 16, 1875

THE LAW OF FELLOWSHIP—HOME TALK BY J.H.N.

We understand by the ascending fellowship, a state in which a person's companionship is with those who are above him in spiritual life, so that the *drawing* of the fellowship is upward; and by the descending fellowship, a state in which a person loves those who are below him in spiritual life, so that the drawing of the fellowship is downward. Everyone will say at once that the ascending fellowship is preferable; it is best of course that all should associate with those who will draw them upward. But still, in order that there may be ascending fellowship, there must also be descending fellowship. If I love a superior, then that superior in loving me must love in a descending direction; so that descending fellowship must be legitimate; and where is the limit? How shall we set this thing exactly right in our minds; I have set it right in my mind thus:

The ascending fellowship—that which draws us upward to God and the Primitive Church, to persons more spiritual than ourselves, visible and invisible—is always in order. It does not need to be limited by us, because those with whom we seek fellowship in that direction will take care that the right limitation is made. We cannot get into more fellowship with God than he chooses to give us. We may always send our hearts freely in the ascending direction.

Now for the descending fellowship. In what cases is that legitimate? How far is it to be allowed and how far limited? How much can we have and still maintain the principle of unity? My answer is this: *We may have just so much descending fellowship as the ascending fellowship directs and allows.* The only principle on which descending fellowship can be justified is that it is sanctioned by the superior, that it is identified with the ascending fellowship and gets its authority from it. All true, legitimate descending fellowship carries with it the inspiration of the superior. It is a pretty stringent doctrine, but it is as fair for one as for another.

Now it is easy to work out the whole problem. Anyone can tell for himself whether or not he has reached a spot where the inspiration of a superior being works through him in a way to make descending fellowship safe for him. There can be no law made about it; for we can see that those who are not established in the ascending fellowship, with the circulation unobstructed between them and God, are unfit for the descending fellowship and must wait until they can grow to that position. They must wait until inspiration turns them downward and gives them freedom by giving them self-limitation.

IV

Criticism

The ordinance of criticism which was, generally speaking, the only
discipline practiced in the Oneida Community, was naturally received by its subjects with varying degrees of enthusiasm. A large
class, they wrote (*Circular,* July 19, 1855), regard it "with the
warmest cordiality," but there was "more or less coolness" in the
feelings of others toward it. They did not "really love it as they
will." Others, a minority, "stood in the attitude of criticizing criticism." A person in this attitude, they said, although connected with
the family, could not be in reality a member of the Association
while they did not wholly sympathize with it in the love of
criticism. Most of those who left after joining had split on the subject of criticism.

There was a difference between the right and wrong spirit of
receiving criticism. It must not be taken as a personal attack. "We
may stand and take it as the fire of an enemy," John Humphrey
Noyes wrote in his pamphlet *Mutual Criticism,* "and so feel
wounded and sore; or we may go over and join the party that fires
at us, in which case we shall feel unhurt. The great secret of going
through the judgment comfortably is to help judge ourselves."

Patience and enthusiasm for improvement, he advised, are the
best spirit in which to receive criticism. "There is nothing that
pleases God more than to see us lie in wait for improvement with
a bright eye and without flurry. Observe that the idea of 'lying in
wait' is not, on the one hand, that of doing nothing nor, on the
other, of bustling about; but to *watch*. The faculty of watching with
fire in the eye is the great secret of power. It requires a perfect

128

balance of spirit between eagerness and self-control. With that balance, criticism may not merely be endured, but welcomed as a positive pleasure."

The system of criticism, developed from Noyes's early experience with the Brethren at Andover, was first put into practice by the group at Putney. Since their number was small and they had come to know each other intimately, the method of public criticism in the evening meeting was feasible. One member would offer himself for criticism. The next evening the person in charge called on the other members to express their views of the character presented. As the membership in the Community grew after their removal to Oneida, this method was often felt to be both too trying to the subject and sometimes too superficial, since it was impossible for every member of so large a group to have a sufficiently intimate acquaintance with every other member to make their criticism apposite. For this reason, although public criticisms were still used occasionally, other methods were adopted. A committee—sometimes called a Club—was appointed, to be changed every three months, to whom persons "desiring the benefit of this ordinance," as Mr. Noyes wrote, might apply, "thus giving all an opportunity to serve as critics as well as subjects." The applicant might, if he chose, have others besides the committee present, or to have as critics only those of his own choice.

"In the great majority of cases," Noyes wrote,

criticism is desired and solicited by individuals because they are certain from their own past experience or from observation of the experience of others, that they will be benefited by it; but in some instances where it is noticed that persons are suffering from faults or influences that might be corrected or removed by criticism, they are advised to submit themselves to it. In extreme cases of disobedience to the Community regulations, or obsession by influences adverse to the general harmony, criticism is administered by the Community or its leaders without solicitation on the part of the subject. Evil in character or conduct is thus sure to meet with effectual rebuke from platoons, or from the whole Community.

"Different methods of truth-telling were adopted," wrote Harriet Worden in *Old Mansion House Memories*.

At one time a committee of four persons was appointed to administer a course of criticism to the whole Community. They devoted several hours each day to the work; first consulting with one another and those best acquainted with the persons to be criticized, and afterwards telling the subjects their faults as plainly as possible and giving such admonition and counsel as the case might demand. In this way the committee went through the whole family. After their labors were closed, the following question was presented, to be answered in writing: *"What has been the effect of our system of criticism?"* The universal testimony was that it had been extremely beneficial.

During the week between Christmas and New Year's Day, 1873, Mr. Noyes suggested that all the members stop work and play and devote their time to a series of mutual criticisms. The plan met with an extraordinary response, a revival, he said, without preaching and almost without leaders; the committees and the Community did the work. As many as fifteen committees served on some days besides public criticisms in the evening meetings, and at the end of the appointed week there remained so many unfilled applications that everyone voted that the good work be continued.

Of this experience Noyes wrote, "One feature of the work was the power of justification that went with the criticisms. Quite a number of persons who have been long regarded as hard cases of fixed character offered themselves for *public* criticism, which is considered the severest ordeal of all; and I was surprised to see how many good things were said about them. With manifest love and sincerity, one after another would acknowledge their improvement, till at last they would come out of the trial with an actual rise of reputation and a new self-respect."

In his pamphlet Noyes discusses Commendatory Criticism. Heretofore they had made more use of criticism in its negative form than in its positive form as praise which should ultimately be the main exercise of criticism. Why should not provocation work the other way and the approbation of the Community burst out in a general manifestation, when persons take a course to excite it? The objection was raised "that so few persons were able to bear praise." There was also "a little danger of exciting envy and jealousy." Mr. Noyes saw no real difficulty in either of these points. "The maturity and general stamina of our society is such that I think it could bear to have praising free, without any danger from the spirit of glorying on the one side, or jealousy on the other."

The case of Mrs. C. is an example of both negative and positive criticism. "Those who have the natural faculty of *usefulness* and a good deal of method and natural decorum are apt to be self-righteous and censorious toward those whose value consists more in their social qualities. The power of making society lively and musical, or of refreshing others by a sweet gentle spirit is often worth more than a great deal of industry with the hands. We are learning that nothing we have done or can do commends us to God: only the fragrance of our spirits pleases him. If Mrs. C. would learn to cultivate in herself the ornaments of the social nature, love, taste, sprightliness, etc., it would improve her very much. She has an excellent mind and strong ambition to overcome the defects in her character. God has a fair chance to work in her—the soil will bear a great deal."

One version of criticism in which the Community grew increasingly interested was what they called historical criticism and which, to the modern mind, has a surprising flavor of Freud and more recent psychiatric thinking. John Humphrey Noyes wrote in the pamphlet cited,

It is found in many cases that present difficulties of experience root themselves in the past life and can be reached only by a process that carries light and judgment and separation clear back to the beginning. A yielding to temptation in former years, by which we admitted the spirit of evil and defiled our consciences, or the entanglements of evil associations through friendship and love, though they may have been long excused and forgotten, were nevertheless vital seeds in our life and are found, on close scrutiny, still active and operating in our central experience. Life is a ball made up by the winding on of the thread of our passing experience; and whatever we have wound in the past, whether good or bad, is still in the ball: it is vitally our own, and in a very important sense enters into our present character. To state the principle in the fewest words, we are what our past lives have made us. With this view, many have entered upon the course of historical self-criticism and the result has been numerous confessions of wrongs in the past that had lain secret—perhaps half forgotten—but necessarily darkening and poisonous to present experience.

But this was not all. They claimed, in fact, to have discovered "a *New Curative.*" A Community writer said,

We have found and seen used with the best effect in many instances of sickness, a curative agent that is not far-brought nor expensive, but which we can confidently recommend to our readers as of exceeding value; viz., *Criticism.* It is a common custom here for a person who may be attacked with any disorder, to apply this remedy by sending for a committee of persons in whose faith and spiritual judgment he has confidence, to come and criticize him. The result, when administered sincerely, is almost universally to throw the patient into a sweat and to bring on a reaction of his life against disease, breaking it up and restoring him soon to usual health.

As an example, "Miss S. P. having a bad cold and symptoms of a run of fever, tried the *criticism cure* and was immediately relieved. The operation was not particularly agreeable—there is no method of cure that is—but it was short and speedily efficacious. One secret of its efficacy is that it stops the flow of thought toward the seat of the difficulty and so tends to reduce inflamation. At the same time it has a very bracing, invigorating effect." Which one cannot doubt.

Many and various, certainly, were the uses of criticism but its apotheosis was left for the leader of the Community to proclaim.

Men have speculated and dreamed for thousands of years as to what is the best and final form of government. We believe we have realized that highest dream in Free Criticism—*The Government of the Truth*—Government by Free Criticism! It combines in itself all that is good in all other forms of government. We believe that it is only necessary for Free Criticism to be generally known in order to be everywhere appreciated and to have a shout go up from all true hearts in its favor. For ourselves we shall do all we can to make it popular. Free Criticism is our candidate for President!

First Annual Report of the Oneida Association, January 1, 1849

SYSTEM OF CRITICISM

In the machinery of religious and moral discipline employed by the Association, a system of *mutual criticism* has held a very prominent place, and indeed has been relied on for regulating character and stimulating improvement more than the meetings or any other means of influence. This system was instituted by the Putney Association during the period of its most rapid advancement in spiritual life. The mode of proceeding was this: Any person wishing to be criticized offered himself for this purpose at a meeting of the Association. His character then became the subject of special scrutiny by all the members of the Association, till the next meeting, when his trial took place. On the presentation of his case, each member in turn was called on to specify as far and as frankly as possible, everything objectionable in his character and conduct. In this way the person criticized had the advantage of a many-sided mirror in viewing himself, or perhaps it may be said, was placed in the focus of a spiritual lens composed of all the judgments in the Association. It very rarely happened that any complaint of injustice was made by the subject of the operation, and generally he received his chastening with fortitude, submission, and even gratitude, declaring that he felt himself relieved and purified by the process. Among the various objectionable features of the character under criticism, some one or two of the most prominent would usually elicit censure from the whole circle, and the judgment on these points would thus have the force of a unanimous verdict. Any soreness which might result from the operation was removed at the succeeding meeting by giving the patient a round of commendations. This system of open and kindly criticism (a sort of reversed substitute for tea-party back-biting in the world) became so attractive by its manifest good results, that every member of the Putney Association submitted to it in the course of the winter of 1846–7; and to this may be attributed much of the accelerated improvement which marked that period of their history. Instead of offences, abounding love and good works followed the letting loose of judgment.

This system was introduced to some extent at Oneida; but the number of members was so large, and their acquaintance with each other in many cases so limited, that it was found necessary to change the mode of proceeding, in order to make criticism lively and effective. Instead of subjecting volunteers for criticism to the scrutiny of the assembly, the Association appointed four of its most spiritual and discerning judges to criticize in course all the members. The critics themselves were first criticized by Mr. Noyes, and then gave themselves to their work, from day to day for three weeks, till they had passed judgment on every character in the Association. Their method was first to ascertain as much as possible about the character of the individual about to be criticized, by inquiring among his associates, and then after discussing his character among themselves, to invite him to an interview, plainly tell him his faults, converse with him freely about his whole character, and give him their best advice.

Second Annual Report of the Oneida Association, February 20, 1850

Anyone who will take the trouble closely to examine the mechanism of our Association will find that the secret of the power which harmonizes it and constitutes its government lies not in any code of laws, nor in the commanding influence of any men, or set of men, but in our *system of Free Criticism.* By this channel the resistless spirit of truth courses through the whole body. It is at the same time the bond of union, and the agent of perfection to all classes, from the most spiritual to the most wayward and immature. We have introduced a fashion of judgment and truth-telling which gives voice and power to the golden rule— "Whatsoever ye would that men should do unto you, do ye even so to them." Selfishness and disorder inevitably annoy the circle around them; and the circle thus annoyed in our Association has the liberty and the means of speaking the truth to the offender. All are trained to criticize freely and be criticized without offense. Evil in character or conduct is sure to meet with effectual rebuke from individuals, from platoons, and from the whole Association. If any member is afflicted with a bad spirit, he finds himself "judged of all, convinced of all, and so falling down on his face confesses that God is in the Association of a truth."

Here is the whole mystery of government among us. Our government is democratic, inasmuch as the privilege of criticism is distributed among the whole body, and the power which it gives is accessible to any one who will take pains to attain good judgment. It is aristocratic, inasmuch as the best critics have the most power. It is theocratic, inasmuch as the spirit of truth alone can give the power of genuine criticism. The whole secret of the "stupendous despotism" which J. H. Noyes is said to exercise, to the terrible annoyance of Rev. H. Eastman, and others of like calibre, lies in the simple fact that he has proved himself to be a good *critic*; for what other means has he of controlling men? He has no military, or political, or pecuniary power; no authority from ecclesiastical antiquity, or from public opinion. *Confidence, secured by manifestation of good spiritual judgment,* is the only possible basis of the "despotism" he wields. Nothing else could give him power for a moment over such a mass of minds as exists in the Oneida Association.

Third Annual Report of the Oneida Association,
February 20, 1851

The spirit of criticism, as it proceeds, becomes more penetrating and refined, more prompt and inevitable in its detection of evil, and, at the same time, more good-natured and genial in its manifestations. Under its operation, we are conscious of real deliverance—conscious that the separation of the great day, between good and evil, has come. And, however painful at the time, the process only increases our love for the truth, which is our deliverer as well as judge. One member, who proved unimprovable under criticism, has been induced to leave.

Another striking feature of the judgment has come out the present year, in the exposure of our past lives, or what we call *historical criticism*. From these revelations, the Community gained a knowledge of human nature, a knowledge of the secret state of the best society in the world, and a preparation for the disclosures of the judgment, such as they never had before. The truth is in the world no man knows his neighbor. Persons meet only in form and appearance, and under the various disguises that are convenient. If a person knows *himself,* his object is to forget a great many things, and, at any rate, to hide them from others; so that the customary respectability is, before God, and in fact to the separate consciousness of individuals, a great sham—a thing used to cover and hide universal misdeeds of thought and action; and this is true, particularly, in the department of sexual relations. The remark that Christ made to the scribes and Pharisees, when they brought to him a woman taken in adultery—"Let him that is without sin among you cast the first stone"—if applied now to any class of persons would show the same result that it did then: all would go out convicted of their own consciences. And yet this subject is particularly covered up in conventional darkness. The real experience of mankind, the sinful, woeful, death-working action of this passion is closely hidden in the heart, and all pass along under the smooth mask of outward respectability. However this surface show of propriety may serve as a useful temporary restraint, we believe the time has come when the mere coverings of character are to be taken off, and when people will be forced to see things just as they really are. They will have to let in the broad daylight upon the whole field of character.

The operation of historical criticism and confession, with us, has been of this kind. It has been like the opening of our inner selves to daylight. And though it requires heroism of faith, thus to betray ourselves to the truth and to retrace with the spirit of judgment our past lives, yet we have found salvation in the result. We have been able to correct our mistakes; to separate our souls from the devil's snare; to untangle and put away from our life the threads of evil that were woven into it; and the effect has been a new feeling of innocence and the peace of God.

The day of judgment is also the day of justification and resurrection; and we think these characteristics fully keep pace, in our experience, with the work of criticism. With the increase of sincerity, there has been a corresponding increase of unity and strength. The power of the resurrection is felt in breaking up habits, displacing the spirit of old age, and in our continual renewing towards the freshness and freedom of youth. This work remains to be perfected; but we have the best evidence that it proceeds in full proportion to the power and entrance which the Spirit of Truth gains among us. It is seen in the continued ascendency of health in the Association—in the unassisted recovery of those who brought serious disease with them—and in the uniform victory which we have had over the ailments which occasionally threaten. There has been no death of an adult believer in the Association since its commencement, and we know of none that are seriously unwell.

Circular, April 4, 1854

Since Mr. A. has left us to return to Wallingford, I have had some very pleasant reflections upon the character of his experience in our Machine Shop. He has been very free from the professional spirit, which made it easy to teach him, and made him apt in receiving instruction. Whenever criticism was needed in relation to his work, he would so readily take sides with the person criticizing, that he made it very easy to perform this duty for him.

His success in his work, although in a business entirely new to him, has been remarkable and he has been but little subject to mistakes or accidents. I have been particularly struck by the fact that in all of his success he never seemed to act as though he had done a smart thing, or in any way to seek praise about it; but would in a modest manner say that he had got through with that job and invite the privilege of doing some other. And on the other hand, when he happened to spoil a piece of work, he would not seem at all mortified or discouraged about it, but in a cheerful, simple spirit, show himself ready to try again, thus providing that the spirit that is not proud or falsely elated by success, will not be ashamed or discouraged when unsuccessful.

Circular, July 15, 1854

MATHEMATICAL CRITICISM

An entertaining method of character examination was lately tried in our circle as follows: The trait under examination was thoroughness—the general habit of faithfulness and order. Each one made a list of the persons present, in detailed order, and then adapting the chronological scale of measuring organs, proceeded to mark against each one's name the figure corresponding to his development of this faculty in the judgment of the writer. The scale being from one to six indicates the degrees—Very Small, Small, Moderate, Full, Large, and Very Large. If a person was thought to have a fair amount of faithfulness he was marked four, signifying Full—if he was noted for reliability in this respect he was set down at five, or Large; each one, however, following his own private judgment in making the estimates. After everyone's list was complete, the sum of estimates against any particular name was taken and divided by the number of critics, which gave precisely the average of the opinions of the whole on each case.

This method might be extended to all the various departments of character, and the result would be in any family or circle of acquaintance a pretty accurate chart of everyone's mental and moral development.

Circular, July 19, 1855

The young men who go out in the neighboring villages with our vegetable wagon and expect to be abroad in this way a good part of the summer invited a family criticism as a means of strengthening their sympathy with the Community and enabling them to represent its spirit in their business dealings. Much love and confidence was expressed toward them and at the same time their faults were freely spoken of and some things in which they could improve were pointed out.

Another criticism this evening by invitation of the subject. The talk last night gave rather a peculiar interest to this case. The individual was one who has had as severe treatment under our system of criticism perhaps as any member of the Association. His faults were not of the hidden, subtle kind, but outstanding, obtrusive, and annoying. He has large self-esteem and extraordinary practical judgment in some respects, which together with an ardent temperament, and large language, made him naturally forward, dogmatic, and oppressive in his intercourse with others, and has laid him open from time to time to the hottest fire of criticism from the Community. Of course, he had difficulty at first in accepting it, but he has gradually grown in love with this treatment and now he instinctively courts criticism when he feels anything discordant between him and those around him. His invitation tonight drew out some criticism but more commendation. He was commended particularly for faithfulness, which is a quality so redeeming that no matter what a person's other traits are if he has that he will get along. His improvement was spoken of in respect to those things for which he had been criticized and his position towards criticism was held up as an example for all.

Circular, April 12, 1855

In the evening the Horticultural Department was offered for criticism. That business was generally thought to be too much set apart by itself—not communized as the trap business has been. Mr. N., as chief of the latter business, was commended for the manner in which he had taken in a company of "barbarians" as it were—men, women, and even children—into his shop, and patiently taught and encouraged them, until now it is fairly a community trade. The Horticultural Department needs popularizing in the same way.

Circular, March 19, 1857

One of the class of boys was criticized. H.'s faults were thought to arise mainly from a deficiency of self-respect. Small self-respect, combined with a great propensity for fun, gives him the character of a *clown.* It is his delight to divert the boys with clownish wit, and he does it to their disadvantage in school and elsewhere. His love of approbation descends now to the boys' answering laugh. With more self-respect, it would lead him to please the Community by manly, praiseworthy conduct. It was thought he had a good heart, and a disposition to improve, and needed to be encouraged by praise and an appreciation of all that is good in him. As to his propensity, let it be civilized and elevated, and who knows but it will find an edifying sphere. Perhaps there is a place for a clown in such a Community as this.

Circular, January 14, 1858

Friday evening the criticism of the spirit of carelessness. Some accidents which have occurred here lately render it very appropriate. The devil seems to have given up trying to make us sick by poisoning us internally, and is contented to bruise and dislocate and disable us by accident. We expect to discourage him in that task presently.

Circular, March 4, 1858

A member proposed himself for criticism in the evening meeting. He had been subject to a variety of unpleasant and painful sensations during the present winter—his health had suffered some and he had been more or less uncomfortable in his mind. He could say he loved criticism for its good effects, but not for *itself* as some profess to do; indeed he thought of it with dread and when he remembered what hard criticisms he was apt to get, he shrunk from offering himself to the ordeal. Nevertheless in view of the good it would do him he invited the family to be free, and he would try and hold still to the utmost that any had to say.

In responding to his request it was thought that Mr. Blank's expression of his feelings towards criticism did not really represent his deepest instincts. In his present state he misjudges himself, and as one appealing from "Philip drunk to Philip sober," so we appeal for Mr. Blank in his present state when he needs criticism, to Mr. Blank when criticism has had its softening effect: *then* he does not regard criticism as a bitter dose. In respect to his faults, it was thought his propensity to *talk* was his greatest difficulty. It sometimes leads him into argumentation which injures his fellowship with those around him; and sometimes it makes him tedious, producing the same effect. Excessive talking is a sure road to spiritual poverty with anyone. Mr. Blank needs repose of character, and more appreciation of unity. He is a great friend of the right of free discussion and individual opinion. The faculty of agreeing is as important as independence of mind, and more so. The spirit of independence may be combined with a true taste for social harmony, and a reverence for the superior judgment of others; and we should be rather predisposed to sympathize with what another says, than to find objections to it.

Circular, October 7, 1858

Nervousness criticized—The spirit that loses self-possession or, which is the same thing, trust in God in the presence of agitating circumstances. The spirit of fear exposes us to the evil we would shun. Women, particularly, indulge themselves in nervousness; they are brought up to think it is true feminine sensibility to go into hysterics at the sight of anything tragical. But the education of faith is very different. So far as we are possessed by faith we are prepared for scenes most appalling, natural or super-natural—we know that the evil one has been overcome, and that in the name of Christ we can defy his power. We can have a self-possession through faith, that is proof against any scare the Devil can get up—women as well as men: and we should be indignant at the tremulousness of fear.

Circular, October 14, 1858

Talk in the evening about table manners and etiquette. The boys came under some criticism for lack of respectful and quiet deportment in the dining room. A stiff, formal silence at the table is not what is wanted, but rather a free flow of conversation promoting a genial sociable spirit—pleasant conversational buzz is good music while eating.

Circular, September 22, 1859

The "principality" as it was called, of the horse barn was criticized; not persons in particular, but the character of the department. This department in the Community includes half a dozen teamsters, with two or three in constant attendance at the stables. The nature of the business was thought to be demoralizing. It is a school of character, and it educates the same qualities that slaveholding does, tyranny and cruelty and coarse brutal will. The threatening and scolding and whipping, which the young teamster has to do, or thinks he must do, are ruinous to his manners. His language and conduct toward his horse will react upon his spirit and he will bring the same language and manners home to be manifested towards those around him. Old ideas that there is no government but the relentless whip are retained. In the world, indeed, a more civilized code is gaining adherence. Gentleness is beginning to be thought one of the prime qualities of a horse-tamer. As the result of our discussion, it was resolved that considering the very bad conditions attaching to the horse barn department, the business, in addition to its positive degrading tendencies, being much removed from female sympathy, and often requiring irregularity at the family meals and meetings and irregular hours of sleep, there should be special care taken to have frequent changes, never to keep the young there long, but to fill the place as much as possible with those who are spiritual and reliable.

Circular, June 14, 1860

Dancing has also had its share of criticism. This is a very popular amusement in the Community, as all classes can engage in it perhaps more freely than in any other. The young and best dancers were cautioned against excess, and against taking any course which would make it unpleasant for the old and less experienced to participate in this beautiful recreation. On the other hand, the less accomplished are urged to seek improvement, and to persevere until they become good dancers. Improvement should be the motto of all, and those who are most capable should generously bear with the deficiencies of the others, and teach them what they have themselves learned.

Those amusements in which the greatest number can join, which are not restricted to the young, or to one sex, and which best promote universal fellowship, are superior to those games which are limited, and which excite antagonism and rivalry. In this view, dancing is superior to ball-playing, chess, and similar games, and should be most cultivated. The life and interest of the young men should not be absorbed by amusements which are in their nature limited; let their chief attention in this respect be directed to those amusements which are best calculated to promote Community fellowship.

Circular, March 1, 1863

A CRITICISM

Criticism of M. this evening. He was commended for kindness of disposition, readiness to serve and oblige others, affection and warm-heartedness, versatility of talent, and force of character; and was censured for lack of purpose, and selfishness in his dealings, for a strong love of dress, or foppishness, and pleasure-seeking in social matters, and for the lack of the spirit of *improvement,* and indisposition to qualify himself intellectually to do business properly. Was advised to withdraw himself from the Peddling Business, and take hold of some steady employment here at home—to put himself to school intellectually and spiritually, etc., etc.

Circular, March 26, 1863

CRITICISM

Mrs. R. is a kind-hearted friendly woman. There is much natural dignity and self-possession in her character. Has a good mind and is quite clear in her intellectual perceptions of truth. But her perceptions of truth are more intellectual than spiritual; more through her mind than through her heart as the result of inspiration. It was thought that she placed a higher appreciation on the intellect and intellectual attainments than on spirituality and that the same was true in regard to social fellowship. It occupied her attention more than spiritual growth and improvement. It was thought she was somewhat affected by a complaining spirit in regard to love. She sometimes makes the remark that she hoped the time would come when everyone would have all the love they wanted. She seems very desirous that others should love her—thinks it very desirable to be loved—which is all true enough—but she does not sufficiently appreciate the profound blessedness of simply *loving,* whether she is loved in return or not—of being so swallowed up in the element of love—in God—that we can be happy and full of joy and contentment, whether we realize any outward returns or not. It is a good thing to be loved; it is better to *dwell* in love, and love for love's sake only. It was thought there was a good deal of pride in her character, and that it had never been thoroughly humbled and subdued. She is self-complacent and whole in her spirit, and it is not easy to bring her into the judgment.

Daily Journal, April 14, 1863

Mr. H. was selected as an Agent to go to Cleveland, Ohio, to reinforce G.W.N. Preparatory to his going, he asked and received a criticism this evening in Meeting. He was criticized for liability to take on the spirit of the world while out peddling; for too much freedom of communication with outsiders in relation to our social matters and principles; for hardness of spirit and an itching to get out of the shop, etc.; a spirit of discontent with his position there. Commended for being a good manager in the shop; as faithful to his responsibilities, and as a good, genial social companion. In pleasure-seeking he was advised to seek spirituality, and keep a good relation with Mr. Noyes.

Daily Journal, December 17, 1863

Mr. Noyes gave a deeply sincere criticism of himself, and history of his late illness and of the experience of the Community the last few days. He compared his own case to an engineer on a train, who got his train under such momentum that he couldn't stop at the Depot but went right on by it.

John Humphrey Noyes, around 1851.

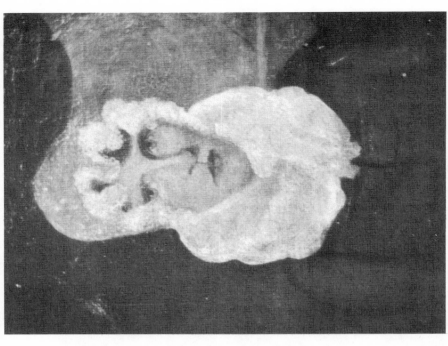

Polly (Hayes) Noyes (1780–1866), mother of John Humphrey Noyes.

The Honorable John Noyes (1764–1841), father of John Humphrey Noyes.

Harriet (Holton) Noyes, who married John Humphrey Noyes in 1838.

Boyhood home of John Humphrey Noyes, "Locust Grove," Putney, Vermont.

Mary Cragin, no date. Mrs. Cragin started the first school for the children in a little shoe shop at Oneida.

Old log hut, predecessor of Mansion House.

Old Mansion House (destroyed in 1870) at far left; Children's House (destroyed in 1868) at left; new Mansion House, center; Tontine at far right. Photograph around 1865.

East front of Mansion House, 1870's.

Front lawn of Mansion House, 1870's.

South view of Mansion House from the garden, 1870's.

Quadrangle, 1870's.

Summer house,
north lawn, 1870's.

Front porch of Mansion House, 1870's.

Fruit House, where the fruit-canning department was located, and Keep, where the Community's fruits and vegetables were stored.

Factory at Willow Place (Sherrill), built in 1864, was the site of the Community's trap and silk manufacturing and the machine shop.

Vestibule and showcase of Mansion House, containing curios given to the Community by friends.

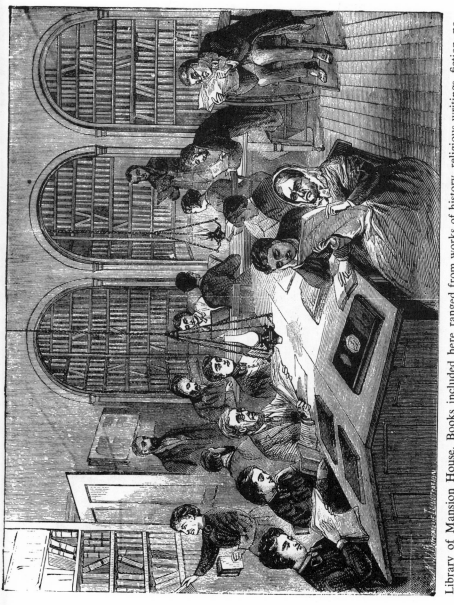

Library of Mansion House. Books included here ranged from works of history, religious writings, fiction, poetry, and translations from Greek, Latin, French, and German to a wide selection of current periodicals.

Oneida Community kitchen.

Upper sitting room of Mansion House, the general gathering place of the Community family.

Big hall, with gallery, was used for concerts, lectures, meetings, and all other occasions when the whole family assembled together.

Community dining room. Note the lazy-susan centers of the tables.

Daily Journal, April 4–6, 1864

EVENING MEETING

A very severe criticism of the legal spirit in the library and dining room, as represented by Mr. Carr and Mr. Delatre, particularly the first-named person, upon whom the criticism centered. As a practical conclusion Mr. Noyes advised Mr. Carr to quit the library entirely—quit reading newspapers and go to studying his (Mr. Noyes's) writings for some time—a year or two—and get acquainted with his spirit. The next evening was a continuation of the criticism of the Legal Spirit as exhibited in the kitchen and among the stewards—Mr. Cragin coming in for a considerable share. Mr. Noyes thought that Mr. C. had better not continue in that position any longer. The feeling of poverty which has come over us during the last few weeks and which has tempted the stewards to scrimp in the provision for the table was criticized very severely. Mr. Noyes remarked that he wanted his army well fed!

Circular, February 5, 1866

Considerable attention is being turned in the family to criticism; it has been thought best to have some sort of organization, which would secure promptness in attending to cases of criticism, and relieve the general meeting from responsibility with regard to them. Accordingly six committees, or clubs of "Inquiry and Criticism," of ten members each, have been appointed. These clubs are to meet once a week or oftener.

Daily Journal, July 18, 1866

In meeting Meroa K. was criticized. Much dissatisfaction was expressed with her present unimproving and disobedient state, and it was thought that if there was not a thorough change in her spirit she would have to be invited to leave the Community. She is inefficient in business, is gross in her alimentiveness, and spends a great deal of time in reading novels and newspaper stories. A committee was appointed to talk with her and find out what her real character and purpose are and determine what course shall be taken with her.

Daily Journal, January 19, 1867

A CRITICISM

Two evenings have been principally occupied with the criticism of the boys that attended Mr. B.'s school. They were not thought to be in as good a state in reference to their studies as they were at the commencement of the winter. Distracting influences have come in, and diverted their attention from study. Besides, they were too much absorbed with each other, and did not enough seek association with persons older and better than themselves. A good deal of interest was manifested for them and a desire expressed that they should take a new start—seek ascending fellowship, and become helpers to Mr. Hamilton and the Community. Much love was expressed for them.

Daily Journal, January 22, 1867

EVENING MEETING

Mr. Hamilton: I have promised myself that I would sometimes criticize the habit of making excuses and apologies when we attempt to do anything. Almost all will remember that Mr. Noyes criticized this habit long ago. If persons had anything to say, he disliked to hear them begin with an apology. I believe we should do better all round if we did just as well as we could and then took credit for what we are able to accomplish. If you fail, don't try to plaster it over with excuses.

Daily Journal, December 10, 1867

A CRITICISM

Mr. I. had asked for help, and the meeting was devoted to a thorough investigation of his state and its causes. Mr. I.'s faults were set before him in a kind but sincere manner. He dislikes responsibility, and has put the foremanship of the machine shop mainly onto John S. so that young men working there hardly know who is foreman. It was generally testified that he had never been the head of his family; that his wife, with all her legality, ruled him; that he was subject to fits of condemnation for having left her as he did; that he had never had control of his children; that he had a great deal of respect for worldly religion; had never studied Christ's character only in a one-sided way, regarding him as the Lamb of God, perfectly yielding and docile to his father, but quite overlooking his character as the Lion of the Tribe of Judah. It was thought there was some of the Lion in Mr. I. if he could only be aroused; but the spirit he is under makes him torpid, spiritually lazy, and inclined to say, Good Lord, good devil, or that all is good. When he first commenced on the silk machinery, he acted like an entirely new man, and seemed full of Mr. Noyes's inspiration. It was hoped he would now take hold and clear himself of this vacillating state, and be a strong man in the cause, not have to be pushed on by others. He must take hold and strike for himself, and be willing to strike a pretty hard blow too, if he would be free. He once knocked a man down; and it was hoped he would now come up to the scratch and do the same thing for this principality that has so long abused him and hindered the work of truth and righteousness.

Circular, January 16, 1868

The habits of disease and old age were spoken of as particularly disgusting, and one elderly member said he didn't want persons to treat him as though he was an old man, and needed care and petting on that account. He thought the best way to overcome old age (which was nothing but a habit) was to ignore it.

Circular, February 5, 1868

A communication from Mrs. C. was read, going into some historical criticism and asking the help of the family. Mrs. C. is at times possessed with a dumb devil that makes her treat persons ill in the way of not answering. She says she does not hear. She was a pet in her father's family which would account for much of her bad experience.

Circular, August 12, 1872

In the past we may have showed that the aspect of criticism was stern and severe. Its application caused a man to sweat, and it was as difficult for him to hold still as it is for a soldier who is under the surgeon's knife. But criticism has another side, and one that it loves to show most often. If it is sometimes severe, it is more often gentle. If it pulls down the old life, it delights to heap praise upon the new. It is quick to spy out good, even where the subject does not suspect it, and this it magnifies and enlarges with a will. Sometimes it is as soothing as a mother's touch and as comforting as a mother's love. At such times, it literally "heals the broken-hearted and bindeth up their wounds." It justifies one who is condemned; it builds up one who is cast down; it exalts the lowly minded.

Circular, January 6, 1873

At the beginning of the holidays when the foremen were busy taking their inventories and making estimates for the year to come, and when it would have been easy to have given way to a great deal of gaiety, it was proposed to have our outside men gather in, have our studies rest awhile, and our books lie unopened, while we got ready for the New Year by a grand time of mutual criticism. It has been no "you-tickle-me-and-I-tickle-you" work, but simple truth-telling, pointing out faults of temper, of tastes, of manner, of character, of attractions and of repulsions, faults of every kind, in short, and all done in kindness with a view to unity and softness of heart, and not for giving vent to pent-up grudges. The fruits are peace and humility, purity, and a new life.

Circular, April 21, 1873

C. has the pride of oddity—a special fondness for differing from others. It had been bred into him, and shows itself on all occasions, particularly in efforts to excel in daring, reckless exploits. This is a fault everywhere cultivated in young people. They think to please by doing things that excite fear as well as surprise. They do not please in that way those whom they should care most about pleasing. Possibly C. may in his exploits seek to please by variety; but he is at least in danger of forming bad habits—such as will make him an "odd stick" in society. Father Richards used to say of B. that he had every kind of sense but common sense. I should advise C. to get in love with common sense. If you find the people around you generally think thus and so, count it all the better for that, and adopt the same thought if you can conscientiously, and not, from the pride or habit of oddity, take the unpopular side of questions. By common sense is meant the sense of people in general. Having established itself in common sense—that is, in sympathy with those around him on all sorts of subjects—then it will answer better for C. to indulge in occasional oddities; but there should be first a basis of sympathy and unity.

Circular, March 16, 1874

A little over two years ago we established a club which we called the "Criticism Club." This club met once each week, and to it came all who were desirous of deliverance from difficulties of the heart and soul. At the beginning of the winter just past, there arose a new love for criticism, and the fear of it so natural to the old life insensibly melted away. "Cleanse thou me from secret faults," seemed to be the prayer of the Community heart. The Club was so pressed with applications for truth-telling, that its regular sessions began to be held twice and then three times during the week, and its members stood ready to be called together whenever their services should be needed. So great was the call that in some cases the applicants were put off from week to week, and one person waited nearly three months for the coveted washing. Not only by committees was the work carried on, but often in the evening meetings the tremendous power of the Community concentrated in a way to thoroughly purify persons of long-standing faults, and bring about almost instantaneous changes of character. Personality in criticism was scarcely to be found, but in its place was a strong desire to do each other good. Criticism no longer rankled and offended, but brought relief and a feeling of thankfulness. J., after criticism so mortifying and severe that to the outward eye it seemed impossible to bear, showed a countenance so unmistakably the reflex of a happy heart that we wondered at her. "Why," said she, "I am happy; after my criticism I felt relieved just as I think Christian did when the burden rolled off his back." F., to whom the truth came suddenly and sharply while in the midst of isolation and pleasure-seeking, said afterwards, "If anyone had told me a week ago that I should have felt so well and happy as I do now I should have said, 'Not unless a miracle is performed';" and every step of the winter's experience has proved beyond a doubt that the age of miracles is not past. The children, too, have caught the revival spirit and asked that they might be clean; and for several weeks parents and guardians have done earnest work among them. Even the four-year olds have had a round of criticism, themselves acting as critics and good ones too. It may seem like trifling that we should introduce criticism among children so young, but far from it; it is a very serious thing to them. By it they are saved from much trouble and unhappiness. In the case of the older children especially, we find that criticism does away with the need for whipping, keeps them soft-hearted, and in good relations with their superiors, teaching at the same time the most perfect sincerity among companions. As to their ability as critics we know that children are gifted with the keenest discriminations of character. The result of this kind of sincerity at the Children's House is very encouraging. Mr. W. reported in a late meeting that at no time since he has acted as father to the children have they pleased him so well. A good harmonious spirit has taken possession of them and they are real comforts.

Circular, March 30, 1874

What if it should be considered the rule of Community etiquette to say *nothing disagreeable to anyone after dinner*—but tell our troubles and criticize others as a general thing in the forenoon; also exclude questions of business as much as possible from the latter part of the day. Let that time be devoted to gratitude, to speaking of the goodness of God, to telling good news and good experience, to provoking to love and good works, making folks around us feel happy. Of course there would have to be exceptions to this rule, but as far as we could carry it out, it would have a good effect.

Circular, August 31, 1874

THE PRIMA DONNA FEVER—REPORT OF A MUSICAL CRITICISM

In searching this morning for the cause of a bad spirit apparent in one of the younger women, I providentially or accidentally hit upon a discovery which seemed so important and had such an important bearing on the present condition of music in the Community that I thought the best thing that could be done would be to bring it before the whole musical fraternity, and have a free talk about it as it is always best to strike while the iron is hot.

The essence of the evil seems to be that among these persons who are in trouble, music has evidently become a selfish, personal thing; they look on their talents, their reputation, ability, and success in music as their own, and are quarreling in their hearts about the matter, just as the world quarrels about money and other selfish rights; music in fact is uncommunized property. I thought that if the strife had become such a nuisance among those younger girls, it might be possible that the whole musical body is so affected by the same spirit. It is astonishing what an amount of *discord* the science of *concord* can make.

The object of this meeting is to uncover the working of the spirit which is striving "who shall be greatest." It seems to be the confession of quite a number of the class of girls, that they are possessed with a spirit that is striving to be greatest. Though they hate it like poison, yet they find it difficult to get rid of it. If that spirit is essentially identified with music, we had better clear music out of the Community.

This selfish spirit which these girls have exposed will work out in some other way, if they do not get rid of it in their music. I should go for giving up music, unless it can be separated from this spirit. If they do not rid themselves of it now, it will show itself in other forms even if they drop music.

Lately we have got our music altogether from the world, and have gone to New York for musical education, and we are suffering the consequences. If we could separate music entirely from the idea of displaying ourselves to visitors, and look on it as something for our own use, we might get back into the old feeling of it. We never had a class of singers brought up on the stage and before the world as much as this class of girls has been. They have been brought up on the stage, and have got the *prima donna fever*.

There are always two sides in the matter of envying. There is one that envies, and there is one that is envied; and sometimes the one that is envied is as much to blame as the one that envies. I wish criticism might reach that part of the game. It seems to me this morning, after this astonishing disclosure in respect to the difficulties between these girls, that I have got a sure diagnosis of the unhealthy condition of music in the Community. We doctors have long been trying to find out what is the matter, and after feeling pulses and looking at the tongues all round, we find that it is the *prima donna fever*. I am going to doctor for that. If we can cure that we shall have music back on its legs again. It is bedridden now and has been for a great while with the *prima donna fever*! That's what's the matter!

Circular, November 15, 1875

This would not be a faithful record of home events did we not record the sorrows as well as the joys that befall us. For a week past the Community here has been under some criticism from the family at Wallingford Community. As all know that family has devoted itself, the past year, with unceasing zeal to start a health revival, and with most marked success. To be sure, we have given Wallingford our hearty sympathy in their work, and have advocated the Turkish Bath, and as our readers know, kept up faith testimony in the *Circular*. But we shall have to confess that we have been tardy in taking practical steps in that direction. On one or two occasions in the case of weak eyes and lame ankles, we have asked the advice of physicians rather than depended on faith, as was our wont, or using the well-tried remedy of the Turkish Bath. This seeming difference of purpose, caused an unpleasant jar between us and Wallingford, and made us deservedly a subject of criticism from them; since which we have earnestly set to work to get at the difficulty. As one suggested, the cause of this unusual occurrence may be that worldly wisdom has too much influence with us, and inspiration not enough. However that may be, we are in earnest now, and shall not rest until we find ourselves under the guidance of the same inspiration that has been at work with the family there.

V

Health

Stemming from what they considered a "faith cure" of one of their members while the group still lived in Putney, the Oneida Communists until their later years were devout believers in such therapy and as far as possible eschewed all kinds of medicine. Although one of the members was a doctor, they were able to testify to very good health and "not a pill or potion left" when questioned in 1853 (*Circular,* May 11, 1853). Although at this time they had abandoned tobacco, they still used tea and coffee and the occasional meal of pork or other meat when they could afford it. All these items were later discarded (*Circular,* December 13, 1855).

Alimentiveness was a subject often discussed in their meetings and in print to "examine our state, criticize our practice, and let in the spirit of resurrection newness." In order to break habit, of which they disapproved, they occasionally declared a fast or a meal of nothing but bread and cheese, passed around in the parlor (*Circular,* September 20, 1855). At another time when an even more rigorous fast was declared, the children too, fasted with no more complaint than a wistful question as to "when the fast would go away" (*Circular,* March 1, 1869). If it was argued that a mixed diet of animals, vegetables, and fruit was best adapted to their wants, the answer was that the abandoning of meat, tea, coffee, and tobacco was not a matter of religious conscience but of "pure instinct and aesthetic taste."

An article by Mr. Noyes from the *Berean,* a Community publication, was sent to Dr. Graham, a popular food faddist of the period, who made a rude reply. The Community was not impressed.

150

Grahamism, they said (*Circular*, July 14, 1859), was "the fiend in the stomach," and cited the case of a woman who had reduced her diet to nothing but bread and water, whereupon she decided that she had been under the spirit of legality and fear, began to eat whatever she liked, and acquired "a healthy, *forgetful* digestion."

The most serious as well as dramatic battle against sickness occurred in the winter of 1863–64 when an epidemic of diphtheria struck the Community. After several shocking losses, the communists decided to abandon conventional treatment and resort to their own brand of healing. By February every member was well enough to celebrate the famous twentieth of February (*Circular*, April 4, 1864).

Some years later, in 1870, a lesser contagion attacked the children—whooping cough—and after tending it and bearing with it for some time, the Community decided that the nuisance had lasted long enough and called an "Indignation Meeting" (*Circular*, February 7, 1870) so powerful that apparently the children responded to it by getting well. Children, they said, throve a thousand times better on such treatment than on pills and syrups.

One winter (*Circular*, February 4, 1858) when a severe epidemic in the nature of a cold visited the Community, although it was a temptation to "putter with remedies," they decided that the less they had to do with them the better. Even the youngest were treated by the faith cure; a small girl who had been crying all night with an earache was told to confess Christ, after which she fell into a quiet slumber and the earache disappeared (*Circular*, March 29, 1855). The children complaining of cold were encouraged to go outdoors and play in the snow which, they said, "false tenderness might consider severe" but which apparently had a beneficial effect (*Circular*, January 15, 1857). Persons with a cold were adjured to resist sneezing and coughing "which a resolute person could restrain," instead of following the Biblical advice to "go now, weep, and howl for the miseries that shall come upon you" (*Circular*, February 10, 1868).

Much bad experience, they believed, was attributable to the "hypo"; that is, a tendency to look too much at evil and give it importance (*Circular*, January 23, 1858). Disease was a spirit, and all difficulties, either bodily or mental, were connected with the spirit. There was a temptation to refer any evil to an outward cause, but by perceiving that it was a matter of the spirit it seemed as though the devil sneaked away. The best curative agent was criticism. Anyone attacked with any disorder could apply for a committee of six or eight persons to come and criticize him. Let the critics, they said (*Circular*, December 24, 1863), seek out the weakest spot in character and conduct, which was the avenue through which disease entered; if the criticism was mortifying, it was only a sign that the remedy was applied to the right spot and was taking effect.

The Community people were normally kind and sympathetic characters, but both their circumstances and their religion recommended fairly spartan attitudes toward the weaknesses of the flesh. One woman with a toothache was advised to consider it a spiritual disease and commit her teeth into God's hands (*Circular*, February 14, 1856). An epidemic of influenza among the children was met firmly with criticism in which the children themselves were expected to join (*Circular*, March 29, 1855). Crossness and stupor, as well as other symptoms, indicated the presence of an evil spirit, and since disease, they believed, came and went through the spirit, they cured it with a course of exhortation and criticism which was apparently just what was needed.

Anesthetics were a recent discovery and their use in dentistry was discussed (*Circular*, August 6, 1866). The dentist—a member—admitted that it was good to pull teeth without pain but he thought that "a little spunk" would be better, and Mr. Hamilton thought pain was good for them, and, if they tried to dodge it, God might corner them and teach the lesson another way. A member who complained of sleeplessness was advised to rise above his dependence on sleep into fellowship with the unsleeping energy of God. Inordinate attention to the body, or, as they called it, "bodytending," was always disapproved, and though they gave their patients good care and "all necessary nursing and sympathy," they said that there should be "chastity and reserve" in the matter (*Circular*, April 30, 1866). The mortality figure given for their children, from birth to fifteen years, was almost half that of the average for the rest of the country at that time, which would seem to speak well for their methods (*Circular*, March 21, 1870).

Only one disease, endemic or epidemic—what we now know as malaria but which they called "fever and ague"—breached their defenses (*Circular*, October 2, 1871). This occurred not at Oneida but at Wallingford, and grew to such serious proportions that at one time more than half the members were affected and a few of the most seriously ill, known as the "refuse lot," fled the infected spot and went back to Oneida. There was even talk of abandoning the Connecticut colony altogether (*American Socialist*, May 4, 1876). However, they stuck it out but the subject came up for severe criticism. Naturally, the Community preferred to trace this "*daimonia*" to a spiritual source and its villain to "the old murderer," the devil (*Circular*, October 2, 1871). They resisted this attack with faith as well as they could but were obliged in some cases to resort to quinine.

This last was an innovation, promoted, perhaps, by the two young men who had been sent to Yale to become physicians. However it was, in 1872 the Community "obtained liberty to use means in the case of disease," which of course meant using "external remedies" as well as faith. The budding physicians must have been persuasive since this item (*Circular*, July 15, 1872) adds that they believed science to be true handmaid of faith and that the two rightly joined would give them "a new and important purchase on the devil and his kingdom."

Two years later (*Circular*, November 16, 1874), at the suggestion of young Dr. Noyes, a Turkish Bath was constructed in the basement of the Mansion at Oneida and another in the dwelling house at Wallingford. The latter was open to the public and during the first year over a thousand baths were given to outside patrons and another thousand to their members. Some of this, they reported (*Circular*, October 25, 1875), was for "luxury and precaution," but they also treated fever and ague, dumb ague, rheumatism, hay fever, colds, dropsy, and paralysis. The number of cures was not reported, but they noted "the buoyance and elasticity of spirit" which resulted, as well as the favorable public opinion created locally.

Wallingford, as the first proponent of the Turkish Bath, was perhaps naturally its most enthusiastic advocate and worked with great zeal to create what they called a Health Revival. Although the members at Oneida sympathized with their work, they, in the opinion of the Wallingford folks, lagged behind in any practical effort in that direction (*Circular,* November 15, 1875). Even more shocking, on one or two occasions in certain cases of illness they consulted physicians instead of depending on faith or the Turkish Bath. This seeming indifference brought down upon them a severe criticism from the Wallingford members who suggested that worldly wisdom had too much influence with them and inspiration not enough. The Oneidans did not try to justify their conduct but promised not to rest until they found themselves under the same inspiration as their sister commune.

Steam heat throughout the Mansion House largely dispelled the dread, especially in the elderly, of the rigorous northern winters, but in its place there was apt to be a temptation to neglect outdoor exercise. In a dwelling containing two hundred inmates there was good society and enough amusements provided so that there was no occasion to go abroad visiting. Even the dining room in the Tontine was connected with the Mansion House by a warmed covered passage. Thus, they said (*Circular,* February 17, 1873), though winter was effectually kept at bay, they must take care lest they become mere hot-house plants and lose the vigor, elasticity, and enterprise which their northern latitude was so well calculated to foster.

Circular, May 11, 1853

DIALOGUE

QUESTION—You have just returned from Oneida, I understand. How is the health of the Association?

ANSWER—Very good.

Q—Haven't they any sick ones there?

A—No. None that are confined at all.

Q—Don't they employ a doctor?

A—Not at all.

Q—One of their members was formerly a doctor, I believe. What does he do?

A—He was tending the circular saw when I was there; but he goes from one business to another, making himself generally useful, as the phrase is at Oneida. He is called upon to pull a tooth occasionally, he is always ready to sew up a cut or do any little office of that kind when asked.

Q—His *materia medica* is all thrown overboard, I suppose?

A—Not a pill or potion left.

Q—Where there are so many children I should think that some of them would be ailing. Don't they have colds? It would be strange if they did not annoy you with coughing.

A—I heard none, and very little complaint of any kind. I was told that the children had been almost entirely free of colds the whole winter.

Q—What does the Association live on?

A—Common vegetables and fruit; good bread of all kinds; tea and coffee; fish, salt and fresh; some salt pork; and once in a great while they have a dinner of fresh meat.

Circular, March 29, 1855

A severe influenza, or epidemic cold, has been among our children lately. Symptoms—headache, sore throat, cough, earache, and in some cases considerable fever. Also, more or less crossness and stupor, indicating the presence of an evil spirit. Acting on our faith that disease comes in and goes out through the spirit, we commence the course of exhortation and criticism with the children who are most affected, advising them to confess Christ as their physician, and invite criticism as their medicine. We commenced with A. He did not seem to mind what was said at the time, but before night he manifested symptoms of returning activity. Next came G.'s case. He was criticized for hardness of spirit, which had come in by being petted. He was in his place the next day among the children at work and at their play. Little M. had symptoms of the croup—quite serious. She was plied with simple remedies for a day or two without much improvement. We urged her to confess Christ, but it did not make much impression; so we gave a dose of truth telling to the spirit that was oppressing her. She appeared refreshed by it and grew steadily better until she was well. L. had been ailing for several days; all attention seemed to no avail. She suffered nights with severe earache, sleeping but little. One morning, when we called the children together for a talk, she was lying on the bed crying with pain. We proposed to invite her to submit to criticism as the only help we could render her. After some little delay she consented, got up and took her seat with us in the circle. The children all told her fully what was in their minds, showing very ready discernment.

A few of the firsh shots appeared to add to her pain, and she was tempted to criticize criticisms; this she was told, which hit the mark; she stopped her mouth and with that, stopped the pain, and she has not felt the first sting of earache since criticism. A good natured, loving spirit immediately took possession of her and she has been bright-eyed and happy ever since.

Circular, August 9, 1855

We used to hear a great deal about the unhealthiness of the evening air—the danger of being out when the dew is falling—of sitting in a draft—or on the damp ground, of wetting the feet, etc., etc. There were thousands of ways of "catching cold," where we lived abroad. But here, nobody says, "you will catch cold"—you do not hear the caution once a year, and yet we are very careless in respect to what we should once have thought exposure. We are out in the evening all we please, and find nothing noxious in the air or the dew. We sleep with curtains waving in the wind. Our women, if the creek is to be crossed and the bridge is not handy, do not scruple to take off their shoes and stockings and divide the rippling stream with their bare feet. If a shower catches them in the hay-field, they are the last to run; one laughs to see how leisurely they take their way home. In short, we are on excellent terms with all outdoors, the air, the dew, the rain, and mother earth. We do not think they are going to hurt us and they accept our confidence and treat us benignly.

Circular, September 20, 1855

In respect to alimentiveness, we find it healthy to bring this subject up from time to time and examine our state, criticize our practice, and let in the spirit of resurrection newness. Perhaps there is no department of human nature in which habit is more disposed to domineer: and it is an axiom with us that the devil works in habit. We find it good then occasionally to break in upon the routine of our table arrangements. Friday of this week we kept a kind of fast. We had a meeting in the parlor at nine and before noon spent an hour in reading and conversation, then plain bread and cheese was passed round and eaten lightly of. This passed for breakfast and dinner. For supper, bread and plums were served in the same way, after a similar meeting. We thought the effect on the whole was more chastening to the appetite than a severer fast would have been. Then it was one in which the children could participate, which they did with the utmost cheerfulness. We have quite fallen in love with this way of taking a meal, and think we have struck a vein that we shall work and get much good from. Our limited accommodations at present prevent all the family from sitting down at one table, but here is a way that we can all eat supper together as often as we wish. The unity which this fashion secures is one good thing. Its departure from routine is another. Thirdly its tendency is to moderation and to the recognition of the Lord's presence, making the meal a sacred ordinance.

Circular, December 13, 1855

When the Association some year and one half ago quit the use of tea and coffee and tobacco, they recognized the leading of God in the movement, and it was accompanied with an expectation that he would lead us on in the same direction of improvement 'til our table should in every respect be conformed to the heavenly idea. Deliverance from bondage to these stimulants was thought to be the beginning of an entire breaking up of habit, and we held ourselves open to a total revolution in our taste and manner of living. Since then vegetables and fruits have been gradually supplanting meat on our board, partly because we chose to confine ourselves as much as possible to home productions, and we produce more of the former than the latter kinds of foods; and partly because meat has been losing its relish. (It is perhaps a natural chord with stimulants we had discarded, and goes with them.) Nevertheless, the old institution of pork has maintained its existence to some extent. We have talked about its abolition, and expected it sometime; but swine have so long had a place in the economy of a farm that it seemed difficult to dispossess them at once. The housekeepers hardly knew how to manage without lard. We had a quota of the animals on hand, and in the time of waiting for the mind of the Association to assume unanimity and a decisive expression of the subject, several of them had been killed at intervals and used in the family with some abatement of the usual methods. The instinct against pork has been strengthening itself however, and a part of the Association have felt free to quietly abstain from it for some time. This evening a member on the other side, so far as there was any, whose mind had been laboring on the subject of alimentiveness, expressed his conviction that we are invited as an Association, by the spirit that is leading us all into improvement, to give up the use of this meat. And his sentiment took so unanimously that a resolution to that effect was forthwith adopted.

All seemed to be ready, and pork was given a *shove*—the baked meats for breakfast being recommended to the soap maker, whose manufacture is useful to us for the present at least.

Circular, February 14, 1856

Suffered considerably with a toothache while at the trap-shop. On my way to the house, stopped at the dentist's office and had the filling removed, which relieved it some. After coming home had some conversations with Mrs. S. She thought I needed to consider the toothache more as a spiritual disease, and commit my teeth into God's hands, and trust him to guide me as to having them filled, etc. I have desired to have the right spirit about my teeth, and I think Mrs. S.'s hints will help me.

Circular, January 14, 1858

M., who presents in his own physique an admirable specimen of a good breather, introduced the subject of ventilation and said he was afraid we were falling into some indifference toward it. To shrink from a gush of pure air is to repel an exhilarating draft. He could only compare the air these charming mornings to the most delicious honey. He should have a whimsical plan for the new house, some way to surround our bodies with warmth and keep our heads outdoors.

Circular, July 14, 1859

Saturday evening an article from the *Berean* was read, entitled Love of Life. It criticizes that inordinate attention to the body, which physiologists inculcate. It says, "the way to shut out the power of health is to crave and seek for it as though it were the one thing needful; and the way to admit and attract that power is to love life and health only according to their true value, and seek first the Kingdom of God and his righteousness." This article was sent to Dr. Graham at the time of its first publication, and the paper in which it was contained was returned with the following marginal note: "The babblings of a fool— not of a natural fool, but of a self-made fool." According to our observation we are forced to believe that Grahamism is the fiend in the stomach of many a poor dispeptic. We heard a woman but lately tell her experiences under that possession. She began questioning her food, and thinking this thing and that thing hurt her, and leaving off one and another until she had reduced herself to bread and water. But when she found her stomach was too delicate for that even, she stopped, and said to herself, "what is the use? Everything hurts me, and it is of no use to choose. I may as well eat what I want. I believe it is this spirit of legality and fear that is sinking me." She immediately stepped into the pantry and ate what she found there, and continued after that to eat what was set before her, without consulting the scruples of the demon, but cultivating faith and thankfulness, and her stomach began to strengthen, and she acquired a healthy *forgetful* digestion.

Circular, May 1, 1862

Vaccination is the order of the day. Smallpox is in the neighborhood, and old and young are taking precautions against it. Almost everyone, except the youngest children, have been vaccinated at some earlier period in their lives, but nearly all have tried it again, and some, to make assurance doubly sure, if the left arm will not work, try the other. This disease is prevailing among the tribe of Indians who live near here; and as they often call at our house to sell the baskets they manufacture, or exchange them for food and clothing, it is necessary for us to be on our guard. It was proposed to try to keep them away for a while; but no plan was suggested by which this could be effected.

Circular, April 4, 1864

A CAMPAIGN WITH DIPHTHERIA

In the last days of last summer the diphtheria first made its appearance in the Oneida Community. The class first attacked was that of the young men. Three of the cases, in quick succession, proved fatal. Something like dismay fell on the Community. The doctors were appealed to for help. All the remedies that could be heard of as successful were brought to bear. Still the enemy steadily advanced. The young women were attacked. Two of them died—the last as late as the 5th of November. During the two months of struggle up to this point, a new system of treatment had been gradually developing itself in the instincts and practice of the Community, and from this time forward was fully organized, and took the brunt of the battle. The usual remedies were wholly discarded, and in their place the following measures were adopted: 1. *General measures of prevention,* such as more liberal diet; instructions for healthy breathing; and increase of faith and courage. 2. *Special measures for actual cases of attack,* that is, the application of ice and criticism. The general method of using *ice* was to provide the patient with a supply of the article, chopped into pieces suitable for the mouth, and by faithful attendance of nurses keeping him eating it or holding it in his throat day and night until the canker disappeared. This treatment was suggested by a paragraph in a newspaper reporting the practice of some French physician.

The disease continued its ferocious attacks from day to day through November, December, January, into the middle of February, till it had prostrated temporarily nearly half the Community. But after the new treatment was inaugurated, no death by diphtheria occurred, and most of the cases were cured substantially in a few hours. The disease, by steady repulse, became gradually more manageable, changed its form once or twice, and finally disappeared from the Community, so that on the 20th of February every member of the family attended its annual celebration. At the end of the campaign, a printed list of questions concerning the points of special interest in the attack and defense of individuals was distributed to every adult with an invitation to answer in writing. From the reports thus obtained, the following summary has been compiled:

Whole number of persons actually attacked by something like diphtheria	112
Of these, cases without canker, though otherwise severe	40
Cases with canker, and all other symptoms of genuine diphtheria	72
Of these, cases that were cured	67
Cases that proved fatal	5
Number of cases treated by doctors	3
Of these, cases that proved fatal	2
Of these, cases that recovered	1
Cases treated with borax, alum, and various "nostrums," without attendance of a doctor, before the adoption of the ice and criticism treatment	9
Of these, cases that proved fatal	2
Of these, cases that recovered	7
Cases of clear diphtheria treated with ice and criticism	59
Of these, cases that recovered	59
Cases treated with ice, *without criticism,* that proved fatal	1

Number of those who acknowledge sensible
   benefit from criticism   50
Of these, cases that received *instantaneous*
   benefit from criticism   22

All who reported, except one, thought that criticism was a powerful and useful medicinal agent: and he thought it was *too* powerful to be used on persons in a certain feeble state of mind.

The following is a specimen of remarks accompanying many of the reports: "My experience in respect to *criticism* was new, and to me interesting. I was taken at night with a sore throat, which continued to grow worse, and the next day I had all the symptoms of diphtheria. Being no better at night, but rather worse, I sent for a committee. Their criticism immediately threw me into a profuse sweat, till I felt as though I had been in a bath; and before the committee left the room, my headache, backache, and fever were all gone. The criticism had an edge to it, and literally separated me from the spirit of disease that was upon me. I slept well, and in the morning called myself *well,* as indeed I was, with the exception of weakness. I attributed my recovery entirely to the Spirit of truth administered in *criticism,* and believe it to be the best remedy for soul and body. I regret my coldness toward it, and my fear of it in the past."

Daily Journal, April 30, 1866

The Saturday evening conversation turned on the care of the sick. It was thought there should be chastity and reserve in regard to turning our attention toward those that are sick. They should have good care, and all necessary nursing and sympathy, but the Community should go about its business and not suffer its attention to be distracted from its work and purpose and turn to the wounded and sick. This is the best way to help the sick. They need to give their attention to Christ and the church, and not to their own bodily ailments and symptoms. The Community is an army in warfare and on the march, and it will not do to stop the march or turn from the fight for the sake of the wounded. They must be cared for by the proper ones, but the fight must go on until the victory is won. The devil would like to divert our attention, and have us all thinking about and taking care of the wounded, giving him a chance to prey upon us where he likes. Even if those who are sick or wounded die, the most that can be said of them is that they are taken prisoners, and will have to be delivered up before the war closes.

Daily Journal, July 14, 1866

Our friend X complains of sleeplessness. We recommend him to adopt our theory that sleep is a far less necessary institution than is popularly believed, and seek a higher method of recuperation. The whole institution of sleep needs to be brought into the light, to be judged and purified, and placed on the basis of Resurrection-Repose. As it now reigns it belongs to the "fashion of the world which will pass away."

Experience is teaching us that six, eight, or ten hours sleep out of each 24 is by no means a necessity, and that there are other means of bodily and mental recuperation far more effective and life giving. We believe others will find this true if they study the matter in a scientific way.

A man may be dependent on sleep, and feel exhausted and weakened from loss of it, or he may rise above this dependence into fellowship with the unsleeping energy and life of God.

Circular, August 6, 1866

THE USE OF ANAESTHETICS IN DENTISTRY

As anaesthetics have recently found their way into our dentist's room, Mr. Hamilton thought it would be well to have some discussion about their use. The dentist said he confessed it seemed quite a fine thing to be able to pull teeth without giving pain, but he did not intend to use ether as a general thing. He thought a little spunk would be better if it could be had; and the grace of God would be a great deal better than either. Mr. Hamilton said, "I have an idea that most of the pain we are called to endure is good for us, and if we cannot get courage to have a tooth pulled without dodging the pain by taking ether, I don't know but God will corner us up and teach us the lesson of endurance another way."

Mr. I. had had good experience recently in having seven teeth extracted at one sitting without the use of any anaesthetic. At first he felt childish about submitting to the operation, but when he once made up his mind to it, he found it a profitable experience.

Circular, March 13, 1867

The whole number born in all the Communes since the beginning of the O.C. was 38; average, $2\frac{1}{9}$ a year.

Whole number of deaths, including Mrs. Martha Burt and Mrs. Jones, was 60; average $3\frac{1}{3}$ per year, allowing it to be 18 years.

The number seceding in that time was 115. On the 20th of February 1866 there were at O.C. 209 members; at Wallingford, 44; at Willimantic Silk-Factory, 3; at New York Agency, including Miss Nunn, 7; in all 263.

Counting Mrs. Bushnell, Mr. Leete, and Mr. Herrick, 22 members have been added the past year and one born.

Of the 209 persons young and old at O.C. on the 20th of February 1866, 63 were born in the state of New York; 60 in Vermont; 18 in Connecticut; 6 in England; 4 in Illinois; 2 in Ohio; 4 in Maryland; 1 in Wisconsin; 1 in Virginia; 1 in Ceylon; 30 in Massachusetts; 10 in New Jersey; 4 in Maine; 3 in Canada; 2 in New Hampshire; 1 in Iowa; 1 in Missouri; 1 in Scotland.

At Wallingford: 16 in New York; 9 in Connecticut; 13 in Vermont; and in Maine, New Hampshire, Massachusetts, New Jersey, Maryland, Michigan, 1 each.

At the New York Agency: in New York and Massachusetts, 1 each. Vermont 2, Connecticut 3.

At Willimantic: in Vermont, Connecticut, and Maine, 1 each.

In February, 1866, there were in the Community the following: Number under 10 years of age was 20; Number over 10 and under 20 was 28; Number over 20 and under 30 was 36; Number over 30 and under 40 was 29; Number over 40 and under 50 was 31; Number over 50 and under 60 was 36; Number over 60 and under 70 was 22; Number over 70 and under 80 was 3; Number over 80 and under 90 was 4.

Average age at O.C. was 37 years and 29 days; at Wallingford 31 years, 7 months and 14 days; at Willimantic, 28 years, 11 months and 3⅓ days; average age of the 6 in New York, was 31 years, 2 months and 5 days. The oldest on the 20th of February 1866 was 86 years and 12 days. The heaviest, 219¾ pounds. The lightest, 18¾ pounds. The tallest, 6 feet 2 inches and a half. The shortest, 2 feet 3 inches. Average weight, 132 pounds. Average height, 5 feet 2 inches and about a half. At O.C. 99 were male and 110 female; at Wallingford 17 male and 27 female; at New York six male and one female; at Willimantic, one male and two female.

Circular, September 28, 1868

COMMUNITY CHILDREN

Some years ago, when our principles were under a darker shadow of suspicion and foreboding than they are at present, there crept among us (whether from abroad or from inside whisperings we cannot say), an insinuation that our social life was "stunting" our young women. Two or three cases of small stature among the girls gave a slight plausibility to the notion. Whereupon the matter was put on trial by systematic investigations and measurements; and it was ascertained that more than three-fourths of our young women were taller than their mothers! And, what is still more curious, since then another set of young women have come on to the stage of womanhood that are taller and larger than any that have gone before them, actually threatening to overtop the men, and fill the Community in a few generations with Amazons and giants! It is now said that twenty-six of our young women are taller than their mothers!

To show what sort of a young crop of both sexes we are raising, we give the following recapitulation of weight:

Recapitulation:
Average weight of males—143¾ pounds
Average weight of females—136½ pounds
Average weight of males and females—139½ pounds
Average height of males—5 feet 9¾ inches
Average height of females—5 feet 4½ inches
Average height of males and females—5 feet 7½ inches

These are selected specimens, of course. Farmers always send their best to the fair. But we had to leave out others as good as these in making out the dozens. They do not exaggerate the strength of our rising generation.

Circular, March 1, 1869

The Community would make a clover field for a contagious disease, if sympathy of numbers were not as good for resisting a bad influence as it is for distributing it. When an epidemic like the influenza gets in among us it spreads fast for a while; but just as soon as the Community fully realizes its presence, and wakes up to a unitary push, it has to budge. Its back is broken at once. Tuesday evening we had some talk about the prevailing cold, and it was suggested that it might be taking advantage possibly of the liberality of our cooks. A family fast was proposed, and warmly cheered. It will be good, we said, for body and soul. It will promote thankfulness by helping us to realize how much enjoyment we have every day in going to our meals. It will strengthen the inward life. So Wednesday no table was spread for breakfast or dinner, though there was free access to the cupboards of course, for all who felt in need. The children made their breakfast on bread and water, having only butter additional for their dinner. They had a great many questions to ask, as "if the fast would go away tomorrow," but entered into it very cheerfully. The supper was enjoyed, of course, as the abstinence had been quite universal. We conclude the next time we wish to make a feast, the best way will be not to load down the board with good dishes, but fast two meals beforehand, and then get a common repast.

Circular, February 7, 1870

Eighteen of our youngest children have been seized, almost simultaneously, with that most disagreeable disease, the whooping-cough. All those who have had any acquaintance with the whooping-cough say that our children are having it "very light," as the phrase goes. None have missed more than one day at school, or at outdoor exercise and play. They were told at the beginning of the cough to resist it—not give way to it nor cough any oftener than they could help.

The other evening Mr. Noyes said to a few who had dropped in to his room: "Don't you think this whooping-cough nuisance has lasted about long enough? I don't believe in its 'having a run,' as they say, and that we must put up with it. We have dealt with diphtheria, measles, and such diseases, in a way to shorten up their visitations. I think we can do so with this nuisance."

A good, hearty, "indignation meeting" was the consequence of this talk and the results reported, so far, are very favorable to this mode of treatment. This morning we stepped into the Children's House and asked how the little ones did.

"Oh! Pretty well," said one of the Children's House women, "most all of them have gone out sliding." The bright red cheeks of these little ones as they came in from their slide suggested anything but sickness, and we did not hear a cough while we were in the room. Children, we believe, fall in naturally with this method of treating their little ailments; they like it, and thrive on it a thousand times better than on pills and syrups.

Circular, March 21, 1870

VITAL STATISTICS

The children born in the Community are nursed and cared for by their mothers until about the age of fifteen months, when they are placed in the care of the Children's Department, until the age of puberty. The period from two years old to fifteen is usually an isolated life, one of considerable risk; mortality even in country places ranges quite high.

The United States Census of 1860 gave the following rates in New England and New York State. They are probably some higher than would be the case in a purely country population, in consequence of the fact that the returns of the two great cities of New York and Boston are included:

> Under two years of age, 25% of total deaths.
> Between two and fifteen years, 20% of total deaths.
> From birth to fifteen years, 45% of total deaths.

Supposing in the city the percentage of infant mortality in the total deaths to be double that of the country, we must make a reduction in the mortality of the first class to represent the country mortality of these states. They will then stand:

> Under two years of age, 20% of total deaths.
> Between two and fifteen years, 20% of total deaths.
> From birth to fifteen years, 40% of total deaths.

Let us now see how this rate of mortality in the two periods of childhood compares with that in the Community.

Under two years of age (the limit to this period is put at the time when the children pass from the care of their mothers to that of the Children's Department which is a little under two years of age) the mortality in the twenty-one years of the Community's residence at Oneida has been 16% of the total deaths in the same time.

Mortality from two to fifteen years (period during which children are cared for by the Community) 8.8% of total deaths.

This percentage is caused by the death of two boys at eight years and one girl at two: they are the only deaths which have occurred in the Children's Department, which has cared for a constant average of thirty children for twenty-one years.

The mortality from birth to fifteen years of age, including both periods, was 24.8% of the total deaths.

Ratio of Mortality to Total Deaths in Two Periods
First Period—Under Two Years of Age

City Mortality (Philadelphia)	31%
Country Mortality (New England and New York Exclusive of Large Cities)	20%
O.C. Mortality	16%

Second Period—Two to Fifteen Years

City Mortality (Philadelphia)	14%
Country Mortality (New England and New York)	20%
O.C. Mortality	8.8%

Both Periods—From Birth to Fifteen Years

City Mortality (Philadelphia)	45%
Country Mortality (New England and New York)	40%
O.C. Mortality	24.8%

With new buildings in process of erection and entering upon an era of scientific propagation, we expect the next twenty years to show still more favorable results of Community life.

Circular, March 6, 1871

The innocents who are yearly tortured, if not slaughtered, by dosing with medicines would envy our children did they but know how the latter fare in this respect. To be sure, our children, with plenty of air, exercise, and amusement, and hardly ever exposed to contagious diseases, are seldom seriously sick. Still they are liable to colds and epidemic influenzas. We have had some trouble of this kind the past year, besides two cases of jaundice, several of hard teething, and various other slight ailments. But Miss A., the head nurse of the Children's Department, tells us that in the course of two or three years past, all the medicine she has used is a couple of doses of castor oil, and a few doses of wormwood. Anyone choosing to examine the shelf where she keeps her remedies would find nothing more potent than bottles of peppermint, glycerin, arnica, camphor, shellac, powdered borax, sweet oil, etc. with a couple of boxes of camphor ice and carbolic salve. If the children are a little ailing—have the headache, etc.—she gives special attention to their diet, keeps them quiet and above all cheerful. This last is the most important item of all. Indeed, Miss A. says that many an apparently grievous pain is entirely dissipated by getting the little ones to stop crying, and diverting their attention with a pretty picture or a story. The children when ailing are always encouraged to confess Christ, say they are not going to be sick, and will scarcely ever admit anything of the sort. It is evident to those who take care of the children that this resistance in their spirits to the attacks of disease does more towards curing them than the most potent remedies.

Circular, October 2, 1871

Old Connecticut, the land of steady habits and of two hundred years civilization, is "grievously tormented" this year with the fever and ague. It visited certain localities last season, but was quite circumscribed and exceptional, and hardly exceeded what is characterized as the sporadic form of the disease. This year it became epidemic, and though it has been most prevalent in the valleys, the hills have not been exempt from it, nor even the seashore. Various are the speculations as to the cause of the appearance of this epidemic here where it has been unknown for generations. One of the most plausible theories is that instead of seeking the cause in superficial, local circumstances, we should trace it to its spiritual source, and then we have a tangible enemy to meet and resist. Whether we deal our blows against *daimonia* or parasites, we are sure that the "head center" and instigator of the whole thing is the devil, the old "murderer," and that faith and courage are as potent in this field of warfare as any other.

Circular, July 15, 1872

Among the subjects discussed in our evening meeting this week was that of the inspired use of means. When our Community movement began here twenty-five years ago, our leader insisted that spiritual interests should occupy the first place in our attention whether we labored or not, whether we prospered externally or not. We adhered to this policy, though for several years we lost money continually, and to the worldly mind it appeared as though our ship must inevitably sink; but at last we reached a point where we could give all necessary attention to business and money-making and at the same time keep our faces heavenward. We have had similar experience concerning education, music, and other things. We have lately obtained liberty to use means in the case of disease. Heretofore we have had to withstand the tendency of the use of means to crowd itself into the place which rightfully belongs to faith, and being resolved that we would have faith whether we lived or died, we abandoned almost entirely the use of external remedies. Science we believe to be the true handmaid of faith, and that rightly joined they will give us a new and important purchase on the devil and his kingdom. Visitors sometimes say, "Why how many *old* people you have among you!" This remark has been made so many times during the last year or two that we began to think there might indeed be a preponderance of the aged among us. Appealing to some curiosity about the matter we borrowed the record-book of our statistician this morning, and running over the census taken January 1, 1872, made the following notes: Between the ages of 1 and 20 we have 63 members; between 20 and 40, 98; between 40 and 60, 68; between 60 and 80, 47; between 80 and 100, 4. There are 161 members under 40, and 119 above 40, leaving a majority on the sunny side of middle life. Upward of 50 of our prominent men and women who are now approaching 60, were scarcely 30 when they put the vigor of their young life into this movement 26 years ago.

Circular, February 17, 1873

We have disarmed winter, thanks to our admirable system of heating, so that we suffer none of the shrinking dread which is often experienced, especially by elderly persons living in ordinary habitations, at the approach of a long, rigorous, northern winter. Our chief concern is that we do not get overheated, living as we do enclosed in brick walls, with a summer temperature maintained day and night from the basement to attic. We are threatened with the enervating influences that pertain to tropical climates, and we have had to earnestly exhort the "heaters" to carry less head of steam. The women occasionally have to bestir one another to take constitutionals. We are under more than ordinary temptation to neglect outdoor exercise. Our great Community Mansion, containing two hundred inmates, provides good society and good distances of travel, so that there is no occasion to go abroad visiting. Our assembly Hall, which is in our home dwelling, makes it unnecessary to step outdoors to attend meetings, hear lectures, or find amusements. The Dining-Room, to be sure, is in the "Tontine"; but it is connected with the Mansion by a steam-heated, covered passage, through which persons who do not choose to encounter the storms and chills of winter may find their way. Thus while we rejoice that winter is so effectually kept at bay, and laugh at the winds and storms and pinching frosts, we must see to it that we do not become mere hot-house plants and lose the vigor, elasticity, and enterprise which our northern latitude is so well calculated to foster.

Circular, November 16, 1874

We have lately introduced into our building a small experimental Turkish Bath. Dr. Noyes thought that the large bathroom in our cellar might be fitted up at trifling expense so as to give everyone a chance to try the Turkish Bath. Then if we liked the effects of it we could erect more elaborate accommodations in the course of a year or two. The women could have the use of the bath during one part of the day and the men during the other part, and thus give all a chance to try it.

This plan was adopted. The family voted the necessary appropriation and the changes in the bathroom were made at once. A partition was put up, which in addition to one already in the room, made three apartments, to be used respectively as, "Hot-Room," "Shampooing and Cooling-Off Room," and "Dressing-Room." Three steam coils, two upright and one laid horizontally under a false floor, were put into the Hot-Room, enabling us to raise the temperature of the room to the desired point. A rubber hose with a perforated nozzle on one end was attached to a combined hot and cold water pipe in the Shampooing-Room, for sprinkling the subject after the shampooing, and so lowering the temperature of the body by degrees. The bathtubs in the Hot and Shampooing-Rooms were supplied with covers, thus making very good lounges.

Suppose you go in and take a bath. Having disrobed yourself in the Dressing-Room, you step into the Hot-Room. The thermometer hanging near the ceiling marks the temperature of the room at 150 degrees Fahrenheit. The object of subjecting oneself to that temperature is to invigorate the perspiratory system and thereby improve the circulation of the blood. You can recline on a lounge, or sit on one of the chairs put there for the purpose. Soon the sweat begins to pour off you. After perspiring sometimes very freely, you step into the Shampooing-Room, where an attendant tells you to lie down on the lounge, in which position he rubs you off in warm water. Now comes the best part of the bath; you are shampooed from head to foot; you are kneaded, rubbed, pressed, patted, spanked, squeezed, and tousled generally; after which you are sprinkled, rinsed, and deliciously soothed, the water being warm at first but colder gradually, till your pores seem to tie themselves up in hard knots. Then you feel tight and elastic. The doctor who has been feeling pulses, and looking after the persons in the Hot-Room to see that they are not affected badly by the heat, says to you as you return to the Dressing-Room, "Don't dress in a hurry, take plenty of time; for if you get to perspiring again you will lose part of the good effect of the bath." You dress slowly, and take your departure feeling much invigorated and certainly much cleaner.

Circular, January 18, 1875

Our Turkish Bath is small and rather inconvenient, it having been "fixed up" more as an experiment than for anything permanent. Small as it is, we find it a great luxury. It is patronized from ten in the morning until ten at night without cessation; the women occupying it until one o'clock P.M., and the men the remainder of the day. So popular has the bath become that our old bathrooms—though fitted up in excellent style with many modern improvements—are really quite forsaken. They are good, but the "Turkish" is better.

It is a "cure for every ill." If you are weary, nervous, headachey or backachey, an hour in the Turkish Bath will set you all right—make a new creature of you. That is, if you are discreet. In this as in everything else you *must not go to excess.* It is a good friend if you use it well; if you abuse it, you must suffer the consequences. There is such a thing as overdoing the matter. Excessive bathing is weakening. Some persons may feel improved by a daily ablution, while you are better off with only one or two a week. Find out what you can bear and then be judicious. Don't denounce the "Turkish Bath" *in toto,* because it does not happen to agree with *you.* The fact that you have some constitutional or acquired weakness which is somewhat aggravated by bathing need not deprive others who have none, and who are benefited and improved by it, from speaking in its praise.

The Turkish Bath has found universal favor with the family here, and we have heard of but two instances where persons have experienced bad results from taking it. It is highly probable that a large and more convenient bathroom will be built in due time. Until then we shall be quite content with such things as we have.

Circular, Wallingford, October 25, 1875

Since the fourth day of June last, the date of our opening of the Baths to the public, we have given 1,066 baths to our own family. As nearly as we can estimate, we put the total number of baths given for the four months ending October 14, at 2,132.

A large proportion of this bathing has been for luxury and precaution, what in medical phraseology would be called prophylactic bathing; but many baths have also been given for specific diseases. Of these we have treated the following cases, that is: chills and fever and intermittent fevers, 67; dumb ague, 85; rheumatism, 31; hay fever, 4; colds, 43; dropsy, 4; and paralysis, 3. The financial part of the summer's work can scarcely be represented by figures, since so many advantages have accrued from the Turkish Bath that they are impossible to compute in money value. As, for instance, the steady attention that our family is able to give to business without the hindrance and distraction of disease; the increased value of our real estate over what it might have yielded if we had forced it into the market as was proposed last winter. [Editor's note: The previous year the Wallingford Community had been so plagued by what they called "fever and ague," i.e., malaria, that they had almost reached the point of deciding to sell the property and wind up that whole branch of the Community.] The buoyancy and elasticity of spirit that all now bring to their work is a mine of wealth to us, and the general effect of the Bath upon the public opinion and on the state of feeling with reference to disease has undoubtedly helped to lift an incubus from this neighborhood. These and kindred considerations cannot possibly be reduced to dollars and cents.

VI

Education

Exactly how soon after their arrival at Oneida the communists were able to take time out for education from their really desperate struggle for existence is not recorded in their press, but study they would; men, women, and children, whether or not they ate, set about it with their customary enthusiasm. Whoever among the members had had experience as teachers, or, failing that, whoever was found to have special acquaintance with or ability in any particular branch of learning was drafted as teacher. Aside from the very young children, who were obliged to attend school a certain number of hours a day, the adult classes were formed by any who applied to join. During most years there was a fever of enthusiasm for education and whenever possible the Community tried to provide it. Five of the young men were actually sent to college and graduated, two as physicians, two as engineers, and one in law. During their vacations at home, these especially gifted boys acted as teachers of classes of students both older and younger than themselves. In music those with outstanding talent or training instructed the others. During the 1870's several of the most talented vocalists were sent to New York City for a brief course of training.

In 1855 there were evening classes in several subjects (*Circular*, October 4, 1855). Four years later *(Circular,* April 14, 1859), the pressure of work had abated enough for Noyes to exhort his members "to work hard this summer so that they might have school next winter." In 1860 (*Circular*, November 22, 1860) a class of the young men was given half of each day to devote to "systematic schooling," while another group, perhaps more deeply involved in the businesses, proposed to take only two hours out of the working day for study.

In the autumn of 1861, classes for various studies, musical practice, an hour for reading aloud, and a lyceum, which had not been mentioned before, filled the evening hours. The children's school was held in the original wooden Children's House which was still extant, but for the older or adult students, a separate school-house was desirable. They needed a university, they wrote (*Circular,* September 4, 1862), a building well-situated and well-planned.

At this time their ideas on education had changed somewhat. Children under six years old should be kept in the nursery, they said. From six to twelve they should be in a school to learn read-ing, spelling, obedience, manners, and prayer; from twelve to twenty they should attend an institute under a system of professor-ships which covered a fairly wide curriculum. After graduating from this, the students should go on and become professors them-selves, the whole forming "a foundation of instruction to the Com-munity at large." Such a system would "move in combination with labor, social and family privileges" (*Circular,* September 4, 1862).

In 1863 and 1864 there appears to have been a particular out-burst of enthusiasm for study. Astronomy, arithmetic, geography, grammar, Latin, French, music, and other subjects were eagerly attended by young and old. Reading for general entertainment preceded the usual evening meetings in the Hall; the orchestra practiced two evenings a week with a concert on Fridays. These and other activities besides and beyond their daily preoccupation in the various industries, presented a view, they wrote (*Circular,* December 17, 1863), of the "systematized intellectual course of the Community."

The next year they expressed some doubts about the schooling of the young folks, at least in large groups when, they said (*Circular,* April 11, 1864), "their mutual influence becomes stronger than the teacher's." In such cases, "horizontal attraction prevailed over the ascending," which was not a good thing. Little children under six taught each other, the younger emulating the older, but those older than ten or twelve were able to "generate a public opinion among themselves which could only be dealt with by a system of divide and conquer." The situation must have resolved itself, for the next fall (*Circular,* November 14, 1864) they had changed the system again and discontinued the infant school, while the older children had regular classes. The elder members of the Community were invited to make out a desired program of studies, and a committee did its best to arrange classes to accommodate as many as possible.

The Community discussed the university as early as 1859 (*Circular,* April 14, 1859). Financially, it was completely out of the question at that time, of course, but failing that they determined to make the Community itself a university for the education of the whole man, to strive for the cultivation of taste. It was a practical matter, too; the love of the beautiful could be made to harmonize with and quicken all kinds of manual industry; it was possible to combine the worker and the artist.

In 1869 (*Circular,* October 2, 1869) a new seminary building was constructed, spacious, light, and airy, and equipped with new desks and seats. The children were delighted with it and to celebrate the occasion were allowed to have supper on the lawn, after which they were drilled in marching exercises to the music of fife and drum. At the end of another year (*Circular,* May 15, 1871) they were examined in analytical geometry, trigonometry, Latin, and thorough bass—the art of harmonic composition. Adult classes also recited in the seminary when the children were not using it. Adult classes were open to all, with recitations of an hour each, meeting at times and places most convenient to the students, from an astronomy class meeting at 6:45 in the morning to late day meetings held anywhere from the Reception Room or the Community Hall to the upper room in the North Tower where Mr. Noyes conducted a class "aimed at a somewhat broader education" (*Circular,* December 17, 1863). This may have been the *Berean* Class, mentioned on pp. 158 and 180, which must have been comparable to a modern Bible class. The *Berean,* written by John Humphrey Noyes and published in Putney in 1847, was announced as a "manual for the help of those who seek the faith of the Primitive Church." It was, Robert Allerton Parker says in *A Yankee Saint,* "a compendium of all that Noyes had written from the days of the New Haven *Perfectionist* to the first article in the *Spiritual Magazine* in 1846. It was characterized as the Bible of the Oneida Community."

The Community's appetite for learning was nothing if not catholic. They studied Greek and Hebrew, astronomy and algebra, arithmetic, spelling, and grammar and many other subjects with passionate enthusiasm. One elderly man read a document relative to "bringing science into the kitchen and having their bread and biscuits, griddle cakes and shortcakes constructed on scientific principles" (*Circular,* August 5, 1867). At Wallingford Dr. Theodore Noyes actually did fit up an old ice house into a handy little laboratory in which he taught a class of nine the science of chemistry (*Circular,* December 2, 1867). Even the tiny children had a primary school which taught them with surprisingly modern kindergarten methods.

After the brick Mansion House was built, the library was an object of great pride and interest to all the members. Even in those days there were occasional lean years when economy was the watchword but even when the fare was meagre, the Community continued to buy new books and subscribe to a number of magazines and newspapers (*Circular,* March 22, 1875). The list of some twenty-five given here must have included some papers which exchanged with the *Circular* and were therefore not an expense, but Greeley's famous *Tribune* and *Harper's Weekly* and *Monthly* must have been paid for.

Circular, October 19, 1853

A visitor at Oneida, expressing her admiration of the enthusiasm for study that prevails there, mentions the following illustration:

"Mrs. N. (over 40 years of age) is very enthusiastic and says that she now cares nothing about her work, but wants to be studying all the time; while she used to be all absorbed in her work, and care nothing for books. She now attends to three regular studies—grammar, German and French—besides reading Cromwell and superintending in the kitchen."

This scholar is in the "sober afternoon of life," according to Mr. Greeley's horology—but quite in the early morning, if we judge by the freshness of her own feelings and tastes.

Circular, April 14, 1859

We should do all we can to make the Community a University for the education of the whole man. A great deal of the cultivation of taste—the love of the beautiful—and the time spent in educating this susceptibility was not thrown away. The love of the beautiful could be made to harmonize with and quicken all kinds of manual industry. The artist does not need to be an idler, a dreamer, a mere speculator. It is possible to combine the worker and the artist. We have begun that work here; the elements of art and industry are combined, to some extent, among us. The experiment is in its infancy, but on looking back a few years, we can see some progress. The office of art and the love of the beautiful, is to glorify labor and make it attractive. We do not want to make ourselves mere horses and oxen, which the mechanical, solitary labor of common country life tends to do. We want the highest kind of industrial energy and at the same time to be able to keep work subordinate to superior ends.

Circular, April 14, 1859

The legitimate object of labor was to secure leisure—leisure for social, intellectual and artistic cultivation. JHN remarked that this idea agreed with the scripture where it says, let us labor that we may enter into rest. He would apply the exhortation thus: Let us work this summer, so that we may have school next winter. Our young men have been deprived of their full term of schooling this winter in consequence of the demand for labor. He was anxious they should have an opportunity for getting a liberal education, for studying mathematics and the languages, and going through a thorough collegiate course. He hoped we should get ahead with the work, so that next winter they would all have the leisure necessary. He thought our ardor for the new house should not throw us out of the channel, the giving of our young men a good education.

Circular, November 22, 1860

A class of 26 young men are to have half of each day (the forenoon) to devote to systematic schooling, with a competent teacher to hear recitations. Another class of some half dozen of the more advanced young men, who depend pretty much on individual effort and ambition for an education, and who are interested to advance the business interests of the Community at the same time, propose to take two hours only of each day out of business hours (from one o'clock to three P.M.) for study. Still another class, denominated the Business Class, and which is principally made up of members of the other classes, is to meet evenings, and spend an hour or two in the study of bookkeeping, and whatever else is deemed essential to a thorough business education. In the absence of a schoolhouse or academy (which convenience we expect to realize at no very distant day in the projected new house), the family offers the school the use of the parlor, trusting that sufficient civilization has been attained to secure orderly behavior, and carefulness of the household rights and immunity. The Community sustains the school at considerable sacrifice from a business point of view, at a time like this, when every man and boy finds study and profitable employment. But education is a vital interest to us which we cannot afford to lose sight of or neglect, and our purpose is not to allow business to usurp the place that rightfully belongs to it.

Circular, November 7, 1861

Within doors, as the days shorten and evenings grow long, we naturally look around for expedients to fill up the interval between supper and meeting. Numerous small classes are formed for various studies or reading. Musicians, singularly or in duets, count themselves most fortunate if they can secure some vacant shop, schoolroom, or remote chamber for an hour or two of practice. The Lyceum and semi-weekly Singing School are attractive centers to the young and old of both sexes. Thus in various ways the busy, teeming life that finds itself repressed and checked by the forbidding frowns of a November sky for much outdoor enjoyment, seeks within for social and intellectual pleasure. The hour from seven till eight is again appropriated as in former seasons to reading aloud for general entertainment in the parlor.

Circular, January 9, 1862

A school for the young men is held daily, Sundays excepted, in the parlor, during the forenoon. It is attended by 22 persons, of ages varying from 14 to 26. The studies pursued are reading, spelling, grammar and composition, arithmetic, algebra and Latin.

A children's school is also held daily in the schoolroom of the Children's House. About four hours a day are occupied in this way; two in the forenoon and two in the afternoon.

Circular, September 4, 1862

I will endeavor to strike out a sketch of what might be accomplished in the educational line in the next few years. In the first place I should say that the interest of education among us will demand very soon the erection of a building adapted to that purpose. Such a building should be located outside and at a little distance from our present building. There I would place the *Community Institute*. When visitors come here they want to know if we have a school. I tell them, yes, but hardly know where to say it is located. It has thus far been movable and liable to be crowded upon by other demands for room. We need a University—a building well situated and planned.

Then for a system of education. I would have children kept in the nursery until they are six years old. From six to twelve I would have them placed in the department of the school where they would be taught reading, spelling, obedience, manners, and prayer. I would not expect more than that before they were twelve years old. With the rudiments of industry and art gained by association with the adults in Community labor, this would be the nucleus of an education. Then from twelve to twenty I would allow them to have the privilege of a school three or four hours a day, from the first of September to the first of March. I would have in this Institute a system of professorships. One, for instance, a professorship of elocution, which should include reading, spelling, oratory and composition; another of geography, mathematics and astronomy; another of languages. The young men should not consider their education finished when they had graduated from the school but should deem that they had only laid the foundation for further advance. They should calculate to go on and become professors themselves in such branches as their inclinations and talents led them to, so that while teaching others they would still continue to be learning themselves. Professorships of other sciences and arts would in time group around these, and the whole would form a fountain of instruction, not only to the young, but to the Community at large, by means of lectures.

Finally the system of education thus indicated would not be an isolated, monastic one, like the college systems of the day, but would move in combination with labor, social, and family privileges, opportunities for practical enterprise, etc., the whole harmonized and controlled by that general education which is the atmosphere of the Community—the science of the heart in our relation to God.

Circular, December 17, 1863

A prominent feature of winter life in the Community is the classes, which, as now organized, draw a large part of the adults into one or more studies and recitations during the day. While the children have their five hours school by themselves, and the young men have half of each day for study, with the privilege of attending any class held during that time, the classes are open as far as practicable to all adults, and occupied generally in their recitations about an hour each. The meetings are held in different places, and at such times as are most convenient to the members. The astronomy class meets in the Reception Room at 6:45 o'clock in the morning. Two classes in arithmetic meet at different times, one in the Community Hall, and one in the schoolroom. An enthusiastic geography class of nearly fifty members, men and women of many ages, attend in the schoolroom at 4:30 o'clock P.M. Maps are found very serviceable in this study. Besides these there is a grammar class of 30 or 40, an algebra class, a Latin class, a Berean class, a French class, music classes, etc. The superintendent of schools devotes most of his time to the instruction of classes and the general interest of education in the Community. While industry goes on with its usual vigor, the men and women of the Community are encouraged to think that they can spend time enough to attend at least one of these classes, and we are confident that no business interest suffers from it. A small class, with whom Mr. J. H. Noyes meets daily, and who aim at a somewhat broader education than the usual classes afford at present, make a studio of the upper room in the tower, four stories from the ground. The usual seven o'clock reading for general entertainment takes place in the Hall, when not interrupted by other occasions, every evening. The orchestra meets for an hour's practice on two evenings of the week, and various singing and instrumental clubs at other times. These operations, together with our evening and Sunday meetings, occasional lectures, and a concert on each Friday evening, present a view of the systematized intellectual course of the Community.

Circular, April 11, 1864

The school for the children is suspended for a fortnight. Friday was examination day. The children bore questioning very well. The outline maps which, unrolled, cover much of the wall of the schoolroom, had evidently made geography "easy." The line of a lake, a peninsula, an isthmus, or a sound is so well defined on these mammoth maps that the little children readily get the idea. There are no names on the maps; but in the recitations the pupil, having studied his geography and small maps, points out the boundary of any state, the course of any river, the location of any city mentioned by the teacher; or perhaps the teacher takes the pointer and asks the name of a country, sea, or city that he touches. There was no examination in grammar. The oldest class has studied it some this winter, but it takes a mature mind to really appreciate and digest this study. In its place the children have been set to writing compositions. Their performances, being read before all, have been subject first to the impulsive comments of the other children, and then to the strict criticism of the teacher. This exercise includes attention to grammar, and spelling, and handwriting, and is a good way to learn them all.

Circular, April 11, 1864

As to schools, they grow less in favor with the Community, only as they may be limited to small children. We prefer education in the family sphere—a diffusion of the young folks in the family, each receiving special attention from some superior associate or private teacher. In schools, much of the strength of the teacher is expended in counteracting the atmospheric influence generated by the aggregation of the scholars. Half the winter has to be spent in getting the moral supremacy, and that generally by hard measures. When children are old enough to be really put to study, the fewer there are together of the same age the better. Little children may be managed in flocks; they are receptive, and a good teacher can magnetize them; but older than 10 or 12, their mutual influence becomes stronger than the teacher's, the horizontal attraction prevails over the ascending. When we go into the nursery and see the little ones together, from the rosy age of five or six down to the toddler of 15 months, we are delighted, and think there never was so nice a way to bring up children. The little toddler wants no better amusement all day than he gets from the three-year old, and they are happy in being schoolmistressed and mothered and housewifed and officered by the class older. They teach each other to sing and say ABC, and rehearse the songs and tableaux of our concert evenings, and never tease to be amused. Example, at that age, seems to go the right way—the younger emulate the older. But when children are old enough to generate a public opinion among themselves, which may become an impenetrable barrier to superior influences, then "divide and conquer." Let them not pack in schools, but be retained in the family circle, and if in that circle there is a lively taste for knowledge, they will get their education by contagious enthusiasm. Where the family is a school, as it is in the Community, the young folks need not be a separate class; and this is a great advantage.

Circular, November 14, 1864

We have reduced our school proper to a minimum this season. It numbers about a dozen between the ages of seven and twelve. We have no infant schools as some of our most respected teachers insist that it is better not to feed children with books till they are full seven. Then they are ready to be put to learning without any dawdling. All above the age of twelve have an opportunity for study in classes which have regular hours for recitation, something after the college fashion. The classes were organized in the following manner: All the members of the Community (over the age specified) were invited to make out a program of the studies they would like to pursue this winter, the time which they could conveniently devote to them, and the teacher they would prefer. A committee was appointed to receive these programs and make arrangements to meet the wishes of all as nearly as possible. Of course the organization of the classes must be accommodated to our situation as a *family,* with business in the shops and out of doors that must be carried on, and women's work of all kinds in the house that cannot be dispensed with. We cannot all be at leisure at the same hour; so the times for the classes to meet were necessarily distributed through the day, to suit the convenience of the greatest number wishing to study particular branches. It was found for instance that some fifty wished to study arithmetic. Three classes were formed under three favorite teachers. One class in the higher arithmetic meets in the evening, consisting mostly of young men, taught by a young man. Another class elected Mrs. T. for their teacher, and meet at 3:00 P.M. This class is composed chiefly of adults, including several grandmothers, not to say many of our responsible housekeepers. Mathematics is found to be an excellent tonic for minds in a condition of more or less disuse, and is sought as a natural regimen by those who wish to increase their mental activity, and get that power of attention which is the first qualification of the general student. A third class in arithmetic meets at 9:00 A.M., and consists of boys between the ages of twelve and fifteen. The teacher of this class is responsible also for their further education, and appoints them to such other classes as he thinks best. There are two classes in grammar, composition included; twenty-six pupils in writing, several proposing to correct hands formed or *not* formed many years ago. Another considerable company proposed to wipe out this winter, with one desperate endeavor, the stain of bad spelling which the lack of education when young has left upon them. Three classes in Latin; four or five in French. These classes are in different stages of attainment. There is a class of young ladies in natural philosophy—a very ambitious class which will put us all to school I expect, and be inventing machinery before the winter is out. Good classes in geometry and algebra. Smaller ones in astronomy, chemistry, and thorough bass. There is scarcely a person in the Community who does not belong to one of these classes—most persons are members of two. The enthusiasm is intense. Where there is a jabber you may be certain it is about some study. Gossip will get the go-by this winter; and all attention to trifles.

Circular, November 16, 1866

The study of algebra is likely to become even more popular with us than it was last winter. We hear of one class that has already commenced, and many of the family are quite enthusiastic to improve every leisure moment in studying it in private. Some are commencing the study for the first time and others are hesitating and the question is heard to drop from their lips, "do you think *I* could learn algebra? Am I not too old and too obtuse to try?"

It appears to us that if anything will arouse persons from their apathy, and awaken their dormant faculties it is algebra. In this respect it seems well adapted to elderly persons, many of whom are averse to close thought and investigation. If the study seems hard at first sight, a little patience and perseverance will soon overcome the difficulty and it will become a real pleasure.

Circular, December 10, 1866

The educational campaign is fairly opened, and enthusiasm for study runs to the highest pitch. Our hired folks have caught the infection and have solicited our people to furnish them with a teacher as we did last winter. The question whether we shall do so remains to be decided.

One of our elderly women got so absorbed in mathematics yesterday that the premonitory stroke of the dinner bell failed to reach her ear and on she plodded, till some past one o'clock. She roused at length and on seeing some man putting on his overcoat preparatory to going away, she said, "What, you are not going until after dinner are you?" This caused a general laugh in the room, which recalled our mathematician from her abstraction to this mundane sphere, and to the physical wants of the body.

Daily Journal, December 11, 1866

Community people in times past have been considered lacking in concentrativeness, but had an observer passed through the Lower Sitting-Room the other day, he would have received quite an opposite impression. The idea of a "school-house on a battle-field," or the man watching the clock with a "here she goes, there she goes," in spite of all interruption, no longer seems impracticable. At the table sit three of the brothers, deeply engaged in the study of algebra. One is reading the example, another performs the operation, while a third demonstrates. These gentlemen perhaps, fancy themselves in class, and consequently their voices are raised considerably above a whisper to say the least. At the other side of the table sits a lady absorbed in arithmetic, apparently undisturbed. Two more are studying their lessons aloud (grammar and phonography), while the sewing machine in the adjoining bedroom keeps lively time. A rather facetious old lady (one of the occupants of the room) perceives the state of things, and proposes to herself to read aloud an article from the *Circular*. This she does in a clear loud tone, without in the least diverting the attention of anyone. All, with one exception, confess that they were ignorant of what was going on around them, and the reader from the *Circular* affirms that she never had so good an understanding of what she read before.

Daily Journal, July 29, 1867

A document was read last night from John Leonard relative to bringing science, particularly chemistry, into the kitchen, and have bread, biscuit, griddle cakes, short cakes, etc., etc. constructed on scientific principles. George E. and Theodore were called on and made some remarks upon the subject; the use of soda, fermentation in breadmaking, etc. It was thought that the kitchen group should study the different combinations in cooking, and as much as possible inform themselves as to general principles. Our bread has been very nice of late, but the biscuit deserves a good deal of criticism. It was thought that the women on the whole had done pretty well, but that perhaps the time had now come when they are to receive a thorough education in culinary science.

Circular, Wallingford, December 2, 1867

The dream we have cherished so long of establishing a university here seems to be taking a practical form. An ice-house which our annual supply of ice outgrew a year or two ago has been fitted up for the purpose of prosecuting the science of chemistry on a modest scale. It is a very unassuming building, only 12 by 13 feet in size; but it is warm and attractive inside. There is a little iron sink in one corner of the room, over which a faucet projects, indicating that water is a servant at command. Shelves have been put up and filled with the many curious and beautiful things which are used in the illustration of chemical facts. Theodore Noyes has commenced teaching a class of nine students who are pursuing the study of practical chemistry.

Daily Journal, Willow Place, December 4, 1867

Our classes are fairly started, numbering six—composition, university and elementary algebra, geometry, grammar and spelling. As we have no schoolrooms we receive our course in geometry and grammar at the tables where our dinner is served up to us. Our algebra and spelling classes seem thoroughly wide awake though they are held in the same room where some of the members are accustomed to spend many hours in sleep. All seem enthusiastic and inclined to improve their time and make the most of their opportunities.

Circular, February 5, 1868

Calling on Portia's school we find she has 17 scholars, five of whom are too young to study much, but she teaches them from a chart of "Familiar objects represented by words and pictures." This helps them to gain correct ideas of the form and color of objects. The older ones study reading, writing, spelling, geography, and arithmetic; and one of the little girls says "We speak pieces sometimes, too."

Circular, October 2, 1869

The children's school commenced this morning in their schoolroom at the new seminary. It is a light, airy room with eight windows; and the new shining desks and seats look very attractive. There are ten double desks (different sizes) with seats fastened to the floor. The whole cost $72.00. The children looked happy enough, as seated in their places they waited for their books that they might commence their studies. They all took their supper on the lawn this evening; after which, with music of fife and drum, they were drilled by Mr. C. in the marching exercises which they learned last winter in the Upper Sitting-Room.

Circular, February 14, 1870

Perhaps the most interesting class of all is that from four to five P.M. It is not a young men and women's class at all, and it does not belong to the regular school, though it recites at seminary. It consists of fourteen members, only one of whom is under thirty, the ages of the rest ranging from thirty to above sixty years.

Circular, May 12, 1873

We have had a revival of interest in the matter of spelling. Every evening between the hours of seven and eight o'clock persons gather in the South Sitting-Room, Upper Sitting-Room and Large Hall, and each one, furnished with a slip of paper and a lead pencil, takes his seat in readiness to write down words as they are put out from a spelling book. The vigilance committee has been appointed and is informed of all egregious errors. It was urged that we should not content ourselves until bad spelling is thoroughly weeded from the Community orthography; those who spell well (and this includes the greater part of our family) should assist in bringing the rest up to the perfect standard; and those who have heretofore been careless should seek criticism until correct spelling becomes a habit with them. There is no lack of enthusiasm on the part of anyone, and we feel sanguine in the belief that faulty orthography in the O.C. will ere long be among the things that "used to be."

Circular, December 8, 1873

An evening school has been started near the trap factory for the benefit of such of our employees as are engaged in the trap shop and silk factory and who live on Willow Street. Mr. Nelson, the station master at the O.C. Midland Depot, has consented to act as teacher; and although it is his first attempt as schoolmaster, he seems well qualified both by education and character to fill the place. Two rooms were fitted up in the old Willow Place house, the building formerly occupied by the Willow Place family, but now partly used as a machine-shop. The conveniences are somewhat primitive, with the exception of a handsome map presented by a friend in New York. The scholars, about 30 in number, ranging from 12 to 25 years, are divided into two classes according to their attainments, and each class meets three evenings in the week from six till eight. A great desire for improvement seems to possess all, and we hope the result of winter's work will encourage us to continue it every year.

Circular, October 12, 1874

Aunt Susan teaches the primary school. Every day, a half an hour after breakfast, and half an hour before dinner, the children go to her school. Aunt Susan has a variety of ways of interesting them. She has charts beginning with the ABC's, and increasing in difficulty to words of two syllables, each letter, word, or story handsomely illustrated in attractive colors; she has a large box which contains all the letters of the alphabet, distributed in small pigeonholes, which they often amuse themselves in forming into words; she has slates and pencils which she gives round occasionally when books are tiresome; she has new primers and picture-books; and above all she has a fund of Bible stories to tell them, which please their infant minds wonderfully. She has no difficulty thus far, in making them learn. They like to go to her room and hardly realize that it is a school; yet they improve all the time. She even finds it necessary to hold them back—they are so interested and eager to read their new books.

Circular, March 22, 1875

The literary "spread" on our library reading desk is something as follows: *The Daily Graphic,* lively, gossipy, and picturesque. *The Daily Tribune,* crammed with information but not always of the juiciest kind. If we add the Utica *Herald* and Utica *Daily Observer* the list of our dailies for the library is complete. The *Evening Post,* semi-weekly, has always been on our list, as also the semi-weekly *Tribune.* One of the best political sheets we take is *The Nation. The Independent* and *Methodist* are the religious papers.

Science is fairly represented by such papers as the Boston *Journal of Chemistry, Journal of Applied Chemistry, Nature,* and the *Popular Science Monthly.* The arts are not left out, as witness the *Scientific American, American Artisan, The Telegrapher,* and the *Manufacturer and Builder.* There are five standard agricultural papers, a paper devoted to music, and one to field and aquatic sports.

There are three health reform papers, two devoted to law and equity, four to spiritualism, and two to natural history. Philadelphia sends us the *Penn Monthly* and the *Journal of the Franklin Institute.* From St. Louis comes the *Journal of Speculative Philosophy.* The press of Boston makes a faint show in *Littell's Living Age,* and the *Youth Companion.* The popular *"Weekly"* and *"Monthly,"* of Harper and Brothers, and in fact the greater part of our current literature comes from New York.

VII

How They Played

Dancing which at this period was sometimes frowned upon by the godly of the outside world was extremely popular in the Community. Beginning in 1855 (*Circular,* November 8, 1855) they made a point of teaching everyone, both old and young, and after that first lesson, given in the wood-house chamber in the Old Mansion House, they danced whenever they could. Everyone enjoyed it, from the babies and the children from the Children's House watching in the gallery to all the grown-ups who took part. If there was a lull in their activities or a special victory to be celebrated, the Community members voted for a dance and it was urged that dancing be made an ordinance of worship and edification, not a "mere pleasure-seeking affair." Dancing was for the earnest and thoughtful as well as the young and giddy. All amusements were good, "so long as the spirit of improvement has place."

In their early days, 1857 (*Circular,* July 12, 1857), they adopted one of Fourier's suggestions and took up marching. If there was an outdoor bee for picking peas or weeding the garden or picking berries, the workers were summoned to the lawn by the notes of a clarinet. There they formed a line and then, to the music of the band, proceeded to march to the field. This ordinance, they said, proved very animating in its effect. How long their enthusiasm lasted is not stated but years later, in 1873, they noted (*Circular,* February 17, 1873) that not all the members danced as they used to do, and so suggested that they have an exercise which would bring them all out on the floor; everybody could walk, so marching was the very thing. They drilled for several weeks and finally gave an exhibition, much to their admiration.

188

The Birthday of the Cause (*Circular*, February 26, 1857), the twentieth of February, was from the beginning celebrated in the Community as the day on which their leader, John Humphrey Noyes, had announced Salvation from Sin. Their exercises were simple but heartfelt. In later years the programs were more elaborate but not more truly enjoyed.

Games of all kinds were popular in the Community, but perhaps croquet was their long-time favorite. Introduced in 1866 (*Circular*, August 20, 1866), the Croqueterie, as they called it, was marked out on the lawn, the stakes and bridges arranged for playing and soon it was all the rage. Even Mr. Noyes caught the fever and characteristically evolved a theory about it (*Circular*, August 17, 1866). Occasionally Croquet Fever got out of hand and the game was proscribed for a time (*Circular*, February 22, 1872), but it was a continuing enthusiasm, and in 1873 (*Circular*, January 1, 1873) it was played all winter by men, women, and children on a court surrounded by walls of snow three feet high.

Baseball was another outdoor game which was very popular. "A game of ball in the East Meadow" was noted (*Circular*, September 30, 1858), but the sport was apparently not really organized until later. In 1862 (*Circular*, May 8, 1862) a number of young men signed up for it and took it up with their usual enthusiasm. Ninepins was spoken of as a healthy exercise. Apparently they constructed some sort of rude outdoor alley, but lack of further mention of it suggests that it did not catch on.

Indoors, chess was "cultivated with enthusiasm" to such an extent that at times they were obliged to make a rule that any game started at noon and not finished when the bell rang for work should be counted as a tie (*Circular*, October 21, 1858). The Community approved what they called "fits of unitary enthusiasm" (*Circular*, November 6, 1871), but they liked to "modulate gracefully from one interest to another after the inspiration had run out." One such modulation was from chess to dominoes which amused them for a time. They favored simple games of chance rather than complicated games of skill, as involving less antagonism. The question of playing cards was discussed (*Circular*, October 21, 1858), and finally such games were dismissed as objectionable. They refused the game "not because it was wicked but that it was not expedient."

Picnics or "ruralizing" were always a popular amusement in the Community for both old and young. The *Circular* records many such excursions, from the earliest days to the latest. They noted (*Circular*, August 25, 1859) that such occasions "educated their children more than by meetings or schools." Another kind of picnic was a favorite—butternutting. Nut trees were plentiful on the home domain, and gathering and cracking the nuts was an afternoon's occupation. Sometimes these excursions were for small groups, but often the whole Community family attended and a picnic meal was added to the affair (*Daily Journal*, September 16, 1867). An expedition to pick mushrooms was another popular event at the right time of year, and their account of it (*Circular*, October 2, 1871) prints their favorite recipe for preparing this delicacy.

Not all their socializing was done by the whole family. The communists found it pleasant occasionally to gather in small groups. Parties were got up in odd, out-of-the-way places, in the sewing-room or the Dairy House for someone's birthday. Such affairs gave zest to Community acquaintance and fellowship (*Circular*, August 19, 1858).

From the beginning to the end, the Community was devoted to music, both vocal and instrumental. In the early days their orchestra was only a few flutes and a couple of violins and perhaps a horn, but as soon as they could afford it they bought more and better instruments, and the enthusiasm for practicing swept the Community. As they said (*Circular*, May 22, 1871), in a musical family of two hundred—this was in the seventies—there seemed to be no part of the Mansion House where someone was *not* practicing anything from a bass viol to the kettle drums, but no one complained. A few years later they were rich enough to afford a small cottage, somewhat removed from the Mansion, where the piano and any other instrument could be played and vocalization could take place out of sight and hearing of the unmusical members.

Parlor music was instituted in 1855 and much appreciated at first. Later (*Circular*, February 20, 1858) the Community was criticized generally for "want of appetite" and a "hypercritical taste." They did not indicate whether or not the parlor music continued in the face of this discouragement, but in 1863 they note (*Circular*, August 27, 1863) that in place of the noon orchestra practice four times a week their public music would resolve itself into an evening concert once a week. The next year during the winter they gave twenty-three weekly concerts to which the public was invited (*Circular,* March 21, 1864). Their organization comprised twenty-two performers besides the conductor. They had also a small orchestra, a choir of twenty-five singers, two or three quartette clubs, and three or four soloists. The children also were taught to sing and dance, and their performances were enormously popular both with the communists and the outside audience.

Theatricals also were popular. Cantatas, five-act plays, humorous skits, and comic songs were in order for some years, but they required a great deal of effort and practice, and later, in 1870, everyone was so busy that these formal performances were given up; instead, as they said (*Circular,* March 21, 1870), their theatricals "did themselves." If anyone had a song, a recitation, or a feat of gymnast they were welcome to perform on any Sunday evening. The Community was surprised to find these concerts so amusing and to discover so much unsuspected talent among their members.

In summer swimming was a delightful sport; after a pond was made at Willow Place (*Daily Journal,* August 17, 1866) both women and men—at different hours—took pleasure in it. They found it so refreshing that they invited the men and women of Turkey Street, at stated hours, to use the pond, and it became a popular if not fashionable watering place. After the cottage at Joppa—on Oneida Lake—was available (*Circular,* November 25, 1872) the Community people enjoyed not only swimming but boating and fishing. The Willow Place pond was also used in the winter, but only by a few hardy masculine spirits, of whom Mr. Noyes was one.

The cottage on Oneida Lake was "lonely enough for those who think it lonely" (*Circular,* November 25, 1872), but the Oneidans enjoyed it immensely. Parties of six or eight went there often in summer, and, with the fish they caught and other goodies from home, their menus were positively lavish compared to the fare at the Community. Thus fortified, one ambitious couple (*Circular,* July 21, 1873) walked the whole twelve miles home, with "very little fatigue but an excellent appetite for supper."

The description of Christmas in the Community (*Circular,*

January 1, 1874) is charming but notable mainly because for many years the communists—partly because they could not afford it—took little notice of the great day. Even in 1874 they do not mention any giving of gifts amongst the adults, but the rapture of the littlest children at receiving their new boots must have given extreme pleasure to their elders who, despite their strictures against "spoiling" the children, doted upon them as fondly as any parents in The World.

Circular, July 4, 1852

FESTIVAL AT ONEIDA

Our strawberry festival yesterday, all agree, was the most exquisite thing of the kind that we ever witnessed. Early in the morning some of our people constructed a bower of sweet scented evergreen cedar in the children's playground, capacious enough to seat 75 or 100 persons, with tables interspersed. Another party engaged in picking and preparing the strawberries of which over seven bushels were gathered before noon from our garden bed. Another party prepared biscuits, etc., for the entertainment. Various groups of rustic chairs and tables of fantastic pattern were arranged in shady spots about the grounds. Everything was done easily and with enthusiasm.

About 80 families of our neighbors and of citizens of Vernon, Oneida Castle, and Oneida Depot had been invited to partake of strawberries and cream. Soon after 3, our friends began to arrive; and though most of them were strangers to a majority of the Community, they were nonetheless welcome. The house was thrown open, and those who pleased were attended in the stroll through the gardens, or were invited to amuse themselves in their own way. Some took their way to the arbor where an abundance of strawberries, cream, and sugar were waiting their acceptance. Parties continued to arrive for about two hours and there was said to be 300 guests. The attendance and singing of the Community children was apparently gratifying to our visitors. The company interested themselves in the house and on the grounds, with picking strawberries and conversation until about 7 o'clock, when all withdrew. We were happy to be able to supply many of them with strawberries to carry home.

Circular, August 9, 1855

On the whole, it is a progressive summer with us. Music—social, industrial, vocal and instrumental—and the art of being happy has been

cultivated with encouraging success. There is considerable private reading and study going on but for the present a suspension of any intellectual exercises in concert. The summer is the season perhaps for social
and physical expansion, in the winter for spiritual and intellectual
growth.

Circular, April 8, 1854

A BIBLE GAME

You heard something of the Bible play we have been inventing
here. I will try to give a clear view of it. For an evening sport we arrange ourselves in a circle around the family fire, forming a class as in
a school. Two or three of the best readers are appointed to take turns
in the office of master. The master opens a Testament at random with
the point of a knife, and reads the first verse that meets his eye, calling
on the head of the class to tell what *book it is in.* If the answer is correct,
the master says, "right," and opens again, putting a new verse to the
next in the class. If the answer is not right, he says, "the next," and so
on until the answer is correct. Then he opens a new verse and goes
on as before.

This is one form of the game but the radical idea admits of many
variations. Instead of ranging through the whole New Testament, we
may confine ourselves to a single book, and opening that book at random
as before we may ask what chapter the verse is in.

Another method might be to confine ourselves to a chapter, and
ask the number of the verse. And on the other hand, we might extend
our range over the whole Bible, and ask for the book or the book and
the chapter, or the book and chapter and verse.

We began with Matthew, and have spent one evening upon it, but
find it necessary to give it another. All are much engaged in studying
the book before the trial. Even the children are going over it. The
mental exercise is as good for all and is exciting as 'tis in chess or
checkers, or any other common games of skill. A good memory and
quick power of calculation will be called for and developed. Then combined with this sport and exercise of mind, we shall be receiving *edification* from what we play with.

Circular, July 12, 1855

We have lately found it pleasant and profitable to avail ourselves
of one of Fourier's suggestions in marching out to our field service with
music; and it proves very animating in its effects. At the sound of the

clarinet, after supper on the lawn, announcing the preparation for a Bee for picking peas, weeding in the garden, or whatever the work is, all hands gather with great hilarity, and form a line under the directions from Captain K. The band then performs some lively marches, to which the whole company march in order to the field, turning corners and changing from platoons to single file, as the width of their way requires it, in regular military style; the sportive nature of which gives us a fine zest for work when we get to the place of its performance. At the close of the work, the music again sounds a call for all to assemble at some convenient point, where we take up our line of march again for home in a similar manner. For the sake of variety, sometimes all join in singing one of our home songs and step to the time of it. On arriving at home Captain K. occasionally gives place to some of the recollections of his former officership, in putting us through a few simple military evolutions, which makes an entertaining exercise for men, women and children. Sometimes we march to the reservoir and parade in order on its green slope to witness the sportive feats of some of the young men, clad in swimming dresses, in the water. This introduction of music to our field work is a somewhat novel feature in our Community life, but we find it chimes in beautifully with the growing spirit of sport and ardor among us.

Circular, November 8, 1855

In the place of our usual classes after tea, we had a general dance, or rather a drill in the first rudiments of dancing, including all in the Association who were pleased to be present and stand up on the floor. For a hall, the lumber in what we call the wood-house chamber (a place for drying clothes in the winter and the general storeroom for beds, bed clothes, boxes, bags, bundles and budgets) was arranged in as compact a manner as possible under the eaves, and a space cleared that would allow 30 or 40 couples to dance at once. It was lighted by hanging lanterns, and looked withall cheerful and unique, the laughing children perched on the piled-up boxes, and musicians seated in a rude alcove reserved at one side.

Floor-masters were appointed who knew how to dance, and we formed ourselves, to begin with, in two rows, across the length of the floor, displaying a greater variety in heights and ages than perhaps ever met for the same purpose before. The first lesson was how to make a *bow*, and as the curtsey loses its grace and fitness in the short dress, both sides were instructed in the same action. Next we practiced the ten steps, first with counting and then with music. Tall men who had never used their feet to any such tricks made their first essay; and thanks to a good free spirit of improvement there was a fair share of aptitude displayed in learning—the feminine half rather excelling, it was said. We danced at last two simple figures, which by a judicious matching of those who could dance, with novices, went off very well. The effect was altogether good. Here was a fascinating pleasure all pervaded and salted with the spirit of improvement. It was a combination of the old and the young, a good object in all social economy. Parents and children danced together. We might have mentioned in our former allusion to the subject this good feature of the amusement and association which does not attend it elsewhere—the marriage of sobriety and playfulness, vivacity and wisdom.

Circular, January 3, 1856

A fortnight ago the boys were much engaged in trapping muskrats, employing their play hours in hunting for traces of these animals along the banks of the creek and setting traps in likely spots. They succeeded in catching a dozen or more, and will not need to buy any fur for their caps this winter. Within a few days, winter whose tardiness we can never blame, has suddenly assumed its sway and put an end to trappings; but to make amends it has frozen over the creek and pond and made a stage floor for the skaters. Scarcely had the first preparations been made when the boys rushed on and their precipitant experiments had to be checked by the wiser part of the Association. Today the dare-danger spirit has met with a good criticism. One of the boys advancing near the dam, the ice on which he was parted from that behind him and shot over the brink with him on it. He had the presence of mind to jump into the water as he descended, and being a good swimmer, got to shore with only a wetting; but it was quite a perilous skate. Circumstances gave occasion for a serious talk in the evening meeting in which the spirit that cannot have sport without the excitement of danger was criticized. Skating itself is an amusement in favor with all in the Association; and it is not right it should be brought under condemnation, as it will be by connection with venturesome bravado. It was thought that there were special temptations in skating and swimming to court danger, and that it required special care to keep these sports simple. The lad who went over the dam was criticized for a little too much zeal in investigation.

Circular, February 26, 1857

BIRTHDAY OF THE CAUSE—PROGRAM FOR THE 20TH

1. Breakfast and Bible reading at the usual hour.
2. The bell will be rung at 11 for leaving work.
3. At 12 gathering in the parlor.

   Exercises
   1. Song, "The Morning Light is Breaking."
   2. Address by H. W. Burnham.
   3. Volunteer speeches, sentiments, and communications.
   4. Song, "The Resurrection Hymn."
4. Dinner. First table at 2, second at one-half past two.
5. General bee for clearing off the tables, etc.
6. "Guy Mannering" continued reading at 4 in the parlor.
7. Dancing at 5:30 in the dining room.
8. Supper and meeting in the parlor at 8.
9. Instrumental music at 9.

What shall we say of the banquet? Where were the stuffed turkey, the roast beef, the savory sparerib, the turnips and onions, the mince pies and plum puddings, the gravies and pickles of old Thanksgiving dinners? They were actually forgotten. We doubt if they were once thought of; while we made our repast of the simple *trimmings* of customary feasts, coffee and wheat bread and butter, preserves and custard pie. The bread and butter were sweet as nectar to be sure, and the coffee, by habitual disuse, was rendered not only a luxury, but a "cup of cheer." This was amusingly manifest by the swell and surge of talk and merriment that soon filled the dining room.

Circular, August 12, 1858

We might tell our friends about the children's picnic today, how they sung on starting—how four large wagon-loads of them with a few attendants, drove to some woods on the west hill some six miles distant, how when there, the baskets of bread and butter, and cakes and nuts and raisins were disposed of, how presents were distributed to each of the children as an acknowledgment of their faithfulness in braiding, how they swung, danced, played blindman's buff, fox-and-geese, and football, how they closed with songs and returned at five o'clock to supper in the schoolroom.

Circular, February 20, 1858

Discussion about our parlor music. Some of the band complain of want of appetite and propose to play only once a week. The family and others of the band voted otherwise. Want of appetite was ascribed to daintiness and hypercritical taste, which is not disposed to enjoy amateur preformances. Plain, common food will not do—we must have oysters and turkey, daily concerts or something better all the time. It was thought that our parlor music, which was instituted about three years ago, had really done more for the interests of the art of the Community than any other thing—that great improvement had been made, and there was everything to encourage its continuance.

Circular, April 22, 1858

Some criticism of the tendency to excessive chess playing manifested by some members. The effect was detrimental to business and to prompt habits at industry. It has been common to see a group gathered around the chess board, the lookers-on apparently as much interested and absorbed as the opponents; and the result has sometimes been that the party would get so deeply enlisted in the game that the bell calling to work would not be heeded, and a half hour would be subtracted almost imperceptibly from the time allotted to business. The exhortation or criticism was thought to be timely, and seemed to be appreciated and thankfully received.

Circular, August 19, 1858

Our large dining room, with its three ranges of tables seating about one hundred persons, is the common and pleasantest resort of all at meal time, but occasionally there are smaller "parties," as they are called, got up in odd and out-of-way places, that have peculiar zest for variety at least. We have the fortune today to be invited to such an entertainment. We were asked by a matron of the family to repair at three o'clock to the sewing room which, in the present narrowness of our quarters, serves also as the office and has the bookkeeper's desk facing the sewing machine.

At about the same hour there happened to be two other "parties"; one of the gardeners and their guests in the dining room, and one by a young girl in the Dairy House on her birthday. Such affairs are not over-frequent, but occasionally they break in pleasantly upon the common course, and give zest to Community acquaintance and fellowship.

Circular, September 30, 1858

Notice on the bulletin at noon: "A game of ball in the east meadow this afternoon—quit work at three. Dance after supper." In the evening a talk on the subject of dancing. It was urged that dancing with us should be made an ordinance of worship and edification and not allowed to become a mere pleasure-seeking affair; and hence the more earnest and thoughtful part of the Community should take the lead in it, instead of the young and giddy. All such amusements are found to work well so long as the spirit of improvement has place but ill when that is displaced by a noisy pleasure-seeking spirit.

Circular, October 21, 1858

The question of card-playing was discussed. Is it expedient to have it in the Community? Chess is cultivated among us with enthusiasm. It is a favorite noon recreation and you may see a game in the parlor after meeting almost any evening, the group around enjoying it equally with the players. Some of us like to play over the games between Morphy and his European competents, and other games between distinguished players reported in chess journals. On the whole we are lovers of chess and sympathize with the enthusiasm of the times on on this subject.

But shall we tolerate cards? To a certain class of persons they are more attractive as a recreation than chess. Are they more objectionable? We think they are. They do not combine improvement with sport. Their associations are evil. They put us in rapport, as you may say, with a diabolical sphere. They are offensive to the best moral sense of the world and we should justly incur the worst suspicions if cards were our pasttime. Let them be refused: not on the ground that it is wicked to play them, but that it is not expedient.

Among the things touched upon was the habit of chess-playing. It was proposed and unanimously voted that we hereafter consider it one of the laws of the game of chess to call it a *drawn game* at the ringing of the bell. No matter how near a *checkmate* at that moment the game should cease, and be pronounced a *drawn game*.

Circular, August 25, 1859

Saturday afternoon we ruralized; the whole family, down to the titmouse of all, adjourned to the woods and spent the half day. The place was about a half mile from home, near the western boundary of the domain, in a grove by the borders of the creek. There the kitchen group had prepared a feast, to which the apiary, the fruit-cellar, etc. had contributed. A cooking stove which sent its steam and smoke up through the trees and served to bake potatoes, etc., made it seem gypsyish and camp-like. The children had a fine swing, and the titmouses were in a delirium of wonder of course. We had music—songs of praise and instrumental music. There was some laughing too, to make the woods echo. . . . This is all very undignified play you will say; but we do not think so much of dignity as some do—we think more of sympathy—of fellowship between the old and the young. We expect to educate our children by social influence more than by meetings or schools.

Circular, May 8, 1862

We overheard a company of young men at work the other day arguing strongly in favor of the theory that "all work and no play makes Jack a dull boy." Afterwards, a notice appeared upon the bulletin inviting those who would like to play baseball occasionally during the coming summer to put their names to the paper underneath. Quite a list of names was soon made out and yesterday afternoon the first game was played. We asked a usually quiet, undemonstrative youth if he intended to join in the amusement. "Yes, indeed!" he replied with energy and added that it was the most fascinating game he knew of. And so it appears, judging from the enthusiasm with which men and boys enter into it.

Circular, March 21, 1864

Our winter series of free concerts, twenty-three in number, was completed on the evening of the fourth. When the proposal was made last fall to give a series of weekly concerts during the winter, it seemed a large undertaking with the great press of business we were under; but remembering that "where there's a will there's a way," we have appointed an executive committee, organized our musicians, vocal and instrumental, and all enthusiastically set about carrying out the plan. As to our *matériel,* there was, firstly, the orchestra of twenty-two performers besides the conductor: six violins, two violin cellos, one double base, two flutes, two clarinets, one piccolo, two cornets, two horns, one base tuba, two drums, and one harmonium. Secondly, the small orchestra of eleven members, five violins, one violin cello, one double base, one flute, one clarinet, and two horns. This organization was used principally during theatrical performances, playing between the scenes.

Another occasional resource was the brass band of nine instruments. Besides these, for filling in, we had piano music, violin and piano, cornet and piano, and other combinations. The harmonium generally accompanies songs.

Our vocal music consisted of a choir of some twenty or twenty-five singers, two or three quartette clubs, one club of eight male voices, and three or four solo singers.

The programs were generally made of about half-and-half vocal and instrumental music, with an occasional selection from the drama, recitation, a tableau, or a dialogue, generally ten or twelve pieces, occupying from an hour to an hour and a half.

Soon after we commenced the concerts we found that, to make them entertaining to all classes, old and young, a sprinkling of a comic was quite necessary, in fact indispensable. According to this idea, we invited H. to give us a weekly contribution from his stock of comic songs. He cheerfully complied, and so successfully that his weekly appearance on the stage was always welcomed with a smile of satisfaction in anticipation of the hearty laugh which never failed to crown his efforts.

The Children's Department also contributed some very effective pieces. A row of little ones from ten years down to two, all singing and acting the well known song, "One Finger, One Thumb Keep Moving," was sure to bring down the house. One of the tableaux in which they took a prominent part was a representation of the Mother Goose melody, "There was an old woman who lived in a shoe, she had so many children she didn't know what to do."

These concerts were started for the benefit of our workmen and near neighbors, being free, however, to all who were disposed to come. During the winter the interest in them increased to such an extent that not infrequently we found the size of our Hall, the capacity of which is sufficient to seat about 900, entirely insufficient to accommodate all that came.

Circular, October 23, 1865

A Game. At two o'clock P.M. there was a rousing game of baseball. Some brilliant exploits might be recorded if time and space allowed. Let it suffice to state that one side scored fifteen runs and the other thirty-five and that all enjoyed the sport.

Circular, January 31, 1866

There seems to be considerable quilting going on among the indoor folks now days. We heard of two quilts under way yesterday. According to our observations these quilting parties are generally ended with a supper, rather more select than the general course, to which a suitable number of the brethren are invited. The event is thus made memorable for a season, and the recipient of the quilt has the satisfaction of receiving with it a pleasant portion of the Community spirit.

Daily Journal, June 27, 1866

A yard is being enclosed on the edge of the pond at Willow Place for the accommodation of bathers. It is to be furnished with steps descending into the water, and a spring plank.

Circular, August 20, 1866

For some time, preparations have been going on for inaugurating croquet among us. Yesterday afternoon the croqueterie being in readiness, an arena was marked out on the lawn in front of the rustic summer house, and the stakes and bridges arranged for playing. Several experimental games were afterwards played. The game bids fair to prove very entertaining and to afford a pleasant and graceful exercise. We have not yet sufficiently mastered it to enable us to speak intelligently of all its beauties, or its scientific points, but it seems to combine in a rare degree many interesting qualities.

Daily Journal, August 27, 1866

Mr. Noyes remarked this morning, after playing a fine game of croquet, that he had got a new view on the subject of competition. He says that accepting our doctrine about the war, that God is on both sides in every fight, as true, we may apply it to all games and in so doing find that there is a legitimate place for competition and that it is a good thing. By loyally recognizing God in the game, and that he controls the result and gives the victory to whom he pleases, we may enter into it heartily and exercise our utmost skill and power to win. In this way it becomes a field for the development and manifestation of character and individual power and destiny, and competition, instead of being a mere exhibition of antagonism, becomes a harmonic cooperation with God.

Circular, September 17, 1866

One secret of the popularity of croquet evidently is its adaptation to both sexes. Then the question arises, how can the men best preserve this social and civilizing feature—the partnership of the women? First, I should answer, that the gentleness and moderation of the women modified the tendency to excess and competition in the men. The violent way in which many of the men croqueted their opponents' balls, seems very directly calculated to spoil the attractiveness of the game, especially for the women, and more or less for all parties. Very hard striking of the balls is clearly at variance with the character and intent of the game, and is repugnant to the more refined and delicate feelings of those who engage in it. Again, violent striking is destructive to the implements, the balls and mallets.

Daily Journal, September 16, 1867

The Community had a grand butternut crack and roast corn picnic yesterday P.M. at three o'clock over on the island. The day was as fine as a day could well be, and everything conspired to make the affair an enjoyable one. Most of the family were present, and also the Willow Place commune. As we approached the spot we perceived active preparations being made for a roast and a crack. Four fires were blazing, and long sharp-pointed sticks for holding the ears of corn while roasting were furnished for all who wished to try their hand at this primitive mode of cookery, the stones and hammers for cracking the butternuts. Heaps of corn and piles of butternuts were in readiness and the hammer and the roaster were soon in vigorous use.

The kitchen group also furnished the company plenty of the nicest kind of bread and butter, to which ample justice was done. Then followed sports—leap-frog, fox and geese, blind man's buff, etc.

Some of our family are addicted to astronomy, and employ an hour or two on clear evenings in tracing the constellations by the aid of Burritt's map of the heavens. A young lady pointed out to me last night six stars of the first magnitude, all visible at ten o'clock; that is, *Regulus, Arcturus, Spica, Vega, Altair,* and *Antares.*

Daily Journal, July 3, 1867

Who does not remember how every Wallingford journalist has very properly eulogized the beautiful river—the splendid accommodations they have for bathing, and how we, thinking of our muddy creek, awkwardly kept silence, well knowing we had no such luxury of which to boast. Will not someone or all of our sisters there, make their very prettiest bow and congratulate us on at last having an excellent bathing place?

Yesterday afternoon, by the kindness of Mr. W., who procured a conveyance and officiated as driver, we (a party of 14 women and girls) had the pleasure of going to the Willow Place pond, where for half an hour our enjoyment was intense. We will not attempt to describe the delight; all who have tried it know the sensation, and those who have not we hope will soon have an opportunity.

Daily Journal, July 26, 1867

A slight change in the hours for bathing was made. It is desirable that the outside women be permitted the exclusive use of the pond from 6:30 to 7:30 as it is the only hour they can have. The pond promises well to become a popular if not a fashionable watering place. The prejudice, if there has been any, among the women of the neighborhood, is gradually wearing off and every day introduces a number of new-comers to the luxury of the bath. A company of them came at their appointed hour this evening, and seeing a number of our men pitching quoits in the orchard, inquired if it would be proper for them to go to the bathing place. They were told that it would be, so they went right along without minding them. Thirty-four women from O.C., including some little girls, came over today. It is estimated that no less than 100 different persons received the benefit of the pond today.

Daily Journal, September 30, 1867

Last night just before ten o'clock we heard the music of voices and the ringing laugh in the old reception room, and, in quest of items, we ventured to look in and see what merrymaking was going on at that late hour; and sure enough there was a company of six, with a basket of butternuts, grapes, bread and butter, cheese and cake, seated in a circle (some on the floor) enjoying a sumptuous repast, not the least of which was, if not "a feast of reason," at least "a flow of soul." The company with four more had started just before night for a picnic, but being overtaken by cold and rain, they retreated, and not wishing to be entirely thwarted in their plans, they had chosen this unique way of disposing of the contents of their baskets.

Circular, Willow Place, November 16, 1868

Punctually at five o'clock, the bathers, JHN, EHH, and WHW, may be seen coming in Indian file over the hill from O.C. After a moment's chat at the stove, they start for the pond, reinforced by several of the Willow Place boys. Let us, being of the male persuasion, go down and watch them spring from the platform into the water, which this morning was covered with a thin film of ice. It is a cold, wintry day, and the water promises to be a "close fit," as they say. The operation of undressing is performed in a twinkling, and there goes George E. on a dead run down the slope, across the platform, and into the water, with a spring that carries him ten feet out into the cold element. Of course he is out nearly as quickly as he went in, laughing and glowing with the reaction which follows the immersion. After him in quick succession go the rest of the company, and in fifteen minutes after they left the house, they are again conversing by the fireside.

Circular, March 21, 1870

Our theatricals do themselves this winter. Formerly it required laborious preparations. The old play of five acts, the cantata, the overture, were brought out through much tribulation of rehearsal, scenic contrivance, and costuming; but this is the era of spontaneity on our stage. If anyone has a song, a recitation or reading, a feat of gymnast, anything for wholesome mirth or sober entertainment, he gives his name to Mrs. M. who prepares a program of what is offered for the following Sunday evening. In this way we have had stage performances every week, and a great part of our pleasure has been in surprise. Who knew that Charles was such a singer? What a comic vein Milford and Lorenzo discover! What athletes we have amongst us! One of the most pleasing performances was worked up in the Children's School, "The Midshipmen," an opera for children.

Circular, January 9, 1871

Our Sunday evening entertainments have taken shape as follows this winter: First on the program is "Weighing of the Babies." Everybody wants to see the babies as often as once a week at least, so this evening we bring them into the Hall (the hour not being late, commencing quarter after six), and there they are weighed in the order of their ages. The scales are like those you see on a store counter, and are placed on a table in the center of the stage. One man puts the baby into the dish, another adjusts the balance and announces the weight, and a third, with the record of the previous weighing before him, announces the increase during the week. This is an original ordinance, and it affords unfeigned pleasure to the simple folk here. It is sport to see the older babes perched in the dish, while one tries to rock himself, another reaches over to meddle with the weights, and another claps and crows. For the smaller ones, a pillow is laid in the dish, and they are passed on it, still in the dish, with care to their mothers.

After the ceremony of the scales, the orchestra with its late addition of kettle drums plays two or three tunes. The orchestra is under thorough drill this winter, with a new score, new music, etc., and this is all we get from them during the week, so we think a good deal of it. After the orchestra follow theatrical varieties to the end of the hour.

Circular, October 2, 1871

Now is the time for mushroom suppers; and this is the way we get them: Take a spare hour some afternoon, it matters not whether it is bright or breezy; take a big basket, for that will show the hope there is in you; take some companions who have mushrooms in the eye; and then go to an old pasture where horses and cattle have fed, walk briskly across the levels, up the slopes and down the hollows, letting your eyes range near and wide and when you see a great white "button" hugging close to the ground and looking like a young puff-ball, break it off close to the earth with your thumb and finger; put it in your basket and then look for more in the same place. Beware of toadstools, for they are poisonous. The mushroom you are after—the *Agaricus Campestris*—has a stem with a ring round it, has a top like an umbrella lined with rosy pink. If the lining is brown, 'tis a sign your dainty is too old for use. "Buttons" and "umbrellas" are all good. When you have found three or four, go half a mile farther to some other pasture and sweep it, making sudden darts this way and that, as the impulse takes you. Maybe you have found half a dozen trophies by this time, and maybe your zeal is down. When you come to know the times and places you will do better. Next, peel your mushrooms, slice the stems, and fry carefully in butter until the mess turns black. If you add a plenty of sweet cream it will improve the dish. Eat with bread and butter and a nice baked potato, and you have a luxury that is more savory than sage and onions.

Circular, November 6, 1871

Though pleasant the summer, yet we welcome the winter with joy unfeigned. We gather ourselves together, and till the soil of the heart and mind. Then beats high the pulse of social unity. Sweetest emulation to promote the happiness and improvement of the family animates all. Are the frosts chilling? We have weekly entertainments we enjoy so much. Do the winds whistle loudly and is the sky overcast? We have lectures, rich funds of instruction. Are the trees naked, and will the lawns and hills be soon but snowy wastes? We are a big but cozy family, and all winter long we shall be together; we shall read together and sing together, study together and play together. Welcome winter! we say.

The Community is a little world; and like the great world has its times of recurring enthusiasm about some art or amusement. At one time music will take a start, and everyone wants to learn to sing or play some instrument. Again, some game like croquet will become popular, and everyone wants a chance at the mallets and balls. We like to encourage these fits of unitary enthusiasm, and we like to learn how to modulate gracefully from one subject of interest to another, after, as we sometimes say, "the inspiration has run out." This winter we have been having a time of playing dominoes, an old-fashioned and simple game, but capable of some amusing variations. Our experience leads us to favor the simpler games of chance, rather than the more complicated games of skill, which involve more antagonism and require to make them edifying an amount of self-control not always possessed by the juniors; and a game to have a genuine "run" should draw in all classes, old and young.

Circular, January 22, 1872

In the evening we had a dance instead of the usual stage entertainment. A Community, family dance: The Hall is cleared a little after six; the tables and chairs are carried into the passageways and piled up on the stage, leaving just room enough on the latter for the musicians, the violins, the double-bass viol, and the horns. Those who mean to dance at first come in and seat themselves on the outer edges of the Hall below. Mothers with the smaller babies, and nurses with the larger ones, come to look on with the rest. Those who mean to wait for the last dance go up into the gallery and look down from the front row seats. There is also a sprinkling of babies up there. When the music begins the little boys from the Children's House seat themselves on the front of the stage—their white collars turned over and their little legs hanging down. Boys want to see, you know, and they want to be pretty near the big drum, too. Mr. George Hamilton, who is six feet two, and has the voice of a stentor, announces the figures and "calls off." The dancers take their places; and in the pauses and while the sets are forming, there is a by-play between the young folks on the floor and the babies in the gallery. Fathers dance with their daughters; sons with their mothers; brothers with their sisters; young with young; middle-aged with middle-aged; the young with everybody. We have quadrilles, contra-dances, waltzes, polkas, schottisches, one or two of each. The waltzes and cotillions, however, are the most popular. A company of cheerful, serious dancers, who for the most part take the old-fashioned step, and don't go cantering the changes in a sort of mad gallop.

Circular, February 22, 1872

A narrow-minded piety will look on our dances with an evil eye, while reckless pleasure-seekers will regard them as no better than the feast of *Barmecide.*

Circular, August 12, 1872

Does anyone know the pleasure there is in self-denial—the happiness to be found in turning from a thing when you most enjoy it? Our life is one series of discoveries in this line. Croquet has been a favorite amusement all summer; but this week we laid away mallets and balls and left the ground to the birds and babies. We make the move voluntarily and unanimously for the sake of promoting the growth of interior life at this time when outward allurements are at the highest tide.

Circular, September 23, 1872

Cool morning, but a day of sunshine followed. A family picnic in the Cragin Meadow and Island adjoining in the afternoon. First on the ground, between the hours of two and three, were a company of men and boys playing a game of baseball with all the enthusiasm of ten years ago. Another company of men, women and children sat near, watching their movements. One by one, two by two, in omnibus loads and wagon loads, the family were soon assembled for the afternoon pastimes. The game of ball ended, and other games were started. Two croquet grounds had been prepared and were filled with players, including children and adults. At a little distance a sack race was started. A few of the girls play at ball tossing, a few of the men are pitching quoits, a few are watching the velocipede, the children and babies take turns riding horseback, and several others are using the swings.

Circular, November 25, 1872

A party of our men went back to Oneida Lake where they have been engaged a week or more in fishing a little, trapping a little, hunting a little, and getting ready to put up a hygienic lodge at the mouth of Fish Creek. This house is to be 24 feet long, 16 wide, and two stories high, and will be furnished with all the conveniences of "a lodge in some vast wilderness." It stands on a tongue of sand amid oaks and pines and in hearing of the Lake when its waters come rushing on before the rough west wind.

The place is lonely enough for those who think it lonely, and populous enough for those who know how to re-people it with those old French and Indian war parties. We can take the cars at our back door and be set down a little way from our lodge; it is, you see, only an extension of our home. We expect it will add to our pleasure and progress.

Circular, January 1, 1873

Notwithstanding the cold weather and frequent snows of the past week, *croquet* continues to have its patrons and indeed bids fair to be an all-winter, outdoor pastime with a goodly number of boys and girls and men and women of the Community. From one to four couples at a time (foremost among whom may be noticed Mr. K., in his 72nd year), may daily be seen manipulating the mallets with healthful zest. Of course, mittens and sacks and overcoats and warm clothing for the feet are not neglected, but with these accompaniments the game seems to be thoroughly enjoyed by many for an hour or more at a time. The women and girls particularly congratulate themselves that they are doing a little of the rugged, and are oxygenizing their blood in an attractive way by this outdoor exercise in zero weather; and the frozen ground, say all the players, makes an improved floor for rolling the balls. Then if snow falls by night or day and covers the ground to the depth of a few inches, someone is sure to be on hand very soon thereafter, with shovel and broom to clear it away, so that a stereoscopic picture of the croquet ground at this writing would exhibit it as an elliptical enclosure surrounded with a snow-white wall from two and a half to three feet in height.

Circular, February 17, 1873

Terpsichore, dainty goddess, tripping with "light fantastic toe," has lately been superseded by Mars, with his measured tread and upright mein. "Squads," "regiments," "captains," and "divisions" are everyday words. We observed that dancing is an amusement in which not more than half the family take part. Let's have some exercise, suggested one, which will bring us all upon the floor. As there is scarcely anybody but can walk in a straightforward manner, marching was hit upon as the thing for us. Mr. Herrick drilled a small company for several weeks to see what might be done in this line. He gave an exhibition of their attainments a few evenings since, and the family were so well pleased with their varied evolutions that a large number of volunteers have entered the lists. The drilled "Squad" act as captains of the raw recruits, and it won't be long before we shall do the "right and left wheel," "double-quick" and all that quite *à la* the Prussian six-footers or the Imperial Guards.

Circular, July 21, 1873

Parties of six or eight are making excursions to Joppa frequently these warm days. Leaving our station on the ten o'clock train, they arrive at the Lodge near the lake within an hour, and have the rest of the time until the evening train of the succeeding day in which to take a respite from the usual labors at home. A ride on the river, a bath in the lake, and some luck in fishing is the usual round. Food has unusual relish after an hour or two of brisk rowing. In the evening all come in for an informal meeting, which is very pleasant minus the mosquitoes. One of the young women accompanied by A.B. tried the experiment on the 14th instant of walking the whole distance home—twelve miles. Starting at Fish Creek Station at ten o'clock, they arrived at the Community grounds at half past four, only stopping at a small farm house an hour and a half during a thunder shower. They experienced very little fatigue, but had an excellent appetite for supper.

Circular, January 1, 1874

CHRISTMAS EVE

The children off to bed and the play room empty. Mr. Ellis enters as Santa Claus, with a well-filled basket on his arm. He has planned a surprise for the little sleepers. In one corner of the room he has made a thicket of evergreens, under the shade of which is represented a gypsy encampment; the rude tent, the tripod of sticks from which suspends a kettle apparently over a fire (crimson flannel being substituted for flames), the queer dishes and coarse food which are spread on the ground in front of the tent, are gypsy-like enough. "The children have never seen a gypsy establishment," says Mr. E., "and I thought I would make them one." Saying this he proceeds to fill the score of stockings that lie on a table nearby with a variety of nuts and other knickknacks. "But here are not enough stockings to go round, what means this?" asks an assistant to Santa Claus. A second assistant brings forward *seven pairs of new boots!* Tiny boots, black and polished, designed for the seven youngest. These Mr. E. crams with good things, and then carefully stows them with the well-filled stockings in the tent; for the fun is going to consist in having the best gifts hidden from view. Pop-corn balls decorate the little trees from lowest branch to topmost twig. Fathers, mothers, uncles, aunts, and many more come in; some simply to observe the general arrangements, and others who have presents to contribute. Stockings, mittens, boxes, pin-balls, spools of silk, and a variety of useful gifts are hung on the trees, and Santa Claus's work is done.

Circular, January 1, 1874

CHRISTMAS MORNING

A grand jubilee below stairs at six o'clock. "Oh! Oh! Oh! And see what we have got!" But this was before the contents of the tent were known. "Now take your seats, children," says Miss Jane, "and you shall have your things." The tent door is opened and the seven youngest are allowed to peep in. Then each one receives his or her stocking and other gifts with loud exclamations of joy. At last the boots are distributed. Everything else is forgotten in the joy of this first pair of boots! The nuts and the figs and the nice popcorn were delightful a moment ago, but they are nothing compared to these boots! They enumerate the beauties of their new prize, while they gaze in admiration at their feet, occasionally putting their heels down with some unction, to test the amount of noise they can make. The older children are happy over their presents, and it is a general time of rejoicing. But of all the Christmas gifts given or received today, we know of none that are appreciated as much as that seven pairs of boots!

Circular, May 17, 1875

Instead of arising the moment our evening meeting hour is closed, and scattering to their rooms in the different parts of the house, the majority of the family remain in their seats, and the transition from meeting to after meeting is mainly marked by a buzz of cheerful conversation. The stage is always well lighted by two blazing chandeliers. On it, after an interim, perhaps, appear some of the musicians, and favor us with vocal or instrumental solos, duets, quartets, and quintets. Mayhap someone repeats a poem. The other evening by special request Mr. Warne had a few of his scholars recite pieces. Their recitations were received with applause and we were delighted by a promise of more from the children another time. This custom helps to keep warm and bright the family feeling in our big household, and prevents our meetings from becoming, or seeming, stiff and formal.

VIII

Business

The history of "doing business as unto the Lord" in the Oneida Community is a record of hard work, hopeful enterprise, occasional failures, and ultimate success. Their theory in relation to business was as uniquely their own as their theory in most other matters. Their Association, they said (*Circular,* April 1, 1858), was a school, and the object of their labor was to support that school as well as to improve their own bodies and souls. The three things most essential were to strive for peace and fellowship, to please Christ by putting away all laziness and shiftlessness, and to assert and maintain the supremacy of spiritual interests, not allowing business to crowd these interests.

As examples, they wrote (*Circular,* October 15, 1853), Mr. A. had faith and courage; it was a habit with him to expect that things would turn out better than he expected. He was constantly watching the good, although he saw the evil in a secondary way. Mr. B. lacked faith but believed that success in business was dependent on prudence and industry and hence he was prone to look on the shady side. He had the spirit that would make persons feel poor under any circumstances, while Mr. A. had the spirit that would make them feel rich and generous and open-hearted whatever happened. Success and the magnetism of "good luck" surrounded Mr. A. all the time, while Mr. B., industrious, prudent, and economical, lived in prose rather than poetry.

Inspired by a faith and courage like Mr. A.'s, the Community, after a few lean years of depending on horticulture to support them, turned to any kind of enterprise which could keep them

212

afloat. One member was clever at making rustic outdoor furniture and for a time they made and sold quite a lot of it (*Circular*, September 19, 1852). Someone suggested that osier willow, manufactured into baskets, might be profitable. They invested $25 in it but gave it up as uneconomical (*Circular*, June 28, 1855). Mr. V. introduced a new branch of industry in the manufacture of gentlemen's embroidered cloth slippers. The idea was attractive and the young girls took it up with enthusiasm but it petered out after a short time (*Circular*, June 28, 1855). They mention preparing to make farm wagons but nothing further was heard about that. They did make wheel spokes and scuffle hoes and mop handles (*Circular*, May 2, 1855) and once attempted to make plows (*Circular*, February 20, 1865), but none of these attempts worked out.

They kept on trying. Although some of their ideas came to nothing, there were also what they called "little industrial sprouts" (*Circular*, April 1, 1854) which actually did develop into healthy plants. Bag-making was started at the Wallingford branch in 1854 (*Circular*, April 6, 1854); the sale of silk thread which they bought from dealers in New York was fairly profitable. For the first few years the making of steel traps, after the pattern invented by a member, Sewell Newhouse, was largely experimental and provided only a trickle of income, but in 1855 (*Circular*, January 6, 1865), after showing their traps rather timidly to a Chicago dealer, a large order directed their interest to trap-making. Larger quarters were provided and within a few years improved machinery was invented to take the place of the hand labor of the early manufacture. Although their main interest was still in the culture and sale of nursery stock and fruits and vegetables in season, they advertised in 1858 "fresh tomatoes, hermetically sealed in glass bottles for family use" and, in small print, "Steel traps" (*Circular*, March 25, 1858). Two more "little sprouts" which had pushed above ground; in a few years not only tomatoes but other vegetables and fruit, at first only the produce of their own gardens, preserved in glass and cans, found a ready sale, and trap orders were coming in faster than they could be filled.

It was not easy. Just as they were getting under way in 1857, a financial panic hit the country, producing general distrust, dejection, the failure of merchants and banking firms, and short time in many large manufacturing companies. Naturally this state of affairs struck the infant industries at Oneida, but the communists comforted themselves that in such conditions it was not surprising that they should experience some diminution of orders (*Circular,* March 25, 1858). Their courage was still good and the business in the shop went on as usual.

To become a real and true business character, John Humphrey Noyes wrote (*Circular,* April 5, 1860), necessitated an advanced state of development, involving the subjection of one's powers to his will and intellect, as well as the denial of his natural impulses to play and pleasure-seeking. Maintenance of a true business character required inspiration, and such a man must live a true and sym-metrical life, of which business was only one part; his attention must be directed to religion and to intellectual, moral, and social matters as well as to industrial affairs. He must have time every day for play. A true businessman was characterized by purpose, fertility of invention, and enterprise. If a man would accomplish anything noble or permanent he must be able to "work some in a treadmill way," but that must not be his whole life. Every day must have a broad margin for play and culture. Again, he would be *economical in regard to expenditures.* When a man was more eager to spend capital than to increase it, this indicated that his character was not balanced. He needed to balance it by association with persons of opposite tendencies. The principle of producing all one can and finding out all possible improvement rendered labor a new thing. The worker was then always on the *qui vive;* his labor became a luxury.

If the Association was a school for such businessmen, its curriculum was certainly varied. In those early days practically every branch of the organization was operated by committees. In 1861 (*Circular,* April 4, 1861), aside from the Central Board and finance committees and various clerical offices, the following were appointed: committees to receive visitors; for the trap department, machine shop, blacksmithing, building department, shoe shop, bag department, tailor shop, printing office, kitchen, farm and dairy, fruit and garden, teaming, stables, silk department, bee keepers, soap and vinegar, washing and stove superintendent, painter, superintendent of water works and machinist, musical director, dentist, inventor and machinist, poultry keeper, dairyman, Children's House, for assigning and transferring help in all departments, compost manager, commissioner of highways, steward, greenhouse, flower garden and shrubbery committee, grist mill, schools, and one committee "to do what they pleased" (supposed to be a rather popular committee). It would not seem that there was much time for pleasure-seeking.

Still, the men and women of the Community did manage to live a symmetrical life; they had time for "intellectual, moral, and social matters," and at the same time worked enough "in a treadmill way" to make their various industries prosper. The silk peddling business, which had been their best earner in the early days, was crowded out by the more profitable trap and fruit-preserving works and was finally abandoned in 1863 (*Circular,* December 24, 1863). The machine shop and small colony in Newark, New Jersey, were closed in 1855 (*Circular,* May 31, 1855), and the master machinist moved to Oneida where later he was of invaluable help in the trap and silk works.

In 1863 they note (*Circular,* October 1, 1863) that, until two years before, all the labor of the Community was performed by their own members. In that year they hired help for ditching the farm. By 1865 they employed in the various departments twenty-seven hired hands. In 1866 they had forty-nine hired workmen and women, and the next year Mr. Noyes recommended raising the wages, unsolicited, and providing an evening school for the boys and girls who worked in the various shops. In 1867 the piecework system was inaugurated in the bag shop (*Circular,* October 26, 1867). "The old vicious hireling system of the world," they said, "was quite distasteful to the Community people."

This gradual hiring of outside labor did not mean that the communists were any less willing than of old to work and work hard. "They had not," they said (*Circular,* February 20, 1871), "allowed themselves to get lily-fingered." In 1868, when there was mood for economizing, they dismissed the hired women from the laundry and did the work themselves, finding that the same number of Community women shortened the work by two days. This may have been owing to "Grand Bees" several times a week by both men and women in what they called "a unitary fever of cheerful industry" (*Circular,* February 20, 1871).

Partly because of lack of room and lack of workers, the printing and editing of the *Circular* was moved to Wallingford in 1864 and the chain-making which had heretofore been carried on at Wallingford was moved back to Oneida where it could be done in direct connection with the trap-making (*Circular,* March 21, 1864).

The year 1866 was a crisis in the Community's affairs. Business had been only fair in the past two years. Heroic measures were called for (*Daily Journal,* March 16, 1866). John Humphrey Noyes rose to the occasion and as always he called upon the Primitive Church to show the way. His *New Principles in Business* announced "Everything for sale except the soul!" The sale and auction which implemented this manifesto, requiring the sale of all "dead property," were drastic, but with the money earned the debt was paid and the Community was back in running order. The businesses which bloomed and blossomed again by midsummer were a reproach to any doubters who had questioned the expediency of reduced prices. The demand for traps was unprecedented.

On February 2, 1866, the *Daily Journal* records a discussion in the evening meeting of the proposal to send one of their bright young men, Charles Cragin, to Willimantic to learn the silk business. This proposal was, as they said, "fully sympathized with," and it was voted that he should go immediately. A week later came the further proposal to send a woman with him and finally Elizabeth Hutchins and Harriet Allen joined Cragin at the Willimantic factory. Meanwhile, Mr. Inslee, their premier machinist, had been sent east, possibly to the same factory although it is not specified, to learn what he could about making the necessary machinery.

Providence, as they said, seemed to be opening the way for them. The three young people learned the techniques quickly and were graduated from their course on June 10. By the middle of July the Community bought its first bale of raw silk and by July 28 the first lot of machinery was in running order and therewith the beginning of silk manufacturing by the Oneida Community. The first skein of manufactured silk, undyed and far from ready for use but still a triumph for Inspiration, was shown to the Community. By the next spring the *Circular* for April 8, 1867 admitted that there were difficulties "met at every step" in this new venture, but they were bound to conquer. No "fair" article would answer the purpose. They must have the *best.* If they carried righteousness and honesty into the business and manufacturing they knew that money and all manner of success would follow.

Among the articles advertised for sale in the *Circular* that spring were steel traps, traveling bags, iron bag-frames, a corn-cutter, preserved fruits and vegetables, jellies, sewing-silk, and paper collars.

The year 1867 was not as profitable as they had hoped and *concentration* was the watchword. In 1868 the *Circular* was moved back to Oneida where a new brick South Wing was to be added to the Mansion House as soon as they could afford it, but the members were cautioned above all things to "get on the platform of pre-payment and get out of debt" (*Circular,* January 20, 1868).

In 1868 two sudden changes of policy came about. If the Community was courageous about experimenting in new fields, it was equally courageous about admitting its mistakes, cutting its losses, and giving up unprofitable ventures. The year before there had been some criticism of the fruit department. One of the agents reported (*Daily Journal,* March 17, 1867) that some people "didn't like our jellies first rate." The agent, brought up in the school of Community criticism, did not try to justify his position but agreed with his critic that the jellies were not just right because they were made with apple juice, which confession, as he reported, "took the starch out of his critic." Whether this criticism affected the decision or not, the next year (*Circular,* September 21, 1868) the Community decided to give up the fruit-preserving business, because "it drew too heavily on time and attention." Earlier that year (*Circular,* January 20, 1868) they had also given up the bag business, as "taking up too much room and requiring too much effort which could be better expended in the trap or silk businesses." They wrote a letter to their fruit patrons, explaining the situation, and received during the next two years such lamentations from their recent customers that they finally went back to canning fruits and vegetables, a business which lasted thirty years after the Oneida Community had ceased to exist.

The *Circular* (April 29, 1867) remarked amusingly that they did not suppose that Mr. Secretary Seward had had special reference to the interests of the Oneida Community in his recent annexation of Russian America (Alaska) to the United States but it was a curious coincidence that the principal want of that country matched their own principal production. They could, they said, afford to make a present to the State Department of a highly finished trap in consideration of the new market opened for their hardware. In the days after the railroad was completed to the Pacific, the *Circular* (April 3, 1871) spoke of orders for traps to be sent entirely by rail, and orders from California mentioned seventy-three bear traps along with the rest of the smaller sizes.

In 1873 merchants all over the country complained of the tightness of the money market and the difficulty of making collections. The Community, through this time of stringency, had such good luck in receiving money when they needed it that they acknowledged God's care of them with deep gratitude. This was a Special Providence just like those in their early days when, in great straits for ready cash, they had had recourse to prayer and were never disappointed. Now (*Circular,* March 17, 1873), once more, the matchings of receipts and payments were as remarkable as in the days of their poverty, which made them feel that the Lord sympathized with their business and took pains to relieve their wants. Luckily, owing to their new principles, they were out of debt, but if necessary, they said, "We can live on mush and apple sauce and wear our old clothes until better times." Fortunately the occasion did not arise. The next year was still hard sledding, but they "met with good Providences and answers to prayer when in want of money." John Humphrey Noyes said (*Circular,* March 9, 1874) that he "would rather be poor all the time than not to have to look to God for money." People like that could not be defeated.

Circular, July 9, 1853

A visitor at Oneida, who is unbounded in his admiration of the general state and character of the Community is anxious that they should be more systematic in their book accounts and have some method of entry by which they can ascertain at any time the exact balance of their income and expenses. The simple truth is if the Association should take the advice of worldly economists, given often with the best intentions, it would destroy the very cause of its prosperity. If our prudent friend could persuade Oneida to drop down into his own spirit and ways, and give primary importance to its good surroundings, he would kill the goose that lays the golden egg. All that he admires so much has been the result of an entirely opposite course—of adhering to the rule—"*take no thought for the morrow, what you shall eat, drink, and wear, but seek first the kingdom of heaven and its righteousness.*" That is the goose that has laid the golden egg; and Oneida will look out that it is not killed by those who do not know it.

Circular, April 1, 1854

Various trades are already in operation among us in the house in a partial and occasional way: First, tailoring, cutting out garments, etc. This is a constant business, employing generally three women and a sewing machine. Secondly, dress-making. Third, shoe-binding. Fourth, cap and sock-making for men and boys. Fifth, mitten-making. This is a branch which keeps one woman busy all the winter. The mittens are made of thick cloth and lined. Sixth, bag-making for the Grist-Mill. This is quite a business when the mill is in full operation in the flouring department. The bags are cut out and made evenings. Several gentlemen join in this work. Seventh, palm-leaf hat braiding in the spring and summer. The children do the greater part of this work and furnish common hats for the men and boys. Eighth, making pickles, vinegar, and sauerkraut; drying tomatoes, plums, cherries, apples, etc. Ninth, rug and fruit-making, etc. Tenth and lastly, general nursery and infant-school keeping.

Most of these *businesses* if not all, though they do not bring us direct income, furnish us with articles that many families buy, or hire made. Besides furnishing our own family, we receive frequent orders from our sister-Communes, and Oneida expects always to give her sons and daughters when they leave her for some other station, a respectable outfit for a year.

Thus you see we have growing quite a number of little industrial sprouts; but I believe that we should be able to do a great deal more if the way opened. As the spring advances we hope to find a plenty for our children to do in the garden.

Circular, September 9, 1854

I have found it quite easy to meet our debts, so far, in advance of the day of payment. The experience I have had within a few days in my department has been encouraging and strengthening to face. The few days since, I promised $103.50 for corn within six days. Our treasury was nearly empty, still I felt confident it would come at the time it became due; I had it and $20.00 left. I then looked at our cash-book and found due for silk $130.00—this was on Thursday—I said, "I must have it Monday morning, and we'll go to the bank for it if it does not come from some other source." When Monday came I had it and more than $100.00 left over. Next was a bank note for $300.00, due the 10th; on the 4th it was paid. One evening lately I bought 21 bushels of wheat at $2.25 per bushel or $47.25, and promised the cash in a week. The next day I was prepared to pay it. Things are continually turning out better than I expect, for which I thank God and take courage.

Circular, May 31, 1855

The business affairs of the Newark Commune, we are glad to hear, are about closed up—the few hundred dollars worth of machinery only remaining unsold and claims of similar amount being on hand uncollectible. The Newark enterprise was not successful in a business point of view; in fact it was a school of considerable tribulation from the beginning; but serviceable in many respects and pleasant to look back upon. It is now closed, its debts all paid, and its members and material disbursed to the other Associations. Good-bye, Newark; *au revoir*.

Circular, July 26, 1855

A departure of silk-peddlers. When these itinerants go out to *retail*, it is in couples, after the fashion of the disciples. In villages they peddle one, one side of the street and the other, the other. Sometimes they separate for the day, and meet by appointment at night. They are in circumstances to nurse friendship, and generally come home much endeared to one another. Today one of the most fatherly of the fraternity took with him a lad of 14, who was born and brought up in the Community, and is now to take his first brush with the world. We appreciate the opportunity the silk business affords for our youth to get acquainted more or less outside.

Circular, October 18, 1855

THE FIRST PRINCIPLE OF BUSINESS

It is to be counted a first principle, that the special blessing of God upon any business is the grand element of a success. There are, undoubtedly, a variety of elements that come in to contribute to success, as skill in doing business, tact in managing the financial concerns of it, the advantage of profitable connections, the patronage of men and institutions, etc. These are elements which are not to be despised in a secondary point of view; but the mistake of the world lies in making them the first and only condition of success—in ignoring entirely the principle that takes precedence of all others, that is, the blessing of God is the special and main element concerned in prosperity. "Except the Lord build the house, they labor in vain that build it; except the Lord keep the city, the watchmen waketh but in vain." The watchmen may be never so correct and faithful in a worldly way, and the laborers never so skillful and industrious; yet there stands the fact.

Circular, November 8, 1855

The question was proposed and discussed how should superiors treat their subordinates when they make mistakes? Should they "pay on" to them as the saying is, and try to make them feel as bad as they can, or should they treat them with gentleness and forebearance? Which is the best course in an *economical* point of view? That is, by which course will a chief of any business get the most work out of his hands? It was decided that any course which tended to provoke wrath and discouragement was bad policy. In a spirit of discouragement a person is more likely to repeat his mistakes; while there is nothing like kindness to provoke improvement. Some experience was quoted in which persons had realized the good effect of forebearance on the part of their superiors. Criticism should never be given under the impulse of personal vexation.

Circular, May 8, 1856

We have a new institution this spring for facilitating business—a Central Board composed of about 15 members selected from all the different departments, who meet twice a week precisely at 11 o'clock A.M., and close the session at noon. Let us attend this session and note the proceedings. The members of the board are mostly present in the parlor, at the appointed time, seated about the tables with a secretary to record whatever is necessary in the transactions of the meeting. The chairman, Mr. K., commences by inviting attention to any unfinished business that was deferred at the last meeting. This disposed of, he proceeds to call over the roll of members present, giving to each an opportunity of bringing up any "bill," plan, or proposal that he thinks necessary relating to his own particular department, or any other.

Circular, September 25, 1856

Orders for traps from all parts of the country are received almost daily, and this branch of business seems to be on the increase with us. The work is admirably fitted for aggregation, and the employment of persons of both sexes and all ages. Considerable nicety and exactness are requisite in fitting the various parts, matching the jaws, etc. The women like the work: it has been a regular employment for quite a number of them to work two or three hours per day during the summer, and it will probably require more help the coming winter, as the demand for traps increases.

Circular, October 23, 1856

Matters in the trap-shop up for discussion in the evening meeting, in pursuance of the plan adopted at the last meeting. Things a little out of order here, persons complaining of the work being unattractive, etc. Criticism of the foremen for worldliness and inattention to the spiritual interests of the shop. In a selection of the workmen, two of our cardinal principles have been deviated from somewhat, viz., the true combination of the old and the young, the spiritual and the unspiritual, and the commingling of the sexes in labor. Too much reference has been had to the immediate results of labor, and not enough to the spiritual tone of the company. There were found to be too many young men and boys employed to preserve a healthy tone, and it was not made sufficiently attractive to the women to join in the work. A change must be effected in these respects.

Circular, January 1, 1857

In the business meeting today a plan was proposed for obtaining a complete statistical view of the industrial operations of the Association during the last year, by means of written reports from persons acquainted with the several departments, to be read New Year's Eve.

Circular, January 29, 1857

One of those instances occurred today which, from time to time, come as vivid reminders of the care of a watchful providence, even in our most minute affairs. Last evening the financial report showed bills requiring immediate payment, amounting to over $500, and only about $100 in the treasury to meet them. The financiers saw no other way but to borrow from the bank. A note was accordingly made out. Mr. K., on his way to the Depot, called at the bank and obtained the money. Arriving at the Post Office, letters were handed him containing drafts to the amount of $462., enough, with the $100. he took from home, to meet the bills. During the day over $700. came in through the mails—the bank note can be taken up and the surplus left of several hundred. It was taken as an indication that a little more reliance on the Bank of Heaven would not be misplaced.

Circular, April 30, 1857

If one should call into the Trap-Shop this morning about 9 o'clock, he would hear, instead of the clinking, rumbling sounds which usually salute the ear, a low hum of voices, and would notice the group of workmen seated together. To explain a little: after the new arrangement of industrial forces took place this spring, by which a number of the shop hands were drawn out to engage in different occupations, it was noticed that the business here was somewhat deranged, and also that there was not quite so commendable a state of spirit prevailing in the shop as before.

This fact suggested to someone the idea of calling a meeting of the shop hands, to talk over their affairs; which suggestion seems to strike all as a good one. After two or three meetings of this kind had been held, it was proposed to continue these morning gatherings on Monday, Wednesday, and Friday mornings of each week—stop the machinery, and collect together for purposes of mutual edification—inviting perfect freedom from everyone to criticize the hands, collectively or individually, or make any suggestion in regard to business; and, above all, the object of these meetings is to promote spiritual improvement and the acknowledgment of the presence and spirit of Christ in the business. These gatherings had thus far proved profitable, and been well attended. If only a short time is occasionally spent in this manner, it is found to affect favorably the business of the shop in different ways.

Circular, May 23, 1857

Left today Mr. F. who has been our visitor for a few days past. Himself an experienced bookkeeper in the leading New York bank and an enthusiast in his business, he has, from the time of his first acquaintance with the Community, been insidious in his endeavors to introduce a perfect system of account keeping among us. Our communal relations not rendering it altogether essential that any rigid account should be kept except with the outside world, we have shown more indifference to his wishes in this respect than we should have otherwise done. But our present bookkeeper, being somewhat an enthusiast in figures, and having been brought to appreciate, in some degree, the superior system practiced by Mr. F., an attempt will be made to introduce it as far as practical.

Circular, December 31, 1857

The annual inventorying of our *matériel* is going on. Well persuaded of the truth of its fundamental principles, the Association has been free to liberally expand its previously acquired means for establishing a better order of things. Let the apparent objections to associated industry be what they may, and let the obstacles that the Community have had to contend with be what they are, yet, to us, it is evident that Communism has nothing in it incompatible with all needful production. To be sure, such is the effect of the *esprit de corps*—making everyone feel stronger and safer—that no one feels nerved up to his old feverish exertion to guard against impending want. The truth is, we are subjectively rich, though not so objectively, and are free to stop and consider the "Whence, Why, and Whither," of things.

Circular, January 14, 1858

Our book accounts were never so satisfactory as this year, but our heart accounts are still more so. The condition of our young folks was considered a great evidence of the moral power that is among us—that in spite of all contrary attractions, they were growing up in fellowship with us and in loyalty to Community principles.

Circular, March 18, 1858

ORGANIZATION DAY

It is our custom early in the spring to appoint foremen to the various departments of labor in the Community, and to make such disposal of our forces as the exigencies of the time and personal attractions for this or that business seem to demand. A meeting of all the men in the parlor at one o'clock to organize the different branches of business. As a preliminary to selecting foremen, it was proposed that everyone should express his preference by writing upon a slip of paper the name of the one whom he would wish to be the chief of each department, as it was called up for organization. A very pleasant unanimity prevailed, and the thing (by the way, a new one) went off with a right good spirit.

Circular, March 28, 1858

Talk about our finances. The Community treasury is "low" nowadays. The "hard times" have diminished our income from the sale of traps very perceptibly; and our income from other sources is proportionately small. We wish to take a cheerful, faith view of the matter, and on the other hand, it is thought expedient to "trim our sails to the breeze," as well as we can—to purchase nothing that we can well dispense with—do all we can to increase our income; and wait hopefully for "better times."

Circular, December 22, 1859

Whatever blank has occurred in the journal this fall may be supplied in the reader's imagination with extra business of all kinds. Industrial activity has redoubled itself. Circumstances of various kinds have conspired to produce this industrial revival, and it has been throughout healthy in its progress and encouraging in its result. The mingling of all ages and both sexes in the enthusiasm of our mechanical department, has a uniting and solidifying effect socially. The material result of our operations is seen in the erection of an addition to our Mansion, additions to the Trap-Shop and Green House, the introduction of new machinery in our business, and in the paying off of our land debt, which, by the loan of a few hundred dollars, was effected on the first of December, so that the domain of 386 acres now rests in the Community's possession with a clear title. We submit that this is hardly carrying out the *program* of those who ten years ago predicted that we should fail financially and not hold together more than six months. We are thankful too, and often hear the sentiment expressed by others, that we have not received much nursing from the donations of rich men or societies, but have been permitted to work out the debt by our own efforts. We recognize the goodness of God in the manner of his past leading as well as in our present situation.

Circular, May 22, 1862

Some new businesses this spring—making strawberry boxes and mop-handles for sale, the latter being a new invention.

Circular, June 25, 1863

The manufactures of the Community have absorbed so much of our force the present season that we have been induced to employ for farm labor several hired men. They board in tenant houses. This extends the connections of the Community in the new manner, and perhaps carries with it new responsibilities. We hope to avoid in some degree at least the spirit of the hirelings system, and that these working men may have no reason to regret their service of the Community. During the present season, we have been induced to try the experiment of putting out work from the traveling-bag manufactory, and now have work done by women and girls at their homes in the vicinity to a considerable extent. The number of applications for this kind of work is greater at present than we can supply.

Circular, October 1, 1863

It is but a short time since the Community performed the labor of farm, household, and work-shop almost wholly within its own ranks and without hiring. Two years ago we commenced another system by hiring two Englishmen to do ditching on the farm. Now the Community employs in the different departments of work a force of 27 hired hands, not including the mason and carpenters that work on new buildings. Arrangements have been made this week with a neighbor for the boarding of most of this company. Two weeks ago we could have said that the new system had not even then invaded our household. But *mores mutantur;* there are now assisting in the laundry for two or three days in the week, a couple of young colored women from the vicinity. Whether this will prove to be an entering wedge for the extended hiring of domestic service as the two Englishmen did on the farm, remains to be seen.

Circular, December 24, 1863

CHANGE OF BUSINESS

Among the changes of the present season we may mention the closing up of the silk business. This business was introduced about thirteen years ago by Mr. O. H. Miller, a member from Putney, Vt., as a help to the resources of the Community which at that time were rather low. The trade was first carried on in a retail way by two or three foot-peddlers, whose stock was carried in his many carpet-bags, and amounted to not more than seventy-five or a hundred dollars each. From this small beginning it gradually expanded into a wholesale trade, employing from four to six persons to travel for a considerable part of the year by railroad, and amounting to several thousands of dollars annually. It was steadily increasing up till the time when the Community decided to abandon it. The reasons for this step were: one, that it was found to be a spiritual expense to the persons engaged in it, requiring them to be absent from home for a large part of the time; and two, that other departments in our home business now call for a concentration of our force for their proper management.

Daily Journal, January 5, 1864

A report was made by the Inventory Committee of the condition of our property on the first of January. The report shows that the Community has been more prosperous the past year than any other year during its existence. The net gains of the year have been over $45,000! The number of steel traps made during the year was some over 232,000! More than $23,000 of our profits are invested in Government Stocks and in real estate—$12,000 in the former and over $11,000 in the latter! The rest of our gains is invested in material for various businesses and in new buildings and so forth. For further particulars see the Inventory Report and Comparative Statement.

Daily Journal, January 7, 1864

A report from Wallingford of the Annual Returns or Inventory was received today and read in the Meeting. From this Inventory it seems that Wallingford too has been prospered the past year more than ever before—the net gains amounting to over $5,700. This makes the gain of the two communes, Oneida and Wallingford together, more than $50,-000! or nearly as much as the whole property at Oneida inventoried when we first commenced inventorying in 1856 or 1857.

Circular, March 21, 1864

Our New Location

The immediate occasion of the removal of the *Circular* from Oneida to Wallingford was this: The Wallingford Community has heretofore been engaged in making chains for steel traps manufactured at Oneida. But as the Oneida business increased, it became quite expedient and even necessary that the chain-making should be carried on in direct connection with the trap-making. At the same time, the printing business at Oneida was crowded and embarrassed by the growth and clatter of the trap machinery. It seemed best therefore for both departments that the chain-making and the printing should change places. This proved to be very convenient, as each of these businesses require about the same number of hands, and the chain-shop, by a slight renovation, becomes an excellent printing office, while the caloric engine which served the chain business, serves equally well to run the press.

If it is understood that the Oneida and Wallingford Communities are entirely one in their character and interests, that they keep no accounts with each other (except as a prudent man keeps account with himself) and that they are in daily communication with each other on all of the concerns of both, it will be seen that the *Circular,* though for convenience sake printed at Wallingford, is still published by the Oneida Community.

Circular, June 27, 1864

THE TRAP BUSINESS

The extraordinary growth of Trapping as an occupation, within the last ten years, stimulated in part by the remunerative price of furs, and in part by the ever-extending area of frontier settlements in the West, but still more perhaps by the improvement in the manufacture of Traps made by the Community under the supervision of its chief in that department, Mr. Sewell Newhouse, will justify us in giving a sketch of the history of the trap business.

The characteristics which Mr. Newhouse possesses as a mechanic are a critical eye, a sound judgment of material relations, nicety of hand, and a conscientious attention to the *minutiae* of any mechanism, on which so often its proper working depends. As a trap-maker his original idea was to make faultless traps, and nothing could swerve him from this point.

The Community established itself at Oneida, about two miles from the residence of Mr. Newhouse, in 1848, and the next summer received him and his family as members. For several years after this, but little attention was paid to the trap business. A few dozens were made occasionally by Mr. Newhouse in the old way, but it was not until 1855, under a call for traps from Chicago and New York, that practical interest was first directed to this branch of manufacture, with a view to its extension, by Mr. J. H. Noyes. Arrangements were then made for carrying on the business in a shop fifteen feet by twenty-five. The tools consisted of a common forge and bellows, hand-punch, swageing-mould, anvil, hammer, and file. The shop so established employed about three hands. The next year it was moved to a larger room in the building connected with water power, and the number of hands was increased. Among them were several young men, who together with Messrs. Noyes and Newhouse exercised their inventive powers in devising mechanical appliances to take the place of hand-labor in fashioning the different parts of the trap. A power-punch was the first machine produced, then a rolling apparatus for swageing the jaws. Soon it was found that malleable cast-iron could be used as a substitute for wrought iron in several parts of the trap. The brunt of the labor expended had always been in the fabrication of the steel spring, and this was still executed with hammer and anvil wholly by hand. Two stalwart men, with a two-hand sledge and a heavy hammer, reduced the steel to its elementary shape by about 120 blows, and it was afterward finished by a long series of lighter manipulations. The attempt was made to bring this part of the work within the grasp of machinery. One by one the difficulties in the way were overcome by the ingenuity of our machinists, until at length the whole process of forming the spring, from its condition as a steel bar to that of the bent, bowed, tempered, and elastic article, ready for use, is now executed by machinery almost without the blow of a hammer. The addition of chain-making (also executed mostly by machine power) makes the manufacture of traps and their attachments complete.

We may add that to complete their arrangements for carrying on this business at the fullest extent of the possible demand for traps, the Community are building the present season a new manufacturing establishment on the water power about a mile from their present works, which will enable them to more than duplicate their production.

Circular, January 6, 1865

Financial History of the Oneida Community

The Oneida Community commenced its business at its present location in 1848, but did not adopt the practice of taking Annual Inventory until 1857. Of the period between these dates we can give but a brief and general account. The Community in the course of that period had five or six branches with common interests, scattered in several states.

The "Property Register" kept from the beginning shows that the amount of property brought in by the members of all the Communities, up to January 1, 1857, was $107,706.45. The amount held at Oneida at that date, as stated in the first regular Inventory, was $41,740.00. The branch communities at Putney, Wallingford, and elsewhere at the same time had property valued at $25,532.22. So that the total assets of the Associated Communities were $67,272.22 or $40,434.23 less than the amount brought in by the members. In other words, between the years 1848 and 1857, the Associated Communities sunk (in round numbers) $40,000.00. Various causes may be assigned for this, such as inexperience, lack of established business, persecutions and extortions, the burning of the Community Store at Oneida, the sinking of the sloop "Rebecca Ford" in the North River, and the maintenance of an expensive printing family at Brooklyn, the publication of a free paper, sometimes twice and even three times a week, etc., etc. But the account may as well be summed up in one word thus: we sunk $40,000.00 in our own Education, which is like sinking an oil-well—expensive at first, but lucrative afterwards, *if you "strike oil."*

In the course of several years previous to 1857 the Community abandoned the policy of working in scattered detachments, and concentrated its forces at Oneida and Wallingford. From the first of January 1857 to the present time, the progress of its money-matters is recorded in the following statistics, carefully collected from the business books of the Community; which have been kept under the monthly supervision and persevering admonitions of J. J. Franks, Esq., the first bookkeeper of the Tradesmen's Bank in New York City, and one of the best accountants and statisticians in the United States.

Summary of Annual Inventories

First Inventory, Jan. 1, 1857

Net Capital . . . . $ 41,740.00

Second Inventory, Jan. 1, 1858

Net Capital . . . . $ 53,552.72
Increase of capital. . . . . $ 11,812.72
Net earnings in 1857 . . . . $ 5,470.11

Third Inventory, Jan. 1, 1859

Net capital . . . . $ 58,724.38
Increase of capital. . . . . $ 5,171.66
Net earnings in 1858 . . . . $ 1,763.60

Fourth Inventory, Jan. 1, 1860

Net capital .... $ 68,779.08
Increase of capital......... $ 10,054.70
Net earnings in 1859........ $ 10,278.38

Fifth Inventory, Jan. 1, 1861

Net capital .... $ 90,426.58
Increase of capital......... $ 21,647.50
Net earnings in 1860........ $ 15,611.03

Sixth Inventory, Jan. 1, 1862

Net capital .... $ 99,987.43
Increase of capital......... $ 9,560.85
Net earnings in 1861........ $ 5,877.89

Seventh Inventory, Jan. 1, 1863

Net capital $118,232.77
Increase of capital......... $ 18,245.34
Net earnings in 1862........ $ 9,859.78

Eighth Inventory, Jan. 1, 1864

Net capital $166,140.97
Increase of capital......... $ 47,908.20
Net earnings in 1863........ $ 44,755.30

Ninth Inventory, Jan. 1, 1865

Net capital $229,386.32
Increase in capital......... $ 63,245.35
Net earnings in 1864........ $ 61,382.62

Total net earnings in eight years $154,998.71

In regard to Wallingford Community, it may be stated that according to their Inventory on the 1st of January 1857, their net capital was $8,343.22. By their last inventory, January 1, 1865, their net capital was $25,182.07. Increase of capital: $16,838.85. Of this increased capital, $7,700.85 is of their own earnings. The united capital of the Oneida and Wallingford Communities, on January 1, 1865, was $254,568.39.

The average number of persons employed by the Community the past year (1864) has been about 100. The amount of taxes paid by the Community the past year was, for State and County, $2,610.26; National, $5,893.30; besides for the School and Highway taxes. The domestic expenses of the Community the past year were $34,000.

Circular, February 20, 1865

FINANCIAL STATEMENT—NUMBER TWO

Whoever has studied the financial history of the Oneida Community has doubtless noticed that the last inventory shows on the one hand net earnings for the year 1864 amounting to $61,000.00, and on the other, a debt of $33,000.00. The earnings are reckoned *after* deducting the debt, and are really *net* earnings, that is, over and above all expenses and exclusive of all "individual deposits," or unearned additions to the capital. Still, the debt is large and needs explanation.

The largest part of our income for the last eight or ten years has come from the trap business. In ordinary years that business has demanded and rewarded all the industry and enterprise we could bestow upon it; and many times and for long periods our orders for traps have far exceeded our ability to fill them. In the fall and winter of 1863–64 we were behind our orders for more than 90,000 traps. And yet this business has periods of stagnation. Its activity depends primarily on the price and demand for furs, and is doubtless affected by all the causes that stimulate or depress business generally. The reader will see by turning to the third Inventory that the net earnings of the year 1858 were only $1,763.60. That year was a period of almost entire cessation of demand for traps. The past year (1864) has been a second period of the same kind. Following the great demand in which we fell almost hopelessly behind our orders has come a year in which our orders have fallen as far behind our manufacture. We have on hand at this time, in finished traps and unfinished stock for traps, waiting for sale, $80,000.00 worth of property, or more than twice the amount of our debt. This will doubtless go off our hands and give us plenty of means very soon after the usual demand returns. But for the present we carry it as dead property, and have to live without much income. This is one cause of our present debt.

How long this cause will continue of course we cannot tell. Such stagnations have never lasted heretofore more than one year. We expect a full flow of orders next fall, especially if the war should close, which has called away many men from trapping to soldiering, and has in other ways obstructed business. The symptoms of a new activity, even in the coming spring, are promising. The prices of furs are high. We have sold more than three thousand dollars worth of traps within a few weeks, though our spring sales scarcely commence, usually, till March.

Another cause of our debt has been the extraordinary expense incurred the past year for *building.* To provide against the overwhelming demand for traps under which we labored in 1863, we purchased a new water power and have built in 1864–65 a new Trap Factory, at a cost (including water works and machinery) of more than thirty thousand dollars. This again, though prospectively a most profitable investment, is for the present a vast expense. In fact it nearly coincides with and accounts for the amount of our debt.

At this very time also, when our sales of traps are small and our expense for building great, we are invited and in some sense compelled by circumstances and the demands of prudence to enlarge our other manufactures. We wish to be a little more independent of a business that is so fluctuating as is trap-making; and for this purpose must widen our basis by putting more capital into other businesses. We see clearly that we can safely and profitably treble our fruit-preserving. The Bag manufacture is going into the large factory vacated by the trap business, and ought to be doubled. We are also just now commencing a new business—that of plow-making. All these works will require stock, and therefore capital; and cannot be expected to yield large returns till next summer or fall.

The result of these complications is, that *we wish to borrow money,* first, to pay such parts of our present debt as are, or soon will be, falling due; and secondly, to supply our enlarging businesses with stock for the coming season.

We have at Oneida over $100,000.00 worth of real estate which we can mortgage if necessary. We have offers from parties in New York City of sufficient loans on bond and mortgage at 7%. But before entering upon this method of supply, we have thought best to make this frank statement of our situation and our wants to the readers of the *Circular.* Two things in the New York method we do not like—the mortgaging and the 7%. We should prefer to find men who believe that our word or our note is as good as our bond, and who would loan us money at 6%.

This then may be considered as an advertisement to the readers of the *Circular* that we will receive proposals for loans on the last mentioned terms, in sums from $100 to $10,000, and for such times as on correspondence may be agreed upon. Notes will be given by the men who hold the deeds of all our lands. Whoever has money and heart for this business will please respond soon.

Also if any of our readers know or can find men or corporations that will lend us money on the terms indicated, that is, on good notes at 6%; or secondly on bond and mortgage at 6%, or thirdly on good notes at 7%, they will confer favor sending us immediate information. Address—John H. Noyes.

Circular, September 18, 1865

Never, we are informed, was the Oneida Community hive in such a state of industrial and mental activity. The trap works have been removed from their former occupancy at the "mill" into the new and enlarged factory at Willow Place, about a mile from the home buildings. The works are as yet scarcely fitted up with complete machinery in their new location, and are not fully manned. The increasing demand for traps will, however, require them to be in full operation at an early period, when they will employ from 50 to 100 hands. In connection with these works is a blacksmith shop, employing three or four hands, and the machine shop. At a short distance from the Willow Place trap works is the foundry, which gives employment to three or four hired men. Nearby is the sawmill, in which most of the lumber used by the Community is prepared.

The bag factory is now located in the mill building, formerly occupied by the trap works and the printing office, where it has spacious rooms for work, storage and packing. It furnishes employment to fifteen of the Community people, men and women, to eight hired men, and about twenty-five hired sewing women and girls, besides the work done by daily bees and otherwise in the Community Mansion. The amount of goods manufactured per month is $8,000.00 worth or more, requiring two men and a woman to tend to their shipment, the preparing of bills, etc. In the same building, connected with water power, is a carpenter shop where the packing-boxes for all the products of the place are made. The fruit-preserving business occupies a considerable part of the building called the "Tontine," a few rods in the rear of the Mansion. It gives steady employment to eight or ten members of the Community, men and women, and several hired girls. The preparation of the fruit for canning is done by volunteers from the family working a few hours at a time, with some help from the children. In the same building is the laundry, the steam engine, etc., which is directed by volunteers in succession from the Community women, and employs several hired persons. The commercial department, comprising trade in sewing silks and other articles, employs two or three traveling agents. The farm is carried on by hired help under the direction of M.K. Besides him, there are, for home convenience, departments of tailoring, shoemaking, lawn and flower garden, etc., etc., each having its chief and either hired or home assistants. The attendance upon visitors, and the providing of refreshments for them, employs about half a dozen persons most of the time.

There is a corps of phonographic reporters and journalists. The central home office employs two men in business correspondence, a business agent, a treasurer and cashier, and one or two bookkeepers.

Such is the organization and means of doing of the Community. It will be seen to be a complex affair; yet the harmonious adjustment of all this working machinery in these various industries is secured by a weekly business meeting of an hour or two in length, in which the foremen are allowed to present the needs of their respective departments and every member may propose whatever he deems of interest to the general success. Thus each business movement is stimulated and helped by the sympathy of the others; and when it is mentioned that the demand on the Community productions is constantly increasing—that on one day this week the orders for only two of their articles of sale amounted to $4,700.00, and that in another department they are some weeks behind their orders, it will be agreed that there, at least, the devil don't put out much of that kind of work which it is said he gives "for idle hands to do."

"But what," the reader will ask, "is the use of working in this way? What does it all amount to?"

It amounts, in the first place, to the satisfaction of being voluntary producers—if not in the highest, at least in the respectable and useful sphere—a satisfaction that is next to the Almighty's in creation.

Secondly, it demonstrates the ability of people to support themselves in Communism; selfishness being laid aside, and all working for a common interest.

Thirdly, it gives employment to many worthy and industrious people who are not members of the Community, and it will perhaps afford an opportunity for the Community to serve them from time to time in matters better than mere employment.

Daily Journal, January 17, 1866

At the machine shop the handles are being fitted to several thousand mop-irons. This job closes up the mop business.

Daily Journal, February 2, 1866

There was conversation tonight about the proposal to send Charles Cragin to Willimantic to learn the silk business. This was fully sympathized with, and it was thought best for Charles to go on to Wallingford this week. He will accordingly start tonight.

Daily Journal, March 15, 1866

Mr. Hamilton last evening called attention to the finances. He said we shall have to pay out quite a large amount of money during the next three weeks, and exhorted all to do what they could to limit the expenses of the family for the present. He thought a little continence in this respect at the present time, would lead to larger liberty hereafter.

Daily Journal, March 16, 1866

Mr. Wager requests that the amount due him on the Willow Place property ($6,000) be paid him on the first day of April, in greenbacks.

Daily Journal, March 26, 1866

Mr. Noyes, this morning, announced the following new

Principles of Business

1. Everything for sale except the soul.
2. Prompt clearing out of all dead property at any price that can be got.
3. The rule of prices—"sell as low as you *can,*" instead of—"get all you *can.*"
4. Pre-payment in buying and selling.

Daily Journal, March 27, 1866

Mr. Noyes has had the new business principles printed in the form of posters which have been put up in conspicuous places throughout the buildings.

Mr. Noyes talked again on business last evening. The nomination of Mr. Cragin as commissioner to sell property, was unanimously ratified, and Mr. Cragin made oath to be faithful to God and inspiration in exercise of the duties of his office. The following were Mr. Noyes's remarks at the opening of the discussion:

"I find that the Pentecostal text I have been preaching on will carry us clear through; that it contains in it all the doctrines, really, that I have put on to that poster of 'Business Principles.' I want our property clear from all encumbrances and in the hands of inspiration, so that God can really own and use it as he pleases. I want to see it free from our covetousness and stickiness. I am not afraid that God will squander it."

Daily Journal, March 28, 1866

TO THE FAMILY

I hereby give notice to the members of the family that I will be in the Reception Room from quarter past six to half past seven P.M. for the purpose of receiving contributions of jewelry or other property that persons may wish to have sold or disposed of for paying off our national debt; also for the purpose of consulting with the members respecting the sale of Community property and other matters relating to the new commission. [Signed] G. Cragin

Mr. Cragin in his new capacity as commissioner of sale, yesterday issued the following notice which was printed and distributed to the Community:

Notice

Members of the Community who hold real estate, mortgages, notes, or property of any description outside of the Community are hereby requested to report the same to me or to those whom I may hereafter appoint as my assistants. The members of the family are also notified that all dead property is to be sold or burnt up. Let nothing remain above ground that has not life in it. Either burn or bury whatever is not convertible into money or use for God and his cause.

Daily Journal, March 28, 1866

The heavens appear to have ratified Mr. Cragin's appointment in a marked way. His first day in office was signalized by the sale of the steam-engine for the sum of $1,050.

Daily Journal, March 28, 1866

The Petrie land is sold; $321\frac{7}{100}$ acres. Price $100 per acre. $775 were paid down, the balance is to be paid between May and September 1. The Community contract is to give a deed on the receipt of full payment.

Daily Journal, March 29, 1866

A large amount of enthusiasm prevails in the family with respect to the proposed auction, and everyone considers himself or herself a member of the committee of the whole, to hunt up dead property that can be sold. The women held a large and enthusiastic meeting on the subject yesterday, and appointed a committee to receive contributions.

Daily Journal, April 3, 1866

The principle and interest due on the mortgage held by Philip Wager ($6,420.) were paid yesterday, and the mortgage assigned to Francis Whaley, who had paid on the same $2,000 and is expected to pay $2,000 more tomorrow. Mr. Whaley assigned back to one of the Community members an interest of $2,000 in the mortgage, so that he owns only a $4,000 interest in it. Mr. Whaley agrees that this $4,000 may run three years at 7% and that the Community may pay it in two years on giving him two months' notice.

Daily Journal, April 3, 1866

In a sense we have failed as a firm doing business on a worldly basis. And now we have made an assignment of all our property to God and Jesus Christ. When a man makes an assignment he has no control of the property after that, unless it is as an agent. It is in the hands of the assignee. We have made an assignment of our property; and hereafter we are attending to the business as agents of the Lord, to whom the property is made over. I believe he will give us his spirit to actuate us in doing business for him. He will help us fix the prices in a way to secure the end he has in view.

Circular, April 6, 1866

I am anxious to push the sale of landed property as fast as we can. I would like to have bills got out very soon offering the Wilson place, sawmill, foundry, etc., and also the stone quarry across the creek on the Wager farm for sale. I have a strong inclination to advertise. I have got by any sensitiveness in reference to having it known that we are pretty heavily saddled with debt, and are anxious to sell off all unprofit-able property in order to pay our debts. I don't know but that we are going to be called upon to sacrifice our reputation for being wealthy, and so lose our credit. I am now prepared to be stripped of everything and have no credit with the business world, and be obliged to pay cash down for everything we buy. We are a great deal better prepared for this now than we were 18 years ago. This is of course looking at the case in an extreme light. But at any rate I want the inspiration of God to control us hereafter in both buying and selling.

When we have been prospered in business our wants have multiplied in proportion. Our expenses have increased without inspiration. Perhaps God is now putting us through a discipline calculated to prepare us for handling any amount of money without being contaminated in having our personal wants multiplied, or becoming puffed up in any way; learning us to handle his property as faithful agents and servants. We must attain to that state where we can have any amount of property around us and not be tempted to anything that is not dictated by inspiration.

Daily Journal, April 9, 1866

Sales at auction on Saturday—$1,234.89. Sales at the Tontine salesroom, $56.57. Two cows, two half-blood calves, and some other property were disposed of at private sale after the auction, making the total sales on Saturday about $1,500. The agricultural implements sold generally at fair prices, and the cows brought nearly their value with two or three exceptions. The musical instruments, bee hives and some other articles went at very low prices; but, on the whole, we have reason to be satisfied with this commencement of the annual sale. The audience was neither so large nor respectable as we could have desired. The goods in the salesroom were well arranged, and excited no little admiration. One table was covered with a fine display of greenhouse plants; another with preserved fruits and jellies; another with all the varieties of satchels and traveling bags we make; another table had a showcase which contained sewing silk, etc.; two other tables were covered with contributions—offerings to the Pentecostal spirit. The walls were hung with pictures and specimens of artistic effort, including three beautiful shell-covered what-nots, two flower wreaths, etc., etc. On the shelves were seen wool hats, steel traps, and "books going at 5¢." Some of us think a room thus filled and ornamented should be one of the institutions of the Community.

Daily Journal, June 18, 1866

The desire was expressed that we might be able to keep self-possessed and not get excited if we have a great many orders.

Circular, August 6, 1866

The opening year projected a new feature in the business of Willow Place. The order came—"prepare for silk-making—forward march!" On the 20th of January, Mr. Inslee went east to make investigations in regard to the construction of the requisite machinery. By the 15th of February, three students, one young man and two young women had been established in the Factory of C. L. Bottum, at Willimantic, whose Machine Twist stands highest in the market, and by the 10th of June they had all graduated. July 17th, Messrs. Hadden and Co. sold to the Oneida Community one bale of raw silk, weighing one hundred and three pounds, Saturday, the 28th inst., found the first lot of machinery in running order, and the part of the fine room devoted to silk-making fitted up. Monday, the 30th of July came, and with it the beginning of silk manufacturing by the O.C. The acorn has sprouted. A vigorous young seedling from the communistic oak, watered by the rain of Special Providence, and warmed by the sunshine of loving hearts. All day a changing group of admiring spectators hovered around the Winder, watching the slender threads as they were slowly reeled off.

"Is it horsehair?" soberly questioned the six-year-old urchin.

"Not much," we replied.

Circular, August 27, 1866

Work in the trap shop now commences at 5:30 A.M. and continues till 7 P.M., half an hour being allowed for each meal. Twenty-two hired hands are employed in the trap shop together with ten of our own folk.

Daily Journal, September 21, 1866

It is only fair that those who doubted the expedience of Mr. Noyes's policy in urging that the prices of our manufactured goods, especially traps, should be reduced—and said that we should "sell as low as we can"—should acknowledge that his policy has been crowned with grand success. The demand for traps is unprecedented; and the low prices of the Community traps prevent competition instead of stimulating it. Mr. Noyes said, at the time the new price list was made out— "I hope we shall sweep the board this fall," and it is being swept quite thoroughly.

Daily Journal, September 26, 1866

The peach stones which have been saved during the season, amounted to nearly twenty bushels and have been sold for $20.

Circular, October 8, 1866

In these days when we are doing so much to cancel our own national debt, Uncle Sam claims a levy to defray his, in the shape of an Internal Revenue Stamp on every can or bottle of fruit we sell. Over

Six Hundred Dollars has already been expended this season on these miniatures of George Washington: the putting them on is quite a business by itself, besides cancelling them.

Daily Journal, January 3, 1867

ANNUAL INVENTORY

Net Profit at O.C. in 1866	$ 17,396.86
Net Profit at Agency Branch in 1866	1,222.95
	$ 18,619.81
Expense more than Income at W.C. 1866	5,421.07
Net Profits of the United Communes for 1866	$ 13,198.74

The increase of capital has exceeded the profits as more capital has been received from new members than has been subtracted by seceders, and there has also been added $3300, not included in previous inventories on account of unavailability; so that the capital now stands:

Capital Inventoried at O.C.	$247,319.92
Capital Inventoried at Agency Branch	8,343.72
Capital Inventoried at W.C.	30,184.56
	$285,858.20
Total Inventoried Jan. 1, 1866	267,681.71
Increase of Capital	$ 18,166.49

The expenses of O.C. the past year for clothing, food, and many other things have been greater than they were last season, partly on account of high prices, and partly on account of improved fare.

Circular, January 21, 1867

HOME REVIEW FOR 1866

Vital Statistics

The number of members of the Oneida Community and its branches at the close of the year 1866 was two hundred and seventy-one distributed as follows: Oneida Community—209; Wallingford—45; New Haven Family—5; New York Agency—12.

During the year 1866 there were two deaths at O.C.—one of a person aged 86, and the other by consumption of a person in middle age.

No loss by death has occurred in either of the other Communities. The average health at the present time is high, only two or three absentees being noticed at the common meals. Number of members added during the year—19; Births—1; Number seceded—7; Deaths—2; Marriages—0; Increase—11.

Finances at O.C.

In addition to increasing their capital during the year by an amount of $18,000.00 the financial condition of the Community has been otherwise improved. The revival of business the present season, with the consequent sale of its products, has enabled the Community to extinguish this debt, the payables and receivables having been for some months nearly equal and at times showing a balance in our favor.

New Operations

During the past year a store has been fitted up, and filled with an assortment of goods for the accommodation of the Community, its workmen, and its neighbors; which investment promises to be fairly remunerative.

A large room at the Willow Place Factory has been furnished with silk machinery (made at the Community Machine Shop), and the manufacture of sewing machine twist is now successfully prosecuted. This is likely to grow into a large business. It has already absorbed $12,000 in machinery and stock, and thus early furnishes employment to a number of our own people besides fifteen hired employees, mostly women.

Costs of Living

The cost of living at the Oneida Community in 1866 was about the same as that of the previous year. We estimate the cost of food per individual at $1.55 per week, not including the labor of the Kitchen Department in preparing it. In 1865 it was estimated at $1.42 per week. The cost of clothing in 1866 was $37.20 to each individual, including in the work account only such part as was made up by hired tailors. Add to these the other necessary expenses of living, and the whole cost will be about the same as that estimated last year, namely, $2.62 for each individual per week.

Family Expenses

The following are some of the totals of expenditure during the year at O.C.: Musical Department, Fuel, Kitchen, Clothing, Shoe Shop, Medical, Laundry, Traveling, Furniture, Dentistry, Library, Stoves, Lights, incidentals, making a total of $34,244.30.

Some of the above items, such as traveling, musical outlay, etc., perhaps should not be considered in the legitimate expenses involved in the cost of living, but still they show the actual expenses of the Community the past year. Adding to the above $2,000.00 as a fair estimate for the use of the buildings, and averaging the sum total among 212 members, we have, average total expense per week of each individual—$3.28.

Trap-Making

This business is regarded in some respects as fluctuating, the demand for traps not being uniform. Some years we have to carry over a large amount of traps and stocks; while in other years it is difficult to supply all the demands. The past year has been rather fortunate for the Trap Department, enabling it to reduce the large stock it had on hand from the operations of the previous year. By our recent reduction of the price of traps, the sales are likely to be increased, but the profits are diminished to a very moderate figure. Number of traps made in 1866—195,000; number sold in 1866—211,898; amount of sales—$88,468.28; value of stock and tools on hand—$34,124.73.

Fruit-Preserving

This branch of business employed more labor and capital than in any previous season. A considerable proportion of the labor was performed by the members of the Community; men, women and children, not otherwise fully employed, volunteering their assistance in sorting the fruit and preparing them for the cans and bottles. At one time, however, there were twenty-nine persons engaged in this department, neighbors and others, who received wages. The articles preserved were: tomatoes, sweet corn, green peas, string beans, pieplant, pears, quinces, plums, cherries, blackberries, peaches, raspberries, huckleberries and strawberries; fifteen varieties of jellies were put up in glass tumblers and cups, the list also included a few varieties of sweet pickles and jams. There was an unprecedented demand for these goods. The sales amounted to nearly $50,000.00. Good luck attended the preserving operations in many respects, and some very gratifying encomiums on the goods shipped have been received.

Bag Business

The profits on this branch of industry have been small the past year, considering the amount of sales, which is accounted for by the fact that the Community has put down the price of its manufactures to a lower rate than heretofore. Number of traveling bags and satchels made—583½ dozen; number of traveling bags and satchels sold—702 dozen; amount of sales—$32,245.13.

Hired Labor

The following table gives the greatest number of hired workmen and workwomen who were employed at any time in the departments named: Bag Factory—14; Fruit Preserving—29; Farm and Teaming—11; Horticulture—11; Laundry—5; Tailoring—3; Silk Factory—15; Machine Shop—4; Trap Factory—62; Total—154.

Of these probably not more than a hundred were employed at any one time. The amount paid for labor in the above departments during the year was $28,000.

Taxes

The tax account shows that $8,809.29 had been paid for school, town, county, and national taxes.

Wallingford Community

The whole expense of living in this Community, exclusive of direct outlay for the *Circular,* was $10,927.80 for the year. This includes taxes, traveling expenses, educational and library expenses, and $500 for buildings and repairs. Divided among the members (averaged at 50) it would give $4.20 as the total individual cost per week.

Circular, April 8, 1867

In starting the silk, we plan on making a good article. No "fair" article will answer the purpose, we *must have* the best. Perhaps there is no business in which there is more cheating than in the manufacture of sewing silk. In attempting to reform and revolutionize this business, we meet difficulties with almost every step. But we are bound to conquer and shall succeed in establishing it on a correct basis. If we carry righteousness and honesty into the business of manufacturing, we are sure money and all manner of success will follow.

There are now thirty-one girls employed in the silk works, of whom six have been engaged this week. Twelve of them are between ten and fifteen years of age, and how to work them economically and yet not oppressively has become something of a problem. After due consultation, the following plan has been adopted for trial. Mrs. Waltch, an assistant whose disposition and temperament became well-adapted for the task, now has the immediate supervision of the girls. Her time is wholly occupied in looking after them—picking out the snarls they make, etc. At 10 A.M. and 4 P.M. recesses of fifteen minutes are given that they may have a run in the open air. How the plan works shall be duly reported.

Circular, September 16, 1867

Some extra exertion being necessary to finish a lot of trap springs, volunteers were called for who thought they could add four or five hours to their usual day's work, without drawing too largely on their reserve force. A caller at the forge shop at any hour before one o'clock at night would find there a busy group of young men. The foreman of the department, a bookkeeper, an M.D. fresh from Yale, one or two men from the silk factory, a machinist, and a foreman of the bag shop, with some regular trap makers, form a very efficient force. A flock of the children went over to the trap shop this morning to put their little fingers into the pie there. It was very inspiring. They did good service, assorting pieces from the foundry to the amount of fifty or sixty hundredweight.

Daily Journal, September 21, 1867

FITTING AMUSEMENTS AT WILLOW PLACE

Last night about quarter to seven a large load of Oneidans arrived and immediately commenced operations in the chain room and vicinity. Fitting, trying, mending, and sorting were all going on, under the management of M. H. Kinsley. Mr. Kinsley, Sr., started the bee, bringing the folks over in the omnibus with a four-horse team. Twelve of the party were women. Just before nine they were invited to the house to wash; after which ceremony ice cream and cake were passed around. A song or two followed when the party started homeward. Myron reports 36 hands at work, 24 from O.C.; work executed as follows: 10,000 "fits" made; 1,500 chains tried; a large quantity of malleable iron sorted, and a lot of swivels "turned"; as much work as 12 boys would do in a day.

Circular, October 26, 1867

The bag business is passing through some changes in the method of conducting it. It is found desirable to improve arrangements. One change inaugurated, which is important, is to have work done by the piece instead of by the day. The old vicious hireling system of the world, which is only one remove from slavery, requires, in order to get the most work for the least money by the day, a kind of driving, quite distasteful to Community people; and in the absence of this, the selfishness of hirelings takes advantage of our lenity to make a great leak in the profits of our manufactures, which are already reduced to the very minimum. We are learning by special tests, as fast as we can get at it, what it is really worth to do each part, and as soon as practicable intend to have it done by the piece. One man who works by the piece earns a third more pay than when he worked by the week, and the work per piece does not cost us so much, all because he has the more helpful motive to accomplish work, rather than the depressing spirit which watches the clock and seeks dilatory expedience to kill time. Doubtless every man who works for money will do much more when he knows that he will get every cent that he earns, and that every blow struck is so much cash in his pocket.

Circular, November 1, 1867

Mr. Noyes's letter recommending the raising of wages without solicitation from employees was received with approbation. This course has been pursued to some extent in the trap shop. Considerable talk followed, on our policy towards the help. Some of the boys and girls in our shop cannot afford to go to school but would like an evening school. Can we not help them, too, in some way; if we could, it would have a good effect on them and on the world round us. We want a spirit of liberality toward our workmen and not the spirit of the world which grinds them down and seeks to get all it can from them for the least money. Next week we shall commence carrying the boys who live at the Castle and Depot to and from the shop, as we do the girls.

Daily Journal, November 19, 1867

What we seem to need is some business that we can carry on in connection with our trap business to which we can shift our help when our trap trade slackens up. A year ago we had sixty hired hands to work for us on traps, and before the winter was over we had to discharge all but about 18 or 20 men. This fall we have had 90 hands, and we have over 60 now, and nearly all of them are good, steady, faithful hands, and they are anxious to work for us and probably would work for less wages if they could have work all winter. In selecting this help we have probably tried two or three hundred hands, first and last, and instructed them more or less in the business, at a great loss, and then they proved to be such help as we did not want. Now unless we have some business besides the trap business, we shall probably have to discharge the most of our help, and then when the trap trade starts up again, go through this sifting process again. The malleable iron business has been mentioned; the objection to that is unless we have a large capital that we want to tie up in our business, we shall have 30 or 40 more hands to discharge when the trap trade slackens. The bag-frame business helped us to keep our help employed last year, some, but the objection to that is we do not have enough of any one kind to make it pay. Let us all watch and pray and see if the Lord has not something more for us to do.

Daily Journal, December 16, 1867

George Cragin said that he had been looking over the books and found that our payments for hired labor between the present time and the first of last January amount to $36,000 and before the end of the year they will probably reach $40,000. We are not so nearly out of debt now as we were a year ago. The time of the men has not been kept as carefully and accurately as it should have been, and the books must determine how much we invest in the different departments. George E. wished everyone to study the matter and see how much we can reduce our expenses this winter. We want to keep constantly before us the fact that we have vowed to get out of debt and keep out.

Daily Journal, December 18, 1867

It should have been reported that we commenced the eight-hour system in the trap and machine shops on Saturday.

Circular, January 20, 1868

FINAL RESULT OF 1867

The Community debt which pressed heavily in August and September has since been reduced by a fair amount of sales; and on closing the books for the year, we find the result, on the whole, satisfactory.

The O.C. itself has added to its capital, while Wallingford, New Haven, and New York have lost. These are the figures:

Net earnings of O.C.		$28,850.85
Deficit at Wallingford and New Haven	$5,192.29	
Deficit in New York Agency	$2,242.52	7,434.81
Net Earnings of O.C. and Branches		$21,416.02
Amount added by new members		2,804.15
Increase of capital of O.C. and Branches		$24,220.17
Capital January 1, 1867		$286,048.20
Capital January 1, 1868		$310,268.37

The lack of ready money during the greater part of the business season made our position a difficult one. Although at the commencement of the year we were nearly free from debt, in August when our various branches of manufacture conspired to absorb capital preparatory to the fall sales, our liabilities exceeded our cash assets nearly $59,000.00. The strain upon our resources at that time caused us much serious study in the adoption of certain conclusions, whereby we trust that we shall be able to clear our affairs from some of the annoyances and dangers that have beset them in the past.

During the early years of the Community the want of profitable occupations was sorely felt. One by one these have been supplied until, within the last three or four seasons, the avenues of lucrative business have so multiplied that we have been tempted to expand beyond our resources. Under a pressure of orders the tendency to add a few improvements here and there, whereby the cost of production may be lessened, is almost irresistible. The experience of the past year has brought us face to face with the problem of continence in money investments. The improvement and expansion of stock added during the year have been over $37,000.00 in value, an excess of $13,000.00 beyond the addition of our capital. The greater part of this sum was expended before September. At that time we made a stern resolve to forego all expense not absolutely necessary. Although we have adhered to our purpose, and thereby seriously disappointed some friends interested in the Midland Railroad, to say nothing of calling out the vituperations published in the *Democratic Union,* we find that the investments made previous to September have added about $10,000.00 to our burden of debt. A year ago we were nearly free from debt; but on the first of the present January our liabilities exceeded our cash assets about $10,000.00. If the coming season shall equal the last in activity, we shall require for business purposes nearly $60,000.00 in ready money between now and August.

In view of these facts the Community has decided to follow up its September resolve by a change in its general policy. For the last four years our policy has been that of expansion; expansion in hiring labor, in receiving new members, in establishing outposts, in education, and in borrowing money. This course has had its use. It has brought us into contact with the hireling system of the world so that we see its advantages and defects, we have received valuable addition to our strength among the friends who have joined us; some of our young men have had valuable business experience in New York. Some have gained a scientific education in New Haven; and finally we have learned the misery of borrowing money. We have made an "out" and now we are going to get "back." Concentration is our watchword. Our plan in general is to contract the smaller communes and outposts and to strengthen the center. The paper will be removed to Oneida. Business there will be reorganized. The Community will make the most of its old members, assimilate its new ones, get onto the platform of pre-payment and *get out of debt*. The details of the change will report themselves as they transpire.

Our friends will readily see that this is the right movement for the present time. Having by our course of expansion for several years gained a start in education, art, and business experience, we will now return and pour the results into the lap of the parent that sent us forth. Oneida herself is yet to be completed as a model of Communism, and all her children will enjoy putting a hand to the work. She needs new permanent buildings in place of the wooden ones now existing. There should be built a proper refectory, a model children's house, an art gallery and a University. These things are necessary before Communism is ready for public exhibition as an integral system. Let us see and show how much God can do for man and society on a single spot.

Circular, January 27, 1868

HOME REVIEW FOR 1867

Vital Statistics

On the first of January, 1868, the Community and all its branches numbered 278 persons. They were distributed as follows: Oneida Community and Willow Place—210; Wallingford Community—44; New Haven Community—8; New York Agency—16.

There was one death at O.C. during the year. The disease was cancerous and the person was 66 years old. No death has occurred in any of the other communities. The general health of the Community has been excellent. Number of members added during the year—9; Births—5; Total—14. Number seceded (a family)—6; Deaths—1; Increase—7.

Cost of Living

The cost of food at Oneida per individual is estimated at $1.46 per week. Last year it was $1.55. The cost of clothing during the year was $38.95 to each individual. Neither of these items include the work done by our own people in preparing food or making clothing. The men's tailoring, however, is done entirely by hired labor, the cost of which is included in the above statement. The expense for boots and shoes per individual was $7.09.

Family Expenses

In addition to the items of food and clothing there are many miscellaneous expenses in every family. Some might be included among the necessaries of life, and others are probably luxuries. The following table shows the total family expense of the O.C. during the year past.

Furniture, library, music, lights, stoves, fuel, laundry, kitchen, clothing, shoe-shop, dentistry, medical, traveling, stationery, watches and clocks, incidentals. Total—$37,041.39.

The item of traveling includes about $1,400.00 expended by Messrs. George W. Noyes and C. S. Joslyn during their tour in Europe last summer. Deducting this, and adding $2,000.00 depreciation of buildings, and averaging the sum total among 210 members, we have; Average total expense per week of each individual—$3.45.

Trap Business

The trade in traps, which is not uniform, was quite brisk this season. We adhered to our reduction of rates which we made last year, and some improvements in the process of manufacture enabled us to realize more from the sale than we did a year ago. Number of traps sold in 1867—300,776; Amount received from sales—$109,922.75

Fruit-Preserving

The bad luck we had with corn and peas last year caused a partial contraction of that business this season. The managers of the department profited by the leisure to investigate new methods of heating, etc.;

and the result is that we have conquered the difficulties in the preserving of corn, and probably peas. The demand for our fruit this season has been far beyond our ability to supply. If we find ourselves at last on firm foundations, we shall make a large business in this line.

Bag Business

The profits in this branch of manufacture have not been very large. The competition with city manufacturers is too close. We are thinking of gradually reducing our stock with a view of withdrawing our capital from the business.

Hired Labor

No satisfactory statistics are at hand to show the exact number of employees in the service of the Community at any given time during the season. The number was some larger than in any previous year. The amount of cash paid for labor was nearly $40,000.00.

Silk Manufacturing

This business has been enlarged during the year. The large room in the east wing of the trap factory has been filled with machinery, and nearly 40 women and girls are now employed. Although with new machinery and new hands no large profit was expected the first year, the results are such as to encourage us. Experience will probably enable us to make this a large and profitable branch of manufacture.

March 25, 1868

EVENING MEETING

Mr. Underwood reread the talk in which Theodore was spoken of as one qualified to take the lead in finances and develop a true policy for the Community. The nomination was received with expressions of satisfaction. It was thought Theodore was well qualified to fill such an office.

Theodore was appointed chairman of the Committee for the disposal of dead property; and this committee was authorized to dispose of any property that it might be thought expedient to part with. This committee may also elect more members if those now serving think it desirable. By request of Mr. Woolworth, Theodore unfolded some of the workings of his mind on the financial question. So far as he has matured any plan, it is to look the books over and learn how the different businesses "have run" for the past four or five years; see how much capital each has required, and put the whole thing in black and white. As it is now, nobody can tell the exact amount of capital invested in the trap works during the busy season. The same is true of the other businesses. We should know just what each business requires. Then the central management could say to each department of industry, "Here, you can have the use of so much capital this year and make what use of it you think expedient." This arrangement would save the accumulation of dead property; educate the foremen of departments in wise financiering; and save overgrown plans in one department that would swallow the capital of the whole Community. Such is a brief sketch of a few of Theodore's ideas.

Circular, April 6, 1868

This is the time of year for the organization of business. We used to have a time every spring of making a thorough re-cast of all departments, foremen included. Lately, however, the enlargement of our industry has seemed to call for more extended plans than could be accomplished in one season, and the foremen now retain their places until some good reason arises for their change.

In connection with our determination to get out of debt we have formed another purpose—to so arrange our business that times of extraordinary pressure from orders shall find us provided with a larger stock of goods on hand than heretofore. For several weeks last fall the shops at Willow Place were the scene of an extraordinary whirl of business—50 or 60 extra hired hands beside all of our people who could be spared from other quarters, and the shops running nights by a large force of volunteers from our own number who worked their full time by daylight. We have since found that some of our weaker members injured themselves through excessive zeal and lack of proper forethought on the part of those whose duty it was to look after them. One evening this week this matter came up for criticism in our evening meeting. It was plainly seen that what at the time we intended for a great good has proved in some cases a very great evil, and needs to be repented of by all concerned. All testified that a valuable lesson had been learned. We must learn to provide time for rest and meditation at all times, even if we have to forego large sales.

Circular, April 13, 1868

Preparations are being made for the removal of the fruit-preserving to the old mill where it takes the place of the bag business. The latter is gradually closing out. We are having the last of the bag bees, which have continued through so many years of the Community history.

Circular, May 11, 1868

The Community has closed its office in New York City. Of the members stationed there, a part have returned to Oneida, and a part have gone to Wallingford; the same is true of its business. The sale of silks, traps, and preserved fruits is transferred to Oneida, while others, making their home at Wallingford (which is about three hours distant by rail, and five hours by rail and boat), will visit the city weekly to do business for both communes. A room in 335 Broadway is retained, with a desk and bed, for the use of our agents when in the city.

The New York Office was started in 1864, a short time after the new series of the *Circular* began at Wallingford, so that there seems to be something rhythmical in the vibrations of the two movements.

The words spoken in our hearts four years ago were *delocalization* and *expansion.* A horror of becoming a narrow-minded, sectarian body seized upon us. We felt called to recognize our unity with humanity, and we saw that if God was bringing truth to birth in us, it was not for us alone, but for the benefit of the world. Worldly wisdom said, "you will make more money by staying at home and rolling on in the same old rut"; but we felt in our souls that if we curled up into a selfish, social cocoon, the Lord would foresake us.

These ideas were not at all clear to us then, but we can now see that these were instincts that work in our hearts and so we moved the paper out of the whirl of Oneida business and started an office in New York City where some of our young men could get a commercial education, and bought a house in New Haven, that we might send others to school at Yale. Since that time, two young men have graduated from the Yale Medical School, one from the Law School of Columbia College; a class of young men and women have taken lessons in music and elocution, and we have developed and matured our business principles, which we have returned to Oneida to put in practice.

Neither the enchantments of pleasure-seeking and amusements nor the skepticism of literature and science have turned our young people away from the deep principles of "Bible Communism." They returned home and with a rugged purpose to devote themselves to the setting up of God's Kingdom in this world, and to carry forward the work begun by their fathers and mothers. Surely the result of this four years campaign is calculated to encourage those whose hearts are open to understand God's program.

Circular, January 11, 1869

FINANCIAL REPORT FOR 1868

The policy of concentration of capital and prudence in investments, which we adopted about eighteen months ago, has had a favorable effect upon our financial condition the past season. Our producing departments have been small, considering the increase in size of the home family, consequent upon the withdrawal of the stations at New Haven and New York.

The following are the net results at O.C. and all its branches.

Increase at O.C.	$ 55,532.02
Increase at Wallingford	5,425.45
	$ 60,957.47
Deduct Loss at New York	2,178.52
Net Increase of Capital of United Communities	$ 58,778.95
Capital January 1, 1868	313,008.22
Net Capital of United Communities January 1, 1869	$371,787.17

Under the cost of living, the following are some of the principal items.

	Per Year	Per Week
Food per individual	$ 86.44	$1.66
Clothing per individual	$ 35.18	.68
Boots and shoes per individual	6.70	.14
Washing per individual	7.22	.14
Other items	47.79	.92
Total expense per individual	$183.33	$3.53

Trap Manufacture

The trade in traps has not been quite as large this year as last. The market opened earlier in the summer than usual, and fell off as the money stringency in the West came on. The business has been allowed more capital than heretofore, and the manufacture has been carried steadily on throughout the year; consequently we have avoided the crowded rush to fill orders in the fall, which so annoyed us a year ago.

Number of Traps Manufactured	278,000
Sales	$99,937.77
Average Number of Hands Hired	38
Average Number of Hands from O.C.	19

Silk Manufacture

The standard of excellence which we have undertaken in the manufacture of machine-twist has caused an increasing demand for the article, and our shop has been driven to its fullest capacity all fall. We are expecting to enlarge the room in the spring.

Average Number of Hired Women and Girls Employed	50
Average Number of O.C. Hands Employed	17
Raw Silk Consumed During the Year, (44 Bales)	4,664 lbs.
Sales	$86,881.58

Preserved Fruit

This business has had a moderate success. But the wear and tear in the height of the season was more than we could afford, while carrying on our other branches of spiritual and industrial enterprises, which suffered some from the imperious demands of spoiling fruit. So it has been decided to abandon the business. Fruit was plenty this season, and no great loss was incurred. Number of cans of vegetables put up—70,866; number of cans of fruit put up—20,281; number of bottles of fruit put up—9,923; number of tumblers of jelly—3,388; sales—$40,722.79.

Wallingford

The number of persons forming this community at the present time is 33. The number up to the time of the removal of the *Circular* office to O.C. was 50; and during our fruit harvest it was 45. The average number has been nearly 39.

Our remunerative industries have been limited to job printing, fruit-raising, and farming. The net proceeds of the printing department (not estimating the labor of the hands employed, at present three men and two women) have been $2,744.54. Including under one head the various branches of garden and farm culture, the total net proceeds of the garden and farm for 1868 were $5,161.26. The cost of living at Wallingford in 1867 was $1.88 per week for food for each member and for clothing $.84. In 1868 the figures were: the cost of food—$2.44, the cost of clothing—$.82. The average total expense per week of each individual was $4.85.

Circular, January 10, 1870

FINANCIAL STATEMENT FOR 1869

The net earnings of the Oneida Community, as shown by its inventory for the present year, are $30,920.55. This is $24,180.20 less than the earnings of last year.

The difference is accounted for mainly by the discontinuance of the fruit-preserving business and the transfer of capital to new enterprises here and at Wallingford, which have not yet had time to mature and become productive.

The net capital of the Oneida Communities is summed up as follows:

Balance of profit at O.C. and Willow Place....$	31,677.87
Net Earnings of Wallingford Community.......	1,906.57
Total Net Gains...... ....$	33,584.44
Capital January 1, 1869..................	371,787.17
Net Capital of United Communities, January 1, 1870.....................	$405,371.61

Cost of Living

The ordinary family expense, after deducting $1,000.00 for the estimated cost of food furnished to visitors, is $45,984.00, exceeding the amount reported last year by over $4,000.00. This excess is more apparent than real, the last year's account of expenses having been reduced by certain transfers of property beyond their true showing. The expense account contains some items, such as music, library, traveling, etc., which are not generally included in family necessities. The amount assigned for clothing, subsistence, washing, and fuel, which commonly comprise what is called the "cost of living," is $36,779.35. Dividing this by 232, the average number of members, great and small, gives $158.96 as the individual cost per year, or the rate of $3.05 per week.

It should be borne in mind, however, that the above is mainly the cost of the *raw material*. The labor of cooking and washing and partly that of making clothing, boots and shoes, is omitted.

Education

A building has been fitted for a seminary the present season, at a cost of $2,500.00, and classes of young men and women, to the number of 65, have commenced a regular course of study in geography, philosophy, the higher mathematics and languages, with recitations and examinations. The teacher is a recent graduate of the Scientific School of Yale College. The design is to combine in the training of our young people, study and labor, giving one half day to each.

Trap Works

The pacification of the Southern States and the opening of the West by the Pacific Railroad operate favorably in the demand for our traps. Number of traps manufactured—337,437; sales—$114,841.20.

Foundry

The business of the foundry is in excess of last year. The articles manufactured are sleigh-shoes, wagon fixtures, architectural columns and window-caps, agricultural castings and sash weights. Amount of iron manufactured at foundry—300,000 pounds.

Silk Works

The standard of quality maintained in our Machine Twist creates a demand fully equal to our present ability to supply. During the year, we have bought a factory at Wallingford, Connecticut, stocked it in part with machinery, and it is now running in connection with our works here. Amount of stock manufactured—6,941 pounds; sales, including brands of other manufacturers—$141,940.00; average number of hands employed—about 100.

A commencement has been made the present season in silk weaving, with looms and workmen from England. About seven thousand yards of ribbon have been manufactured, but the enterprise is yet in the stage of experiment.

Machine Shop

This is the vitalizing department of the whole, employing about ten men. Its services are so diffused in all directions that a specific account of them cannot well be given. The two following items, however, show its relations to our main producing agencies. Value of silk-machinery manufactured—$7,000.00; value of trap-tools manufactured —$2,000.00.

Building

The main works in this line have been the fitting-up of the Seminary, the erection of a manufacturing building at Willow Place, the renovation of the Wallingford factory, and the building of a large wing to the Mansion at O.C. The latter, from its size and thoroughness of construction, has been costly and is still unfinished. Steam heating apparatus has been introduced to the Community dwelling at a cost of $5,600.00. It is estimated that the whole amount of our net income for the present year has been invested in new buildings.

Cash Paid for Hired Labor

Hardware Department	$20,199.00
Silk Department	15,708.00
Farm and Garden	9,564.49
Building	9,825.94
Clothing and Boots and Shoes	500.74
Laundry	824.22
Total	$56,532.39

Circular, January 24, 1870

WALLINGFORD COMMUNITY—STATISTICS FOR 1869

Capital January 1, 1870	$49,904.40
Capital January 1, 1869	41,728.98
Increase in Capital	$ 8,175.42
Deduct Funds Advanced by O.C.	6,268.85
Net Earnings of Wallingford Community in 1869	$ 1,906.57

Cost of Living

The subsistence account of the Community, comprising expenditures for food, clothing, fuel and laundry, were a total of $6,390.92.

If to this amount we add $500 for rent, there is a total of $6,890.92

to cover what is expressed in the lowest terms as the "cost of living." Dividing this sum by forty (the average number of the family) gives a result of $172.27 as the cost of subsistence for each member per year, or $3.31 per week. The aggregate expenses of the Community (omitting rent, but including the account for taxes, traveling, library, education, etc.) was $9,500—equivalent to a weekly rate of $4.56 for each person.

Circular, March 21, 1870

MONEY MATTERS

The progress of its money-matters is recorded in the following statistics, drawn from its annual inventories (since January 1, 1865):

In 1865, Net Earnings.............$12,382.81
In 1866, Net Earnings............. 13,198.74

Total net earnings in ten years, $180,580.26; being a yearly average income of $18,058.02 above all expenses. The succeeding inventories show the following results:

In 1867, Net Earnings.............$21,416.02
In 1868, Net Earnings............. 55,100.83
In 1869, Net Earnings............. 30,920.55

Being an average for the last three years of $35,812.46 per annum.

Oneida Circular, February 12, 1872

COMMUNITY JOURNAL

At the beginning of the O.C., our account-keeping was made just as small as possible. There were no accounts between the Community and its members; and none between the different departments, although they helped one another in many ways. In the infancy of our Communism we were determined to have nothing to remind us of separate interests; everything was laid at the feet of love and good feeling. Our account-books at that time would have hardly done credit to a farmer who meant to know just how he stood. By-and-by, as our business began to grow, we were compelled to keep accounts with our customers. Our books were then as simple as those kept in a small country store. Mr. J. J. Franks, an experienced accountant, becoming interested in the Community, soon taught us to keep our books by "double-entry." But this did not lead to thorough account-keeping between our departments, though we could see that we were always more or less in the dark as to the profits of any particular business. Feeling thus, we have by degrees crept along toward a thorough-going system of accounts. It was thought last year that our Communism had become robust enough to stand a good deal more bookkeeping. At the beginning of the year each department, whether for production or consumption, is now charged with a certain amount of capital, including cash and goods and material on hand. This the foreman uses to the best of his ability; he is charged with all monies paid him and all bills against him, and he is credited for all his unemployed cash as well as for all the money and goods he furnishes any one of the departments. This system is not only favorable to economy, but it makes our business thoroughly intelligible and systematic. Of course, there is still no account-keeping between the members; and even so, with our present method, Communism saves a deal of figuring.

Circular, April 8, 1872

A writer in the last Circular, April 1, 1872, characterized the last year as one of special economy in the history of the Community, and set forth the self-denial the members exercised in respect to dress. It occurs to us that this writer did not represent the full extent of the self-denial which was practiced in the Community last year. Personal expenses, it is true, were materially curtailed, but these had been only a fraction compared with the outlay yearly made in building and other improvements. During 1871 building was practically suspended, and every department of expense was kept at the minimum. Instead of giving the departments of business carte-blanche (which they had substantially had), in respect to expansion and outlay, a definite appropriation of money—as much as the prosperity of the business and the general financial condition would allow—was made to each, and this appropriation fixed the boundary of expansion and investment. Departments, as well as individual members, chastened their desire for "new clothes" last year; and the result told favorably on the general prosperity. Some of our enterprises had become such vigorous shoots that they needed just this "pinching in," and a stronger and healthier growth is already manifest.

Circular, June 10, 1872

Some of the papers say that if Mr. Noyes takes a pinch of snuff all the Community sneezes. We can tell a story about one pinch that he took. Our great expenses year before last in building and our increased investment in silk business reduced our available resources to a low point. About the first of January, 1871, Mr. N., who, if a visionary, is at least a remarkably practical one, said in a talk recommending honest retrenchment, that he wouldn't have any new clothes for a year; *and that if the rest of the men were of his mind the tailor should send his "gooses" to grass and be drafted into some other business.* All the men of the Community "sneezed," and (what is more) all the women too. In laughing about it afterwards, Mr. Noyes said he called that a sneeze worth several thousand dollars. Several thousand dollars! This is no expression at all of its worth. The effect of the fast on our treasury is not to be compared with its spiritual effect. It brought us nearer to God, and added to our domestic happiness.

Oneida Circular, January 6, 1873

THE EARNINGS OF THE COMMUNITY

Our custom of reporting in the *Circular* the financial results of our labors at the end of each year was pleasant. Part of the comfort of success was in telling of it; and we presume our readers were entertained and pleased as well as we when we had a good story to tell. How we came to drop that custom it would be difficult to say. Probably a feeling crept over us that it was impertinent to call so much attention to our private affairs. But we can hardly be said to have any private affairs; and on sober second thought we will take the liberty to go back to our old way. The following are the figures on our balance-sheets for the last two years:

1871

Earnings of the Oneida and Wallingford
Communities above losses and expenses
in 1871 .... $ 55,386.98
Add Balance of Property brought in by
members above that withdrawn.......... 8,446.61
Net Increase in 1871..................... $ 63,833.59

1872

Earnings of O.C. and W.C. above losses
and expenses in 1872................. $ 71,010.93
Deduct balance of property withdrawn
by seceding members above that
brought in 3,557.23
Net Increase in 1872..................... $ 67,453.70

Recapitulation

Earnings of O.C. and W.C. in 1871	$ 55,386.98
Earnings of O.C. and W.C. in 1872	71,010.93
Net Earnings in two years	$126,397.91
Add balance of property brought in over that withdrawn in two years	4,889.38
Increase in two years	$131,287.29

Circular, October 20, 1873

Financial panics, like fire, try men's works, and not unfrequently discover a hollow interior, when all was solidity to outward view. Perhaps some of our readers may like to know how the late crisis affected us. While we have several hundred thousand dollars invested in manufacturing operations, we must unavoidably feel the influence of such financial storms. Our busiest time of year is September. In that month all our principal industries are generally so active that we have for several years required the use of more or less borrowed capital during the summer and autumn. This we have obtained from our banks, and by taking, contrary to our usual custom, four or six months' credit, on our principal articles of raw material. The temptation has been strong to make permanent use of our credit in this way, and so extend our operations beyond the limits set them if we should wait until the requisite capital should be earned. But a community like ours cannot afford to run risks, and two or three years ago we determined to work into a position in which we can pay cash for everything we buy. A considerable gain in this direction has been made, but not enough to prevent our feeling the recent financial crash, in the sudden stoppage of remittances from our customers. For the first ten days of the month we received only about a quarter of the money due us, and which in ordinary times could be confidently counted on. Having a considerable sum to pay in the shape of notes coming due, it seemed for a few days as if we could scarcely meet our obligations promptly, but providentially receiving a loan and other means from unexpected sources, the critical point was turned, and all our legal obligations promptly met. The payment of many of our small debts has been delayed beyond the customary period of thirty days, but we are now making collections fast enough soon to catch up with them. At one time we were puzzled at the outlook as to supplies of currency for paying off our numerous work people, but the dearth of exchange on New York in the West caused some of our customers to send us currency by express so that we had plenty for all necessary purposes. But the unpleasant sensation of finding ourselves liable to sympathetic cramp when Wall Street is undergoing a convulsion; of worrying for a few thousand dollars when ten times as much is due us from prompt paying customers, leads us to renew our resolution of getting at once in a situation to "pay as we go." Then, if the whole country becomes bankrupt, the worst that can happen to us will be a temporary cessation of manufacturing; but having no debts to pay we can live on mush and applesauce and wear our old clothes till better times. Our cause is too precious to risk in the arena with the bulls and bears, and we shall gladly bid good-by one of these days to the credit system with all its allurements.

Circular, October 27, 1873

Our silk and trap trade, contrary to our expectations, still continue very good. Orders for traps, countermanded during the panic, have been renewed. Wholesale trade in silk is dull, but the retail trade is very good. But fearing to accumulate a stock of goods on a falling market, we have reduced the running time of the trap factory and silk room to eight hours. The silk department keeps its full complement of hands, and the rate of wages per hour remains unchanged.

Circular, January 12, 1874

The Community businesses suffered the past year from the general financial depression of the country, and our profits, as shown by the inventory just completed, were somewhat less than half what they were in 1872; but when it is considered that some of the oldest and best established firms in the country went down in the great autumnal storm, the fact that our obligations are in better shape than they were a year ago and our assets have been increased by about $25,000, leaves us certainly no cause to murmur.

Circular, March 9, 1874

Twenty years ago Mr. John R. Miller was our financier. His custom was to pray for money when the Community needed it, and always to trust God when appearances seemed most forbidding. His daughter is now our financier, and she has inherited her father's spirit about money matters. We have, in a number of instances lately, met with good providences and answers to prayer when in want of money. About two weeks ago we had some large bills to pay but we could not see where the money to meet them was coming from. There was a firm in a western city that owed us $2,000 which was not quite due. We thought of writing and asking them to pay part of it; the next day, without our writing, a letter came from them enclosing a thousand dollars. At another time we needed a large sum to meet payments and asked our Wallingford friends by telegraph if they could make a deposit in our New York bank; they made the necessary deposit. It was a good providence, for they have not had anything to spare before for a long time. Last week we needed money and asked one of our customers for a note, and he sent us a check. We feel like recognizing these providences as the care of God for us. Mr. Noyes said he "would rather be poor all the time, than not to have to look to God for money."

IX

Complex Marriage

Far more widely known than for its theological heterodoxy or even its experiment in eugenic breeding which, after the best part of a hundred years have tended to fade from the public mind, the Oneida Community is known—where it is still known at all—for its radical innovations in social and sexual theory. Although from the beginning members published widely the argument upon which they based this theory, which they called Complex Marriage, they encountered in their own time most often either the violent opposition of prejudice or the perhaps more understandable misunderstanding of ignorance.

However it was, they were stigmatized in the popular mind as Free Lovers. This they denied widely in print but it must have persisted to such an annoying degree that as late as 1871 they began to announce in the masthead of the *Circular* a corrective Special Notice: "The O.C. and Branches are not 'Free Lovers' in the popular sense of the term. They call their social system *Bible Communism* or *Complex Marriage,* and hold freedom to love only within their own families, subject to Free Criticism and Male Continence."

The original statement of their social theory, which they called The Bible Argument, was published in their *First Annual Report* on January 1, 1849. This, and a compilation from the first three *Annual Reports,* under the title *Bible Communism* which was published in 1853, were sent by Noyes to the Governor of New York State and to other men prominent in public life. No official reproof was forthcoming although gossip, rumor, and scandal were rife both in the press and by word of mouth. The virulent attack by the

265

New York *Observer* in 1851–52 and the wholly illegal proceedings of the Oneida County District Attorney against them in 1850 were examples of the ordeals that the Oneida Communists endured.

In an article replete with errors of fact, the *Observer* (February, 1852) remarked in closing that with their own sense of decency they were able to give "only the vaguest and most distant intimations" of the depths of depravity in which that institution wallowed. Two weeks later the *Circular* noted that "the newspapers, following one after another in the wake of the N. Y. *Observer,* have been giving us plenty of publicity." Even their neighboring *Oneida Telegraph,* although it admitted that it had always heard the Community folks spoken of as "industrious, well-behaved people," intimated that there were rumors afloat, "too revolting to be credited."

By the next week, March 7, 1852, the combined attack from at home and abroad had evidently reached such a pitch that the communists published a manifesto covering their past, their present, and what they believed to be their future. In the past, they said, their course had been neither seditious nor unchaste; their household habits would show not a licentious spirit but the opposite of licentiousness. Still, at present their liberty was looked upon with jealousy and offense by surrounding society. Therefore they had decided to withdraw from the position they had held and formally to resume the marriage morality of the world.

"We land," they wrote, "from our long voyage of exploration, improved and refreshed, with a large store of various experience." In May they wrote that "the Oneida Community has, in a certain sense, discharged its mission. Let us treat of that as in the past, without broaching the question whether its principles will again be asserted in the world." A month later, in an article referring to the *Observer* affair, they said that although they had not suffered from actual violence as had the Primitive Church, nevertheless the shame of public censure and public opinion was now vastly more powerful than in the early times." Still they had "found it possible to live in the fiery furnace unharmed."

No further manifesto was issued then or later in their publications touching any change from the position announced in the Manifesto of March 7. In late August they printed a *Theocratic*

Platform sketching "their new state of society" which included the *"Abandonment of the Entire Fashion of the World*—especially marriage and involuntary propagation" and next *"Cultivation of Free Love, Dwelling together in Associations or Complex Families."* In December they reprinted the *Theocratic Platform* as before, with the exception of substituting "Cultivation of Universal Love" for "Free Love," as in the first version.

In January, 1853, in an article in the *Circular* entitled "The Bible on Marriage," they gave the rationale for their new position. "The doctrine that *death* is the legitimate end of the contract of marriage is distinctly conceded by all. Paul and Christ found a way to introduce what may be called a posthumous state into the world, by the application of the death of Christ. Their doctrine was that, by believing in Christ, we are crucified with him. If one died for all, then all died. This doctrine of the believer's death and resurrection by union with Christ was, with the Primitive Church, the very core of the Gospel. They realized that they were past death and so were delivered from sin and legality." It was "the grand apostasy of Christendom" that had lost sight of the truth. The Oneida Community, they said, would follow Christ and Paul who led them unmistakably to the expectation that marriage would be done away and the only question was, what next? Complex Marriage, they still believed, was the true answer.

The *Bible Argument* lays the scriptural foundation for the practice of Complex Marriage. "In the kingdom of heaven, the institution of marriage which assigns the exclusive possession of one woman to one man, does not exist (Matt. 22: 23–30). In the kingdom of heaven, the intimate union of life and interests, which in the world is limited to pairs, extends through the whole body of believers; i.e., complex marriage takes the place of simple (John 17: 21). The abolishment of sexual exclusiveness is involved in the love-relation required between all believers by the express injunction of Christ and the apostles and by the whole tenor of the New Testament. 'The new commandment is that we love one another,' and that not by pairs, as in the world, but *en masse*. The restoration of true relations between the sexes is a matter second in importance only to the reconciliation of man to God. Bible Communists are operating in this order. Their main work, since 1834, has been to develop the religion of the New Covenant and establish union with God. The second work, in which they are now specially engaged, is the laying the foundation of a new state of society by developing the true theory of sexual morality."

The practical working out of this theory required much deliberation and heart-searching. Noyes, its author, was the final arbiter but others of the so-called central members were consulted, and the women among them spoke for the feminine point of view. Since Male Continence was not only their basic tenet but an absolute necessity in a group which could not afford children, it was thought best for the young of both sexes to be initiated into the method by older persons who had learned self-control.

Robert Allerton Parker has written in *A Yankee Saint*:

After prolonged deliberations, the "central members" decided that they must devise some system of supervision. Exclusive, idolatrous bonds between two members, attachments "unhealthy and pernicious to the whole system of complex marriage" must never gain foothold in the Community. Hearts must be free to love all of the true and worthy. This precaution suggested the intervention of a third party—so that all attachments might be brought under the inspection of the Community; so also that women members might, without embarrassment or restraint, decline proposals that did not appeal to them. No member should be obliged to receive—to this they pledged themselves—at any time, under any circumstances, the attention of those they had not learned to love. The Community promised to protect its members from social approaches that might, for one reason or another, either temporarily or permanently, be deemed unattractive. Every woman was free to refuse any, or every, man's attention. When two members aspired to closer relations, an intimation to that effect was given by the man, but always through the medium of an older woman who represented the Community and was authorized to control such negotiations. This was for the double purpose of overseeing and advising the young people, and of allowing the woman so approached to be perfectly free to decline without embarrassment.

As John Humphrey Noyes wrote in a pamphlet entitled *Male Continence,* published in 1877:

The Oneida Community in an important sense owed its existence to the discovery of Male Continence, and it has evidently been the Committee of Providence to test its value in actual life.

The testing Committee, thus qualified has been in session thirty years. Two hundred and fifty sober persons have lived together more than a quarter of a century under the rule of Male Continence in constant observation of its tendencies and effects. Their experiment has gone through all the vicissitudes that reach from one generation to a second. Many applications of their sexual discovery which were in the far-off future when it was first published are now matters of experience. They have tested Male Continence even in its application to Scientific Propagation. In a word, the infantile theory of 1848 has reached the manhood of robust embodiment in 1877.

This necessary method, which he published in various forms and at various times, was explained in simple terms:

Simple congress of the sexes, *without the propagative crisis,* is the order of nature for the gratification of ordinary amative instincts; and the act of propagation should be reserved for its legitimate occasions, when conception is intended.

First Annual Report of the Oneida Association, January 1, 1849 (Bible Argument: Propositions XVII, XVIII, XIX, XX)

Dividing the sexual relation into two branches, the amative and propagative, the amative or love-relation is first in importance, as it is in the order of nature. God made woman because "he saw it was *not good for man to be alone*" (Gen. 2:18), i.e., for social, not primarily for propagative purposes.

The amative part of the sexual relation (separate from the propagative) is eminently favorable to life. It is not a *source* of life (as some would make it) but it is the first and best *distributive* of life.

The propagative part of the sexual relation is in its nature the *expensive* department. While amativeness keeps the capital stock of life circulating between two, the propagation introduces a third partner.

How can the benefits of amativeness be secured and increased and the expenses of propagation be reduced to such limits as life can afford? A satisfactory solution of this grand problem must propose a method that can be shown to be natural, healthy for both sexes, favorable to amativeness, and effectual in its control of propagation.

We insist then that the amative function—that which consists in a simple union of persons making "of twain one flesh" and giving a medium of magnetic and spiritual interchange—is a distinct and independent function, as superior to reproduction as we have shown amativeness to be to propagation.

Simple congress of the sexes, *without the propagative crisis,* is the order of nature for the gratification of ordinary amative instincts; and the acts of propagation should be reserved for its legitimate occasions when conception is intended.

Here is a method of controlling propagation that is natural, healthy, favorable to amativeness, and *effectual.* It is *natural.* The idea that sexual intercourse, pure and simple, is impossible and therefore not natural, is contradicted by the experience of many. It is certainly natural and easy to spiritual men, however difficult it may be to the sensual.

Our theory, which separates the amative from the propagative, not only relieves us of involuntary and undesirable procreation, but opens the way for scientific propagation. We are not opposed, after the Shaker fashion or even after Owen's fashion, to the increase of the population. But we are opposed to involuntary procreation. We are opposed to excessive, and of course oppressive procreation, which is almost universal. We are opposed to *random* procreation which is unavoidable in the marriage system. But we are in favor of intelligent, well-ordered procreation. We believe that the time will come . . . when scientific combination will be applied to human generation as freely and successfully as it is to that of other animals.

Second Annual Report of the Oneida Association, February 20, 1850

The condition of the Association is a matter-of-fact witness of the *feasibility of our Social Theory.* Amativeness, the lion of the tribe of human passions, is conquered and civilized among us. If it were not, we could not possibly hold together and prosper as we have done, for four years since the beginning, and for two years since we commenced the experiment on a larger scale at Oneida. All men of sense will say that amativeness, in a really licentious state of freedom, will inevitably breed bad business habits, social discords and explosions, bad health, and illegitimate propagation. Accordingly, assuming from the character of our principles that we are licentious, the world anticipates these ruinous results, and confidently predicts our speedy dissolution. But these results have not appeared. Good business habits, social harmony, good health, and very limited propagation are the phenomena which the moralists and prophets must consider and account for. The fact that but one child has been born at Oneida that was begotten in the Association (and that not undesignedly or by accident) testifies loudly for the reality of the victory which we have obtained in separating the social from the propagative in the sexual relation. That fact, and one other—that of our good health—are palpable and unanswerable contradictions of the hue and cry in certain quarters against our licentiousness. We give our enemies physical facts—statistics—"figures that cannot lie." The syllogism we present, is this: Licentiousness inevitably leads to disease and illegitimate propagation; but there is no disease or illegitimate propagation among us; *ergo,* we cannot be licentious. Will the moralists ruminate on this?

From the basis thus established, we may fairly rise to the more general affirmation that the condition of the Association *is a demonstration and realization of our original doctrine of* SALVATION FROM SIN. Sin, considered as an offense against God, is *unbelief*; but in its social phasis, it is properly defined by the general term *selfishness. A visible proof of Christ's power to save from sin on the scale of social life,* i.e., proof of the actual abolition of selfishness, was needed. This proof is now before the world. We may defy any sober man to account for the continued prosperity, peace, and health of the Association, under its system of community of property, free labor, and free love, without acknowledging that the grace of God has conquered selfishness among us. We have admitted from the beginning that our free principles in regard to property, labor and love, could not be carried out without the actual abolition of selfishness; so that our success has been avowedly staked on the answer to the old question, "Can we be saved from sin in this world?" And the world, looking on, has predicted our downfall, because it assumed that salvation from sin in this world is a chimera. But we have succeeded. So much realization is secure, whatever may be our vicissitudes hereafter. Homer says, "Jupiter (we say Satan) himself has no power over the past."

Circular, February 1, 1852

VOICE OF THE PRESS

The New York *Observer* gave Perfectionism a prominent notice last week. The editor apparently disapproves of our principles, but he gives his readers considerable valuable information about our social doctrines, Associations, publications, etc. His method of exhibiting us to disadvantage consists in culling from our First Report such detached expressions and sentences as best suit his purpose of making an unfavorable impression about us. We frankly confess that we have followed his reverend example, in culling the following scraps from his article to suit our purpose.

He informs his readers that "the founder" of the new order "is a graduate of a New England college, a student in two theological seminaries, and now, the editor of a paper published in this immediate neighborhood," meaning the *Circular*; that "the center of the sect is in the Town of Lenox, Madison County, New York, where about 150 persons live together in one house"; that "the sect is by no means confined to Oneida and Madison Counties," but has incipient churches "in New York, Brooklyn, Newark, N.J., and in many other places"; that "the adherents of this sect were but recently members of othodox, evangelical churches, some of them well educated, and most of them respectably connected." In regard to the principles of the new order, he says, that "the Bible is their nominal Constitution," and that their social doctrine, startlingly as it is, "is taught, and the attempt is made to defend it from Scripture." "There is no shrinking," he remarks, "from the boldest and frankest avowal of their faith and practice. On this point (he thinks) the Oneida Associationists are honorably contrasted with the Fourierites of this city, who refuse to be held responsible for the consequences to which their doctrines inevitably lead." He gives a pleasant account of the reforms which our ladies have instituted in hair-dressing and costume, and sensibly says in respect to the latter, that "this is plainly the germ of *Bloomerism*."

We regret to see in the conclusion of this article the mortifying and gloomy admission that "the first half of the 19th century," with all the labors of the New York *Observer* and other salt-sellers, "has made no improvement on past generations in morality." We hope the world is doing better than he imagines.

In the language of the editor, we may observe in closing, that with our sense of decency we are able to give "only the vaguest and most distant intimations of what is set forth" in the article we have sketched. We have confined ourselves to its most truthful statements, leaving out what is scurrilous and suggestive of obscenity.

Circular, February 22, 1852

WHICH IS WHICH

The editor of the New York *Observer* couples the Perfectionist Community with Mormonism, and treats our social principles as of the same class and character with the new developments at Utah. This is perhaps the most natural conclusion of a hasty and prejudiced "observer," but it is certainly a very mistaken view. At the risk of startling the reverend editor, we must still insist, and shall proceed to prove that our Society is the furthest opposite of the Mormon polygamic system, that it has in fact much less sympathy and congeniality with Mormon ideas than the ordinary system of which he is the champion.

Circular, March 7, 1852

THE PAST, THE PRESENT, AND FUTURE

Our position as a community in regard to marriage and the relation of the sexes has always been more or less an offense to the world, and has been much aggravated recently by the gross misrepresentations of sectarian opponents. But it should be observed on the other side that we have been from the beginning perfectly frank in the avowal of our principles, and, as we believe, not illegal in our practices—at least according to the laws of this State. At the outset of our movement at Oneida, we placed a copy of the First Annual Report, containing a full disclosure of our Social Theory, in the hands of the Governor of the State and various high functionaries, including the distinguished Representative of our district in the national Congress. No objection was made in any quarter to our movement, and the latter gentleman, we understood, expressed the opinion that we had a right to proceed on our new social basis, without interference. By openly publishing our platform in three successive Annual Reports, and by special advertisement of the highest general and local authorities, we satisfied in equity, if not in form, our obligations to the state. This was clearly evinced by the fact that for four years we lived undisturbed. It strikes us as rather ridiculous for the New York *Observer,* at this late date, to sound the alarm of discovery, and call on the legislature to put down Perfectionism as a new-found heresy!

As our course has not been seditious, neither has it been unchaste; and those who are fond of imputing indecency to us, simply by inference from our free principles, only show that they have no confidence in their own virtue, except as it is secured by law. "Mormonism," "Mahometanism," "Heathenism," are epithets easily applied by surmisers of corruption; but they are all false as applied to us. A legal scrutiny of the household habits of the Oneida Community during any period of its history would show not a licentious spirit but the opposite of licentiousness. It would disclose less careless familiarity of the sexes— less approach to anything like "bacchanalian" revelry—vastly less unregulated speech and conduct than it found in an equal circle of what is called good society in the world. That we disclaimed the cast-iron rules and modes by which selfishness regulates the relation of the sexes is true;

but with these conditions we affirm that there was never in that Association one-tenth part special commerce that exists between an equal number of married persons in ordinary life. This statement can be substantiated by the oath of the Community, as our general modest behavior may be verified by the testimony of disinterested persons who have often visited their friends here. And if this is not enough, let the proof of our morality be found in the broad fact of the general health of the Association. No death of an adult member has ever occurred at Oneida, and not a doctor has been employed; many who joined us sick have become well; and the special woes of women in connection with children have been nearly extinguished. The increase of population by birth, in our forty families, for the last four years, has been considerably less than the progeny of Queen Victoria alone. So much for the outcry of "licentiousness and brutality."

The Present

Still, with all this ground of vindication in reason and conscience, our liberty on this subject is looked upon with jealousy and offense by surrounding society. And in view of the fact, we have decided to forego it, and withdraw from the position we had held. *It may be understood henceforth that the Oneida Association, and all Associations connected with it, have receded from the practical assertion of their views, and formally resumed the marriage morality of the world, submitting themselves to all the ordinances and restrictions of society and law on this subject.*

Our experiment has been carried through successfully, both subjectively as relates to our own education, and objectively as developing the principles of heavenly society. The main thing is gain; and we have graduated in a sufficient state of spiritual freedom, so that we can now afford to accommodate ourselves to others and seek the salvation of all.

We land from our long voyage of exploration, improved and refreshed, with large stores of various experience, which we shall be glad to distribute for the general benefit, as they are called for. *That* voyage with its gales and icebergs and elemental perils is done—passed into history; and we emerge now under new circumstances, ready for new enterprises. Our present transition is like that of the insect passing from its chrysalis state revivified by experience, and shedding its envelopment. The forms that we leave behind are mere cast-off *exuviae* which the New York *Observer* may tear to pieces at its leisure. We shall be found elsewhere.

The Community organization will remain, bound together more firmly than ever by the ties of a common faith and imperishable regard. The Community as a corporate institution is perfectly legal and in fact popular where it is best known. We expect now to have our hands loosened for vigorous movements in business and improvements of all kinds, *looking towards the central object of a Free Press.*

The Newspaper Pressure

The notoriety that we are getting in the world in connection with such misrepresentations as the New York *Observer* circulates about us naturally brings down a good deal of criticism from the conservatories of public opinion. It is a pretty serious thing to lie under the general and outspoken censure of mankind, but we have lived through several such pressures on a smaller scale, and are conscious that our strength has increased in proportion to the increased extent of the present emergency. And to those who are sustained by the conscious justification of Christ, there are some consolations in such circumstances that others who go along in a smooth current of popular favor can hardly know. It has always been the lot of the best to be misunderstood and abused in this world—to have "all manner of evil said against them falsely"; and whether we belong to that class or not, we have some chance of knowing how it feels, and therein rejoice as we are commanded.

If we are appointed to bear a part in their condemnation, most gladly do we accept it, if we may successfully breast the unrighteous, hypocritical judgments of men and afford a shelter from the current which so wrongfully and rapidly bears its victims to perdition. We are conscious that we have that power. We have sailed through this hell-gate, and all round it, without bilging; and no amount of scurrility and defamation such as the *Observer* indulges in, can affect our moral security and self-respect.

Circular, May 23, 1852

THINGS PROVED

The Oneida Community has in a certain sense, discharged its mission, and may be looked upon as in the past. By its change of position last winter, it surrendered the distinctive and peculiar characteristic which constituted its individuality, and fell back within the lines of worldly toleration, and under the forms of selfish law. Of course, it is no longer, as to outward force and feature, the original Oneida Association. Let us treat of that as in the past; and without broaching the question whether its principles will again be asserted in the world, let us inquire what the demonstrated results of that movement were, when it did exist. It is certain that the Oneida Association did stand for four years before the world as a living fact—a new social and religious experiment, founded on principles unlike those of the world, though claimed to be those of the Bible. This is a fact which cannot be altered; it is safe in the past, and so also are the true conclusions and deductions which that experiment served to demonstrate. Whatever questions were fairly involved in the trial are now matters of fact; whose demonstrated force will remain good, whether the world chooses to avail itself of them in the future or not. Let us see what some of the points are that are established by the experience of the Oneida Community.

It proves, for one thing, the possibility of *salvation from sin*. This was the professed theory of the Association, and a prerequisite without which success was impossible. The world has assumed that salvation from selfishness was impossible, and on that ground have always foredoomed our failure; though it was not until they got tired of looking for it that the philosophers interfered to stop the experiment. But we have not failed; we have succeeded, and made the voyage, and can do so again, with perfect assurance, and the promise of unlimited success, whenever there is candor enough to call for and appreciate it.

Circular, June 27, 1852

THE FEAR OF MAN

The anathemas of the *Observer* last winter made these faint hearts tremble. *Our* equanimity was undisturbed; we were prepared—we had nothing to lose; but this surrounding circle of half-committed friends were unpleasantly affected; and in some instances thrown into ludicrous consternation.

There are many considerations which reconcile us to temporary disgrace. The truth is the most important public before which we are acting our parts is the Father, Son, and the holy angels, and the martyred church of the first resurrection. There is a reputation to be gained in higher circles than any on this footstool.

The fear of man that we have overcome is different in some respects from that which the Primitive Church contended with. They suffered violence and deadly persecution; we do not suffer violence, but the shame of public censure; and public opinion is vastly more powerful now than in their day. There was no public opinion then, in the sense which we have to confront. A nation is now as connected as a city was then; and a report started in the newspapers soon makes the circuit of the world, so that a vastly greater weight of odium can be brought to bear on a single point now than then.

Nevertheless we have found it possible to live in this fiery furnace unharmed.

God now wants witnesses that will with great boldness testify to the resurrection and Second Coming of Christ and not be ashamed of them. We are not ashamed of the men and women that have embraced these truths. They show for themselves. Their honesty, good sense, refinement, victory over disease, and freedom from ordinary curses of sensuality, their faithfulness in business, general enterprise, their good will towards men, and harmony with one another—all these things speak for themselves. We are not ashamed of the fruits of genuine Perfectionism. Faith and love, which are the things the world most needs, have grown under its influence. We are not ashamed of its social principles— we believe they contemplate a glorious emancipation for man and woman, and the highest improvement of the race.

Circular, August 29, 1852

THEOCRATIC PLATFORM

The editor of the *Circular* in a recent letter sketches the Platform of our new state of society as follows:

Sovereignty of Jesus Christ, dating from his Resurrection and manifested at his Second Coming.

Union with Christ and the Primitive Church, by faith and love.

Unity of All Believers, in this world and in Hades, with one kingdom in the Heavens.

Resurrection of the Spirit, resulting in salvation from sin and selfish habits.

Resurrection of the Body, preventing or overcoming disease, renewing youth, and resulting in the abolition of death, and the loosing of the captives in Hades.

Community of Property, of all kinds, with inspiration for distribution.

Abandonment of the Entire Fashion of the World—especially marriage, and involuntary propagation.

Cultivation of Free Love. Dwelling together in Association or Complex Families.

Home Churches and Home Schools.
Meetings Every Evening.
Lord's Supper at every Meal.
Cultivation of Free Criticism.
Horticulture, the leading business for subsistence.
A Daily Paper as the gathering point for all separate Associations.

This may properly be called the Theocratic Platform. The ideas suggested will be found to comprehend the main features of the Revolution which we believe is as the Kingdom of God. Our readers, we are sure, will study it with interest, and agree with the remark of Mr. Noyes, accompanying the above, that "a Discourse or Series of Lectures, which shall develop these ideas in their true proportions and connections, so as to make an available science of them, will deserve a premium." The different points and subjects of this sketch will engage the warmest attention of the *Circular* and offer an inviting field of discussion to our correspondents.

Circular, December 11, 1852

PROGRAM OF THE MILLENNIUM

In our last paper we invited the various Christian sects to specify their views of the Millennium: or, borrowing a figure from the custom of the times, to throw in their several proposals of the work each is willing to contract for, in bringing about that long desired period. It occurs to us that our views on this subject are contained in the outline in the Theocratic Platform, which was published some time since. We insert the same again, inviting attention to it, as a fair "bid" for the Millennium, and appending a few remarks:

(The Theocratic Platform is the same as the one published on August 29, 1852, except for items 8 through 10 which occur as follows. Editor.)

8. *Abandonment of the Entire Fashion of the World*—including marriage and involuntary propagation.

9. *Cultivation of Universal Love.*

10. *Dwelling Together in Association,* or Complex Families.

The reader, however, will see that on the basis of resurrection unity, and sovereignty over evil in body and soul, the succeeding points will naturally follow, viz.: *Community of Property of All Kinds; Abandonment of the Entire Social Fashion of the World; Cultivation of Universal Love; and Dwelling Together in Associations, or Complex*

Families. These, as nearly as can be expressed by any formula, are the social and material arrangements that correspond with the genius of Heaven. They give the invisible kingdom its appropriate body through which it can permeate and transfigure the whole outward life.

The institutions of Community life carry naturally with them the perpetual exercise of religious ordinances, and the highest means of spiritual, intellectual and moral improvement.

Circular, January 1, 1853

THE BIBLE ON MARRIAGE

And now we must come nearer in our inquiry as to the precise position of Paul and Christ on the subject of marriage. It is plain that the absolute constitutional principle which they stood on personally, towards which they were leading the church, and which they expected would expand itself, and occupy the field which is now occupied by Monogamy, Polygamy, etc., is declared in that saying of Christ's, "*In the resurrection they neither marry, nor are given in marriage.*"

We have then their position defined, negatively at least, with perfect certainty—a position not in favor of divorce, not in favor of Polygamy, and finally, not in favor of marriage itself; but tending to abolish it altogether. Such a view of their position and such alone, will reconcile their various sayings and doings on the subject.

The doctrine that *death* is the legitimate end of the contract of marriage is distinctly conceded by all. "A woman is bound by law to her husband as long as he liveth; but if the husband be dead she is loosed from the law of her husband." Paul and Christ were certainly not in favor of divorce by any other power than that of death (with the single exception in the case of adultery). They went for marriage *for life,* without any restriction or exceptions. *But they found a way to introduce what may be called a posthumous state into the world, by the application of the death of Christ.* Their doctrine was that, by believing in Christ, we are crucified with him. "If one died for all, then all died." It may be said that the Apostle did not intend to apply the death here spoken of to marriage. We reply he certainly did apply it as a release from the other worldly ordinances. The whole Jewish law was over the church, and it was like the law of marriage, in that it was over them *for life*; and the only outlet from these ordinances, to the conscientious Jew, was by death. Yet Paul everywhere proclaimed release from them, by union with the death of Christ. Though he did not carry the principle out in reference to marriage, it is perfectly clear that the same logic that would make an end of any part of the Jewish law, would make an end of marriage. If that is a substantial principle of the gospel (and it seems to us the very *center* of it), then we can see how they could go against divorce and yet go against marriage as a whole, in reference to the *posthumous* state that was to come in this world, by virtue of the death and resurrection of Christ. They could contemplate that posthumous state, and were pressing toward it; and in view of introducing it to the world, they went against marriage; preferring not to encumber themselves with transitory ties, but seeking rather with their whole hearts the resurrection state.

And here we will remark again, that this doctrine of the believer's death and resurrection by union with Christ, however foolish it may seem now, was with the Primitive Church the very core of the gospel. They realized the fact that they were past death, and so were delivered from sin and legality by the cross of Christ. This is the meaning of those frequent declarations of Paul, "I am crucified with Christ"—"I am determined not to glory save in the cross of Christ, whereby I am crucified to the world and the world to me." This doctrine and belief had a tremendous practical matter-of-fact bearing upon their character and position; and it is the grand apostasy of Christendom, that it has since lost sight of it. It is the spiritual truth which must be restored to the throne of Christianity; and in this particular application of it, viz. the cross of Christ putting men through death and into a posthumous state.

This principle, as we have said, was not carried through to its bearings on marriage; but Paul *did* carry it out so far as to demand that the *heart* should assume the posthumous state, for he says, "let them that have wives be as though they had none" so that in fact he gave his word for abolishing marriage, in the heart, on the spot.

The whole question lies between the doctrine of the Shakers, that there is no sexual relation or constitution in heaven; and the doctrine of what may be called *Pantogamy,* which recognizes the continued existence of the sexual relation, but excludes ownership, and replaces human beings where they were as children—in friendship and freedom, without selfish possession. These are the only two theories that are possible as to the resurrection state; which state Christ and his disciples adhered to as far as possible in this world and contemplated introducing in its fullness.

We shall follow Christ and Paul, and let the path lead where it will. It has unmistakably led us to the expectation that marriage is to be done away and the only question is, what next?

Circular, January 12, 1853

CONSTITUTIONAL CHRISTIANITY

The question how we shall follow in their footsteps in the application of that constitution to the present time is a somewhat complicated problem; and the conscientious man will search long and seriously for some clue by which he may be sure that he is carrying out their intent—following out the principles which they stood upon. We will not undertake now to show how these principles are to be applied by us as followers of them at the present time, but this much we do say: that as loyal believers with them in the gospel of Christ, and receivers of their understanding of the Constitution of Christianity, we are bound now and at all times, in all places and forever, to hold forth the constitutional principles which have been stated. We are bound to accept a posthumous state as the Constitution of Christianity; we are bound to follow them by believing that Christ died and rose for us, and that we are baptized into him. We are bound to sweep the field of all obstructions to the clear view of that fact; and if any institutions now rise up and deny God's right to have a posthumous church in this world, then we shall have to face them, and demand in the name of the living God, the rights of Christianity in this respect.

That is the broad ground we stand upon. The original faith of "Christ crucified" must not only be revived, but it must have the liberty of expansion and growth: and the things that belong to this world must make room for it. This is *Constitutional Christianity*; and we are sure it will ultimately sweep all before it. There is no answer to it: it is safe, and the power and inspiration of God will go with it.

Circular, February 6, 1865

FREE LOVE

This terrible combination of two very good ideas—freedom and love—was probably first used in our writings about fifteen years ago, and originated in the Oneida school of socialists. It was however soon taken up by an entirely different class of speculators scattered about the country, and has come to be the name of a form of socialism with which we have but little affinity. Still it is sometimes applied to our Community; and as we are certainly responsible for starting it into circulation, it seems to be our duty to tell what meaning we attach to it, and in what sense we are willing to accept it as a designation of our social system.

The obvious and essential difference between marriage and whoredom may be stated thus:

Marriage is a permanent union. Whoredom is a temporary flirtation.

In Marriage, communism of property goes with communism of persons. In Whoredom, love is paid for by the job.

Marriage makes the man responsible for the consequences of his acts of love to a woman. In whoredom a man imposes on a woman the heavy burdens of maternity, ruining perhaps her reputation and her health, and then goes his way without responsibility.

Marriage provides for the maintenance and education of children. Whoredom ignores children as nuisances, and leaves them to chance.

Now in respect to every one of these points of difference between marriage and whoredom, *we stand with marriage.* Free love with us does not mean freedom of love today and leave tomorrow; or freedom to take a woman's person and keep our property to ourselves; or freedom to freight a woman with our offspring and send her downstream without care or help; or freedom to beget children and leave them to the street and the poorhouse.

Our Communities are *families,* as distinctly bounded and separated from promiscuous society as ordinary households. The tie that binds us together is as permanent and sacred, to say the least, as that of marriage, for it is our religion. We receive no members (except by deception and mistake), who do not give heart and hand to the family interest for life and forever. Community of property extends just as far as freedom of love. Every man's care and every dollar of the common property is pledged for the maintenance and protection of the women and the education of the children of the Community. Bastardy, in any disastrous sense of the word, is simply impossible in such a social state. Whoever will take the trouble to follow our track from the beginning will find no forsaken women or children by the way. In this respect we claim to be a little ahead of marriage in common civilization.

We are not sure how far the class of socialists called "free lovers" would claim for themselves anything like the above defense from the charge of *reckless* and *cruel* freedom; but our impression is that their position, scattered as they are, without organization or definite separation from surrounding society, makes it impossible for them to follow and care for the consequences of their freedom, and thus exposes them to the just charge of licentiousness. At all events their platform is entirely different from ours, and they must answer for themselves. *We* are not "free lovers," in any sense that makes love less binding or responsible than it is in marriage. JHN

Circular, March 21, 1870

The term Free Love as understood by the Oneida Community, does *not* mean any such freedom of sexual proceeding as this. The household arrangements of our families provide separate sleeping apartments for the sexes, and as far as agreeable, for individuals. The theory of sexual interchange which governs all the general measures of the Community, and which it is bound to realize sooner or later, and as soon as it can, is just that that which in ordinary society governs the proceedings in *courtship*. It is the theory of the equal rights of women and men, and the freedom of both from habitual and legal obligations to personal fellowship. It is the theory that love *after* marriage and always and forever, should be what it is *before* marriage—a glowing attraction on both sides, and not the odious obligation of one party and the sensual recklessness of the other.

Besides all this, Oneida Communists have a special theory in regard to the act of sexual intercourse itself, which places it under unusual restrictions. They hold that two distinct kinds of sexual intercourse ought to be recognized; one simply social, and the other propagative; and that the propagative should only be exercised when impregnation is intended and mutually agreed upon. So far as this matter is concerned, Free Love, in the Oneida sense of the term, is much less free, in the gross, sensual way, than marriage.

Circular, April 18, 1870

CHASTITY

The principle of Male Continence held by the Community, shifts the responsibility of the maintenance of chastity from woman to man. This is right. Nature and justice alike cry out against the wrong done to society and to woman, by imposing upon her weakness a task which man with all the advantages of superior strength and superior position shrinks from assuming. The world is certainly upside down on this point. Licentiousness is a gigantic foe, carrying havoc through the length and breadth of the land. Society places woman, the weaker member, in the front of the army and requires *her* to fight the battle, at her own cost and for both sexes. She has the enemy in front and all sides and ruin stares her in the face if she yields an inch. Man on the contrary, free and easy, has little responsibility, and fears no social degradation if he secretly or even openly goes over to the enemy. What but defeat and ruin, widespread and hopeless, can come from such an unequal fight? What but just the state that actually exists in society? Women fall by thousands and tens of thousands into social ruin, disease breaks up the camp, and dismay at the enormity of the social evil seizes the stoutest heart.

But let the responsibility be shifted. Let man assume that chastity is preeminently a *masculine* virtue, that his *honor* and *courage* are both at stake in this matter—that failure in chastity will involve *him* in social degradation and ruin and what is the result? A new line of battle is presented to the enemy. The strongest battalions go to the front. The courage that spends its force in war and conquest finds a nobler field in conquering its own uncivilized passions. That high sense of honor that resents the slightest hint of disgrace, will guard its own and others' chastity to the death. "A new world, my masters!"

Circular, March 18, 1872

Evening meeting was devoted to a consideration of the relations of the sexes. Not because these relations in the O.C. are unsettled or unsatisfactory, but because the question is thrust on us from time to time by the discussions outside. Notwithstanding, we have our own solution to the problem, in which we are happy and agreed; we never refuse to consider the attempts of others to work it out. We can read John Stuart Mill with pleasure; Mrs. Stanton and Miss Anthony and *The Women's Journal* with attention; but when it comes to doing anything for ourselves, we have to refuse to look at men and women as mutually independent and in a state of competition.

Circular, July 8, 1872

CORRESPONDENCE OF THE "CINCINNATI COMMERCIAL"
Hamilton, Madison County, N.Y., May 1, 1872

Legal Persecutions

About the year 1850 some persons from the town of Lenox went to the Grand Jury of Madison County at court time and entered a complaint against the Oneida Community, charging them with being freelovers and advocates of licentiousness. This complaint was evidently prompted more by bad feeling to the Oneida Community than by sympathy for law and morality. The object of the complaint was to obtain a bill of indictment against the Community, with a view of breaking it up. Several of the jury knew something about the Oneida Community; others knew but very little, and cared still less about them, but were disposed to hear the complaint. On examining the complainants and their witnesses, it turned out that they knew nothing of what they were complaining about. All they brought against the Oneida Community was what they had heard others say, and things that they had not heard of they guessed at. When asked what they did, of themselves, know of the Community, they acknowledged that they knew them to be peaceable, quiet and industrious people, they were apparently good, kind neighbors, honest in their dealings, very truthful, and to all appearances a law-loving, law-abiding, and law-supporting people. On learning these facts concerning the Oneida Community from their enemies, the jury were unanimous in dismissing the complaint, "without prejudice to the Community."

After this some evil-minded persons went before the authorities of Oneida County with complaints against the Oneida Community similar to those brought before the Grand Jury of Madison County. These proceedings were allowed on the ground that the Community, though not inhabitants of Oneida County, had possessions adjoining. Accordingly, some of the Community men and women were brought before the authorities of Oneida County to answer to the charge of immorality. They underwent a searching examination by the District Attorney, without assistance of counsel on their part. Nothing being found to hold them to trial, they were discharged, but with a reprimand, and threatening. They were told that it was the intention of the authorities to break up the Oneida Community; that if they continued to live in a Communistic manner they would again be arrested and severely punished.

Those members went home and told their friends the treatment they had received, and the threats against them if they remained, the family in council concluded it would be best for them to seek another home rather than provoke any further persecution. Accordingly they commenced making preparations to dispose of their property, by getting what they could for it, or sacrificing it if necessary.

The late Hon. Timothy Jenkins was then living at Oneida Castle near the Community. He was a man of influence and respectability, having been a member of Congress two terms, and standing at the head of his profession as counsellor at law. He had been a constant friend of the Oneida Community and gave them freely of his social and legal advice, which was always considered good. When he heard of the treatment the Community were receiving at the hands of the Oneida authorities, he was displeased; and on learning that the Oneida Community were about to yield to their persecutors and leave the place, he determined to prevent it. He accordingly drew up a document expressing in strong terms the wish of the neighboring inhabitants that the Community people should be allowed to remain where they were, and promising that if they would they should be protected. He signed this document and made it his business to circulate it in the vicinity of the Oneida Community and other places. Nearly all signed it that had opportunity, and scarcely any opposition was made to the movement.

This unsolicited expression of their neighbors was presented to the Community. They received it in good faith as a pledge of friendship and protection. At the same time Mr. Jenkins and other prominent citizens strongly remonstrated with the District Attorney, and insisted that the legal proceedings should go no further. Under these circumstances the Community abandoned the resolution they had formed of leaving the county, and concluded to make Oneida their permanent home.

To complete the history of the attempts to persecute the Oneida Community, I have one story to tell. About ten years since four individuals appeared at the Madison County seat, at Morrisville, asking an audience of the authorities to make a complaint against the Oneida Community for lasciviousness. In order to accomplish their business they went to the District Attorney to get him to open the way for them to go before the Grand Jury. The attorney, on hearing what they proposed to do, told them that the Oneida Community had been living in the county many years, and had many friends; that he did not believe one of the jury would listen to their complaint; and that even if they did, and were to find a bill against the Community, he as District Attorney should not feel it to be his duty to prosecute it. He assured them that they would only make themselves ridiculous in the eyes of the jury by making such a complaint against the Oneida Community, and advised them not to do it. They took the attorney's advice and went home, leaving the business unfinished. [Signed by Carlton Rice]

Oneida Circular, November 10, 1873

The *Fulton Times* (November 5) volunteers a wise and well-written reply to the denunciations of certain clerical bodies against the Oneida Community. Will the *Utica Herald* and other papers which have vented the denunciations accept and copy the article from the *Times* as our answer, at least for the present? For peace's sake it is better at this early stage of proceedings that somebody should speak for us rather than that we should speak for ourselves.

We observe with surprise that the Presbyterian "Synod of Central New York," which met at Utica last week, stated in one of its official documents (published in the *Utica Herald,* November 5) that it held its sessions *"within the bounds of the Oneida Community."* What does this mean? If our bounds extend 25 miles all round we certainly have a big parish on our hands and must be looking after the conventicles that hold sessions in it. We knew before that we lived at the exact center of New York but were not aware that we *were* Central New York.

Oneida Circular, November 17, 1873

WHAT WE SAY FOR OURSELVES

In the late denunciations against us, our general morality and good behavior are admitted; no charge of trespass on society around us, sexual or otherwise, is pretended; the only averment is that the intercourse of the sexes, within our own circle, is unrestricted—subject to no regulation whatever.

With this charge we take issue, and reply:

It is not true. It is not near the truth. It is the reverse of truth.

The facts that sustain this reply are well known to all who have read our publications, and indeed to all who have in any way the slightest acquaintance with our principles and practices.

To those who have no such acquaintance we offer the following advice:

Do not believe this great falsehood. It is the inconsiderate assertion of prejudiced and ignorant men, who cannot really believe it themselves; for they know that human society cannot exist without some regulation of sexual passion.

Take pains to ascertain the truth for yourselves. When you do, you will find that the intercourse of the sexes in the Oneida Community is under more stringent regulation than it is in general society.

We aver (1) that the intercourse of the sexes in the Oneida Community is open to the criticism and controlled by the good sense of the entire body, instead of being left, as it is in marriage, to the mercy of each man's passions dealing with woman in single-handed and irresponsible privacy; (2) that the intercourse of the sexes in the Oneida Community is, next to religion, the great subject of scientific and conscientious study, instead of being left, as it usually is, to the sensual drift of fashion and ignorance; (3) that the intercourse of the sexes in the Oneida Community is restricted by the voice and heart of all to entire abstinence from the propagative act, except when propagation is agreed upon by the parties with the approbation of the Community; (4) that the practical result of these regulations, and others similar, is a state of society approaching much nearer to the self-denial of the Shakers than to the imaginary anarchy with which we are charged.

At a regular meeting of the Community the foregoing expression was accepted by unanimous vote and ordered to be published.

(A true copy) and signed W. A. Hinds, *Chairman*

Oneida Circular, July 13, 1874

COMMUNITY JOURNAL

On Friday, July 3, we received a friendly call from Professor Mears of Hamilton College at Clinton. Dr. Mears, while appreciating the economic cooperation and wishing that among Christians, as friends and neighbors, more mutual help could be encouraged, spoke of our social system in terms that made it evident that he does not yet sufficiently appreciate the improvements which we have made upon the monogamic system.

Oneida Circular, November 23, 1874

WHAT THE PRESBYTERIANS SAY

Just before going to press we have received a copy of the "Report of Synod of Central New York on the Oneida Community." It was unanimously adopted by all the Presbyterian clergymen assembled at the late meeting at Oswego. We have not time to give the matter an extended notice, but hasten to give our readers some of the more interesting and important paragraphs from the report, leaving further comment until next week. Here is what they say:

"In fact, it is the successful business arrangements of the Community that are blinding or reconciling the public to their grosser features. By their thrift, their industry, their activity, they have vastly improved not only the large farm which they occupy, but the neighborhood generally has risen in prosperity. Land is more valuable. The poor have employment. Considerable transactions and articles produced by the Community give stir and life to an otherwise very quiet region. The Community does good work, and has an excellent business reputation. Here is a mantle broad enough to cover a multitude of sins. People easily grow indulgent to an evil which contributes to their worldly prosperity. They do not care to hear about the mischiefs that may be lurking in a pursuit which, for the time being, is facilitating their business or raising the value of their estates.

"Hence the Oneida Community has actually raised up a large and influential circle of friends, a constituency, they might also be called, who are prepared to do battle for it when assailed on the ground of immorality. Respectable and religious people are found who deprecate any interference with the concern. The moral tone of the people of Vermont, where the Community was first founded, was apparently quite different. They could not endure the presence of a social monstrosity. The Community, which was driven from Putney, found a refuge in a field of prosperous activity in our own neighborhood, and we have tolerated it for 27 years. Newspaper press of the State has come to observe a policy of profound silence, varied rather by favorable intimations and outgivings, than by the contrary. In some cases they have actively espoused the cause of the Community. The announcement that this Synod has expressed an opinion and appointed a committee of inquiry on the subject, drew forth a number of newspaper articles, which, with a single known exception, were more complimentary to the Community than to the Synod itself."

This last fact need not discourage the Synod. If they will industriously attend to their own business for 27 years and do good work, as they say we have done, they also may earn an excellent reputation and draw out complimentary notices from the press. There is room for all of us.

Oneida Circular, November 30, 1874

THE PRESBYTERIAN SYNOD VS. THE ONEIDA COMMUNITY

The late report of the committee of the Presbyterian Synod of Central New York appointed last year is of a character so remarkable in itself, and appears under circumstances and with concomitance so peculiar, as to deserve some notice at our hands.

No one can fail to notice that this report is not an indictment of the Community alone. It is an indictment of the press of Central New York generally, and of the masses of the people who surround us. They say "one would not think there could be a Christian minister, a Christian man or woman, or a person of ordinary virtue, whatever his profession, in Central New York, but would be conscious of intense disgust and keen personal annoyance at the existence of such a moral defilement in his section. Yet the policy of silence and long-continued toleration would seem to contradict the supposition. Nay more: the frequent visits of large companies and even the assembling of excursionists in crowds, not unfrequently of the young and of Sunday schools . . . would go to prove that the existence of the Community is regarded as an accepted fact."

If these things are true, they certainly do represent a strangely anomalous fact in human experience. One of the members of the committee (Professor Mears) before the appearance of the report, published another paper of similar purport, in which this state of things is characterized in still stronger language. He says, "there are editors of journals considered respectable, who can become almost pathetic," over the injury of interfering with the Community; that editors are "like dumb dogs that cannot bark," and the press needs to be "unmuzzled," and that the tone of public sentiment in the state is generally demoralized in respect to such establishments. Perhaps this is all so, but how came it so, if the Community is really so like that "nocturnal animal" that is referred to in the report, if it is really the "pestiferous weed" which the Synod asserts it to be.

Oneida Circular, December 7, 1874

THE PRESBYTERIAN SYNOD VS. THE ONEIDA COMMUNITY

Last October at the session of the Synod at Oswego, the committee made its report, or at least, a report was made by someone on its behalf. As we stated last week, Rev. Prof. Mears had previously published a paper of similar purport in the *Watchword* at Ilion, N.Y. This was still more bitter and denunciatory in its tone. It was reported in the public prints that on the original presentation of the report to the Synod, it elicited considerable discussion and was recommitted.

That the legal members of the committee should have drawn up this report is scarcely credible; and yet it must be said in its favor, that, unlike the essay of the Rev. R. C. Fox and previously published articles of Prof. Mears, it studiously avoids charging that the Community exists in "defiance of the laws of the state," and only ventures to say that it is "an institution in open hostility to the foundations of social order." That judicial minds should under such circumstances allow themselves to characterize with such vile epithets a body of persons, living even in Complex Marriage is somewhat puzzling. One might suppose that in such minds the inquiries would naturally have arisen, if the Community cannot really be said to be violating statute law, and cannot be suppressed, as the report intimates, without new or addition legislation, whether there might not, after all this ado, be some mistake as to its real character; whether its members are so "scandalously impure," so "corrupt and shameless," as some people say; and whether there is not a good deal of imagination about the whole matter.

This report says that our form of social life is one which combines the "debasement" of both "polygamy," which it describes as "a custom which only a low degree of civilization and a licentious tone of society can tolerate," and "polyandry," which it says is a practice "so vile," that "only the most degraded heathen nations allow themselves in it," and yet, new legislation seems to be necessary to reach it.

In taking such a view of the matter, it does not seem to have occurred to the gentlemen of the committee at all what an indictment by implication they were thus finding against the "Empire State" and its "advanced Christian civilization."

No wonder the report has fallen so flat upon the public ear as it appears to have done! No wonder that last year, in view of the facts in the case, newspaper articles should have been drawn forth "more complimentary to the Community than to the Synod itself!" No wonder that the report gets into print as "published by request," and that even the religious press of the country scarcely notices it at all! No wonder that when published, newspapers should accompany it with remarks such as these: "Thus the Presbyterians of the State in Synod assembled have spoken, and these views *in the abstract* are doubtless endorsed by the great majority of thinking people. But who is there that does not expect to see the Oneida Community stand a fixed and permanent institution after their report has been forgotten? We fear there are but exceeding few that expect any different results."

Those who would tolerate us are right. Only with our public or social influence, with our acts as they affect others in their rights of person and property, may society deal. And we challenge investigation by the Synod as to that. They say we have industry and thrift, and that thereby, not only has the Community prospered, but also our neighborhood generally. They say we benefit the poor by giving employment. As they view us, this is an anomaly. For the world over, lewdness and harlotry is accompanied by idleness and unthrift, by depreciation of property and waste, instead of production and improvement.

Now we affirm that *we have done as much for the morality of the sexes in our neighborhood as we have for its material welfare.* If the Synod will send its committee here and honestly inquire, they will find that even ordinary marriage has been elevated here; that in the tone of society under our influence there is far less lewdness and obscenity than elsewhere; that the fountains of social and domestic virtue are less corrupt, and there is a degree of unity and fidelity in married life corresponding to the material prosperity we have wrought.

Oneida Circular, February 8, 1875

(FROM THE FULTON "TIMES")

On the first page of this paper will be found a document which has been variously denominated, owing, doubtless, to the fact of its having been sent into the world without a name by its projectors. By common consent it is called a report; and calling to our aid some previous publications having reference to this matter, we are justified in characterizing the document as the Report of a Committee consisting of Theo. W. Dwight, the Hon. John C. Churchill of Oswego, Judge Lord of Utica, Daniel Hall, Prof. J. W. Mears, of Hamilton College, the Rev. Mr. Jessup and Dr. Striker, appointed by the Utica Synod at the session of 1873, "to confer with other religious bodies on the expediency of taking some action relative to the Oneida Community."

We must ask the reader, as he peruses the Report, to keep in mind this statement of the functions and scope of the committee; and if he does this we think—if he is careful and unprejudiced—he will discover that this pretentious "Report" is not the result of investigation of Community customs, nor of a "conference with other religious bodies"; but that it is simply an essay giving expression to the sentiments of the Committee on the subject, or, more correctly, of the particular member of the Committee who penned it; and lastly, that the document is not authenticated by the signatures of the members of the Committee, nor of any portion of them. It is a vehicle of invective rather than of argument. Its statements are general and denunciatory, evidently because its conclusions were made up in advance.

The first assumption in the report, that the Community "is in open hostility to the foundations of social order," is repeatedly and successfully contradicted by the report itself; for it is declared therein to be "well organized, prosperous, and with growing relations to the surrounding community. For over a quarter of a century it has maintained itself undisturbed."

The practice of the Community of holding all property in common is denounced by the Committee. Of course a strict construction of the Committee's requirements would prevent associated efforts in any direction, and restrict all business operation to individuals.

But it is evident, notwithstanding the Committee's spasmodic references to other topics, that the burden of the Report is aimed at the Community's views of the relation of the sexes. This is a delicate subject—in fact too delicate to be treated in the obscure, ambiguous and unsatisfactory way the Committee has chosen. We don't quite know what those views are; we don't know from the Report quite what is condemned. We are sorry to believe either that the Committee did not understand what it was talking about or was not willing to communicate that understanding to its readers. Can a Committee of Christian men justly denounce what it does not understand; or can it justly withhold from others the evidence upon which it expects others to denounce?

You claim the right to manage your own families on your own plans. So far as its own desire and preference go, the Community is a private family—worshiping in its own way, devoted to its peculiar creed, and sincere in and faithful to its convictions. The members of the Community are clean and neat in habits and apparel; courteous and polite in demeanor; friendly and obliging in their intercourse with strangers; and they submit to the many, and often impertinent and silly questions that are propounded with a degree of patience and calmness possible only in the higher development of Christian feeling. To say that "mischiefs," and "glaring immoralities," and "worldwide infamy" hide themselves beneath such disguises as these—consistently worn and regularly maintained for a quarter of a century and not detected by those who have known the Community best and longest, is to say that there is no frankness, no honesty, no conscience in the world.

We ask—with not much faith that the question will be answered—Have Prof. Mears and the Committee fairly observed the Golden Rule in their Report on the Oneida Community?

X

Women

After the first and continuing public outcry against the Oneida Community's heterodox theology and their even more heterodox "Social Theory"—Complex Marriage—the feature most universally vilified and satirized was the costume of the Community women— the short dress. In an era of sweeping flounces, it indicated—but did not actually expose—the legs. In 1848, John Humphrey Noyes wrote (First Annual Report), "Woman's dress is a standing lie. It proclaims that she is not a two-legged animal, but something like a churn, standing on castors! When the distinction of the sexes is reduced to the bounds of nature and decency, a dress will be adopted that will be at the same time the most simple and the most beautiful; and it will be the same, or nearly the same, for both sexes. The dress of children—frock and pantalets—is in good taste, not perverted by the dictates of shame, and it is well adapted to the free motion of both sexes. This, or something like it, will be the uniform of vital society."

This hint was all his followers needed. By midsummer of their first year at Oneida, three of the women—Harriet Noyes, John's wife, Harriet Skinner, his sister, and Mary Cragin made a daring invention; they cut off their skirts to knee length and used the discarded material to fashion straight ankle-length pantalets. Not beautiful, not always becoming, but always both comfortable and practical. Under the same inspiration, they cut their hair short, a really shocking innovation in a time when false hair was not only fashionable but could be measured by the pound. Thus costumed, however, the Community women were prepared to work shoulder to shoulder, if necessary, with their men.

294

And especially at first, it was necessary. They were often adjured to "get rid of effeminacy" (*Circular*, February 15, 1855); to be "as independent of the weather as man"; not to "retreat before the cold but put the weather on the defensive." They resolved not to let a day pass without "engaging in some *manly* occupation" (*Circular*, April 26, 1855). Some years later, it was voted to furnish the women with a horse and carriage for their own use. When someone suggested that this might lead to accidents, Mr. Noyes gave the women a rousing criticism as a class for "cowardice and feminacy" and exhorted them to cultivate "manliness and robustness of character." The next spring they were thrilled to be appointed as the Express Agency; two women were to "run" a horse and carriage for light errands daily to Oneida Depot. This, it was agreed, would "extend woman's sphere" (*Circular*, April 25, 1864).

Actually, in 1865 (*Circular*, May 22, 1865) Mr. Noyes made up for his criticism by writing a special tribute to the women of the Community. He said that he was proud of them and that, remembering the unflinching obedience to discipline all had shown in their fifteen-year warfare with the fashions and passions of the world, he wanted to praise and thank them. The next year (*Circular*, January 29, 1866) he evolved a theory that women were "the legitimate critics of men in social life." In the "slave-holding position of marriage," men refused to look on women as equals, but in the dispensation of the Community, women were set free to express their own tastes and feelings and their criticism was the proper looking-glass for a man.

In 1866 (*Circular*, August 6, 1866), during a discussion of the university which they dreamed of but never achieved, it was agreed that girls should be encouraged to study everything that boys did; they should be admitted to all the sciences and to the whole course of education considered useful to men. They went even further and suggested that if women were properly educated, the education of men would take care of itself. It was a good indication of their appetite for cultivation that already many of the women were reading Malthus, Plato, and Greek history and literature.

In possibly more practical fields, in 1867 (*Circular*, March 15, 1867) they added up the number of their "most efficient women occupied outside of the common household world." Total, twenty-six, besides twenty-six a day at bag bees. Moreover, when there was special pressure of orders at the trap shop the women were invited to bees at the Willow Place factory (*Circular*, October 14, 1866). From seven to nine o'clock in the evening the women riveted jaws, tried swivels, and arranged chain for testing. This, after a full day's work elsewhere, but they said that they slept sweeter for the exercise.

During the several periods of financial stringency, the women of the Community joined heartily with the men in the campaign of economy. They did not feel poor or cramped, they said (*Circular*, March 30, 1868), and it was a good ordinance to bestir themselves energetically against the encroachments of the fashions of the world. To this end they decided to do their own housecleaning, washing, and fruit-preserving and to dismiss the hired women from the laundry. There was hardly any limit to their opportunities for usefulness, and they expected "a fruitful harvest from the united industry of so many cheerful hearts."

It must have been an understandable trial to the women when not only the writers who described them in books and newspapers but even the guests who visited them frequently remarked disparagingly of both their strange costume and their unbeautiful appearance. Occasionally, in the *Circular* or the *Daily Journal,* the women defended themselves. For one thing, they said (*Circular,* April 18, 1870), the men *ought* to look better than World's men because they did not indulge in tobacco, tea, coffee, or late hours. On the other hand, the same simple habits ought to make the women equally fair, although they admitted that their short hair and uncorseted waists did detract from their beauty to the common eye. People might sneer at their simplicity, but at least they were *genuine* from head to foot.

When in an article the Reverend Mr. Beecher rather condescendingly praised "the quiet fidelity of the 'she' " who was willing to "dishwash her life away for 'him,' " the Community women answered smartly that condolence came to *them* in action rather than words (*Circular,* July 1, 1872). In the Community, they reminded the Reverend, "he" not only washed dishes with them but, by their inventions, had reduced that drudgery to a minimum, so that "she" could now wash "his" dishes with cheerful grace. With unregenerate women, they said scornfully (*Circular,* November 14,

1870) the more they had the more they wanted. Women in the Community did not have to coax their husbands for the things they needed. "Let us then be smiling and cheerful and do all in our power to make home pleasant."

In a period when women outside were beginning for the first time to agitate the subject of Women's Rights, the women of the Community wished it to be understood that they had already dealt with the matter to their own satisfaction. In the *Circular* for January 1, 1874, they wrote,

Our readers do not need to be informed that the Community took high ground on the subject of Women's Rights years and years ago. Curiously enough though, the movement did not originate with the women; nor was it urged forward by Women's Conventions or by the use of the ballot or any of the usual methods of insurrection. Yet certain it is that some way we have obtained our dearest rights and so have no occasion to get up meetings to talk about them as a separate concern. The spiritual and social questions that agitate women's meetings outside are freely discussed by us, but to confess the honest truth, we find ourselves criticizing ourselves oftener than we do the men.

First Annual Report of the Oneida Association, January 1, 1849

SHORT DRESSES

In connection with this new fashion of making rooms, it will be appropriate to allude to one or two other novelties which the Association has fallen into by free-thinking. Early in the summer, in consequence of some speculations on the subject of women's dress . . . some of the leading women in the Association took the liberty to dress themselves in short gowns or frocks, with pantaloons (the fashion of dress common among children), and the advantage of the change soon became so manifest that others followed the example, till frocks and pantaloons became the prevailing fashion in the Association. The women say they are far more free and comfortable in this dress than in long gowns; the men think that it improves their looks; and some insist that it is entirely more modest than the common dress.

CHANGE IN HAIR-DRESSING

Another new fashion broke out among the women in the following manner. The ordinary practice of leaving the hair to grow indefinitely, and laboring upon it by the hour daily, merely for the sake of winding it up into a ball and sticking it on the top or back of the head, had become burdensome and distasteful to several of the women. Indeed there was a general feeling in the Association that any fashion which requires women to devote considerable time to hair-dressing is a degradation and a nuisance. The idea of wearing the hair short and leaving it to fall around the neck, as young girls often do, occurred frequently but Paul's theory of the natural propriety of long hair for women (I Cor. 11) seemed to stand in the way. At length a careful examination of this theory was instituted and the discovery was made that Paul's language expressly points out the object for which women should wear long hair and that object is not ornament but "for covering." In this light it was immediately manifest that the long hair of women as it is usually worn, coiled and combed upward to the top of the head, instead of answering Paul's object of covering actually exposes the back part of the head more than the short hair of men. It then occurred also that Phrenology, in pointing to the back of the head and neck as the seat of amativeness, has given a rational basis to Paul's theory of the propriety of women's making their hair a covering. It was evident moreover that the hair is not needed as a covering where the person is covered by the dress. These considerations seemed to establish satisfactorily the natural and scriptural propriety of women's wearing their hair in the simple mode of little girls, "down in the neck." Accordingly some of the bolder women cut off their hair and started the fashion, which soon prevailed throughout the Association, and was generally acknowledged to be an improvement of appearance as well as a saving of labor.

Circular, July 23, 1853

Our women had a meeting a few days since, to inquire into the experience about labor, and make all free to express the choice if they had any. It was very wonderful to see the unanimity there was in expressing contentment and good appetite in all the departments of labor; not more than two wanted a change because there were drags; but on the contrary most testified to increasing enjoyment in it. We surmised that there might be some discontent but were pleased with the result of our inquiry. We know there is a great deal more work done here than there used to be; but it is done easier; and the resurrectional-life working more and more makes what work is done sport, and a positive means of health and energy. The sewing-room women spoke of the ease with which they executed the orders for the sister Communes; the work was done before they knew it, and with fewer mistakes than common.

Circular, June 12, 1854

Our women were thoroughly initiated into our outdoor business last season and are now quite ready to volunteer their services on all proper occasions. Notices on the bulletin board of a bee for hoeing corn or a call for extra in the garden are certain to be responded to by them as well as the men. Last Saturday evening the Community were invited to march down into the meadow after supper and engage in ball-playing and other amusements. The ladies were specially requested to participate in our sports, and several took their first lessons in playing ball and acquitted themselves very well, all things considered. There is no sufficient reason why women should be deprived of any amusement of this kind, and we are exceedingly thankful that the women of this Association are becoming free from the restraint which the spirit of the world imposes to such matters.

Circular, February 15, 1855

If women wish to get rid of effeminacy, they must be willing to wear thicker shoes and fabrics of coarser texture than they have been accustomed to. Why should not woman be as independent of the weather and outdoor elements as man? Is there any reason in her original constitution for the inequality which exists? The speaker referred to the present extreme cold and the temptation there is in such a time to curl up, shrug the shoulders, and hover over the register and around the stove; and remarked that so long as we act on the defensive merely, and *retreat* before the cold, it will crowd us. *We must put the weather on the defensive*—take the initiative of war. Instead of seeking protection by outside appliances, we should arouse the center, and let courage conquer both fear and cold together. This was the value of our Brooklyn practice of a daily plunge into the salt brine of the harbor, which some of us enjoyed quite regularly until we left the city in December.

Circular, April 26, 1855

Some conversation this evening on woman's education, and the new course she has entered upon here. It was resolved that our women ought not to let a day pass without engaging in some *manly* work. A lesson in manly work every day would do more for their education than ever so much playing on the piano, or sewing and sweeping. We calculated that every woman in the Association could give as many as two hours a day to outdoor manly industry, and a proposal to this effect was well received. The profit of health, spirit, and value of character, it is expected, will show six months hence. A thorough experiment for converting farm work and gardening from drudgery into sport will be tried here this summer. The social harmonies and the virtue of frequent alternatives, change of groups, etc., will be brought to bear. If there is any power in youth and beauty in feminine attractiveness, it is not going to draw towards the house and laziness, but towards useful industry and productiveness on the domain.

Circular, January 23, 1858

Mrs. F. said I will not detain the ladies long, but would like to say a word. I am a woman's rights advocate but my ideas of her rights are peculiar perhaps. The grand right I ask for women is to love the men and be loved by them. That I imagine would adjust all other claims. It is but a cold, dismal right, in my opinion, to be allowed to vote, or to acquire and hold property. I want the right of the most intimate partnership with man, not in politics particularly but in business, in his studies and pleasures, and in the occupation of his whole time. I would rather be tyrannized over by him, than to be *independent* of him, and I would rather have no *rights* than be separate.

Circular, April 25, 1864

What's the excitement now? What's this buzz in our bee-hive? What are the women talking about that makes them look so important? Well, they have been promoted in business. They have received a sort of agency—an Express agency. The Community necessarily have a great deal of business at the Depot, and it is of two kinds; one involves heavy freight and important transactions, and the other consists of light errands. The women are to "run" a horse and carriage for light errands; for the mail for instance. The Board of Expenses has appropriated a horse and carriage this spring for the women's exclusive use. But it is deemed almost an effeminacy by Community women to ride for no object but to ride, and if this business had not been given them we doubt whether the previous gift of the horse and carriage would have been worth much. As it is, a sense of usefulness will make excursions attractive. And if this thing grows, perhaps we shall have the credit by and by of extending "woman's sphere." It is proposed that it shall be regular and rhythmical, always up to time. If we can do the business and do it in time, and withall learn to *manage a horse,* shall we not have made some advance in the direction of our "rights"? ("Woman's Rights" is a term we always prefer to quote as borrowed; it is not indigenous in the nomenclature of the Community.)

Circular, March 6, 1865

We may state that the short dress is worn very commonly as a working-dress by the most respectable classes about Oneida, especially by the families of farmers and country people south of the Community. We judge from observation as we pass in that direction, that the improved fashion has been adopted at nearly every house for some miles. We have seen a statement too that it has been adopted by some of the factory girls in New England.

Circular, May 22, 1865

To The Community:

I can truly say that I am proud of our *women,* young and old. I see that in will and principle, and to a good extent in practice and feeling, they have conquered the fashions of the world in themselves, and are substantially free from bondage to the spirit of dress and ornament, and special love. The long discord I had with them about these things has passed away. They have, in many respects, had to bear the brunt of the battle for Communism. The reproach of the short dress and our social theory has fallen on them more than on the men. And when I look back and remember the terrible scenes that some of them went through at Putney; and the shame that others endured and despised here when they were brought before magistrate; and the steady, long-continued, unflinching obedience to discipline which all have shown in our fifteen years warfare with the fashions and passions of the world inside from without, I wish to praise and thank them. They have proved themselves good soldiers; and they will have their reward. Already it is evident that the short dress, which our women invented and have bravely won the right to wear, is coming to acceptance and honor in the world. And so it will be with every social improvement that they have suffered shame for. Their time of honor is coming. God bless them! John H. Noyes.

Circular, December 4, 1865

From a Letter from a New Arrival

I see here, women employed as bookkeepers, business correspondents, packers and shippers, and managers of large manufacturing establishments. The policy of the Community is leading more and more in the direction of this enlargement of women's avocations. They have a taste for it, and it makes them happy, as well as doubly useful.

Circular, January 29, 1866

Women are the legitimate critics of men in social life. They have discernment and distinctive good taste in social matters that God has put into them to teach man. Any man who is not respectful to the teaching of women around him, and does not seek criticism from them, does not know his own wants or coarseness. I confess myself indebted to women in the manifestation of the repugnance of women, and their criticism, more than to anything else, for what I have learned of social music. The longer I live, the more I feel indebted to God for chastening the masculine by the feminine. God made women with their finer tastes and sensibilities, and has placed them around me, and if I go on regardless whether I please them or not, it is a revolt not against my inferiors, but against God. It is refusing to take the conservative influence that God has placed around me to improve me and make me a gentleman. In the slave-holding position of marriage, men refuse to look upon women as equals, and refuse to regard their feelings and impressions; but the dispensation we are called to is one in which women are not men's slaves, but loosened from the bondage of marriage, are set free to criticize men and express their own tastes and feelings, which are really the true standard in all social intercourse. Their criticism is the proper looking-glass for a man.

Circular, March 6, 1866

WALLINGFORD

One subject of interest in our evening meetings lately has been the education of women. In our future University it is determined to make the education of women a prominent object. Girls shall have all the advantages of boys. They shall be encouraged to study everything that boys do. We have made a beginning in having our girls learn to swim. They have been admitted to a field there which has belonged to men alone, and it appears that they excel in swimming. They shall be admitted to all the sciences, to the whole course of education considered useful to men. We maintain the ground that if the women are thoroughly educated, the education of men will take care of itself. The subject of systematic reading has engaged attention. The appetite for good strong standard works should be cultivated among the women. There are certain books which may be called the tap-roots of learning to which the literature of the day is but as the leaves on the outmost branches of the tree. That a taste for solid reading has already somewhat developed among our women and girls, appeared in the fact that there were classes reading Malthus and Burges's translation of Plato, with great relish. G.W.N., having himself a new attraction for Greek history and literature, is giving us the benefit of his research in lectures and reading on the subject.

Daily Journal, July 12, 1866

The fashion is growing to favor among the mothers and women here of loving and especially caring for other children than their own. The plan works well, and is enlarging and communizing to the hearts of those who enter into it. The children seem to like it, and some of them behave much better when with their adopted mothers than with their natural mothers.

Circular, August 6, 1866

You will remember the failure of the attempt to introduce female bookkeepers into the departments at Washington. I am happy to be able to say a similar experiment here has proved an entire success. It is less than nine months since the new movement was commenced, and now, at the Home Office and at the Bag Factory, the account keeping is nearly all performed by young women. They receive and distribute the business letters, keep the ledgers, the journals, the sales books, the cash books, the bank books, and the workmen's accounts; and we have yet to hear of any fault found with the new *regime*—yet to hear any comparisons drawn unfavorably to the present bookkeepers. They may for the present occasionally require advice from the men in respect to matters which their experience has not made them familiar; but they are quick to learn; and, judging from the result of the experiment thus far, I should say women are as naturally and as well adapted to the labors of the counting-room as the men.

Some idea of the amount of business performed by them may be obtained from the fact that they have to keep three ledgers, two journals, and five sales-books, receive and acknowledge the receipt of all monies, and answer most letters of inquiry. A sixth sales-book has been kept for several months past by Anne B. who has at the same time had charge of packing the goods sent from the Bag Factory, and of the correspondence connected with that department. In this connection I may mention that the Bag Factory has for nearly two years been superintended by Helen C. Noyes; and for some portion of the time over forty hired persons have been employed therein, besides a large number of the Community members. Other important departments of business are under the superintendence of women.

These facts are only indications of the general movement and the purpose of the Community to give its women a fair chance with the men for development and education.

Circular, March 15, 1867

As there seems to be quite an appetite for statistics at the present time a paragraph concerning women's business, and business women, may not be amiss. It may be interesting to some to learn how many of our most efficient women are occupied outside of the common household world. The counting-room has 4 appropriated to it, the store 1, the silk factory 3, printing office 4, dentistry 1, bag shop 7, bag bees 1, shoe business 1, green-house 1, schoolteaching 1, librarian and company 1. Total 25; besides an average of 26 a day at bag Bee. Then from June to November three women are entirely appropriated to the fruit business, and four to the company business, with continuous bees through the season of *all* the women and children that have any time to spare.

From the 111 females that we now number, take these 25, or average for the year 28 or 29, and also deduct the 28 who are disqualified for the labor department by infancy, age and infirmity. Of the remaining 53, 6 are under 15 years of age, and 6 are *over* 65, so you have left 42 reliable women to attend to the household work.

Cooking, washing, dairy, bringing up children, all the sewing, dressmaking, hat-making and braiding; preparing bedding for the boarding-houses; and one woman to oversee them. To assist in the house-work, 6 men are appropriated and 4 hired girls.

Circular, July 15, 1867

As three or four of our girls were passing down the stairway from the hall, on the 4th of July a stranger was seen to stare at them with a good deal of earnestness in his countenance, when turning around, he said to those nearby, "Well, them gowns *is* pretty."

Circular, October 14, 1867

A young lady who attends the evening bees at Willow Place trap works thus describes the scene: Our great omnibus, which holds fifteen or sixteen persons on a squeeze, starts from the house at six and a half o'clock in the evening, and we get fairly at work a little before seven. Sometimes we put together links to be "fitted," then again some of us rivet jaws, try swivels, and arrange the chains for testing. The noise of the machinery, the flickering of dozens of little kerosene lights, the talking, laughing, and occasional singing of the people make a lively attractive scene. We women and girls like the work very much, and it does not take long to collect a company to go to the shop. At nine o'clock Myron goes round and says, "Time's up." We all jump up, and such a time as we have washing our hands with soap and sand! Going home, our omnibus is more loaded than ever, the boys having to ride on top, and by looking out the windows we can see a row of feet hanging over the side. We get home in good season for bed, and I guess we sleep all the sweeter for our exercise.

Circular, March 30, 1868

The Community women held a meeting one afternoon of the present week for the purpose of devising ways and means by which they could economize their expenses, and thus help their brothers in solving the great finanical problem. Ready hands and brave were present at the gathering, and a lively ambition was expressed by all—both old and young—to do whatever was in their power to help forward the good cause. We don't feel poor nor cramped, and aside from all financial considerations we find it a good ordinance to, from time to time, bestir ourselves, energetically, against the encroachments of the fashion of the world; and to resist indignantly the tendency that will sometimes creep in to make us effeminate. As Community soldiers we want the broadest culture—physical as well as mental; we want strong bodies and spirits, that we may cooperate in every department of useful labor. With this twofold object in view we shall dismiss the hired women from our laundry and supply their places with help from our own number. Heretofore, much of the house-cleaning has been performed by hired help; but this spring we are going to dispense with that also. Looking about us there is hardly any limit to our opportunities for usefulness; and we expect a fruitful harvest from the united industry of so many cheerful hearts.

Circular, November 30, 1868

A model shoe, especially a woman's model shoe, has been an exciting topic this week. On the approach of winter, high-laced boots have reappeared, albeit they were condemned in the O.C. last spring. Our shoemaker, who is obliged to stock his shop with more or less foreign make, says he cannot find anything like what we want and it has seemed rather extravagant (though it has been done here a good deal) to buy the fashionable Balmorals and Gaiters, and then cut them down and pare off their heels. The tendency to backslide has brought on a new discussion, which has led to a new determination to stick to our fashion of low shoes and low heels. Several patterns have been designed and exhibited during the week, all just saving the ankle—just below, we mean. The Gaiter style, with rubber in the sides, is the favorite, on account of the facility with which it is put on. It is a matter of strife here, by the way, who shall dress the quickest, one minute being all that the most expert demand. After we have fixed upon a fashion we shall be able, no doubt, to get them made somewhere. The children's feet are to be treated scientifically—never deformed by misshapen clumsy boots.

Circular, December 7, 1868

Each woman and girl who is able and not too busy in some public service has the care of one or more of the men's clothes, and she is called that man's "mother." As no particular attention is paid to the matter of consanguinity, some funny relationships are made up. Because Mr. X. is your husband or G. is your son, you do not necessarily take care of his clothes; some other woman is quite likely to do it. Uncle Joseph, by frequent changes of residence, lost his mother. Today the women held a caucus, and it was asked "Who will take care of Uncle Joseph's clothes?" No answer! Finally, one said, "I will take care of his shirts"; another said, "I will take care of his stockings"; and presently he had a mother for his pants and vests; another for his collars, towels and handkerchiefs; and two volunteered to share the responsibility of mending and sponging his coats.

Circular, January 10, 1870

As to our costume in its detail, we will gladly describe it. It is not complicated and, with the exception of a few radical points is not so very different from many prevailing, simple modes. To be sure, the pantalettes, which necessarily accompany the short skirt, give our costumes a *toute ensemble* strikingly in contrast to ordinary feminine attire.

To begin with the dress. The skirt is cut just long enough to fall two inches below the knee, and is faced or hemmed according to the material. As to fullness, five breadths of calico is our criterion in using different materials, whether narrower or wider. If the material of the dress is cotton, the skirt is gathered onto the waist; if worsted, plaited according to taste. As to the waist, the fan-shaped Garibaldi, yoked and plain modes, are most in vogue among us, the taste of the wearer and the material dictating. The sleeves are mostly made after the mutton-leg pattern, with slight variations for cotton goods; for woolen materials, various patterns are used, from tight sleeves with puffs at the top, and coat-sleeves, to the mutton-leg. The pants, or as we call them, the pan-talettes, are always of the same material as the dress, among us. In length, they reach from the ankle to half way above the knee.

If, in wishing to know what is best suited for "home wear," you mean merely what is best to work in, we should say calico and common delaine, and for winter, common flannel or linsey-woolsey.

Circular, November 14, 1870

A Lady's Meeting was held the other day that the women might exhort one another to be *thankful.* It is almost proverbial of the unregenerate woman that the more she has the more she wants; the more devoted a man is to her welfare the more exacting she is. "The men of the Community are constantly providing us with new comforts and luxuries," said one; "Let us be grateful and express our thanks, and not bother and tease them with minor wants that can well be put aside." "Women in the Community do not have to coax their husbands for the things they need, but everything is furnished before we ask for it," said another; "Let us then be smiling and cheerful, and do all in our power to make *home* pleasant." And so around; everyone gave grateful testimony, and expressed a desire to enjoy the present, instead of longing for additional comforts in the future.

Circular, April 3, 1871

At our last ladies meeting this afternoon (which was called for the purpose of discussing household matters), an article was read from a recent exchange paper on the enameling process to which fashionable women subject themselves. Many exclamations of disgust and horror were heard. People sneer at our dress, and talk slightingly of our looks; but, alas! they know not what they say. We have no "heavers," nor "plumpers," nor "false calves," nor "rouge"; and perhaps we don't look as well as your city belle who is puffed and padded and painted; but we are *genuine* from head to foot.

Circular, November 4, 1872

A printed notice, yellow with age and in a little black frame, has hung for several days in the Summer Court. Attached to it is the following in JHN's handwriting:

Here is the program of eating arrangements which JHN and HAN adopted during their first year of housekeeping (1840) at Putney, and continued to live by about two years. This card thus framed, hung on their pantry door during that time:

Health, Comfort, Economy and Woman's Rights

Believing that the practice of serving up in a formal manner three meals of heated food daily is a requirement of custom and not of nature—unnecessary and injurious to health and comfort—subjecting females almost universally to the worst kind of slavery—we hereby notify our friends that we shall omit, in our ordinary domestic arrangements, *two* of the usual meals, that is, dinner and supper, and instead of them shall keep in this pantry a supply of variety of eatables, which we invite them to partake of at such times and in such manner as appetite or fancy may suggest.

[Signed]

John H. Noyes
Harriet A. Noyes

Circular, February 10, 1873

A woman superintends the spooling department in our silk works. Five women spend several hours each day in the family machine-shop, running lathes and learning the use of machinery. This is a new industry and a most fascinating one. One woman is teacher in the elementary school and three others instruct classes in music, writing, and drawing. The *Circular* is edited by a woman. Another woman has charge of mailing the paper, keeps the subscription-book, and attends to the foreign correspondence connected with our publications. From three to four women are employed as compositors in the printing-office. Phonographic reporting is done by women. Making paper boxes for our silk manufacturers is a new home industry lately started. This gives employment to two women and several children. Still another home business is making trap-chains. It is carried on in a well warmed and lighted room in the basement. This is a business well adapted to women and children and promises to "draw" well. Two women are employed in ticketing and labeling silk boxes. Two others have the entire business of putting up skein silk. They work in a pleasant west room in the same building (the Tontine), where are the printing-office and boxroom. A number of women find pleasant and profitable employment in skeining silk. This is chiefly done in the Upper and Lower Sitting-Rooms. The financier and two bookkeepers in the general business office are women who take a large share of the duties and responsibilities connected with the accounts and money transactions of the Community.

Circular, January 5, 1874

In our last women's meeting Mrs. C. had a report for discussion and acceptance. A change of system was proposed. The plan that had been pursued for several years was to have a certain sum appropriated for clothing in the beginning of the year, so much for men, so much for women, and so much for children. Another sum was set apart for "incidentals," a word of very comprehensive scope. A woman of good judgment and great patience was appointed to the office of keeper and distributor of goods, and another of like qualifications was associated with a man of experience in doing the greater part of the buying. Each woman made out a list of the articles she needed and selected them from the goods we had on hand, or sent or went for them to our neighboring merchants. This plan worked well in many respects, but it has some disadvantages. The women in charge had to be constantly adjusting and deciding little matters in order to make the wants coincide with the appropriated sum. Many unforeseen demands came in and at the end of the year they inevitably exceeded their bounds. This year the clothing committee in consultation with the financiers propose to adopt another plan. To appropriate a sum in the beginning of the year large enough to cover all reasonable demands, and then, after setting aside special funds for children's clothing, traveling wardrobes, infants' wardrobes, and incidentals, to divide the remainder into as many equal portions as there were women in the family. Each woman then assumes for herself the responsibility of making the two ends meet at the close of the year. It was thought it would be a great advantage to each woman, and particularly to every young girl, to know just what her clothing, from her hat to her shoes, costs. The plan too allows of great variations in way of making presents and helping one another when there is a surplus, or when there is no need, leaving it untouched in the treasury. After due explanations and discussions the women voted unanimously to try the new plan.

Circular, January 5, 1874

That inflammatory, seditious watchword, "a women's meeting in the Hall," is often posted on the bulletin board—and the women gathering there do a vast deal of talking, lecturing, and voting all by themselves. Such meetings are not often called for. Usually we assemble to consult together about family politics. New circumstances are always forming, requiring new arrangements. Our Children's Department is always a fruitful topic; so is our kitchen. The accession of new members by birth or otherwise, the care of the sick, improvements in housekeeping conveniences, the clothing department, criticism of carelessness, and the thousand and one matters which the single housekeeper has to meet and sink under alone, are talked over and settled by the united strength and wisdom of a hundred women.

Circular, January 5, 1874

We have what we call a family machine shop, instituted partly with a view to admit the women. It is in the parlor of the old Willow Place house. This room contains five lathes. Mr. Inslee, whose skill and experience have had very much to do with the manufacturing success of the O.C., presides over this shop and has afforded the women not only the benefit of his instruction but the most hearty encouragement. They began with turning chuck screws of various sizes. Then they were set to cutting the threads of these screws, a nice operation, particularly in the case of the smaller ones; but Mr. I. reports that they have succeeded in cutting the finest screws in first-rate style. He appreciates the women in the shop not only for their work, but for the influence of their inalienable tidiness and order, not to say anything about the attractions of their personal presence, to which he is the last man in the world to be insensible. On the whole he thinks women can do many kinds of light work on the lathe just as well as the sex who have heretofore monopolized its use. Admitted to the machine shop, perhaps the next census will record women inventors.

XI

Children

The Doll Story, which is told in an excerpt dated 1874, I still find as heartbreaking as it seemed to me when, as a small child, it was told to me by my grandmother, herself one of the little girls who gave up their dolls. Even today it seems to me extreme and fanatical to connect the "doll-spirit" with the worship of images.

This occurred, it should be noted, in 1851, in the very first flush of the Community's religious enthusiasm, when they were certainly more intolerant of any slightest deviation from the path of strict rectitude than they later became.

In general, the bearing and rearing of children was of the first importance to the Community; as they often wrote, it was their dearest project and the children were their pride and joy.

From the first settlement at Oneida in 1848, the children between two and twelve years of age were housed in a separate building with their nurses and teachers. Later, in 1849, the first Children's House was built just north of the first wooden Mansion House. In 1869 the south wing of the addition to the new brick Mansion House was especially designed and fitted for the children of various age groups, from babies to twelve-year-olds. This wing, too, was always called the Children's House.

The *Circular* for October 29, 1857, notes that the boys from twelve to seventeen worked at "various employments of the family," and that the class of young girls from ten to twelve "considered as having graduated from the Children's Department were similarly distributed to household duties."

In the 1850's, when the Community was barely keeping its head

311

above water financially, even whatever labor the children could contribute was a help. The older boys worked several hours a day in the trap shop, the shoe shop, the bag shop, on the farm, and so on. Their moral and spiritual improvement was taken care of on Sundays. The young girls were similarly put to work at household duties. The younger children had chores assigned to them, "apportioned according to their capacity." Sometimes they were summoned to a bee for picking up butternuts or potatoes, or the older ones were allowed to braid palmleaf hats. But there was always a generous portion of time for play, indoors and out, their meals were supervised, they got plenty of sleep and plenty of affection.

Too much, in fact, as some of the Mothers and Fathers of the Children's House complained. On one occasion it was thought that parental partiality was to blame for a growing disobedience in the children (*Circular*, June 16, 1859). Children needed more than their own parents to guide them; they needed the strength and wisdom of the whole Community. For one thing, they should learn to like everything that was good to eat. The Community made a point of abolishing the "dainty, narrow spirit" that was always picking and choosing (*Circular*, August 1, 1861). Such a habit, if allowed to persist, would become chronic and was to be deplored.

In 1863, after many discussions of the parental relation, a report entitled General Principles was issued (*Circular*, January 29, 1863). It said flatly that in parents the love and care of children should not interfere with their love as man and woman; amativeness took precedence over philoprogenitiveness. Rearing children should be carried on *in connection* with self-culture but not be allowed to encroach upon it. Conversely, it was the duty of the Community family to supply such care of the children as to enable their parents to leave them in safety and comfort. After some discussion these principles were unanimously adopted.

Another discussion dealt with the mother's and grandmother's overindulgent tenderness which led to insubordination in the children (*Circular*, November 5, 1863). There must be masculine power and execution at the center. But whoever wielded the power, the children seem to have been extraordinarily healthy and happy. And they liked to work. One day they went to the trap shop and sorted fifty or sixty hundredweight of iron in a few hours. On another day (*Circular*, January 1, 1868) they had an exhibition and spoke pieces, one of which ended with the immortal line, "a grasshopper's feelings are not understood," which brought down the house. In fair weather they played outdoors half the day (*Circular*, April 6, 1868). In bad weather they had an excellent playroom with all kinds of toys and equipment for interesting play.

The Community made a special effort to "communize" the children, as they said, "making them the property of the whole Community" (*Circular*, June 15, 1868). Every child donated his store of toys to a large collection to be used by all in common. They were enthusiastic about it, too, and the Community believed that by so doing they had got a good draft of the Pentecostal spirit. During the Children's Hour every evening, the little ones were given a lesson in theology (*Circular*, January 4, 1869), by which was meant the idea of *a Providence*; that somebody bigger and wiser than themselves was watching over them. A part of their daily routine was the Children's Meeting from four to half-past, in which they confessed Christ, got reproof and criticism, and learned to be quiet (*Circular*, May 13, 1872). Actually, when required, some of their members got a thorough-going criticism from their peers. The children were excellent critics, it was said, sincere and without malice, and the effect on the subject was to baptize him in the Community spirit.

Not only the parents but all of the Community took a very serious view of the spiritual state of the children. It was thought at one time that they were in need of a genuine revival; needed to have their hearts softened by the influence of the Holy Spirit. Even the youngest must learn the use of prayer and the confession of Christ. Those who had the care of them should bring them under the influence of a good contagion. They must make sure that the rising generation was brought up in the "nurture and admonition of the Lord" (*Circular*, April 24, 1871). If every other business suffered, they must look to it that this department did not; they must be united in casting out a bad spirit whenever it took possession of their children.

All this sounds like a pretty severe and rigorous upbringing. The evidence, however, weighs heavily on the other side. In summer there were a thousand pleasures for the little ones in the broad lawns and shady groves of the Community domain. Every morning for the youngest there was a circuit of the lawn and a peep at the calves and sheep in the barn, then perhaps a game of croquet at which they were surprisingly dextrous (*Circular,* August 9, 1872). Or they were fitted out with an iron spoon and an old coffee pot and allowed to play in their favorite dirt pile which was their best sport. Occasionally there were excursions to Willow Place where everything was new and different, where there was a kitty to pat, a fox and a pink-eyed rabbit to see, stones to throw in the pond; and one little boy was allowed the rapture of breaking a dozen eggs for custard pies (*Circular,* February 19, 1872). Later there was supper with jelly tarts and nuts and raisins and after supper the thrilling ride home in the omnibus, almost the best fun of all. Their caretaker remarked, after one such occasion, that for some inexplicable reason it was necessary to make *two* loads of what had been *one* load coming over; but then, she said (*Circular,* February 19, 1872), children grow very fast sometimes.

In the fall they were taken again in the omnibus to the pine woods where they had a fine time swinging, running over the soft pine needles, and covering themselves with leaves, and, as a special treat, they had liberty to make all the noise they pleased (*Daily Journal,* November 7, 1867). In winter there was the thrilling business of sliding down hill, "in pairs, triplets, quartets, astride, sideways, sprawled or face downward." There was, their mentors remarked (*Circular,* November 8, 1875), a slight flavor of peril in it which even the youngest appreciated, but they were carefully supervised and rosy cheeks at dinner testified that it was healthy exercise. Visitors remarked that the Community children were the jolliest little creatures they ever saw, and the communists, ever alert for the moral of the story, added that they cried so little because from the earliest dawn of intelligence they had been taught self-control (*Circular,* November 17, 1873).

The picture of the eight "little prattlers" eating their breakfast is one of the most charming we have of the Children's House inmates on the approach of their favorite dish. Why the potato thrilled them more than any other food is hard to understand but apparently it was so. Surprising also, in view of modern dietetics, is the proportion of starchy food in their diet—barley porridge, potato, mush and bread and butter—with only milk and apple-sauce to vary it. Still, it must be admitted that the diet of the adults for those early years was heavily weighted with carbohydrates: potato, buns, potato, pie, biscuits, cake, toast, potatoes, crackers, and so on, meal after meal. And yet the fact was that they all seemed to thrive on it, and at least one generation of Oneida Community children, the so-called Stirpiculties, was not only stronger physically, healthier, larger in stature, and longer-lived but possibly also more intelligent than the average for their time or even for our own.

The children had a play room and later a Play House to them-selves, they had interesting toys, they had work to do to make sure they were not bored, they had a croquet ground for themselves which they helped to make, they had sleds and a wonderful hill to slide on. If they were criticized for occasional naughtiness, it was likely that some adult was also criticized for fostering this naughty spirit. Certain persons, the critics said (*Circular,* March 9, 1874), made idols of babies, in other words, simply a case of "special love," which they ought all to be able to understand. It was pos-sible to love children without petting them.

But the criticisms were not too frequent. If there had been tribulation, then perhaps, to make sure that both parents and chil-dren had a good spirit and were happy, they all drove off for a day at the lake to sail in a small schooner which enchanted the children, to picnic by the shore in what they called a "grove saloon"—at one period every place they inhabited was apt to be called a "saloon": the "trap saloon," the "milking saloon," the "wood-cutting saloon" —to pick berries in the woods (*Circular,* June 16, 1859). Back at their starting place they found a waiting audience for whom the children danced. Then "home again, all safe to welcoming arms."

Circular, October 29, 1857

THE JUVENILES

The class of boys from 12 to 17 numbers about 20. They are distributed in the various employments of the family as follows: 8 to the trap-shop, one to the shoe-shop, 1 to the bag-making business, 1 to the horse barn, 2 to the garden, 2 to the farm, 1 to the carpentry business, 2 to tree planting and improvement of the grounds, 1 to the kitchen—they are under the general care and supervision of Mr. B. who has had long experience as father of the Children's House and who holds meetings with them for moral and spiritual improvement on Sundays and other times.

The class of 8 young girls from 10 to 12 are similarly distributed to household duties and are considered as having graduated from the children's department, though subject still to some oversight from their proper guardians. The schools are in vacation now, though some classes for writing and a class in Latin continue their sessions. Of the children below the age of 12 there are 30, constituting the proper children's department, living in a house a few feet apart from the large mansion and having a system of regulations of its own. One man and three women have charge of the children and give most of their time to their care, working and playing with them, governing them and attending to their wants.

A day's routine at the Children's House at the present time is somewhat as follows: the man in charge lights a fire and rings a bell at the foot of the staircase at 25 minutes before 6. The ding-dong of the bell is answered instantly by the thump of the children's feet springing from their beds on the floor above and the crowd comes pattering downstairs. Dressing then goes on in the large common room where the children have each a hook on which to hang clothes.

There are, of course, hard knots to untie, stiff shoes to help onto little feet, laggards to spur on, etc. Twenty minutes being given to wash, dress, and comb in, there is generally an opportunity for a run in the garden before breakfast. At a word, the children gather and form in an orderly manner to walk down to breakfast, and are in their seats at the table before the breakfast bell sounds. After breakfast they return to their house, and amuse themselves in a quiet manner 'til the bell for Bible reading in the parlor, which they attend for 15 minutes. After this they are gathered and seated for a short time whole their attendants review the state of their clothes, shoes, etc., and administer any criticism or advice that may be required. They are sometimes invited to confess Christ the Savior from evil, and in doing so each one mentions the fault to which he feels most addicted.

The smaller ones go to their play and the larger to the performance of such errands and chores as are assigned to them. At 8 o'clock the bell rings for braiding, and all who are not otherwise engaged braid palm leaf for an hour and one half. The smaller ones having stints apportioned to them according to their capacity. At the close of the braiding a lunch is passed round and all are dismissed for a time to exercise within certain limits as they please. The playground at this time is generally busily occupied with swings, skipping-ropes, etc. Sometimes a bee for piling wood, picking butternuts or potatoes, or some other suitable job follows, or the children are called together for a half hour's practice in singing, under the care of a teacher.

After dinner the children are allowed to attend the instrumental concert in the the parlor, or occupy themselves in other ways until half past one o'clock when they have another spell at braiding—then liberty, then outdoor business of some kind when possible. At 5 o'clock a certain number of the children go to their parents and remain with them the remainder of the day.

Before supper the children are made to be seated and become quiet; attention being given to their personal appearance in preparation for the table. Supper at 6, served by adult waiters who take turns in sitting at the children's table. At half past six the children are again in their place and the next half hour is spent in serious or entertaining talk in preparation for bed. At 7 the smaller children retire, lanterns are lighted in the hall and attic above and a man and woman, selected from a list of volunteers, come to relieve the regular officials at the Children's House. The larger children have an hour with their books and pencils around a table, and go to bed at 8. After that the night watchman visits all their sleeping rooms once or more in the course of his round.

Circular, June 16, 1859

The meetings this week have had considerable family interest, a spirit of sincerity and faithful criticism having scope. Among other things the superintendent of the Children's House was invited to free his mind, and he brought in some complaints of motherly interferences which embarrassed those who had charge there, mentioning persons and instances. His criticism was sustained and received, and it was voted to support the government at the Children's House thoroughly, and if any fault was to be found let it be brought out in the meeting. We had better abandon our system altogether and put the children all under their parents again, than have it half-and-half—Community government checked by parental partiality. Children who are committed heartily to the Community are easily subjected and readily controlled, but the double-mindedness of the parents shows itself immediately in the disobedience of the children. Sometimes parents who are loyal at heart, and really mean to confide their children to the Community care, are tempted by their philoprogenitiveness, which is as blind a passion as ever love was represented to be, to keep a kind of possession of them, that shields them from the faithfulness of their appointed guardians. We have proved abundantly that there are a great many children who need more than their parents to govern them; they need the strength and wisdom of the Community.

Circular, August 11, 1859

Well, the children had their postponed ride today. They were off early in the morning, attended by guardians in sufficient number and the brass band; the whole company reckoning as many souls as went down from Canaan into Egypt. The weather was all we could wish and the morning ride on a dusty road was very pleasant. At the lake, a small schooner and a sail-boat were engaged, which took in our whole party. Now "Blow, breezes, blow." But no! The breezes did not blow and what a helpless thing a sailing vessel is without a wind! In a steamboat the captain is master, but the captain is partner with Providence in a craft of this kind. We moved very slowly however, making perhaps a mile an hour, and the children, who were all in the schooner, enjoyed the novelty of being on the water while they watched the progress of the other boat as it made rather better progress and listened to the music which came from it, mellowed by the lake. The dinner hour found us opposite an eligible landing place, where the women and children were put ashore, while most of the men remained behind for aquatic sport. The landing and shipping of our little army was quite an affair, as we had to take and leave our vessels twenty rods from the shore, and make the distance in two small rowboats, which went and returned several times. We soon found a grove saloon, and when the men rejoined us had our lunch— no qualms of a rough sea putting us out of conceit with our food. After eating, the children rambled in the woods for berries, and we enjoyed the new effect of music in the woods. We were towed back some faster than we went, by oars and lusty arms in a skiff. On arriving at the house on the shore, we found the neighborhood gathered to see our children dance; so they danced a simple figure in the tavern hall. An old man expressing his gratification, said it was "worth five dollars—they *took the steps* as folks used to." Home again, all safe in welcoming arms.

Circular, August 1, 1861

One of the first and most important principles to be instilled into children is that they should like everything that is good. They should never be permitted or encouraged to say "I don't like this or that," but should be taught in a liberal, universal, acceptance of all the good things God has made. We should abolish the dainty, narrow spirit, that can be satisfied only with certain things, and is always picking and choosing. The first manifestation of this spirit is generally in reference to food. Children, if allowed, will take an aversion quite unreasonably to some kinds of food that common use pronounces good and acceptable. This dainty habit will grow upon them—and follow them through life, and extend from things to persons, so that at last discontent is sure to become a chronic thing with them.

Circular, January 29, 1863

Some time since, a member brought up for discussion and investigation the question of the parental relation, and the principles which should govern in the care and treatment of infants and young children. After some preliminary remarks the matter was referred to a committee with power to examine and report. Last evening the committee presented the following synopsis of:

GENERAL PRINCIPLES

1. The love and care of children in parents should not supplant or interfere with their love as man and woman. Amativeness takes precedence of philoprogenitiveness, and parental feeling becomes a usurpation when it crowds out a passion which is relatively its superior.

2. The child is best brought up in an open Community element, and not in a closed circle of family relatives.

3. Parents should not sacrifice the spiritual welfare of their children to their mere bodily comfort.

4. Inspiration and strength come by attention to objects that put us in communication with the *general* service and enthusiasm, rather than by exclusive devotion to the single department of children.

5. Parents should seek above all things blessing of God on the exercise of their philoprogenitiveness, and in so doing should look not so much at their children, as to the object of *pleasing God.*

6. Rearing children should be carried on in connection with self-culture, and the appetite for universal improvement, and not be allowed to seriously encroach upon them.

7. The transition from the mother's care to the Children's Department should be made easy, and to this end each child should be early accustomed to recognize as friends and parents those whom it meets in the family.

8. If the foregoing are true principles for the guidance of parents in the Community, there are certain corresponding obligations bearing upon the conduct of the Community. If it is the duty of parents to be partners, to some extent, in the general service and interest of the family, it is the duty of the family to supply such care of the children, enabling the parents to leave them in comfort and safety, as the objects above stated require.

Free conversation was had on the several propositions, after which they were unanimously adopted.

Circular, November 5, 1863

The government of children forms one of the hardest knots of discord in common society, and it is not without its difficulties in the Community. There are two poles of influence to be seen and conciliated, one represented by the father's exacting and truthful severity; the other by the mother's and grandmother's indulgent tenderness. We have had the Children's Department administered, first with one principle at the head and then with the other. A full discussion and examination of the subject this week leads to the conclusion that the reaction against what seemed severity in the past has gone too far, and allowed maternal feeling to usurp the place of good government, and the consequence begins to be seen in insubordination and untruthfulness among the children. The family of children governed by mere motherly feeling is like a wheel with the hub left out. There must be masculine power and execution at the center and the mother's philoprogenitiveness must be loyally organized into that. The open discussion of this matter in several evening meetings, together with some practical measures, has turned the current towards a sounder state of things.

Daily Journal, May 19, 1866

The regular weekly ablution of the infantile population took place in the Tontine wash-room yesterday. It was the first of these at which the two little E.'s have been present. When they saw the whole swarm casting off the "fetters of the falser life," they seemed to be in some hesitancy, till, amusing to relate, George drew Emily aside and held a private consultation with her, after which, both submitted at once cheerfully to be stripped and washed. The precise terms of the *tête à tête* have not been divulged, but the result was good.

Circular, October 22, 1866

The children of the Community, after infancy, are brought up together in the Children's House, under the organization of that department. This gives them two sets of pas and mas. The mothers also sometimes exchange children, or adopt temporarily those not their own, which increases the pa-and-ma-hood. And when a child goes to Wallingford to stay a while, it may have still a new set of parents there. The consequence of which is that the little ones get a rather mixed way of talking about their relationships which is puzzling to strangers. Yesterday a carriage, containing some fashionably dressed ladies, drove round the buildings and passed in front of the Children's House. Conspicuous among a group of children at play was Temple (four years old), first on an inverted wheelbarrow. The carriage stopped.

"Where are your parents, little boy?"

"My Papa Noyes and Mama Miller are at Wallingford."

Now, the ladies evidently felt themselves on the right track. Another charge as successful as this might result in storming the fortification.

"Miller! That's a nice name; and what is your own name beside Miller?"

The reply had such amplitude, such rolling fullness, such *naivete* and simplicity, that we record it: "My name is Temple Noyes Dunn Burt Ackley!"

We scarcely need add that the enemy was astounded, repulsed, utterly discomfited, and sped away.

Daily Journal, November 5, 1866

We propose to facilitate the working of organization by carrying it into the Children's Department in a more thorough way. We have found in our past experience that children become tired of play-things in a few days, however nice and costly they may be, while ordinary things frequently changed give entire satisfaction. Our plan is to have a set of play-things for every day. Each to close by putting them all away, with the expectation of new ones tomorrow.

Circular, July 15, 1867

A lady who called here yesterday seemed very curious to know all about our children—asked a great many questions and among others if we ever whipped them.

Miss Pomeroy—Certainly we do if they deserve it.

Lady—You whip those that are not your own?

Miss P.—Oh, they are all ours.

Lady—Do you use a machine?

Miss P. (laughing)—Yes, the machine that every faithful mother uses in correcting her children.

We have found cooperative industry as economical in the Children's Department as any other, reducing the work of good training two-thirds; but we do things by hand here pretty much. Though there is wonderful intelligence in machinery sometimes, we shall not commit our children to it right off.

Daily Journal, September 9, 1867

The coming of the children this morning to help in the trap shop was quite inspiring, they were so enthusiastic and hearty. They were accompanied by Mr. Hatch, M.D.P., and H. M. Worden, their teacher, who worked with them. They did good service, of sorting between 50 and 60 hundredweight of iron in a few hours, a piece of work which would have occupied as many hired boys all day, and who would have been paid 10¢ each hour. A vote of thanks for the children's help was proposed in meeting this evening and unanimously passed.

Circular, January 1, 1868

The children had a little exhibition on New Year's Day, and a small company were gathered in the schoolroom to hear them speak their pieces. They looked bright and happy and full of the importance of the occasion. All acquitted themselves creditably and the little ones "brought down the house" everytime they spoke. Mabel related the trials of a grasshopper, ending with, "A grasshopper's feelings are not understood." She seemed fully to enter into the spirit of the song and a general burst of laughter from the company followed.

Circular, April 6, 1868

Among the fresh impressions which we newcomers take is that of the fine accommodations for the children. When we young folks were children we were pretty much confined to our play-yard for amusement, and never could go to the "big house" where the grown people lived without asking leave of those who took care of us. But now the larger children have considerable scope about the house, and they all range from one end to the other of the extensive lawns. Almost any hour of the day they can be seen—even the four-year-olds—frolicking about on the grass, playing horse, "King, king, castle, who dare wrastle?" and numerous other games which are as familiar as ABC to all who have ever been romping boys and girls. Passing through the Children's Department this morning, we noticed with interest a pleasant room which is devoted to the special jurisdiction of the juveniles. A royal teeter, with cushions both ends and a box in the middle for some tot to ride in who isn't big enough to hold on astride the board, lay aslant along a high stool. There is a swing made of iron ropes fastened to some stationary posts; there is an attractive-looking work-bench with a machinist's vise attached; there are bars for climbing and balancing; while wagons, blocks of wood, and other childish joys are strewed in charming confusion about the floor. Happy creatures! They live in such harmony together, that one always feels lighter-hearted for having watched them in their innocent sports.

Circular, June 8, 1868

The juveniles are out barefoot. This is one of the results of the "lame ankle crusade." The mothers were a little loath at first, afraid of broken glass, anticipating stone bruises and spreading toes, but after some talk we came to the unanimous vote, mothers and all, that the children of the O.C., up to ten years old, should go barefoot three months in the year, for the sake of what toughening they will get in that way. We see many benefits in poverty that we are unwilling our children should lose.

Circular, June 15, 1868

We have made more thorough work this spring than ever before of communizing the children—making them the property of the whole Community as completely as we have all other possessions. Heretofore, mothers have had the care each of her own children's clothes, and kept up more or less special connection. The children, besides the common stock of playthings, have also had little things of their own, presented to them by friends. The clothes are now put into the hands of those who are in charge of the Juvenile Department, the mothers gladly consenting. There was a charming scene among the little ones the other day. Each one brought his store of toys and made a large collection to be used by all in common. They were very enthusiastic about it, and enjoyed the draft they got of the Pentecostal Spirit as much as anybody. No one says now "me" and "mine" but "ours" and "we."

Circular, July 6, 1868

I must tell you something of the way our children are passing their vacation. They are not spending it in idleness, playing, and seeking various methods of whiling away time, but in joining us grown folks in carrying out the true spirit of industry; attending bees and *working* while there, too. I would not have you think it is all work and no play with them. No; they work one, two and three hours and then have a fine relish for play. I had the pleasure of picking peas with them an hour or more the other afternoon, in company with "Mr. Edwin," as they call their new father at the Children's House. Said one, "Let us see how long we can go without speaking." "Agreed!" When the signal was given all hands fell to work in good earnest, and not a word was spoken for some time. The scene was amusing. Such intense silence and such nimble fingers! Occasionally, one would be anxious to communicate something, and in order to get the attention of her companions would clap her hands, and give her ideas by pantomine. C. and E. picked in the same basket like persons working for a wage, neither of them speaking for nearly three-quarters of an hour. On arriving at the house, a team was ready to take them with attendants to Willow Place Pond, where they had a nice time bathing, and the older ones swimming. This is one of their richest treats.

Circular, January 4, 1869

"The Children's Hour" continues to draw. It is as good as a theater. A new feature has been introduced this week. After twenty minutes of unbounded freedom in which they make as much amusement as they get, the bell is rung and they all sit down and take a lesson in *Theology.* Now don't think we try to indoctrinate them in some sectarian creed, or even in the Bible. No, we mean their principles of religion shall be based on *positive science,* so that they will never have to unsettle them, never, but grow stronger and stronger in them as long as they live. So we begin below the Bible, in the idea of *a Providence.* That is an idea that a child can appreciate, because it is the first idea it gets, as you may say, beyond the impressions of its senses. The first thing a child knows is that somebody is watching over it bigger and wiser than itself. We tell them that we parents have been watched so we know that somebody is taking care of *us,* as parents take care of their children. We instruct *them* to watch.

Circular, July 3, 1871

The Children's House you know is one wing of the family Mansion, communicating with that by various passages in every storey. The Children's House corps consists of one man and five women. Three of the latter there at present have children of their own among the rest. One takes the general management. The others help. All are great-hearted, patient, motherly women. They are not burdened. They are not all on duty at the same time. Their care does not include all the wants of the children. They attend them at the table, but have nothing to do with the preparation of their food. They dress them but do not have to make or mend their clothes. They see to their getting up and going to bed, but do not have the chamber-work to do. The industries of the older children are overseen by other persons, and the school, musical instruction, etc., are in charge of other persons. Those who keep the Children's House have it for their care to make the children good, to mold their habits, to know where they are, and go in and out with them, giving them all suitable change and amusement, and attending to every little incidental want. It is strictly parental care.

The East Room, which is the babies' room in particular, is large, high, and airy, fronts on the south and east, and has a bay window. There they have their playthings, their picture-books, blocks, wheels, tops, etc. There the other children come to play with them when permitted. There the other babies come when their mothers want to take them a-pleasuring. There the fathers come to see them, particularly after dinner, and there the mothers come at any hour. It is ridiculous to have to say it, but the natural relation is anything but extinguished. The babies do not love their parents less, but they love some of the rest of us just as well.

Do you think it is cruel to put our babies into the Children's House at fourteen or fifteen months? We pity a mother who has no such place for her child at that age. It is cruel sentimentally perhaps, but actually it is merciful. We have proved it over and over again, that the mother's care is like hot-bed warmth, while the Children's House care is like the open air and sunshine; and that about fourteen months is the judicious time to transplant. When a mother takes her child away for an hour, you should see how pleased it is to get back. The babies in the Children's House sleep with adults in different rooms.

Mothers and babies are well—indeed they are in excellent health. The babies have never been sick only as they have ailed a little with teething. Altogether they have not given us a dozen watchful nights since they were born, not counting the first week. Not one of them has had a touch of the cholera infantum or anything of the kind. They are put into the bath tub every day—the water not too cold. They are kept outdoors in pleasant weather. The mother's milk is supplemented if necessary with pearl barley porridge—one-third milk. They are weaned at nine months, and after that live on bread and milk, baked potato, and mush made of coarse wheat flour dressed with cream and sugar. All the weaned ones eat strawberries lustily and are not hurt.

Circular, September 11, 1871

Miss Harriet Allen, at the Children's House, tell us that she has twenty-four children under her care. Five of them are large babies that run and talk some. The children get up from six to seven, as they awake; all take a full bath and go to breakfast and then to play, until a quarter past eight when the seventeen older ones have a Bee for doing some kind of light work, like husking corn or shelling beans. This lasts from an hour to an hour and a half. After this they wash, have a fruit lunch, and go to school until noon. At one o'clock they sometimes go on to the stage to sing. Twice a week they have a singing school from two to half-past two; the older ones sing four times a week. At half-past three the girls sew for half an hour and the boys do some chore. Another moderate fruit lunch. From four to half-past four they have a meeting, in which they confess Christ, get reproof and criticism, and learn to be quiet. Supper at five or a little after. Then racing and running on the lawns till half-past seven. At eight o'clock they are all in bed. This is the routine of the Children's House as near as we can give it. It is of course subject to variation. Some of the older girls practice on the piano, and one of the boys has an exercise on the violin. They go to ride in the omnibus; they bathe in the creek; they go to gather butternuts. They all have more variety and play than is shown here. This year will be remembered by some of them as the one in which they learned to work. The work they do makes them happy and gives them a keen relish for play. They do not suffer from *ennui* as they might.

Circular, November 27, 1871

Our "Children's Hour" has begun its winter course, but not as usual. The plan for the present is this: Various persons about the house are engaged to take a child an hour in the evening, doing their best in the time to instruct and amuse him. After a day spent together in study and play, it is thought the effect will be good on the children to separate them a while before going to bed, and let them associate with those older. So, when six o'clock comes, the children scatter to the rooms to which they are invited, where they stay until seven. They go to the same rooms for a week, and then pass on to others; and so a mutual acquaintance between children and adults will be promoted all through the Community. We went the rounds the other night, and found some playing, some looking at pictures, some writing compositions, some listening to or reading stories, and so on.

Circular, May 13, 1872

The Children's Meeting is a daily meeting held with the children by the heads of the department in one of their own rooms and is an immemorial institution, having begun with the organization of our Children's House more than twenty years ago, and been kept up with little intermission over since. It was formerly held in the morning at eight or nine o'clock, but at present the hour is from four to five in the afternoon. Its length, however, is frequently shortened. Its object is moral effect by a variety of exercises, such as reading, conversation, confession of Christ and criticism. One of their number was criticized in the meeting yesterday—a boy of nine or ten. His spirit and manners had given offense for some time and he was advised to offer himself for criticism. He was old enough to know that it would do him good, and he had grace enough to want to improve, so he offered himself. Two or three of the family were invited in. The children were very sincere. Every one of them had something to say about the boy's selfish, inharmonious ways. Even youngsters of six or seven had been outraged in their sense of what is right and wrong. There was no malice in what the children said. They are too ingenuous to hold a grudge. The truth is, a formal criticism finds you in the most dispassionate frame of mind. The subject takes an attitude that virtually says, "I have done wrong," and you forgive him any personal grievance. You tell the truth about him without any bitterness. The effect on him is not to provoke or discourage but to soften him and baptize him with the Community spirit. The children are forbidden to "tell on each other," as the saying is, on common occasions, but we give them a legitimate opportunity for making complaint from time to time, in a way to get a benefit all round. In these criticisms they take lessons in the highest aesthetics—aesthetics of character.

Circular, September 9, 1872

Every morning at just a quarter before seven our eight little prattlers are ready for breakfast. It takes four women to supply the demand of their insatiable little appetites. First each must have a drink of barley-porridge; then they are ready for their bread-and-milk, nice morning's milk right from the cow, with sweet baked apples or applesauce; then comes the favorite dish of mashed "totato." Eight pairs of little hands and feet fly up and down in joyful anticipation when it is set before them, and even the youngest joins in the chorus, "Oh, the totato—Oh, the totato!" When it is given them, they eat with a relish most refreshing to behold. The next course is mush, which they value for the "sugar on it," rather than for any charm in itself; then each is allowed a small piece of bread-and-butter, another drink of barley-porridge then they are done. They jump down from their little high-chairs, and run to have their hands and faces washed, when they are ready for their morning walk, or ride, as the case may be. The house rings with their happy voices as they are preparing to go out doors, for merrier little company never lived under one roof.

Circular, January 27, 1873

Besides the work at box-making the children now work at chain-making. Messrs. Woolworth and Hutchins have lately fitted up a room in a warm and well-lighted basement where they carry on this business. Our trap chains are made of malleable iron, and in a manner just adapted to a household shop and to the children. Our steam heating and various other conveniences do away with numerous stoves, the tending of fires, the bringing in of fuel, and numberless chores, which in common homes serve to keep the children busy and happy, so we have had to seek pleasant and profitable employment for them.

Circular, May 12, 1873

Monday evening a notice on the bulletin read, "The small orchestra will meet in the Hall at half past six o'clock." So up we went, and were just in time to hear the word of command, "March," in a sharp, quick voice; and on looking whence the sound proceeded, saw Miss Constance at the head of a file of "infantry!" Each soldier carrying a musical instrument in one hand. In military style they marched onto the stage and formed themselves into a semi-circle, and at the proper signal began playing, when our ears were greeted with sounds most indescribable from fifteen willow whistles, blown in the most violent manner by fifteen ardent little performers. We were told this was the "Overture to the Spring Whistle!" But unlike most musical artists they soon tired of their own music, and began biting the bark off their instruments, and would have destroyed them *in toto,* had not Miss Constance interfered, giving the order to "play" as they marched off the stage.

Circular, November 10, 1873

Our small children (the youngest two years) now eat but two meals a day and take no lunch. Their breakfast is at eight and their dinner at three. It is astonishing to see how kindly they take to the system. Some of us hardly believed it possible, remembering the frequent lunches with which we were wont to be fortified in childhood. Much of the ease with which they adapt themselves to this method is doubtless due to their diet, which is largely composed of coarse wheat flour and fruit. They go to the table with splendid appetites and are allowed to eat all they wish, often prolonging their sitting to three quarters of an hour. They never tease for food between meals, and will even play with the apples at the paring bee without apparently thinking of such a thing as tasting. The little creatures are evidently happier for allowing their stomachs time to rest; they certainly are far less restless at night and rise in the morning bright-eyed and buoyant.

Circular, December 1, 1873

How to dispose of children on rainy days is a problem which every mother is compelled to study more or less. "What shall I play with now, mama?" asks the restless boy who has been confined in the house all day by the dripping clouds, and is tired of top, rocking-horse, and marbles and is sighing for a race in the fresh, outdoor air. There are some inactive children who have to be urged to the rougher sports of the yard and meadow; but to your regular "romp" an all-day restriction to such amusements as may be had in the parlor and sitting-room is a fate most dismal. In our labyrinthian cellars a room has lately been fitted up for the purpose of satisfying this demand. It is warmed by steam, and a nice floor of wood covers the cement bottom. There are swings and other arrangements dear to the heart of childhood; but the most interesting feature is a carpenter's bench, where the boys can learn the handling of tools. They have great plans of what they shall make. Flying-machines, we understand, are among the simplest of their projects.

Circular, March 9, 1874

The managers of the Children's House and the whole family had better look into the matter of "petting" small children. It is very common for certain persons, and had been for many, to take possession of babies when they just begin to act prettily, and make idols of them. I observed in the case of C. that this tendency is connected with a tendency to special love towards older persons, male and female. Let us study the subject and see whether the spirit of special love does not establish itself in this stronghold first of all; whether the petters and the pets are not soaking in special love. We have a great deal of experience in this matter; and we ought to be able to understand the effects of petting, both on the petters and on the pets. This seems to be one of the very important lessons that Stirpiculture is setting before us.

Circular, June 8, 1874

A few evenings ago attention was called to the Children's Department. We have fifty children under the age of twelve, who need a great deal of care and counsel. An increasing responsibility rests on the Community to bring them up properly. This branch of human development is certainly the most important interest we can have; and those who act as guardians and teachers to the children should realize that theirs is the most important office, and spare no pains in fulfilling their duty. As we value the future of Communism, we must see to it that our children— the rising generation—are brought up in "the nurture and admonition of the Lord," else they will some day rise up against us and become a curse. If every other business suffers, we must look to it that this department does not. Let us choose strong men and women for this place, and add to their strengh by giving them the support of the whole family in making the little ones obedient. It is good for all to turn attention towards the children occasionally. We shall accomplish great results fighting specific evils if we are thoroughly united in casting out bad spirits whenever they take possession of our children.

Circular, October 5, 1874

A new croquet ground has lately been made for the Children's Department. It is situated a little south of the main buildings near a clump of evergreens which serves to shade the players from the sun in the latter part of the day. Among this group of trees west of the ground is a little house for mallets and balls, and from thence a path winds up the steep bank leading to the door at the South Tower. The larger children were very enthusiastic in helping Mr. K. in grading this new croquet ground, often getting up at five o'clock in the morning to work with their shovels and wheelbarrows. They seemed to enjoy the work very much. Since the ground was finished, happy groups of children may be seen most any hour of the day (except in school and box-bee time) with their mallets and balls, each one doing his best to make the round and get home to his stake before the rest. Yet they seem to be very free from strife and contention about the game. They often invite some of the older folks to play with them.

Circular, October 19, 1874

Our children have a great variety of amusements, and many playthings such as delight the heart of a child. But one toy is banished from our play-room—that idol of little girls—the wax doll! This was discarded many years ago, and for good reasons, as will be seen from the following paper drawn up by Mrs. Cragin, and which Mother Noyes lately found in an old bundle of letters. It was written at Brooklyn and addressed to the flock of children—the girls more particularly—at Oneida. As this document gives a correct history of the doll-revolution, we copy it in full:

Brooklyn, Feb. 2, 1851

The dolls having given us some trouble lately, Sarah Burt, Mary Prindle, and Mrs. Cragin formed themselves into a committee and agreed to report on the subject which they did the next day, as follows:

Sarah Burt—My doll seduces me into a heedless spirit. At Oneida, Harriet Worden and I were criticized for neglecting to come down to breakfast in time, and the reason why we did not was that we stopped to dress our dolls before dressing ourselves and that made us too late. Several times when we older girls were told at a certain time to come downstairs and wash and dress the little children, we forgot all about it, because we got so taken up with our dolls. At Brooklyn I notice that as soon as I begin to play with my doll, I get frivolous and do not love to study. I have asked Christ to help me to do the thing that will please him about it, and should rather put my doll in the fire and see her burn up than play with her any more; because I think that she gets my attention away from Christ.

Mary Prindle—I have had a great deal of trouble with my doll, because when I play with her, I get silly and frivolous, and then I have to be criticized.

One of the boys—I do not like dolls—we have to be babies ourselves when we play with them, and think and talk just as we guess a little baby thinks and talks, and that makes us superficial.

Mrs. Cragin—It is such a common thing for little girls to play with dolls that I have never looked into the matter much with the idea that it was hurtful to them. Accordingly I gave Sarah and Mary each a doll, and encouraged them to teach themselves to sew, by making dolls' clothes. I noticed every little while that the girls were too much taken up with them, and we would have them give them up for awhile. They went without them for a week or more, and then asked to sleep with them and did so. In the morning they made quite an ado over them, talking to them as though they were living children. In talking the matter over we [the committee] came to the following conclusion:

1st—That playing with dolls, admiring them and treating them as though they were living beings, is acting and speaking a lie, and that we do not mean to speak or act lies.

2d—That we do not want our philoprogenitiveness to grow any faster than God sees is best for us. We wish to learn more of the "fear of the Lord" which is the beginning of education before we try to learn to become mothers.

3d—That, because in order to play with the dolls, we have in spirit to become babies ourselves, and think baby thoughts, and talk baby talk; that it tends to make us forget that our tongues belong to God, and tempts us to talk foolishly with each other.

4th—We think that this doll-spirit that seduces us from a Community spirit in regard to helping the family and that prevents us from being in earnest to get an education is the same spirit that seduces women to allow themselves to be so taken up with their children that they have no time to attend to Christ, and get an education for heaven.

This report was read to Mr. Noyes and Mr. Hamilton and others, who heartily approved of it. Mr. Noyes added this remark, "This doll-spirit is connected with the worship of images. Men in the infancy of the race worshiped images, and children worship images of human beings. It is a species of idolatry, and should be classed with the worship of graven images."

The children being determined to make an end of the pleasure-seeking spirit, and being well satisfied that the doll-spirit had seduced them into frivolity and lying, voted that they be burned up. Accordingly, they were stripped without delay and laid on the coals and burned up with a merry blaze, and all hands rejoiced in their condemnation.

[Sarah Burt, Mary Prindle, M. E. Cragin]

This was the signal for "voting dolls out of the Community forever." When the above was read to the Oneida children, there was but one voice in the matter—the little boys were loud in their clamors for the great massacre, and the little girls, after a few struggles, were ready to make the sacrifice of their idols. At the hour appointed, says the writer of *Mansion House Memories*, "we all formed a circle round the large stove, each girl carrying on her arm her long-cherished favorite, and marching in time to a song; as we came opposite the stove-door, we threw our dolls into the angry-looking flames, and saw them perish before our eyes."

That was an effectual work. The children that have followed since have never had dolls, some of them have never seen any, and we opine they are all the better for it.

Circular, December 21, 1874

During the autumn months, the landscape committee, in consultation with the Children's Department, graded the hill south of the dwelling-house into just the right incline for sliding, and now our whole flock, down to the very youngest in pantaloons, can be trusted with a sled. Every morning after breakfast the whole tribe is muffled in caps, thick sacks, over-socks, and mittens, and sent out to play. Sliding is the chief sport. At this the youngsters never tire. Many of them will stay out for an hour or two without asking to go indoors to warm.

Circular, May 3, 1875

The head nurses of the Children's House and the mothers of the children in this department held a meeting in the Hall this afternoon. The points discussed were the most judicious way of clothing the children and their outdoor exercise. All were enthusiastic in favor of having the children dressed, for the greater part of the day, in such a manner that they can be allowed to play in the dirt to their hearts content without any fear of soiling their clothes. Many visitors marvel that we manage to keep our children so clean, and some of us have thought that perhaps we were too careful in respect to their trimness and neatness. However that may be, we are determined to allow them all opportunities for hardy, healthful exercise, even if very sunburnt and dirty hands and faces are the result. Mr. Allen, one of the superintendents of the Children's House, has purchased some wheelbarrows, carts, and shovels for the children, much to their delight.

Circular, August 23, 1875

The children's Playhouse is so far completed that the juveniles have taken possession of it today. This will be a fine retreat on rainy days, and a relief for the older folks; for it is a fact that forty children imprisoned within doors will make a noise. The new Playhouse is to give them that liberty.

Oneida Community family, late 1860's.

Oneida Community family, around 1860. John Humphrey Noyes, with arms crossed, stands in right foreground.

A hoeing bee, no date.

A bag bee, no date. Note the man, right of center, reading to the group.

A pea-shelling bee, before 1860. John Humphrey Noyes is seated at left background, behind woman with glasses.

A game of croquet, 1860's. Old Mansion House in background.

ONEIDA COMMUNITY.

ONEIDA COMMUNITY—FRONT VIEW OF THE MAIN BUILDING.

SEASON OF 1878.

The Community beg to announce that as more of their members are residing at home than at any time for many years past they have promised themselves the pleasure of making an unusual effort to entertain the crowds of friends and visitors who make summer excursions to their place. They will furnish refreshments, a variety of vocal and instrumental music, some theatrical performances, opportunity for dancing with suitable dance music, etc., etc. They have also reduced their prices to suit the times, as the following table will show:

SCALE OF PRICES.

Tickets for full Community Dinner (reduced from 75 cts.), each,... 60 cts.
Tickets for Plain Dinner, good food but less variety, each, ... 35 cts.
Tickets for Grand Entertainment in O. C. Hall, each,.. 25 cts.
Tickets for First-class Dinner *with* Entertainment, each, ... 75 cts.
Tickets for Plain Dinner *with* Entertainment, each, ... 50 cts.
Lunches, Ice Cream, Soda Water, Confectionery, etc., at popular prices.
☞ **TEA AND COFFEE will be furnished at every meal.**

MUSIC AND THE ENTERTAINMENT.

The Community have organized, for the season of 1878, a Grand Military Band which will play out-doors on suitable occasions, without charge. A Quadrille Band, with use of a large and airy Dancing Hall, may be had for a small sum. For particulars inquire at the office.

A mixed entertainment, consisting of choice vocal and instrumental music, theatricals, readings, etc., lasting an hour or more, will be given just after dinner, when large parties desire it. On these occasions the Community children will also appear on the stage and sing songs, act pantomimes, etc. ☞ *All persons who buy dinner at the Community will be admitted to the entertainments for fifteen cents additional.* To others the price of tickets will be twenty-five cents.

☞ Guests who purchase tickets for refreshments, or for the entertainment, can have their parcels and wraps checked without extra charge. To others the charge will be ten cents.

FREE TO ALL!

The Flower Gardens, Lawns, Croquet Grounds, Swings, the principal rooms in the Home Buildings, the Museum, Collection of Stuffed Birds and Animals, etc., etc., will be open to all visitors without charge.

N. B.—The N. Y. & O. Midland Railway Company authorize us to announce the following reduction from their regular rate of three cents per mile to all parties visiting the Oneida Community from any point on their road: To all parties of from 10 to 60 persons the fare will be two cents per mile,—**a reduction of one-third**; to all parties of 60 persons or over the fare will be one and one-half cents per mile,—**a reduction of one-half.** These rates may be relied on.

The Community require to be notified beforehand when large parties are about to visit them, in order that all necessary arrangements for their comfort may be made. Managers of excursions should write as early as convenient, stating the number of persons they will bring, the day, train, etc., and making arrangements for any special music they may desire.

Address all letters on this business to

F. WAYLAND-SMITH,
Oneida Community,
Oneida. N. Y.

An entertainment broadside, printed after excursions of interested "outsiders" began when the Midland Railroad was completed in 1869.

A rare photograph of the family group at the Wallingford, Connecticut, branch of the Oneida Community, early 1870's. John Humphrey Noyes, right of center, holds a little girl on his knee.

Community women in their famous short dresses and short hair, no date.

A bag bee, no date.

Community women, no date. Note their short hair, styled with convenience in grooming a high priority.

Community men, no date.

John Humphrey Noyes, 1870's.

John Humphrey Noyes, 1870's.

Dr. Theodore R. Noyes, son of John Humphrey Noyes. Dr. Noyes introduced Turkish baths to the Community.

Community babies.

Children at the Summer house, north lawn, 1870's.

The children's hour in the upper sitting room of Mansion House.

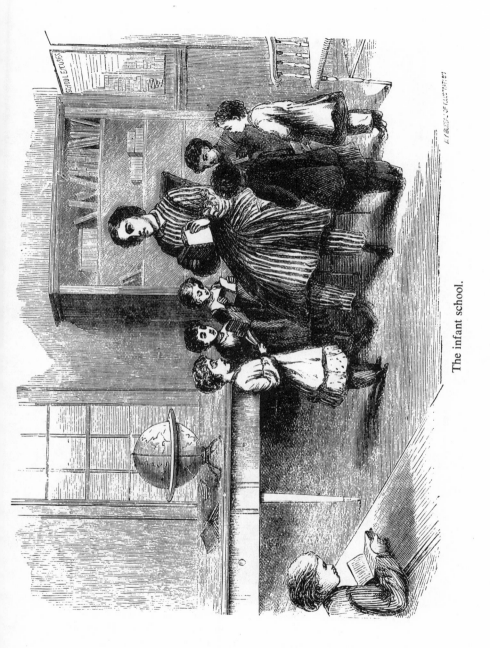

The infant school.

A group of Stirpicults, 1875. Left to right, front row: Ruth
Barron, Richard (Noyes) Wayland-Smith; second row: Ruther-
ford (Noyes) Towner, Dorr (Burnham) Kelly, Humphrey
Noyes; third row: Pierrepont Noyes, Blanche Perry.

XII

Stirpiculture

Stirpiculture, a word invented and used by the Oneida Community, is a compound of two words, of which the first is *stirpes*, the Latin word for race, and *culture*, an English word meaning cultivation with a view to improvement. The whole word, therefore, means *race-culture* and the products of this culture were called by the Community, Stirpicults. This was a darling project from their earliest days but was only achieved after twenty years of continence. Not until 1869 were they secure enough financially to venture a deliberate addition to their numbers. The plan was voted on unanimously by the entire Community and the young men and women selected offered themselves as subjects for mating at the behest of a specially chosen committee. A major ambition was about to be realized.

The two excerpts from 1858 (*Circular*, January 23, 1858) and 1859 (*Circular*, May 26, 1859) stated the Community's principles bravely; childbearing to be a voluntary affair; a just and righteous freedom accorded to the woman and "the sympathy of all good influence should concur." However, they were obliged to add rather sadly that the subject had for various considerations been postponed. Truth to tell, they were so poor at this time that they were hard put to it to support their present numbers; the addition of unwanted babies at that time might have been disastrous. They had to content themselves with adjuring their women to cultivate robust health. If ladylike habits prevailed and the women grew delicate and feeble, they said rather ominously, their future propagative prospects would be very poor.

335

The "keen appetite for having children," which they confessed to in 1859, had increased as time passed and the Community's economic situation improved. During the six years between 1859 and 1865 eleven children had been born in the Community. In some cases, women who would have been beyond child-bearing age if they waited for a dubious prosperity to strike were permitted to have children. In other cases it was simply a mistake. During the twenty-one years between 1848 and 1869 when the Stirpicultural experiment began, only thirty-five children were born to a Community population of upwards of three hundred persons. From 1869 to 1875 thirty-four Stirpicults were born. Their conception in every case was planned by a committee and agreed to by both parents.

In 1869, the Community was prosperous enough to put their theories into practice. At this time (*Circular,* June 13, 1870) they were obliged to announce that in view of this new preoccupation they would be forced to refuse to accept any new members "except those who came by another entrance—in the baby state." Not less than a dozen were expected in the first year, but the Communists were thankful that their means were increasing so that they could hope to rear and educate these newcomers properly. They chose to economize in numbers in order to give abundant care to those they had.

Motherhood, they said—and this was shocking—was not the chief end of a woman's life; she was not made simply for the children she could bear. She was made for God and herself. In marriage, as Mr. Noyes had said, women were most often mere "propagative drudges." They were not that in the Community. The testimony of both a foster mother and a young mother whose baby had just been put into the babies' room bore this out.

The former said that the natural mothers were in full sympathy with the new system, that the babies did not suffer from the separation and that not only the parents but baby-lovers throughout the Community found a new source of enjoyment in visiting the newcomers. The latter, mother of a small baby just introduced to the new baby room, wrote that she was convinced that her baby had better care than she alone could give her and that for herself, relieved now of the anxiety she had always felt about her child, she could enjoy it more than ever before. She signed herself, "Yours for giving up everything that stands in the way of improvement and revival."

If the Oneida Community did not, as they hoped, produce a generation of geniuses, they did certainly produce a crop of fine, healthy children, most of them beyond the average in stature and many of them beyond the average in intellect and character. What succeeding generations of Stirpicults might have been no one, of course, can say since the Oneida Community as an organization came to an end in 1880 when the first of the class of planned children was only about ten years old. The later lives and careers of this class, so far as they are known, suggest that the experiment was at least a successful beginning.

The documents relating to the Stirpiculture experiment were, unfortunately, destroyed after the death of George W. Noyes. Prior to this, Robert Allerton Parker had access to these papers when writing *A Yankee Saint*. In this book, therefore, are the only existing accounts of the Stirpiculture undertaking derived from the Noyes archives. The following two excerpts are from *A Yankee Saint* (pp. 256–57 and 259–61).

For twenty years (1849–1869), the Community had deliberately refrained from bringing children into the world, increasing its number less than two a year in a population of some forty families. This policy, is was explained, was dictated by temporary expediency. Like all prudent parents, the Community awaited "responsible maturity and favorable circumstances." In entering its regime of scientific propagation, the Community claimed that it had reached its earliest marriage stage. Twenty years had tested the practicability of its sexual principles. The men from the original Putney group had no children in the so-called Children's House—with the exception of George W. Noyes, who was the father of a boy of seven. This was an intentional exception.

Early in 1869, they were ready to inaugurate their daring venture in planned, scientific procreation. They decided to name it Stirpiculture, because that word seemed to Noyes and his counselors to express the highest and most sacred art that humans could cultivate. The idea the word expressed could never have originated in the minds of debauchees. It must have first been coined and brought into use where human offspring was most highly prized, where they received the most loving and intelligent culture.

As a result of these deliberations, fifty-three young women of the Oneida Community solemnly signed these resolutions:

"1. That we do not belong to ourselves in any respect, but that we belong first to *God*, and second to Mr. Noyes as God's true representative.

"2. That we have no rights or personal feelings in regard to child-bearing which shall in the least degree oppose or embarrass him in his choice of scientific combinations.

"3. That we will put aside all envy, childishness, and self-seeking, and rejoice with those who are chosen candidates; that we will, if necessary, become martyrs to science, and cheerfully renounce all desire to become mothers, if for any reason Mr. Noyes deem us unfit material for propagation. Above all, we offer ourselves 'living sacrifices' to God and true Communism."

A corresponding statement, signed by thirty-eight young men of the Community, was addressed to Father Noyes:

"The undersigned desire you may feel that we most heartily sympathize with your purpose in regard to scientific propagation, and offer ourselves to be used in forming any combinations that may seem to you desirable. We claim no rights. We ask no privileges. We desire to be servants of the truth. With a prayer that the grace of God will help us in this resolution, we are your true soldiers."

This man in his sixties was destined to sire, during the next ten years, at least nine of the fifty-eight children born under the Stirpicultural regime. The mothers were chosen from the ranks of the young women who had signed the pledge quoted above. Each felt honored at the privilege of having the patriarch as the father of her child.

One year after the inauguration of the Stirpicultural program three children had been born, and five more were known to be on the way. This sudden expansion was accepted as proving at least two things: first, the general faithfulness of the men of the Community to male continence in the years past; secondly, that their virility had not been impaired by this practice. Fathers of four of these "Stirpicults" were veterans of the first generation who had practiced male continence longest and most. The other four fathers were young men of the second generation, who had never known any other practice. These births also refuted the prediction of female sterility as a result of the Community's "social" practices.

The bold venture into scientific procreation, of which the Community made no secret whatever, was denounced by interested moralists as an attempt to introduce the "ethics of the barnyard" into a human group. But the experiment was widely discussed, even across the Atlantic. In an essay on "The Evolution of the Family," published 1877, even Herbert Spencer referred to "Father" Noyes and Stirpiculture.

The curiosity of outsiders now became even more insatiable. Certain visitors pried endlessly in their efforts to learn the names of the Community children, partly to satisfy themselves that each youngster actually possessed a name.

"Is it true that the children here really know who their parents are?" asked one lady.

"I suppose that they are in the same condition in that respect," answered her courteous guide, "as the children in ordinary society. They have to accept the testimony of their parents on that particular point."

One hundred men and women of the Community participated in the Stirpicultural experiments, and eighty-one of these became parents. Fifty-eight live children were brought into the world; there were four still-births. During the earlier years, couples desiring to undertake a Stirpicultural experiment applied to the cabinet of central members to decide upon their fitness. This meant that in reality John Noyes directed the mating, and in certain cases strictly forbade it. On January 25, 1875, a formal Stirpicultural Committee was appointed by the Community. This committee was composed of six men and six women. Two of its members were graduates of the Yale medical school and the rest were chosen for their exceptional experience and sagacity. However this committee functioned during a period of only fifteen months. After April 20, 1876, direction of the Stirpicultural policy passed again into the hands of the central members of the Community. These changes of policy seem to indicate some inner disagreement.

Records of the Stirpicultural Committee indicate the general methods of selection. In the majority of cases, application to the Committee was made by couples desiring to become parents. After due consideration, the Committee either approved or vetoed the selection. If an application were disapproved, the Committee would always undertake to find other combinations satisfactory to all concerned, which it could approve. Occasionally the Committee itself took the initiative in bringing about combinations which, in its opinion, were specially "indicated."

Fathers of the Stirpicultural infants averaged in age 12.2 years older than the mothers. This average was brought up, undoubtedly, by the mating of the leader members—the founder and leader taking the initiative in this respect—with the younger women. Quality of offspring, the central members were convinced, was more dependent upon selection among fathers than among mothers.

Out of fifty-one applications from men and women desiring to become parents, nine were vetoed on the ground of unfitness, and forty-two were approved. Care of the children was in accordance with the already established custom of the Community. During early infancy they remained in the care of their mothers. When able to walk, the child was admitted to the day nursery department of the Children's House, the mother continuing the night care. From the beginning of the play stage until adolescence the Children's House had complete charge, though parents visited their children and received visits from them. Much attention was given to diet, clothing, sanitation, and profitable activity. Epidemic diseases common in outside society were vigilantly excluded; sickness among the children was rare. In case of illness good medical attendance and the best of nursing were immediately available. There were also facilities for quarantine, night watchers, and appliances for comfort and convenience, such as few private families could afford. During the forty years, 1841–1880 inclusive, in which a total of one hundred and ninety-three children were cared for, only five deaths occurred in the Children's House. At adolescence a young person graduated from the Children's House, and took his place in the general organization of the Community.

In the pioneer days of the Community, it has been estimated, approximately ten out of forty-four babies died before the end of the first five-year period. Out of the fifty-eight live births during the Stirpicultural period, only six deaths had occurred in September, 1921, when the oldest "Stirpicult" was fifty-two years of age and the youngest forty-two. According to actuarial computation based on the Elliott tables for 1870, the deaths of forty-five out of these fifty-eight would have been nearer normal. Selection of parents is not entirely accountable for this low death rate. Other factors, such as exceptional care provided by the Community, and excellent hygienic conditions, decreased the infant mortality rate. Of the children of these Stirpicults, out of a total of ninety-eight births, only three failed to survive the first twelve-months, and there were no stillbirths. One professional statistician has expressed the opinion that two-thirds fewer deaths occurred among this group than if typical rural conditions and customs had prevailed. Full credit must be given, of course, to the hardy New England stock represented in the Stirpicultural matings, as well as to the exceptional intelligence applied to domestic and personal hygiene in the Community house. The results are said, by actuarial experts, to be unprecedented in the records of contemporary vital statistics.

Circular, January 23, 1858

The subject of bearing and rearing children, though second to none in interest, has been for various considerations postponed until we should arrive at it in the due order of things. Childbearing, when it is undertaken, should be a voluntary affair, one in which the choice of the mother, and the sympathy of all good influences should concur. Our principles accord to woman a just and righteous freedom in this particular, and however strange such an idea may seem now, the time cannot be distant when any other idea or practice will be scorned as essential barbarism.

Circular, May 26, 1859

Criticism of the fine-lady spirit which would always be glad to creep in and install itself in the place of our principle that it is good for woman to associate with man in his work outdoors. We started here with the principle of mingling the sexes in labor and cultivating a robust race of women; but the law of habit and worldly fashion resist our purpose with great force and pertinacity. There is a keen appetite rising among us for having children and great hopes of this kind wait on the improvement of our accommodations, but if ladylike habits prevail, and the women grow delicate and feeble, our propagative prospects are very poor. Maternity requires rugged health. If our female branch is sickly, propagation that is worth anything is out of the question. All who are anxious we may advance in the direction of propagation should be equally anxious for the true physical development of the women.

Circular, March 27, 1865

SCIENTIFIC PROPAGATION

A writer on sheep-breeding and its influence on the product of wool, says:

"Wool is increased in succeeding generations of sheep, by breeding, just as every other desirable quality is thus increased, that is by coupling those males and females together which possess it in the greatest degree."

How long will it be before people will discourse in similar style in reference to breeding human beings? Why should not beauty and noble grace of person and every other desirable quality of men and women, internal and external, be propagated and intensified beyond all former precedent by the application of the same scientific principles of breeding that produce such desirable results in the case of sheep, cattle, and horses? Farmers and herdsmen all over the civilized world are enthusiastic in regard to matters that relate to the improvement of stock. Societies are founded, principles are discovered and practically applied, and the ends of the earth are ransacked for desirable animals with which to cross and develop new excellencies. For while this is true of the animals below us, man leaves the infinitely higher question of his own propagation to the control of chance, ignorance, and blind passion. The place where science should rule most of all is ruled by the least science; the subject around which the highest enthusiasm should cluster is viewed with the most indifference. Yet human breeding should be one of the foremost questions of the age, transcending in its sublime interest all present political and scientific questions, and should be practically studied by all. May the time hasten when this shall be!

Circular, April 3, 1865

STIRPICULTURE

Assuming it to be granted that improvement in the race should be sought, among other ways, by attention to the *principle of breeding*, the question at once arises, what is the special line of improvement to be followed? Animal breeders have a special point of view towards which their efforts at development are directed. In some cases it is fineness of hair or plumage; in others bulk and symmetry; in others speed or endurance; and others docility and an educated instinct. Whatever standard they aim at in these several respects they pretty surely attain.

Assuming then that we have to deal with a science in breeding that gives definite results, we refer again to our question, what is the point to be first aimed at in the improvement of the human stock? Shall it be physical perfection, beauty of form, strength, complexion, health? Shall it be sagacity, acuteness of mind? Shall it be amiability of disposition? These are questions for consideration. Again, shall we adopt some fixed type, as the Anglo-Saxon man, or the classical Greek type, and selecting the most beautiful examples of one of these classes, breed to them as a standard? Or shall we recognize the variety of nature as the rule, and seek only to perfect the multifarious types that are now extant, each according to its own peculiarities of style and constitution? These points are to be resolved by careful thought. The subject is new, and will have to be approached by degrees, until practical experiment shall have thrown its light upon the broad pathway that, through truthful, scientific propagation, must lead the race up to its ideal development and destiny.

We will, however, venture two or three ideas that seem to us to offer themselves as guides in this speculation. First, in addition to the process of natural selection that has been at work on the race from the beginning, tending to raise it by weeding out its poorest stock, the Lord himself has exercised the herdsman's right of selection in a more direct manner, and carried on a course of scientific breeding with reference to the production of a specific result. The highest attainments of civilization, society, science, and art exhibited in the world today may be traced to the direct influence of the divine manipulation in the breeding of a certain stock of mankind in the past. First, the main progeny of Adam were set aside as worthless, and one man, Noah, was selected with his wife to a new breed. A few generations later, another selection of one man, Abraham, was made with whom to commence again an improved strain; this last variety was followed up by a course of close culture, or breeding in and in, until the divine purpose was accomplished, and the result stamped itself forever on the world's consciousness as a perfect work.

Let us see now, as far as we may, what were precisely the aim and product in this case. What special quality or qualities did the Lord breed to in selecting Abraham and his decendants? Evidently two: that is, receptivity to *inspiration and obedience*. These attibutes, belonging not to the outward, physical person, nor to the knowing faculty merely, but to a condition rather of the *solar plexus*, or central nerve-region of the body, were deemed of paramout importance, and became the object of the providential care throughout all the training of the Jewish nation.

As providence, in its dealings with men, does not repeat its work, this exact course of culture will not doubtless be called for again. The effects of what was attained are secure to mankind. Regeneration, by union with Christ, is offered to the race, by which, whatever were the circumstances at their first birth, they may be raised to the standard of his obedience and inspiration. But is this the end of improvement by selection and the laws of breeding? We think not. On the basis of the perfection which Christianity offers in its social unity and its exclusion of selfish fashion, we may force a superstructure to be reared of scientific procreation, tending to develop every child that is born into the godlike symmetry of an immortal. In fact, Communism, which is the flower of Christianity, has just brought mankind to the point where a scientific use may be made of the sexual passions and faculties. Heretofore society has produced, here and there at rare intervals, and by wholly unknown laws, what are called "born geniuses." They illuminate and delight, with the splendor of their endowments, the generation in which they live; and when they die men mourn and wonder and inquire when, by some fortuitous chance, their like will appear again. Investigation, we believe, will prove that the advent of such person is not fortuitous; that it is governed by the definite laws of breeding. It will be the business of Communistic societies to find out those laws and apply them; and we see no reason why, in the "good time coming," every child that is born should not be a "genius," fitted to supply to society, in some of the multifarious chords of which its music is composed, the harmonies of a celestial nature.

Circular, April 10, 1865

We may now go further, and give attention to the fact that several agencies have been providentially arranged to bear on the production and preservation of improved varieties of the race. The dispersion of mankind into separate nationalities with languages so diverse as to obstruct communication is one. Difference of religion is another. Exclusive marriage is a third. Each of these agencies has operated as a fold or enclosure, secluding that part of mankind contained in it from promiscuous mingling with other parts, and confining it to an inbreeding process by which its peculiar traits have been strengthened and perfected. If a breeder wishes to develop or preserve the variety, he provides for a careful separation of his animals. So diverse nationalities, languages and religions, and marriage, have been the separate breeding-yards of the race, hitherto. The consequence has been that each of these types has had the opportunity to develop and perfect whatever was peculiar or valuable in it, as a distinct variety.

This is one side of the Providential plan of Stirpiculture. The Lord has hitherto shown himself a producer of improved seedlings on a majestic scale. But there is another department of the art, besides that of preserving varieties by seculsion, that is of skillful crossing and combining of varieties, whereby the special value of two or more are reproduced in a third. This, we believe, is the stage to which the divine art of Stirpiculture has now arrived. We look now for the unification of mankind in a race that shall combine in one all the good that has been attained by separate culture.

This movement culminates in the renunciation of exclusive marriage and the substitution for it of a system by which scientific combination of the sexes, for the sake of progeny, can take the place of the crude and mainly instinctive unions of the past. Observe that while exclusive institutions have served a good use as breeding-folds for the production and preservation of varieties, they have also lasted till they could put the interest of human propagation into the hands of their true successors, science and inspiration. There is to be no interregnum—no dropping down from what has been gained to a lawless and degrading promiscuity; but everything being right for the change, the accumulated materials of the past are to be transferred without reserve to the direction of science and the Higher Law, for an unlimited advance.

Circular, January 10, 1870

All properly collated facts bearing on the subject of parentage are valuable. The fact that a certain number of aged women have had large families does not show that all women would be benefited by having numerous children. It proves only that some women of peculiar constitution and under certain favorable conditions (of which perhaps a congenial marriage is one) have thriven in the business of childbearing. But before we can form any valid generalization on this subject, applicable to the whole case, we have to consider a mass of facts of a different kind. We should have to ask how many women have broken down after having the second, third, or fourth child, and disappeared by a premature death. This class of facts, so easily ignored by longevity collectors, should be placed beside the other in order to arrive at a sound conclusion; and from them it may appear that different classes of women are differently adapted to the work of procreation.

It may still be a question whether mere longevity is the all-important consideration in the case. The rearing of children is a great function undoubtedly, but it may not be the highest of which woman is capable. It is certainly shared by the ignorant and degraded as well as by the refined, and in fact seems to predominate in nature, just in proportion to the lowness of the race which exercises it. It appears that some higher considerations than that of mere maternal vigor should enter into this question.

We should inquire: 1. The improvement, mental and spiritual, of the mother. 2. The highest quality in the offspring.

1. In respect to the first of these points the standard of female character is continually rising. Women feel that they are capable of development in a thousand ways apart from maternity; and hence the problem is one of the correlation of force. If they are to be educated and act in the mental sphere, they cannot devote their life wholly to childbearing. The signs of the times indicates a great change in this respect from the condition of the past.

2. It deserves inquiry whether, in the matter of progeny, quality is not often sacrificed to quantity. A mother may be long-lived and prolific, and so may be pointed at as an example of the benefit of propagation, when in fact she leaves but a deteriorated stock in her children. The second generation from great breeders as a whole is not apt to be bril-

liant. Why not condense the dozen or twenty children into one quarter their number, whereby they would be better born and cared for, and the results would be at least equal in point of power?

This brings us to the position of the O.C. Our views on that subject as printed in our First Annual Report in 1849 are the following:

Our theory, which separates the amative from the propagative, not only relieves us of involuntary and undesirable procreation, but opens the way for scientific propagation.

This has been the position of the Community for twenty years, and we see no reason to regret it. If we have had somewhat less children than society in general, those we have had have been at least well cared for.

Circular, March 21, 1870

STIRPICULTURE

This word (meaning race-culture), applied to the improvement of human beings by scientific breeding, is beginning to have place in the minds of the thoughtful. Darwin's discovery of the principles of natural selection and the survival of the fittest among the lower forms of life leads right on to the idea of improvement of man by voluntary selection. If strawberries can be developed by care in selecting and crossing, from the insignificant field variety to the magnificent *Triomphe de Gand*; if pigeons can be made into pouters and fan-tails; if, as Lord Somerville has said, the sheep-breeder can chalk out the form which he fancies on paper, and in a few generations can bring his flock to that exact pattern, what sense is there in neglecting to apply this agency to the elevation of the human race?

In ordinary society the application of science in this direction is almost impossible. Experiment is forbidden. Good results are only obtained by chance. Mating is left to the same irresponsible, careless guidance that prevails among the buffaloes and antelopes of the prairie; and if a mistake is made there is no remedy. Yet notwithstanding this general impotence of society, history still shows that all the good that has yet been accomplished in the world has resulted from providential direction in the matter of parentage. If men have neglected to work by science, God has not. The history of Abraham and the Jews is a splendid example of Stirpiculture, with Christ and Paul as specimens of the result.

The world now begins to see the importance of this subject, and demands that it be investigated. Science points out the conditions. The O.C. fulfills them. In the Community are the requisite numbers, the requisite culture and character, the varied development, the theory and practice of self-control, and above all the freedom for experiment that are necessary to found a bureau of Stirpiculture. The science is in its infancy; everything has to be learned. We may make mistakes, may have to observe long and patiently; but there could be no mistake about the final result, which will be to place the science of human breeding at least on the level with that which, in the case of plants and animals, has produced the race horse and *Triomphe de Gand.*

Circular, April 11, 1870

O.C. EXPERIENCE IN PROPAGATION

Objectors to Male Continence say that "it is impracticable." If experience has produced an answer to that, they say, "it is unhealthy." If facts are opposed to that, they say, "it will ultimately produce sterility: it will disable the men, and render the women infertile." To these last objections we have not been able heretofore to oppose many facts, because we have not been in the way of experiment. For twenty years and more, we have refrained from having children to a great extent, counting less than two in a year in a population of forty families. This has not been for Shaker reasons, but for reasons of temporary expediency. The individual waits for maturity and favorable circumstances; why should not a community? The O.C. is only now at the earliest marriageable age. These twenty years have well tested the *practicability* of our social principles so far as abstinence is concerned. The original Putney men have no children in the Children's House, and none anywhere between the age of twenty years and infancy, with the exception of G.W.N., who has a little boy of seven years—an intentional exception. The same is true of most of the other principal men who were in at the foundation of the O.C. But since the change of our policy last year and inauguration of the era of Stirpiculture, some pretty decisive facts have made their appearance. Three children have been born, and not less than five more are known to be on the way. Here is a sudden expansion which proves at least two things, viz., first, the general faithfulness of the men of the Community to Male Continence in years past; and secondly, that they have not lost their male potency by their continence—which last deduction is strengthened by the fact that the fathers in four of these cases are veterans of the first generation who have practiced Male Continence longest and most while the other four fathers are the young men of the second generation, who have never known any other practice. This expansion also casts to the winds the prediction of sterility on the part of the women as the result of our social practice. And withal it must be borne in mind that what has been done is only a cautious beginning, and not at all a test of what we can do.

Circular, April 25, 1870

Right along with this dying of marriage has risen the clamorous demand for scientific propagation. Darwin has been dealing out the law of Stirpiculture by wholesale to the scientifics, and the phrenologists and popular physiologists have retailed it to the masses till everybody is under conviction about it. It is wonderful to see how unanimous the acknowledgment has become that we ought to be doing for man what has been done for horses, swine, and potatoes. With all the cursing of the O.C. that is going on, not a word is said against our movement in favor of scientific propagation. Everybody commends it. The times are evidently ripe for a positive movement in this direction, whether the O.C. has commenced that movement or not.

Here then are two notable things together—marriage dying, and scientific propagation coming to the birth. Is there no discoverable relation between them?

Certainly scientific propagation is impossible so long and so far as mating is done by promiscuous scrambling, which is the very nature of marriage. If the time has really come for scientific propagation, then the time has come for the departure of marriage and the reconstruction of society on principles which will allow science to lay its hand on the business of mating.

Circular, June 13, 1870

It will be well for us to take some pains to understand God's policy in regard to our taking in new members. Our inspiration and practice is evidently very different now from what it was in our early history, when we kept our doors wide open to nearly all comers; and the question naturally arises why this difference? One reason is plain to be seen; that is, then we were poor and persecuted, and so it was safe to keep our doors open, because people were not likely to want to join us, unless they were sincere and in earnest for Christ; whereas now we are rich and in some sense popular: and thousands are ready to rush in for the loaves and fishes. With this selfish rush pressing upon us, our only safe way is to shut our doors entirely, even if we shut out some that are worthy. At least we must keep them shut until we can devise ways and means to separate the worthy from the unworthy. And just at the time when this necessity is upon us of barring out the crowd of worldly applicants, we have reached the stage in our own experience where we can safely take hold of the business of home progagation. It should be considered that we are really taking in new members in the baby state quite often nowadays. We shall probably admit not less than a dozen within the present year; which would be considered a fair quota if they were outsiders. This then is the change that has come, that is, we have not really shut our doors; but are taking in new members by another entrance. And now let us be content until God gives us new orders; let us turn our hearts away from the outside rush, to the coming regiment of babies, and do our best to make the Community a model, self-perpetuating institution, in the home-producing way. Our means, which at first were small, are constantly increasing, and with the ability to properly rear and educate children we shall doubtless have plenty of them. Meantime, the principle of self-control which has worked in the men, and of self-improvement in the women, forms a basis of mutual respect, favorable to the development of science in the whole matter of propagation.

Circular, July 11, 1870

It will be said that we do not have the common proportion of children. Indeed, we don't. We think it is awfully extravagant to bear a great many children for early death. We choose to economize in number and give abundant care to those we do have. Money will not buy the care a child needs. A lady from New York had a wet nurse with her for her babe. We should consider it a calamity to be obliged to accept such care for our children. We trust them only with our own family, those we have lived with many years, and love as fathers and mothers and brothers and sisters. They are never left to inexperienced hands—to servants, or older children even. If sick, as last winter with the whooping cough, they have the best attendants out of all the family, one set of attendants relieves another, and the doctor lives in our own house. Unregulated propagation by which more children are produced than can have good care, will certainly be condemned by advancing civilization, and it will be found that the isolated family can hardly give good care to one child.

Circular, September 19, 1870

THE FINAL ANSWER

"Do children in the Community know their own parents?" For twenty years this question has been asked; for twenty years we have patiently answered, "yes." Our patience and good nature still hold out, and might for twenty years longer. Still, it is desirable for all parties that a complete answer should be given to this oft-repeated, ever-interesting question. Such an answer we have in the simple fact that the Community believe in scientific propagation, and are earnestly endeavoring to have this principle modify and control all their propagative experiences. Now every intelligent person knows that scientific propagation is utterly impossible without careful attention to pedigree. No bovine will be admitted into the herd books unless the owner proves that its blood has no foreign admixture for at least six generations, and no equine is entitled to the designation "pure blood" unless it can be shown that its ancestors for at least eight generations have not included any "mongrel" animals. So it becomes of the utmost importance that the Community, in favoring the production of pure-blood races of men, should keep accurate pedigree accounts; and we assure our curious friends that this will be done, and that, as time rolls on, we shall be able to tell them not only who the particular parents are of any child born in the Community, but who its ancestors were for many previous generations. A child knowing his own father will not be accounted "wise" among us, as is said to be true in other circumstances: he will have to know his great-great-great-great-great-great-grandfather. This would be too much to ask of children, or adults even, in ordinary society, where the greatest confusion prevails respecting this matter of propagation; for there no scientific reason exists for keeping a careful pedigree record: selfish family pride and property interest furnishing the only motives for it. It is not, therefore, surprising that few can trace back their pedigree for more than two or three generations. Their records, compared with those which scientific propagation necessitates, are mere "chalk marks." They will answer well enough for "mongrel" society; but are wholly unsuitable to the approaching era of Stirpiculture. It ought, therefore, to be a thoroughly satisfactory answer to all who inquire whether Community children know their own parents, to say that the Community believe in and practice scientific propagation. Scientific propagation and sexual confusion and incontinence are absolutely incompatible: they cannot exist together for a single day.

Oneida Circular, July 3, 1871

STIRPICULTURAL

The idea of race-culture has taken firm hold of public attention. Believers and disbelievers in the Darwinian hypothesis alike recognize and proclaim its unspeakable importance. The right to be born well will soon be asserted as the dearest of human rights. It matters little whether man is descended from a monad or made outright, according to good old Orthodox idea; that is a question of fact and theory about which there may properly be much discussion; but the subject of Stirpiculture is of immediate and practical interest. Every man of ordinary reflection acknowledges, to himself at least, that human beings should make as rapid and great an improvement as the inferior animals; and in most cases draws the natural inference that if they do not it is because less science is brought to bear upon human than upon animal propagation. Those who think most deeply have the strongest convictions on this subject, and most earnestly arraign existing society and most fearlessly expose its false conditions.

Circular, May 6, 1872

The material economies of bringing up a dozen children together are very great, but after all the economy, the moral training is the chief advantage. We do not say you can train a dozen children together as well as you can one alone, but we say that you can train a dozen children together *better* than you can one alone. Lay out your labor on the first two or three. Have their parents the best. Let them be the children of Stirpiculture. Then train them in all that is generous and pleasing, teaching them the confession of Christ, and for the rest of the dozen you may trust a good deal to imitation and sympathy. The principle operates in common families no doubt, the oldest child influences the character of all that follow; but a disparity of two or three years is less favorable than a disparity of a few months. You must not put your example at a discouraging distance. The sympathy of comparative equality is necessary to make it most effective.

Oneida Circular, August 12, 1872

THE LOVE OF CHILDREN

It is certainly to the credit of Bible Communism that it guarantees a woman the possession of her own person; that it holds that it is her undoubted right to choose when and how often she shall bear children. This right is inviolable in the Community, and it is only upon the freest consultation that children are begotten. It is to this freedom that we attribute much of the attraction for children which exists in the Community. Freedom and attraction go hand in hand, and children are chosen with pleasure and loved with a mother's love and with a Community's love.

Oneida Circular, April 7, 1873

COMMUNITY JOURNAL

In our Evening Meetings lately we have listened to the reading of a capital paper on Scientific Breeding by Mr. S. L. Goodale. It treats at length and in a very interesting manner of the great economic value of good breed; the law of resemblance of offspring to parents; the law of variation whereby new breeds and varieties are started; atavism, or the resemblance of children to ancestors rather than to their parents; the great influence of a first male on all the subsequent offspring of the female; the points in which children resemble the father; the points in which they resemble the mother; in-and-in breeding—its value and limitations; crossing and its uses; the formation of new breeds . . . and so on.

Circular, June 23, 1873

There are certain hearsays about the Community which are as inexpungable as the Canada thistle. You may rout them out year by year but they reappear with the visiting season as persistently as the white daisies in the meadow. One of these is that we take the babies away from their mothers at a frightfully early age and after that the poor little things never know their mothers from the rest of womankind. Heretofore we have been able to repel this odious impeachment *in toto*. We could say that our babies were left in the entire care of their mothers till their fifteenth or twentieth month, according to their comparative development. But the era of scientific propagation is leading us into new courses, and now we shall have to own up to the first half of that immemorial hearsay. We have four babies under a year—from seven to eleven months—and we are trying the experiment of putting them together through the day. Instead of each mother taking care of her own child in her own room, we put the four into one room, and under the care of two women *not* their mothers. Perhaps if we tell more about it, and the mothers themselves are heard on the subject, this will not appear such a "awful disclosure."

Of course our reasons for this move connect with our Community principles and our Community circumstances. First as to our circumstances: If mothers are to have the chief care of their own babies, the Community is not so good a place on some accounts as the isolated family. The mother in a private household has a round of cares and duties which force her to turn off her child and make it learn to take care of itself. She is compelled to be wife and housekeeper as well as mother. Then her second child soon crowds out the first, and she cannot stop to dote. But the young mother in the Community is under no such necessities. Her housekeeping is all done for her. She has no cooking nor washing nor ironing to do—no imperious calls of any kind. These are circumstances of temptation. A baby soon finds out how much care it can have and exacts more and more. Let a fond mother have no compelling cares, and there is great danger that her child will enslave her and get spoiled itself for want of wholesome neglect.

Then on the other hand Community circumstances are always teaching us new economies and better ways of doing things. We have found that children a year and a half old can be brought up together to a great advantage. They can have the best kind of care at a vast reduction of cost—better, far better care than a weak and overburdened mother could give them; better care than a mother under any conditions could give them. A child that has been in the way of teasing its mother half to death and making itself sick with its innocent restlessness, will go into our nursery and soon become well and happy. Here is philosophy, as everyone knows that has studied the habits of children. In a department on purpose they can have selected guardians—the most gifted infant-culturists we can find among us—and so the best kind of training is insured. Well, why not begin earlier—as soon as the baby is weaned, at least? We resolved to have the benefits of the gregarious system as soon as possible.

Our Community principles in regard to "Woman's Sphere" have governed in this movement. We do not believe that motherhood is the chief end of woman's life; that she was made for the children she can bear. She was made for God and herself. She has a spiritual nature which lifts her up to God, and there is in her highest sphere, where there is "neither male nor female." Then in association with man she was not made first of all to be the mother of his children, but to be his companion and lover—to be what she is in courtship rather than what she is in marriage. Set aside sentimentalism and exceptional cases and woman's sphere under marriage is well characterized by Mr. Noyes in his Bible Argument as that of a "propagative drudge." She is not that in the Community. She has children only by choice, and her drudgery as a mother is to be reduced to the minimum.

The babies are all weaned—the last within a week, its mother choosing to wean it at seven months, rather than wait as she would have to do till cold weather. They continue to sleep with their mothers, who dress them and give them their breakfast and keep them till half-past seven. At that hour they are carried into the drawing-room where their foster mothers are waiting to receive them. The "drawing-room" is in the Children's Wing and was used through the winter to take our next youngest into for a change, but their play yard serves a much better purpose at present. It is a large, airy room, 28' by 12', four windows to the east; is carpeted and furnished with cribs, a low bed, etc. The two in charge are relieved by other motherly women at meal times and fixed hours, and with the fathers to take the babies to ride and the little girls to amuse them and kind hands on every side, they are not overtaxed. The mothers take their babies at six again.

Testimony by a woman who is one of the new foster mothers of the children of the babies' room.

"The feeling that the mothers are in full sympathy with us gives us good heart, and the babies do not suffer from the separation as they would if their mothers' hearts were bleeding. I have never felt so interested and given up to any work that I have ever been in as this, and it was never so easy for me to ask God for help in any work as this. The babies are all well. We spread an old quilt on the carpet and they sit on it with their play things a good share of the time, and seem to think it is the nicest place in the house. Their fathers come in often and give them a tossing, and baby-lovers all through the Community find a new source of enjoyment. The four are getting into the habit of taking their naps at about the same time, which gives us a chance to rest."

Testimony from one of the young mothers whose baby had just been put into the new babies' room.

"Corinna has now been in the nursery two weeks, and as my room is nearby I've had a chance to observe the working of the new plan and am convinced that she is happier and has as good if not better care than when I had entire charge of her myself; and when I go every evening at six to get her she is always delighted to see me and I, feeling rested and fresh instead of tired and often impatient, take more real comfort than before. The love I've had for my baby has never given me the happiness that I expected to realize, for with it has been a feeling of anxiety and worry lest she should be sick, and perhaps taken from me, or that some accident or other might come to her; but since I gave her up that trouble has been taken from me, and in its place I have a feeling of rest and thankfulness. I now realize as I did not before, that the old way of each mother caring exclusively for her own child, begets selfishness and idolatry; and in many ways tends to degrade woman. The new system works well in every respect, but particularly do I appreciate the opportunity it affords me of not only joining in public work but of self-improvement and 'going home' to God every day.

"Yours for giving up everything that stands in the way of improvement and the revival."

Circular, September 22, 1873

Our youngest is unnamed. It is the fifteenth boy out of 25 children born to the Community within four years. "Sarah said, the Lord hath made me to *laugh*, and all that hear will laugh with me." We have heard this laugh of the mother-to-be, from whom the gift has seemed to be withholden, and it is the happiest laugh in the world. It is the running over of pure joy. It has rippled and echoed in all the quarters of the house where we room ever since the year began. Will she laugh in her extremity? we said. She carried it through with smiles between, but the laugh came when she saw her baby—the same laugh with super-added joy—and all that heard laughed with her, except the father who vented his feelings in a flood of tears.

Oneida Circular, December 6, 1875

HEREDITARY PERFECTION

Stirpiculture has a new interest to me lately from the fact that it answers a very deep, puzzling question that comes up in my mind every little while in relation to human experience. The question is, how is there ever going to be an end of suffering or troubles of the flesh as a means of teaching us wisdom? We see that we have to learn lesson after lesson by terrible experience; generation after generation passes away with people arriving at real wisdom only at the end of their lives when they are just quitting the world; that one generation does not love another, but the second comes up just as foolish as the first, and has to go through the same troubles; worrying along through life, and finally getting to be wise just when they are ready to drop into the grave. The question arises, how long must that last; how long must we be born and grow up fools and only grow wise by suffering as our fathers did before us? Well, Stirpiculture answers that question to me. I can tell just when all this repeating of troubles over and over is going to end. It will be when wisdom and righteousness are fixed in the blood, so that the lessons which the parents have learned by experience, the children will have in them when they are born. If you can tell when that will be you can tell when the end of all these tribulations is coming, for it won't come until then. Lord hasten the day, is my prayer.

Epilogue

The withdrawal of John Humphrey Noyes from active participation in the life of the Oneida Community in the spring of 1876 may be said to mark the end of the first long phase of the Oneida experiment. For this reason it seems logical to divide the total history of the Oneida Community into two parts: the first part comprising the first twenty-five years is a scene in bright sunshine; the second part —the last five years before the break-up—is dark and tragic. What may have been the causes of this painful change the reader may perhaps divine from the members' accounts of themselves, straws in the wind, perhaps, even in their sunny years. If there is such evidence, they were not aware of giving it. In any case, it is both meagre and unconscious.

One possible straw might be a brief piece in the *Circular* which expresses the hope that the Community will be strong enough to convert its own children. If not, the Community would perish in the second generation. Such pessimism seems strange, coming in 1861 when they were thriving and happy. Another possible straw might be a talk by John Humphrey Noyes on "the inspired use of natural means," which, translated, meant the use of medicine to cure illness. This was explained as "the coming conjunction of faith and science" which is surprising since faith cure had been one of their firmest beliefs.

Such evidence is certainly not proof positive and there is very little of it. Later, during the years from 1875 to 1880, there is a plethora of it, although judges may differ in their assessment of the guilt or their acquittal of the accused.

356

Generally speaking, the chief general cause of the fatal change was a gradual loss of the religious faith which was their original reason for being, the cement which had held them together through so many vicissitudes. When they lost this, they began to lose everything—their security, their agreement, their selflessness, their happiness. What brought about this irreplaceable loss may be a point of debate. It may be as simple a fact as that faith cannot be inherited or is not transmissible from one generation to another. Or possibly the most important cause was the ageing and then the retirement of their leader, John Humphrey Noyes.

His intelligence, his wonderfully magnetic personality, his strong influence and control, his extraordinarily intuitive dealing with the human problems involved, or perhaps most of all his absolutely unflagging faith could not be reproduced, even with all the good will in the world, by his successor. From a distance he advised, he tried to instruct and persuade, but it was useless. New ideas, modern science in the place of mysticism, were new wine in old bottles which could not contain it.

The younger generation which took over after John Humphrey Noyes left Oneida—specifically his eldest son, Theodore, and a few associates—strove earnestly to fill the void with all sorts of new theories, new panaceas, new regimens, from Darwinism and evolution to spiritualism and Turkish baths. Although they had given up Complex Marriage, they and most of the other communists were still convinced of the desirability of communal living, but not all their good intentions were able to achieve this in a group now deeply divided. Common faith and a single strong leadership had meant agreement and the successful continuance of the Community. Loss of faith under a divided and weak leadership spelled disaster.

It seems evident that if this internal dissension had not eroded the inner structure of the Community, the second attack by the clergy which struck at this time could never have breached their defenses. They had withstood as much or more at other times in their communal lives, fought it off, endured. This time, really leaderless, they surrendered—but surrendered more to their own disunion within than to the enemy without.

The history of this disaster which meant the end of Bible Communism, the end of the old Oneida Community, the end of a remarkable experiment, and after that end, the later slow recovery in "The World" as a joint stock company, is another story. Dark as was its beginning, another decade saw the light begin to brighten once more. Not everything was lost, as it had seemed at the time. Some of the old faith—in brotherhood, in equality, in agreement—was strong enough to persist in a new form of living and working. However impossible it had seemed at the time, the dark story of dissolution had a happy ending which must be told in another book, for without it any account of those first bright years is truncated, inconclusive. Nevertheless, so far as it goes, it is a kind of idyll, worth relating for its own sake and in its own terms.

A Note on Sources

Two excellent biographies of John Humphrey Noyes and—in part or in full—of the Oneida Community are: *The Religious Experience of John Humphrey Noyes* and *John Humphrey Noyes, The Putney Community*, both by George Wallingford Noyes, and *A Yankee Saint* by Robert Allerton Parker. The two Noyes volumes were intended as the first parts of a definitive history of the entire communistic experiment under John Humphrey Noyes, from Putney to Oneida. This project was, unfortunately, cut off by the death of the author. The Parker book, written while George W. Noyes was alive, benefited by his generous help and advice, and, perhaps even more important, by access to the compendious archives which he possessed. At some time after his death in 1941, most regrettably, the largest part of those invaluable and irreplaceable papers was destroyed. For this reason, the only remaining primary sources relating to John Humphrey Noyes's family, childhood, education, and young manhood are in the two Noyes volumes. The quotations given in the Introduction to this book are from diaries, journals, memoirs, and family letters as cited in the two George W. Noyes books. In many cases, dates and other desired information are lacking but cannot now be supplied except as they appear in the above works.

In his preface to *The Religious Experience* the author says: "The intention had been to present all documents precisely as written. But since many of the documents consisted of imperfect reports of extemporaneous talks, it was soon seen that some condensing and arranging would be highly desirable. . . . The editor has, therefore, allowed himself considerable liberty as reviser. He has, of course, scrupulously avoided any alteration of the sense. His aim throughout, in both these changes of the plan, has been to put the reader in possession of the essential thought or fact in the fewest possible words and with the least possible obscuration from the literary medium."

The editor of the present volume should add that absolutely no changes of any sort except omissions in the interest of necessary brevity have been made in the excerpts. They were transcribed exactly as they appear in the various numbers of the *Circular, The American Socialist,* the *Daily Journal of the Oneida Community,* and the few other Community publications cited, plus quotation in the prefaces from identified sources.

One other note on the sources from which the excerpts in this book were made. Although it has not been the intention of this present book to emphasize or deal particularly with the religious aspect of the Oneida Community as it appears in its publications, it will perhaps be noted by a reader of these excerpts, or by a reader who attempts the daunting task of reading through the entire file of the *Circular* and *The American Socialist* from 1851 to 1879, that a change of emphasis occurs in the progression from early to late.

In the first volumes, especially from 1851 to 1855, the principal body of articles printed dealt with various religious subjects, with only occasional references either to secular matters or to the affairs of the Oneida Community. Gradually the emphasis shifted; there were fewer religious articles—aside from a weekly Home Talk by John Humphrey Noyes—and more homely items of news under such headings as The Community Journal, The Oneida Journal, Home Items, Things at Oneida, and so on. They also began to print news of the world, especially war news. The Crimean War, the Civil War, and the Franco-Prussian War were all followed with interest. A curious assortment of articles on miscellaneous topics from "Skating in Central Park" to "What Mr. Gotocede Thinks of Democracy" or the "Life of Jonathan Edwards" appeared more and more frequently.

In the final avatar of Oneida publication, *The American Socialist,* the religious note is seldom sounded. Except for times of crisis such as the attack by the clergy in 1879, the Oneida Community is only occasionally mentioned, and the paper, as it avowed in its prospectus, is largely devoted to "the progress of socialism everywhere."

Following the four other publications with which John Humphrey Noyes had been associated during the previous nearly twenty years— *The Perfectionist* (New Haven), 1834–1836; *The Witness* (Ithaca-Putney), 1837–1843; *The Spiritual Magazine* (Putney-Oneida), 1846–1850; *The Free Church Circular* (Oneida), 1850–1851—*The Oneida Circular* was first issued from the Brooklyn branch of the Oneida Community in 1851. Later, in 1855, it was removed to Oneida where it remained until 1864 when it was again moved to the branch commune at Wallingford, Connecticut, and then finally back to Oneida in 1868. The

Circular ceased publication under that name in 1876 and its successor, *The American Socialist*, edited by John Humphrey Noyes, began publication at Wallingford in that year. It ceased publication in December, 1879. *The Daily Journal*, from which excerpts are taken, was a small leaflet, sometimes of four, sometimes of eight pages, printed at Oneida and intended as a private and local news bulletin for the members of the Community. It is often more particular and more detailed than the accounts of events which appeared under the title "Oneida Journal" in the weekly *Circular*. It was published regularly for not more than three years, from 1866 to 1868, after a brief early period in 1863–1864.

For the first four years—1851–1854—the *Circular,* published in Brooklyn, New York, and distributed gratis, was edited the first year by J. H. Noyes, for the next two years by "J. H. and G. W. Noyes," and the next year "by A Community." This signature was used for one year. Thereafter, following the removal of the printing office to Oneida, the editorial signature was "By the Oneida Community," no editor specified. After the removal to Wallingford, the masthead is "Mount Tom" and no editorial signature is given. A third removal, back to Oneida in 1868, continued with no editorial signature until 1871 when "Wm. A. Hinds" is given as editor for the ensuing two years. In 1873, Tirzah C. Miller was editor until December and thereafter H. M. Worden until March, 1876, when the *Circular* ceased publication. *The American Socialist* announced its beginning publication in that same month with John H. Noyes, William A. Hinds, and F. Wayland-Smith as "responsible editor, resident editor and business manager," respectively.

The Daily Journal had a period of publication from January 1, 1863, to September 15, 1864. No editor is cited but the following Prefatory Remarks are signed "A.W.C." presumably Amasa W. Carr.

PREFATORY REMARKS

It is the design of the following Record to furnish material for the future History of the Community; & the Entries will embrace, primarily, brief notices of important Discussions in our Evening Meetings; Criticisms; Lectures; Social Changes & Developments; Business Transactions of much importance; Applications for Membership; the Reception or Expulsion of members; Transfers of Members from one Community to another; & in general, whatever events, or transactions, that are of historical value, or importance, with full reference to letters and other documents, which may describe them more in detail.

A secondary object, will be, to note all important *arrivals & departures,* including those of Peddlers, Agents, & other Business Men (when their trips are of much consequence), as well as the visits & departures of outside Believers. Likewise, such other occurrences or transactions as may be desireable to note for temporary reference or convenience.

A.W.C.

Oneida, N.Y., January 1, 1863

The second period of publication of the *Daily Journal* of the Oneida Community began January 4, 1866, and continued under that name until January 24, 1867, when the name was changed to *O.C. Daily,* under which title it continued publication until December 30, 1867. No editor was ever specified for this publication.

Various persons worked in the printing office, wherever located, and occasionally certain ones are mentioned as being responsible for Home Notes in either the *Circular* or the *Daily Journal,* but no over-all editor is ever mentioned for the *Daily Journal.* With the exception of certain selections from articles by John Humphrey Noyes and one or two other Central Members, which were signed with either name or initial, none of the excerpts is signed by the author. Especially in the later years of the *Circular* and *The American Socialist,* various articles were reprinted from outside publications, but aside from Letters Received, no other outside contributions were used. There were, however, a large number of outside subscribers, paying, or non-paying.

Publication of some sort was, from the earliest days of his conversion to the doctrine of Salvation from Sin, the dearest project of John Humphrey Noyes. The Putney Corporation, as an organization, published twenty-six numbers of *The Witness* (Putney), 1837–1843; *The Spiritual Magazine* (Putney and Oneida), 1846–1850, when the first number of the *Oneida Circular* was published from Brooklyn, New York, in 1851.

During the Brooklyn period, which was a time of great financial hardship for all the communes, John Humphrey Noyes insisted upon continuing the publication of the paper. As Robert Allerton Parker notes in *A Yankee Saint*: "Let the private fortune of the Oneida Community be what it may, its first business is to see that God has a Press. If it does that, it will have God's blessing as I have had it."

BIBLIOGRAPHY

Confessions of John H. Noyes. Part 1. Confession of Religious Experience: including a history of Modern Perfectionism. Oneida Reserve: Leonard & Company, Printers, 1849.

First Annual Report of the Oneida Association: Exhibiting its History, Principles, and Transactions to January 1, 1849. Published by order of the Association. Oneida Reserve: Leonard & Company, Printers, 1849.

Second Annual Report of the Oneida Association: Exhibiting its progress to February 20, 1850. Published by order of the Association. Oneida Reserve: Leonard & Company, Printers, 1850.

Third Annual Report of the Oneida Association: Exhibiting its progress to February 20, 1851. Published by order of the Association. Oneida Reserve: Leonard & Company, Printers, 1851.

Religious Experience of John Humphrey Noyes, Founder of the Oneida Community. With seventeen illustrations. Compiled and edited by George Wallingford Noyes. New York: Macmillan, 1923.

John Humphrey Noyes; The Putney Community. Compiled and edited by George Wallingford Noyes. With twenty-four illustrations. Oneida, N.Y., 1931.

A Yankee Saint, John Humphrey Noyes and the Oneida Community, by Robert Allerton Parker. New York: G. P. Putnam's Sons, 1935.

Bible Communism; A compilation from the Annual Reports and other publications of the *Oneida Association* and its *Branches;* Presenting, in connection with their history, a summary view of their *Religious and Social Theories.* "The multitude of them that believed were of one heart and of one soul: neither said any of them that aught of the things which he possessed was his own; but they had all things in common." Acts 4:32. Brooklyn, N.Y.: Printed and published at the office of the *Circular,* 1853.

Faith Facts; or, A Confession of the Kingdom of God, and The Age of Miracles, edited by George Cragin. Oneida Reserve: Leonard & Company, Printers, 1850. Free Church Tracts, No. 1.

Essay on Scientific Propagation, by John Humphrey Noyes. Oneida, N.Y.: Published by Oneida Community, n.d.

Salvation From Sin, The End of Christian Faith, by J. H. Noyes. Wallingford, Conn.: Published by the Oneida Community, printed at the *Circular* office, 1866.

Dixon and His Copyists. A Criticism of the Accounts of the Oneida Community in "New America," "Spiritual Wives" and kindred publications, by John Humphrey Noyes. Published by the Oneida Community, 1871. 2nd ed. 1874.

History of American Socialisms, by John Humphrey Noyes. Philadelphia, Pa., 1870.

Male Continence, by John Humphrey Noyes. Oneida, N.Y.: Office of the *American Socialist,* 1872.

Mutual Criticism. Oneida, N.Y.: Office of *The American Socialist,* 1876.

Health Report of Oneida Community Children, by T. R. Noyes. Oneida Community, August, 1878.

Paul's Prize. Report of a Home Talk by J. H. Noyes, n.d.

The Oneida Community: A record of an attempt to Carry Out the Principles of Christian unselfishness and Scientific Race-improvement, by Allan Eastlake. London, 1900.

American Communities: brief sketches of Economy, Zoar, Bethel, Aurora, Amana, Icaria, the Shakers, Oneida, Wallingford, and the Brotherhood of the New Life, by William Alfred Hinds. Oneida, N.Y.: Office of *The American Socialist,* 1878. 2nd revised ed. 1908.

My Father's House; an Oneida Boyhood, by Pierrepont Burt Noyes. New York: Farrar & Rinehart, 1937.

A Goodly Heritage, by Pierrepoint Burt Noyes, New York: Rinehart, 1958.

The Days of My Youth, by Corinna Ackley Noyes. Oneida, N.Y.: privately published, 1960.

Old Mansion House Memories, by one brought up in it, by Harriet M. Worden. Oneida, N.Y.: privately published, 1950. A reprint from articles in the *Circular,* 1871–1872.

The First Hundred Years, 1848–1948. 1848—Oneida Community. 1880—Oneida Community Limited. 1935—Oneida Ltd., by Walter D. Edmunds, with photographs by Samuel Chamberlain. Privately published by Oneida Ltd., 1948.